ARAB ECONOMIES IN THE TWENTY-FIRST CENTURY

This book examines the relationship between demographic growth and economic development in eight Arab countries. Despite a slowdown in demographic growth, the labor force is increasing rapidly because of the change in the age structure of the population. In other parts of the world, similar developments have enhanced economic growth. In the Arab world, however, many of the opportunities presented by demographic transition are being lost, resulting in serious threats to the political stability of the region. The main reason for this is that the region has missed out on industrialization.

The book goes beyond conventional analysis to ask two closely related questions. The first is why were governments so slow in tackling stability? The second is why has the response been similar in apparently different economies? Answers are provided using new literature in economics and economic history.

Paul Rivlin is the Sandra Glass Senior Fellow at the Moshe Dayan Center for Middle Eastern and African Studies at Tel Aviv University. He is the author of three other books: *The Dynamics of Economic Policy Making in Egypt* (1985), *The Israeli Economy* (1992), and *Economic Policy and Performance in the Arab World* (2001), as well as numerous monographs, papers, contributed chapters, articles, and reports on economic development in the Middle East and on international energy markets, defense, and trade economics. Educated at Cambridge, Harvard, and London Universities, he taught undergraduate and graduate courses on Middle East economics at Tel Aviv University, Ben-Gurion University of the Negev, and London University, and he has been a visiting professor of economics at Emory University. He has lectured in the United States, Canada, China, Egypt, India, Japan, Turkey, and Europe.

Arab Economies in the Twenty-First Century

PAUL RIVLIN

Tel Aviv University

CAMBRIDGE
UNIVERSITY PRESS

CAMBRIDGE UNIVERSITY PRESS
Cambridge, New York, Melbourne, Madrid, Cape Town, Singapore, São Paulo, Delhi

Cambridge University Press
32 Avenue of the Americas, New York, NY 10013-2473, USA

www.cambridge.org
Information on this title: www.cambridge.org/9780521719230

First published 2009

Printed in the United States of America

A catalog record for this publication is available from the British Library.

Library of Congress Cataloging in Publication data

Rivlin, Paul.
Arab economies in the twenty-first century / Paul Rivlin.
p.   cm.
Includes bibliographical references and index.
ISBN 978-0-521-89500-2 (hardback) – ISBN 978-0-521-71923-0 (pbk.)
1. Arab countries – Economic conditions.   2. Arab countries – Economic policy.   3. Arab
countries – Population – Economic aspects.   4. Political culture – Arab countries.
5. Unemployment – Arab countries.   6. Labor market – Arab countries.   7. Arab countries –
Foreign economic relations.   I. Title.
HC498.R578   2009
330.917′4927 – dc22   2008031270

ISBN   978-0-521-89500-2 hardback
ISBN   978-0-521-71923-0 paperback

Contents

Figures and Tables

Figures

Tables

Preface

This book is the result of research carried out at the Moshe Dayan Center for Middle Eastern and African Studies at Tel Aviv University. It was funded by the Sandra Glass Fellowship. I am grateful to Asher Susser, former director of the Center, for his assistance and to three reviewers for their valuable comments on drafts. Francois Crouzet and the late Paul Bairoch encouraged me to take a long, historical view of contemporary economic problems in the Arab world, and I am grateful to them for the time they spent with me discussing European and Middle Eastern economic history. My thanks to Scott Parris and his colleagues at Cambridge University Press for their encouragement and assistance and to Tammy Berkowitz, who provided vital technical assistance.

Some of the demographic material in Chapter 5 is based on an article published in the *Middle East Review of International Affairs*. Chapter 6 uses material published in an article in *Orient*. I am grateful to the editors of those journals for permission to use them.

My greatest debt is to my family, to whom this book is dedicated with love and thanks. Rosemary read and improved much of the text and produced the graphics; Ben assisted in producing the diagrams and coping with bilingual and two-directional software. Alex made many pertinent and thoughtful comments on contemporary economics. Thanks to my mother, Zena, who taught me to ask questions and to my parents-in-law, Brenda and Michael Josephs, for their interest in my work. I am, of course, responsible for all errors and omissions.

ONE

Introduction

This book examines the relationship between demographic growth and economic development in Egypt, Iraq, Jordan, Morocco, the Palestinian Territories, Saudi Arabia, Syria, and Tunisia. It shows that, despite a slowdown in demographic growth, the labor force is increasing rapidly because of the change in the age structure of the population. This is known as *demographic transition*, a phenomenon that has enhanced economic growth in other parts of the world. In the Arab world, however, many of the opportunities presented by demographic transition are being lost, which results in serious threats to the political stability of the region.

The main reason for this situation is that the region has missed out on the Industrial Revolution that has spread through Europe, North America, East and Southeast Asia, and now to India since the nineteenth century. Demographic growth, albeit at a decelerating rate, and the change in population age structure against a background of slow job creation is a major cause of political instability and even terrorism. This poses severe challenges for all Arab countries, despite the differences between their economies. This book goes beyond the conventional analysis of demand and supply to ask two closely related questions. The first is why did governments act so slowly in response to the problem of unemployment, given the danger that it poses for social and political stability? The second question is why has the response been similar in very different economies? Answers are provided using new literature in economics and economic history. The book also examines the role of oil in retarding economic development and especially the way in which it strengthens the state and its relations with the governments of oil-consuming states. It also examines two countries that have suffered conflict: Iraq and the Palestinian Territories. The book places the effects of conflict and occupation into their historical context and shows both the similarities and differences between these economies and those of other Arab states.

1

States in conflict usually fail to produce good data and are, therefore, omitted from much of the economic literature. Conflict within Arab states and sometimes between them is endemic and the economic and socioeconomic conditions of those states need examination even if the data are weak.

Chapter 2 outlines the main demographic and economic trends in the region. Demographic growth has slowed and demographic transition has increased the share of the population that is of working age. It then looks at the labor market, with population viewed as the supply side and economic development as the source of demand. Economic performance has not been strong enough to significantly reduce unemployment. The reliance of many economies on different kinds of rental incomes and the weaknesses of the industrialization process are analyzed in order to explain the pattern of economic growth.

Chapter 3 evaluates the explanations of Arab economic performance. It analyzes the characteristics that Arab economies have in common and puts forth explanations for the persistence of policies despite serious economic problems. It covers the explanations for weak economic performance given in the Arab Human Development Reports and by others in and outside the region. These have increasingly blamed such factors as discrimination against women, poor education, and the lack of political freedom. They do not, however, explain why Arab countries remain in this situation. The answer is found in the way in which these countries have developed, and new literature in economics and economic history is used to explore these developments. This covers the role of geography and the resource base, culture and religion, and institutions. The weakness of the middle class, a group that has played a key role in the politics and economics of other regions, is central to understanding the predicament of Arab states. The role of Islam is highly controversial: Although economists and economic historians have been much more willing than many other Middle East scholars to examine its effects, there is no consensus.

Chapter 4 compares the economic development of Arab countries to that of East Asia and Latin America, with emphasis on industrialization. It shows how basic conditions varied between the regions and how these were much more successfully built upon in East Asia than in the Middle East and South America. It also shows that as a result of oil income and cautious capital account policies in the poorer countries of the Arab world, financial crises accompanied by debilitating capital outflows were avoided. This is despite the fact that a huge amount of Arab capital has left the region.

Chapter 5 is about Egypt, a political and cultural leader in the Arab world, with the largest population. Egypt faces huge problems, many of which derive from demographic growth. This presents challenges in terms of the provision of social services and infrastructure. The labor force is growing rapidly and there are high levels of hidden and open unemployment. This chapter examines the effects of education on fertility and the role of women in the labor force. Despite many reforms, Egypt's main productive sectors – agriculture and industry – suffer many constraints and have not provided increases in productive employment on the scale hoped for. Many of the problems are due to the unwillingness of the government to complete the reform process in the widest sense. Egypt has, however, grasped a prickly nettle by overcoming internal opposition to the creation of Qualified Industrial Zones (QIZs), designed to export to the United States with limited Israeli content, thus securing hundreds of millions of dollars of manufactured exports and thousands of jobs. Egypt is important because of its size and importance as a cultural leader in the Arab world. It permits free debate about economic issues, although those debates have seldom influenced the decisions taken. The economic success or failure of Egypt is a matter of concern for the region as a whole as well as for many outside the Middle East.

Chapter 6 provides a historical perspective on Iraq's current economic problems. For many years it has played a major role in the region and has fought three wars. The Ba'ath regime was the most totalitarian in the Arab world and it squandered the country's human and natural resources on an unprecedented scale. As a result, it is often excluded from the analysis of the region. Despite the huge destruction, Iraq has economic potential and it will play an important role in the future. It shows how, since the 1950s, Iraq has favored the oil sector at the expense of others. This is done through an analysis of how oil revenues were invested and how, until 1980, huge volumes of funds were unused. From 1980 until the present, Iraq sustained massive losses that have caused extensive damage to the economy and to the welfare of the population. U.S. policy proposals, partly implemented after 2003, are scrutinized and it is suggested that they repeat some of the errors of previous Ba'athist policies.

Chapter 7 analyzes demographic and economic developments in Jordan. It suffers from high rates of unemployment but also imports labor. The economic reform program designed to tackle underlying structural problems is then examined. Jordan has gone further than most Arab states in trying to change its economy, especially its foreign economic relations. In this connection the creation of QIZs is analyzed. These have come to rely on cheap, imported labor and show some of the problems of industrialization in a developing economy. The chapter also looks at the history and development of entrepreneurship in Jordan. In many respects, the economic policies of Jordan have been brave: there have been large and successful investments in human capital and attempts to industrialize using Western economic models in the face of huge demographic, social, and other challenges. Success has been limited and this – together with the country's geo-political importance – justifies the examination of its economic development.

Chapter 8 shows that Morocco introduced many reforms but these have not cured its huge socioeconomic problems. It has done much that the International Monetary Fund (IMF) and the World Bank demanded and as a result its financial position has improved and it has avoided balance of payments and foreign debt problems. Morocco was also one of the first countries in the Middle East to experience demographic transition and now benefits from slower population growth. Economic performance has been less satisfactory: economic growth remains very unstable, excessively influenced by fluctuations in the harvest due to the vagaries of the weather. Despite large-scale emigration, Morocco has very high levels of unemployment, especially among young people. It also suffers from mass poverty. The international environment has not been helpful: most exports go to Europe and face increasing competition. The private sector's room for maneuver is limited by the royal palace as well as by other weaknesses and this has limited industrialization and foreign investment, with the notable exception of tourism. Morocco demonstrates how difficult the implementation of economic reforms is even in the context of a relatively free debate within the country and a much freer political system than prevails in most other countries in the region.

The Arab Human Development Reports and many other studies in the Arab world have blamed the conflict between Israel and the Palestinians for the lack of economic development in the region as a whole. Without subscribing to the causation implied, Palestine is important in itself and because of the effects of conflict. Chapter 9 shows how the creation of a healthy economy in a future independent Palestinian state was affected by Israeli policies after 1967. The refusal to permit or encourage industrialization was the most serious blow because it left the Palestinians dependent on other sources of employment. With the deepening of conflict with Israel, the Israeli labor market was closed and the Palestinians suffered huge losses. The creation of the Palestinian Authority in the mid-1990s was also a profound disappointment. It granted monopolies to those close to the leadership and replicated the corruption prevalent in other Arab countries. The result was the alienation of much of the population, the exit of much of the West

Bank middle class to Jordan, and the rise of the fundamentalist Hamas that rejected attempts to reach a peace agreement with Israel. The Second *Intifada* resulted in major loss of life and massive destruction. Despite, or perhaps because of this, the population has grown faster than nearly anywhere else in the world, contributing to a large fall in per capita income.

Chapter 10 examines the paradox of why Saudi Arabia – a country with huge oil resources – suffers from high unemployment. This has been accompanied by the import of millions of workers from abroad. The kingdom's problems stem from the policies developed during the oil boom of the 1970s. First, it adopted a pro-natal policy that resulted in rapid demographic growth. Second, it increased the size of the civil service to supply services to the population and to provide employment. Third, it did little to develop technical, technological, and scientific education. The public service often offered higher pay than the private sector and the latter increasingly relied on imported labor. Saudis therefore preferred to work in the public sector. After oil prices fell in the mid-1980s, the government could only maintain the public sector by large-scale borrowing. Investment was cut and the economy went into crisis. Since then the financial position has improved immensely. However, the education system still fails to sufficiently train Saudis for work in the private sector and many of those who have a technological or scientific education leave because of the stifling political system. In this environment, fundamentalism and terrorism have increased. Many, though not all, of the issues faced by the Saudis have been present in the development of the other, smaller Gulf States. It therefore serves as the example of oil-based development.

Chapter 11 analyzes the Syrian economy. It has the richest agricultural sector in the Arab world, oil and gas, and magnificent tourist attractions. Despite both this and its dominance over Lebanon for many years, the Syrian economy is one of the most backward in the region. Syria suffers from rapid population growth, even faster labor force growth, and high unemployment. Its industrial sector is underdeveloped and is held back by extensive government intervention and by the lack of a modern banking system. The country is isolated from the international economy: it is now among the most inward-looking countries in the Arab world. Oil production has declined and oil revenues are falling, leaving the government with even less room to maneuver. Despite cutbacks in military spending, Syria maintains a large army and the conflict with Israel is central to all considerations in Damascus. The Ba'ath regime in Syria is much less violent than that in Iraq and so Syria has suffered much less conflict. Despite this, the extreme centralism and incompetence of the economic system have had huge negative effects. Syria also presents an interesting parallel to Tunisia. In 1960, the two countries had similar-sized populations and economies. The paths that they have followed, measured by growth of national income per capita, have been quite different and the reasons for this are explored here.

Chapter 12 deals with Tunisia, the most industrialized economy in the Arab world. It has experienced years of economic growth as well as the advantages of demographic transition. Major efforts were made to improve the efficiency of agriculture so that it would not be exposed to the effects of the drought, and these have had considerable success. They have also helped to limit the pace of urbanization. The labor force is growing at 2.5 percent a year, more than twice the rate of growth of the population and this is one of the main reasons why unemployment, especially among the young, is high. Tunisia seems unable to break through a glass barrier to faster and higher technology industrialization. One of the reasons is the tight hold that the government has on the entrepreneurial class and its apparent unwillingness to devolve power.

Chapter 13 presents conclusions as to the causes of Arab economic problems. Based on the ideas outlined in Chapter 3, I put forward the concept of an "Arab equilibrium" and suggest that the current balance of power is one that opposes change, despite the dangers posed by unemployment and even terrorism. This is reinforced by the region's relations with the rest of the world that are dominated by the sale of oil and gas that is government-owned and permit rents to play a major role in the political economy of the region.

TWO

Demography and Economics

During the last twenty-five years, all of the countries examined in this book have experienced significant declines in their demographic growth rates. This is mainly the result of a fall in fertility rates that started in North Africa and later spread to the rest of the Middle East. Despite the demographic slowdown, the rates of growth in most of the countries remain high by international standards and the absolute increases of the population in all of them are large. In 2000–05, the population of eighteen Arab states rose by more than six million a year or about 2.2 percent annually (see Table 2.1). One of the consequences of demographic change has been the creation of a large young population of reproductive age. Another is a rapidly growing labor force. None of this is expected to change in the next twenty years. Although the population of working age has grown, so has the size of the dependent population and as a result the pressure for public sector spending on social services such as education, health, and welfare has increased, often beyond the financial abilities of governments.[1] In the non-oil states and those with small oil incomes, taxation was the main source of funding for government spending and was usually under pressure. This was particularly true during periods of recession and when stabilization programs were being introduced. In the oil-rich states, the problems were much less acute, but they have occurred during periods of low oil revenues.

Demographic growth, insofar as it is the main cause of increase in the labor force, can also be thought of as a supply factor. The task of the labor market is to balance the supply of labor with demand. When there is an

[1] Williamson Jeffrey G. and Tarik M. Youssef. "Demographic Transitions and Economic Performance in the Middle East and North Africa," in Sirageldin, Ismail (ed.), *Human Capital: Population Economic in the Middle East.* London and New York: I.B. Tauris, 2002. 22.

Table 2.1. *Demographic transition in the Arab world, 1970–2015 (millions)*

	1970	2000	2015 (forecast)	Annual growth rate 1970–2000 (%)	Annual growth rate 2000–2015 (%)
Arab population	122	281	385	2.82	2.12
aged 0–14	55	107	129	2.24	1.25
aged 15–64	63	164	240	3.24	2.57
age 65+	4	10	16		
aged 15–64/total*	51.6	58.4	62.4	0.41	0.44

* The demographic gift is growth rate of the working population minus that of the total population.
Source: Dhonte, Pierre, Bhattacharya, Rina, and Yousef, Tarik. (2000). "Demographic Transition in the Middle East – Implications for Growth, Employment, and Housing," IMF Working Paper No. 00/41, http://www.imf.org/external/pubs/ft/wp/2000/wp0041.pdf.

excess supply, then unemployment results. To understand conditions in the labor market that led to very high rates of unemployment in all Arab states (some 15 percent in 2000 and nearly 11 percent in 2005), it is necessary to look at the sources of demand for labor. These depend on the structure and growth of the economy. In all of the countries examined here and in all other Arab states, the generation of employment has been weak. This was partly because of unstable or low economic growth rates, but even when growth rates were fast, the pattern of growth was such that employment growth was limited. The main reason is that the region has largely missed out on the process of industrialization, which has transformed much of the world economy. Industrialization also transforms societies and their politics, generating new interest groups – both capitalists and workers – that have interests in pro-growth economic policies. Here again, the Arab states have, to a considerable extent, missed out on a process that is much more than economic but that has profound economic effects. The weakness of the industrialization process was in part because of government policies: both in countries that espoused Arab socialism and in those that did not, governments have played, and continue to play, a dominant economic role. It is also reflected in the weakness of the private sector, an important theme in this book.

The eight countries analyzed here are fairly representative of the Arab world. They include states in the Mashreq and the Maghreb, oil and non-oil as well as low-oil economies. Among them are those in varying states of war and those at peace, some with low and others with higher income per capita, monarchies and republics.

Between 1960 and 1985, Arab economies grew by an average of 2.5 percent annually, which permitted major improvements in human development indices. Although the growth of per capita income was very low, the benefits of growth were spread throughout society as a result of socialist policies in some countries and welfare policies in both socialist and nonsocialist states. The remittances earned by millions who went from the poorer states to the oil states to work flowed home with beneficial effects on income levels and distribution. These factors helped to reduce poverty levels; as a result, in 1990 only 5.6 percent of the Middle East population lived on less than one dollar a day, compared with 14.7 percent in East Asia and 28.8 percent in Latin America.

In the mid-1980s, oil prices slumped, incomes fell, and economic growth decelerated; so did remittances and the demand for labor in the oil-rich states. This had a ripple effect throughout the region. Since the mid-1980s, poverty has increased and, as will be shown, the region has been unable to take advantage of the "demographic gift" of an expanding supply of educated labor. In 1985–94, growth slumped to −1.1 percent a year and as a result, per capita incomes fell significantly. Furthermore, the volatility of growth increased. In the period 1995–2000, there was a modest recovery to 0.3 percent.[2] In the period 2000–05, there was an improvement mainly as a result of higher oil prices. The growth record since the mid-1980s has meant that poverty and unemployment have risen. There was also an increase in the number of people suffering undernourishment, from an average of 21.7 million in 1990–92 to 24.7 million in 2000–02, an increase of 14 percent.[3] This increase suggests that income inequality rose and that the ability and/or willingness of governments to maintain welfare levels declined. It also reflects the enormous pressure on the economy of demographic growth.

The Arab economies share three closely related features. The first is a deep and prolonged employment crisis. The second is the very limited development of the manufacturing sector and of industry in general. The third is the major role played by rental incomes. These are examined in this chapter.

Population Growth

The underlying supply-side reason for the employment crisis is demographic, specifically the very rapid rates of population growth that prevailed in the 1970s and 1980s. Population growth in the Middle East is the fastest in the world, despite the deceleration of recent years. In the second half

---

[2] Elbadawi, Ibrahim A. "Reviving Growth in the Arab World." *Economic Development and Cultural Change* 54 (2006). 293–326.

[3] Calculated from FAO, *The State of Food and Agriculture 2005.* http://www.fao.org.151.

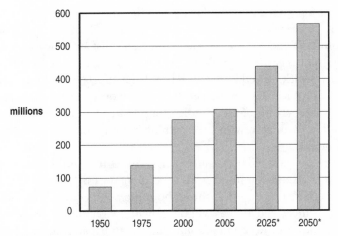

Figure 2.1. The Arab Population, 1950–2050 (millions). *Source:* Population Division of the Department of Economic and Social Affairs of the United Nations Secretariat, "World Population Prospects: The 2004 Revision and World Urbanization Prospects: The 2003 Revision, Medium Variant," http://esa.un.org/unpp.
* forecasts

of the twentieth century, demographic transition – the progression from a population with short life spans and large families to one in which people live longer and have smaller families – in the Middle East was marked by a decline in mortality that preceded the fall in fertility. In 1950, the total population of 18 Arab states was 73 million. By 1975, it had risen by 97 percent to 144 million and by 2005 it had reached 307 million (see Figure 2.1). The rate of population growth accelerated from 2.5 percent a year in 1950–75 to 2.75 percent in 1975–2000, whereas world rates fell from 1.9 percent to 1.6 percent during the same period.[4]

During the late 1970s, the crude birthrate averaged 42 per 1,000, resulting in 6 million births a year while the crude death rate was 12.2 per 1,000, resulting in 1.8 million deaths a year. As a result, the population rose by more than 4 million annually. In 2005, birthrates were estimated at 26 per 1,000 in North Africa and 27 per 1,000 in West Asia; crude death rates were 6 per 1,000 and 7 per 1,000, respectively.[5] Death rates in the Middle East and North Africa (MENA) fell because of improvements in health. Relatively

---

[4] Population Division of the Department of Economic and Social Affairs of the United Nations Secretariat. *World Population Prospects: The 2004 Revision and World Urbanization Prospects: The 2003 Revision*, Medium Variant. http://esa.un.org/unpp.

[5] Population Reference Bureau. *World Data Sheet 2005*. http://www.prb.org.

simple methods were employed to reduce or eliminate contagious diseases; improvements in the provision of clean water and knowledge about basic hygiene had major beneficial effects. As a result, the infant mortality rate fell and life expectancy rates rose.

Fertility rates fell as a result of the increased use of contraceptives. This was, at least in part, related to the improvement in women's education as well as that of men. The fact that more women delayed the age of marriage and went to work also reduced fertility rates.[6] Ironically, the improvement in women's health was a factor that increased already high fertility rates as well as reducing mortality. Urbanization and the increased survival rates of infants and young children also contributed to lower birthrates.

Table 2.1 provides data on population growth between 1950 and 2000 and United Nations' forecasts for 2025 and 2050, based on its medium variant assumptions. The table shows that there were significant differences between trends in the North African states of Algeria, Morocco, and Tunisia and the Middle East states, with Egypt in between, both geographically and demographically. The demographic transition started earlier in North Africa than in the Middle East. As a result, North Africa began the later phase of transition – that of lower population growth rates – earlier. Many Arab countries – most notably Saudi Arabia and Syria – encouraged population growth in the 1970s and 1980s and have lived with the consequences ever since. The populations of the Gulf States were also boosted by immigration of workers, first from other Arab states and then from outside the Middle East. More worrisome was the huge demographic growth experienced in two of the poorest countries in the region: Sudan and Yemen.

Between 1965 and 1990, the economically active population (aged 15–64) in the Middle East rose by 2.88 percent annually and the dependent population (aged 0–14 and 65 and older) increased by 2.37 percent. The net economic impact is defined as the excess of growth of the economically active population over that of the dependent population. The net economic impact from population growth was 0.51 percent annually. In East Asia, in contrast, the economically active population rose by 2.39 percent annually in the same period while the dependent population rose by 0.25 percent annually, giving a net economic impact of 2.14 percent.[7]

---

[6] "United Nations Population Fund: The Arab Population," in *The Arab World Competitiveness Report 2000–2003*, New York: Oxford University Press for the World Economic Forum. 2003. 34–43.

[7] Williamson, Jeffrey G. and Tarik M. Youssef. "Demographic Transitions and Economic Performance in the Middle East and North Africa." 20.

The Role of Economic Factors in Declining Fertility

The decline in Middle East and North African fertility has been associated with the increased use of contraception and later marriage. Morocco was the first country to experience a consistent decline in fertility: between 1973 and 1977, the fertility rate fell from 7.4 per 1,000 to 5.9 per 1,000 and it has continued to decline ever since. This was a period in which the price of Morocco's main export – phosphates – collapsed on international markets and government income fell sharply as a result. The government reacted by increasing taxes and encouraging women to go to work to maintain family incomes. Between 1960 and 1980, the labor force participation rate of women aged 20 to 24 rose from 10 percent to 37 percent. Changes of a similar order in fertility rates and female labor-force participation rates occurred in Saudi Arabia in the mid to late 1980s, when oil revenues declined, and in Egypt from 1986.[8]

Between 1980 and 1990, the population of eighteen Arab states increased by 31 percent, or 51 million. Between 1990 and 2000, the rate of increase slowed marginally, to less than 30 percent, but in absolute terms the population increase was larger: just over 63 million. As a result, the population doubled in twenty years. A similar trend is forecast for the period 2000–10, with an increase of 23 percent, or almost 64 million. This compares with increases in the world population between 1980 and 1990 of 19 percent, between 1990 and 2000 of 15.3 percent, and a forecast increase between 2000 and 2010 of 12.5 percent.[9] Between 1950 and 2050, the total Arab population is forecast to increase 7.75-fold while the world population is forecast to increase 3.6-fold. The Arab world has thus been, for the last fifty years, the fastest growing demographic region in the world and will continue to be over the next fifty years.

Because of the very fast growth over the past thirty years, the population is very young and the working-age population has grown faster than the population as a whole. In 1950, in twenty-two Arab countries, the population aged 15 to 59 accounted for 52.9 percent of the total population; in 1975 the share was 50.3 percent but in 2000 it rose to 55.6 percent. It is expected to go on increasing over the next fifty years.[10] The working-age

[8] Courbage, Youssef. "Economic and Political Issues in the Fertility Transition in the Arab World – Answers and Open Questions," *Population and Environment: A Journal of Inter-disciplinary Studies.* 20, no. 4, 1999. 352–80.

[9] UN. *World Population Prospects, 2004 Revision.*

[10] "United Nations Population Fund: The Arab Population," in *The Arab World Competitiveness Report 2000–2003.* 40.

population of North Africa (Egypt, Libya, Algeria, Tunisia, Morocco, and Mauritania) increased from 45 million in 1970 to 105 million in 2000. In the five other most populous Arab states – Iraq, Saudi Arabia, Sudan, Syria, and Yemen – the increase was even more dramatic: from 59 million to 146 million.[11] Between 1990 and 2000, in both groups of countries, the average annual increase in the working-age population was nearly 6.5 million a year. The increase in the working-age population, together with the increase in labor-force participation rates, was the main explanation for the rise in the labor force. The number of women entering the labor force has increased, but so has the number of women of childbearing age.[12]

Demographic Transition

Demographic transition is the move from preindustrial high fertility and high mortality rates to postindustrial low fertility and low mortality rates. Declines in mortality precede those in fertility and benefit the young most. The increased rate of survival results in a gradual reduction in the number of children, but as this takes time the number of young people increases.[13]

The result is a change in the age structure of the population. Table 2.1 shows that between 1970 and 2000, the Arab population aged 15 to 64 rose by 160 percent compared to a total population growth of 130 percent. The population aged 0 to 14 grew by 95 percent and that aged 65 and older rose by 150 percent. Between 2000 and 2015, the IMF forecasts that the working-age population will increase by 46 percent, the total population by 37 percent, the 0 to 14 age group by 21 percent, and the 65 and older age group by 60 percent. The table shows how the working-age population as a share of the total population rose from less than 52 percent in 1970 to just over 62 percent in 2015. As a result, the ratio of dependents to those of working age fell from 0.94 in 1970, to 0.71 in 1980, and is forecast to be 0.60 in 2015. These changes offer Arab countries the opportunity to reduce the burden of supporting dependents and thus increase income per capita and savings. These factors were found to have made a significant contribution to economic growth in East Asia and could do the same in the Arab world. (See section "The Role of Economic Factors in Declining Fertility".) They

---

[11] Calculated from UN, *World Population Prospects, 2004 Revision.*
[12] Richards, Alan. "Economic Reform in the Middle East: The Challenge to Governance," in Bensahel, Nora and Daniel L Byman (eds.), *The Future Security Environment in the Middle East.* Santa Monica, Calif.: Rand, 2004. 65.
[13] Bloom, David E. and Jeffrey G. Williamson. "Demographic Transitions and Economic Miracles in Emerging Asia," *World Bank Economic Review.* 12, no. 3, 1998. 419–55.

also pose a threat because large numbers of unemployed young people may threaten social and political order. Conflict in Sudan, the Western Sahara, between Iraq and Iran, between Palestine and Israel, and within Lebanon may well have been exacerbated.[14]

The economic effects of population growth depend on the balance between the growth of the population of working age and that of the dependent population. This balance is determined by the extent to which a population is experiencing demographic transition. The Middle East is in a much earlier stage of demographic transition than East Asia and other developing areas. The difference between the growth of the population of working age and that of the dependent population represents the net demographic addition to the productive capacity of the economy.

Between 1970 and 2000, the *demographic gift* (defined as the difference between the growth rate of the working-age population and that of the total population) in the member states of the Arab League (Afghanistan, Iran, and Pakistan) was 0.41 percent a year. In the period 2000–15, it was forecast at 0.44 percent a year.[15] The acceleration was because growth of the population of working age increased and that of the dependent population decelerated. For this to benefit the economy there has to be sufficient demand for labor. In many neoclassical models, the problem of employment is assumed away if the right economic conditions apply. In Keynesian models, the problem of employment is endogenous and the evidence presented here suggests that this is a more realistic description of the situation in the Middle East.

The effect of the increase in the dependent population is felt in terms of growing demand for social services and infrastructure, and this affects the pattern of investment. In countries with a larger net demographic impact, investment was concentrated in the direction of *capital widening*, defined as an increase in the quantity of capital in an enterprise or an economy without necessarily changing the proportions in which the factors of production – land, labor, or capital – are used. This increases the productive capacity and level of output of the economy faster than investments in social services

[14] According to the Population Action Council, countries that experienced new conflicts in the 1970s, 1980s, and 1990s were cross-referenced with their age structure at the beginning of each of those decades, and very young age structures were found to have the strongest correlation with the outbreak of civil conflict. Leahy, Elizabeth with Robert Engelman, Carolyn Vogel Gibb, Sarah Haddock, and Tod Preston. "The Shape of Things to Come: Why Age Structure Matters to a Safer, More Equitable World." *Population Action International*, 2007. http://www.populationaction.org.

[15] Dhonte, Pierre, Rina Bhattacharya, and Tarik Yousef. "Demographic Transition in the Middle East: Implications for Growth, Employment and Housing." IMF Working Paper WP/00/41, 2000. Table 2.18.

and infrastructure. Another effect is on the rate of savings. If there are more dependents, then the family cannot save as much. If there is pressure for more public spending, then the government cannot save as much. This has a negative effect on the growth of national income. In 1965–90, both investment and savings rates in the Middle East were lower than in East Asia and South Asia. The demographic burden in the Middle East therefore accounts for a significant share of its lower gross domestic product (GDP) per capita growth relative to that in the high-performing economies of East and Southeast Asia.[16]

In East Asia the growth of the working-age population that results from demographic transition has had a powerful, positive effect on the growth of national income while the growth of the total population has a powerful negative effect, after controlling for other factors.[17] The IMF has concluded that demographic transition in the Arab world presents both a challenge and an opportunity. The demographic gift could contribute 1.1 percent a year to real GDP growth in the period 2000–15. The so-called augmented demographic gift, which focuses on the ratio of employment to the total population, could contribute 2 percent annually.[18]

Population growth in the region has been one of the fastest in the world (see Figure 2.2). Despite the deceleration over the last thirty years, in 2005–10 estimated population growth in the Arab world was more than three times as fast as in East Asia and nearly 50 percent faster than in South America (see Figure 2.3).

The Labor Market

In comparison with many other developing regions, the Arab world has one of the most problematic labor markets. It has the fastest labor-force growth rate, the lowest female labor-force participation rate, by far the largest share of employment in the public sector, and second highest unemployment rate. The data in Figure 2.4 is for the Middle East but there was no significant difference if Iran was excluded from the figures.

---

[16] Williamson, Jeffrey G. and Youssef Tarik M. "Demographic Transitions and Economic Performance in the Middle East and North Africa," 31.

[17] Bloom, David E. and Jeffrey G. Williamson. "Demographic Transitions and Economic Miracles in Emerging Asia," *World Bank Economic Review* Vol. 12, no. 3, 1998, pp. 419–55, 453.

[18] Dhonte, Pierre, Rina Bhattacharya, and Tarik Yousef. "Demographic Transition in the Middle East: Implications for Growth, Employment and Housing," IMF Working Paper WP/00/41, 2000. 7–8.

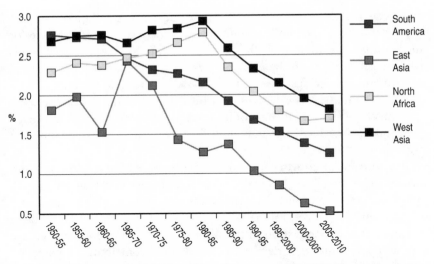

Figure 2.2. Population Growth Rates, Annual Averages, 1950–2010. *Source:* Population Division of the Department of Economic and Social Affairs of the United Nations Secretariat, "World Population Prospects: The 2006 Revision and World Urbanization Prospects: The 2005 Revision, Medium Variant," http://esa.un.org/unpp.

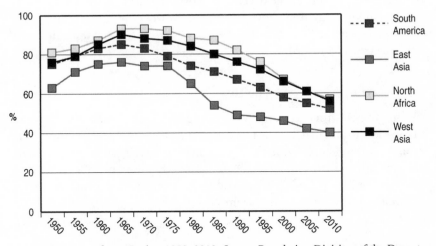

Figure 2.3. Dependency Ratios, 1950–2010. *Source:* Population Division of the Department of Economic and Social Affairs of the United Nations Secretariat, "World Population Prospects: The 2006 Revision and World Urbanization Prospects: The 2005 Revision, Medium Variant," http://esa.un.org/unpp. The dependency ratio is defined as the ratio of the sum of the population aged 0–14 and that over age 65 to the population aged 15–64.

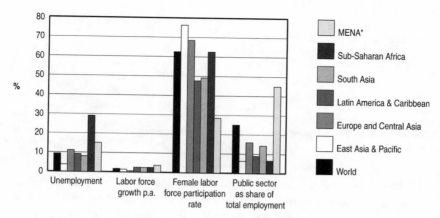

Figure 2.4. International Labor Market Indicators, 2000. *Source:* World Bank, Jobs, Growth, and Governance in the Middle East and North Africa (2003).
* Arab States and Iran

Labor-force growth rates have accelerated in Egypt, Iraq, Jordan, Syria, and Yemen. The International Labor Office (ILO) notes that the Middle East and North Africa labor-force growth rate rose from 3.3 percent a year in 1993–2003, to 3.4 percent in 1994–2004.[19] These high rates have been applied to larger bases, resulting in what is called *demographic momentum,* which results in increasing absolute additions to the labor force[20] (see Figure 2.4).

In the 1970s, the average annual increase in the Arab labor force was 1.1 million. By the 1980s it had increased to 1.6 million. In the 1990s it rose to 2.5 million. As a result, between 1970 and 2000, the labor force increased by an astonishing 2.8-fold. According to the World Bank, in the period 2000–10 the annual increase will be 3.1 million and only in 2010–20 will a deceleration occur, when it will be just under 3.1 million (see Figure 2.5).

An alternative measure has been given by Youssef Courbage.[21] He measured the number entering the labor market minus the number leaving. The former is determined by demographic factors, such as the number of people reaching the age of work (e.g., ages 15–20) and their rate of participation.

[19] International Labour Office, *Global Employment Trends Brief,* February 2005. http://www.ilo.org.
[20] Richards, Alan. "Economic Pressures for Accountable Governance in the Middle East and North Africa" in Norton, Augustus Richard (ed.), *Civil Society in the Middle East,* Leiden, New York, Koln: E.J. Brill, 1995. 59.
[21] Youssef Courbage (n.d.). "New Demographic Scenarios in the Mediterranean Region," http://www.ined.fr.

Table 2.2. *Annual changes in the Arab labor force, 2000–2025 (millions)*

	2000–2005	2005–2010	2010–2015	2015–2020	2020–2025
Accessions	6.215	6.522	6.279	6.039	6.182
Exits	0.921	0.981	1.150	1.463	1.833
Balance	5.294	5.541	5.129	4.576	4.349

Source: Calculated from Youssef Courbage (n.d.). "New Demographic Scenarios in the Mediterranean Region," http://www.ined.fr.

His forecast of the pressures on Arab labor markets is given in Table 2.2. This shows that the annual average number of people entering the labor force in 2000–05 was an estimated 6.2 million. As 900,000 retired each year, the net rise was almost 5.3 million. In the period 2005–10, the balance of accessions and exits will be 250,000 higher than in 2000–05 and only after that will it decline.

Labor-Force Participation

One of the most important developments of the last twenty-five years has been the increase in the share of people of working age who go to work outside the home. Middle East (including Iran) labor-force participation rates rose from 54.5 percent in 1970 to 57 percent in 1990 and are expected

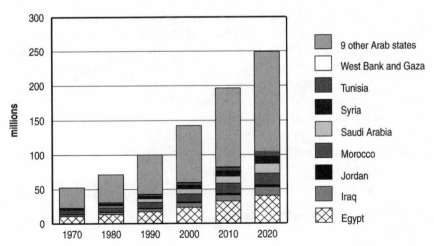

Figure 2.5. The Labor Force, 1970–2020. *Source:* World Bank, *Unlocking the Employment Potential in the Middle East and North Africa* (2004).

Table 2.3. *Labor-force participation rates, 1980–2003 (percentage of 15–64 year olds)*

	1980			1990			2003		
	Total	Female	Male	Total	Female	Male	Total	Female	Male
Egypt	56.4	29.3	83.5	56.9	31.5	83.4	59.0	38.9	82.3
Iraq	48.7	16.2	80.1	46.0	15.0	76.1	48.2	20.9	76.3
Jordan	47.7	14.7	78.6	48.4	17.9	75.9	55.3	29.3	79.7
Morocco	61.0	38.1	84.7	61.7	40.4	83.4	63.2	44.6	82.3
Saudi Arabia*	53.6	9.7	86.3	58.0	16.4	85.9	57.1	23.9	78.8
Syria	52.9	23.5	82.5	52.3	24.6	80.4	54.8	31.7	80.7
Tunisia	59.5	34.5	84.7	58.5	34.4	82.8	62.1	41.3	83.0
West Bank and Gaza	37.0	6.5	66.2	38.0	6.6	67.4	41.4	11.0	72.0

* Including non-nationals.

Sources: World Bank, "Unlocking the Employment Potential in the Middle East and North Africa," 2004, and "World Development Indicators," 2003.

to reach 61 percent in 2010.[22] Table 2.3 shows the increase between 1980 and 2000.

The female labor-force participation rate in the Middle East and North Africa was and remains the lowest in the world: about 25 percent in 1995 and about 29 percent in 2005.[23] Nevertheless, Table 2.3 shows that the increase in female participation in the labor force more than outweighed the decline in the male rate that occurred in six of the countries listed. The female rate rose because of improved education, the operation of economic incentives, and other changes that enabled or encouraged women to work outside the home. It was also affected by economic necessity: recession resulted in increased male unemployment and so women had to supplement family incomes. It may also have been affected by rising living standards. The female participation rate for young women (aged 25–29) increased by up to 50 percent in Algeria, Egypt, Libya, Oman, Saudi Arabia, Syria, and Yemen. It is not clear whether wealth or poverty was the cause. If these economies grow, then they will need more labor and thus women will be attracted to the labor market. Recession could have the same effect, however, as has been observed in the past.

Between 1980 and 1990, the male rate fell because of rising unemployment. At the margin, men were replaced by women in the labor force. Applying average rates for the Middle East to the Arab states, the following

[22] World Bank. *Unlocking the Employment Potential in the Middle East and North Africa*, Washington, D.C.: World Bank. 2004. 225.
[23] International Labor Office. *Global Employment Trends Brief*, June 2005. http://www.ilo.org.

calculation can be made. If a constant labor-force participation rate of 54.5 percent in 1970 and 2000 is assumed, then the rise in the working-age population accounted for 95.6 percent of the rise in the labor force. The increase in the participation rate from 54.5 percent to 57 percent therefore added the additional 4.4 percent to the labor force. This means that 95.6 percent of the 52.8 million increase in the labor force between 1970 and 2000 was because of the growth of the working-age population and 4.4 percent was because of the increase in participation rates, ignoring the effects of migration into the region.

Public Sector Employment

The period since the Arab states gained their independence has seen a massive increase in public sector activity and employment, especially in the civil service. Part of this was due to the Arab Socialist Movement, which began in the 1950s in Egypt, Syria, Iraq, and Yemen, and in the 1960s in Algeria. Using the Soviet model, these countries nationalized economic assets and used central planning and control to develop their economies. The creation of employment by the public sector was a key policy designed to increase welfare, maintain social stability, and encourage political loyalty. Nonsocialist countries such as Jordan, Morocco, and the Gulf Cooperation Council members (Bahrain, Kuwait, Oman, Qatar, Saudi Arabia, and the United Arab Emirates [UAE]) also used the public sector to push economic development forward.

Since the 1980s, most countries in the region have moved away from the socialist model toward free markets and many have privatized assets. This has not, however, reduced total public sector employment. For example, the Egyptian bureaucracy expanded rapidly after independence: from 350,000 in 1952 to 4.8 million in 1992.[24] In the period 1988–98, despite reforms, the civil service grew rapidly, providing 1.82 million more jobs while 306,000 were lost in the rest of the public sector. In 1999, one million were employed in state-owned enterprises and the number was higher if public authorities were added.[25] In Egypt in 1990–98, despite the implementation of structural adjustment programs and a reduction of the share of government in the

---

[24] Rivlin, Paul. *The Dynamics of Economic Policy Making in Egypt.* New York: Praeger, 1985. 21; Assaad, Ragui. *The Transformation of the Egyptian Labor Market, 1988–1998.* Economic Research Forum for the Arab Countries, Iran and Turkey, August 2000. Table A11.

[25] Assaad, Ragui, Table A11.

economy, the civil service was the fastest growing sector of employment. In 1988 it accounted for 19 percent of total employment; in 1998 it took almost 24 percent.

Algeria is an example of a country that gained its independence with a very small bureaucracy. When the French left in 1962, they withdrew their civil servants, who had been running much of the administration. Algeria was thus left with fewer than 30,000 civil servants, all of low rank. By the late 1980s more than 800,000 were employed in 26 ministries and about 39 public organizations.[26] In 1995, there were 1.2 million civil servants and a further 1.2 million were employed in public sector enterprises, equal to about 32 percent of the labor force.[27]

What about states that did not experience Arab socialism? In 1962 there were 37,000 civil servants in Saudi Arabia; in 1981 there were 232,000.[28] In 1999 the Saudi government employed 900,000 people or 12.8 percent of the labor force. Of these, 716,500 were Saudi citizens and they constituted almost 22 percent of the labor force made up by Saudi citizens.[29] In Kuwait, the civil service expanded from 22,000 in 1963 to 146,000 in 1980 and to 160,294 in 1987.[30] The number of Kuwaiti nationals thus employed increased from 25,000 in 1966 to 58,000 in 1987, equal to about one-third of all Kuwaiti citizens in employment during that period.[31] In Jordan in 1998, 69,000 or 16.4 percent of the labor force was employed in public administration and defense. Another 10.3 percent were employed in education and health. Together these categories accounted for 27 percent of the labor force, but the share of the public sector was much higher if workers in publicly owned industries are included.

Government in the Arab world is oversized. In the late 1990s, the bureaucracies in Egypt, Algeria, Saudi Arabia, and Jordan employed almost seven million. If Syria, Morocco, and Iraq are included then the figure was at least eight million and possibly as high as ten million. This does not include those in public sector industries or organizations. The huge numbers of civil

---

[26] Ayubi, Nazih N. *Overstating the Arab State.* London: I.B. Tauris, 1995. 305.
[27] Calculated from Ruppert, Elizabeth. "The Algerian Retrenchment: A Financial and Economic Evaluation." *World Bank Review*, 13, no. 1999; IMF: *Algeria: Statistical Appendix*, Report no. 01/163, 2001.
[28] Richards, Alan and John Waterbury. *A Political Economy of the Middle East.* Boulder: Westview, 1990. 211.
[29] Saudi Arabian Monetary Agency. *Annual Report.* no. 37, 2001.
[30] Richards, Alan and John Waterbury. *A Political Economy of the Middle East*, 211.
[31] Kuwait, Ministry of Planning. *Annual Statistical Abstract, 1988.*

servants form a vested interest and this inevitably comes into conflict with liberalizing trends.[32] These are not the only forms of public employment.

Military Employment

In 2005, an estimated 2.6 million people were employed in regular and paramilitary forces in Arab countries, excluding the police.[33] Large armies provide employment in a region that suffers from large-scale unemployment. They maintain control systems, operate intelligence, and encourage loyalty. The large size of armies and security forces means that the state has an overwhelming monopoly of force, something that limits opposition to regimes in the Arab world.

Unemployment

The Middle East and North Africa have the highest unemployment rates in the world (see Table 2.3). The overall rate has risen over the past twenty years and remains high.[34] This holds true for all types of economy: the oil-rich, the mixed economies, and the poorest. Unemployment has risen because the traditional sources of employment growth have weakened and have not been replaced. The primary source – the public sector – took the brunt of the crisis that hit the region in the 1980s. Governments that previously guaranteed jobs for graduates could no longer afford to do so. Reforms in agriculture as well as diminishing returns in that sector meant that adding labor did not result in increased production. As a result, migration from the countryside to the towns increased. Moreover, the opportunities to move from poorer to richer Arab states declined as the oil income of the Gulf States diminished. At the same time, the working-age population grew and the average level of education rose. Jobs for an increasingly educated workforce were not forthcoming on the required scale: there was a mismatch between the number and types of job available and the supply of labor. This resulted in higher unemployment rates among those who had completed secondary education than among those who had completed (or not completed) primary school only. Unemployment among young people in the

---

[32] Weiss, Dieter and Ulrich Wurzel. *The Economics and Politics of Transition to an Open Market Economy in Egypt*. Paris: OECD, 1998.

[33] Stauber, Zvi and Yiftah Shapir (eds.). *Middle East Military Balance 2004–2005*. Brighton, Portland: Sussex Academic Press for The Jaffee Center for Strategic Studies, 2005.

[34] ILO. *World Employment Report 2004–5*. 57.

Middle East (the Arab states and Iran) averaged 25.6 percent in 2003.[35] It is now necessary to examine the demand for labor, a function of the rate and pattern of economic growth.

Economic Growth and Industrialization

Between 1980 and 2000, the performance of the economies in the Middle East and North Africa was disappointing. In the 1980s, per capita income fell by an average annual rate of 1 percent, a worse performance than in any other part of the world except Sub-Saharan Africa. In the 1990s, GDP per capita grew by 1 percent a year, an improvement over the previous decade but still very weak compared with most other parts of the world.[36] Since 2000, as a result of the increased price of oil, growth has accelerated in much of the region.

In 1990, eleven Arab countries, including Egypt, Kuwait, Morocco, Saudi Arabia, Syria, Tunisia, and the UAE, accounted for 0.9 percent of the value added in world manufacturing industry. At that time they accounted for 0.8 percent of world income and 3.1 percent of world population. In 2001, although their share in world income had more than doubled to 1.8 percent and they accounted for 3.4 percent of the world's population, their share in world manufacturing value added remained unchanged. The growth in income was largely accounted for by the rise in oil income.

In 1990, fourteen Arab states (Algeria, Egypt, Iraq, Jordan, Kuwait, Lebanon, Morocco, Libya, Oman, Qatar, Morocco, Saudi Arabia, Syria, and Tunisia) exported $137 billion of merchandise, equal to 3.9 percent of world merchandise trade. In 2001, they exported $274 billion or 3.5 percent of world merchandise trade. Between 1990 and 2001, world merchandise exports rose by 121 percent and that of the fourteen Arab states by 100 percent, most of which was due to the rise in the price of oil. In 1990, the fourteen Arab states exported only $23 billion or 0.7 percent of world merchandise exports, excluding oil, gas, and minerals. In 2003, non-oil exports of the fourteen Arab states came to $47 billion, about 0.7 percent of the world's total.[37] In 2000 the Arab world accounted for 0.6 percent of world manufactured exports. By 2005, this had increased to 1.3 percent.

[35] ILO. *Global Employment Trends 2004.* 19.
[36] The Economic Research Forum for the Arab Countries, Iran and Turkey. *Economic Trends in the MENA Region, 2002.* Cairo: The American University in Cairo Press, 2002, 1.
[37] World Bank. *World Development Indicators 2005*, World Bank, Washington, D.C., 2005. 214–16.

If the UAE is excluded, then the shares were 0.3 percent and 0.6 percent, respectively.[38]

Both in terms of manufacturing output and exports, the volumes and shares were very small. To a considerable extent the Arab world has failed to industrialize. The share of manufacturing in total employment was therefore low and this sector, despite its growth in some countries, failed to provide the basis for employment growth that it did in the Industrial Revolution in Europe and the United States in the nineteenth century or in East Asia in the twentieth century.

In many Arab countries, manufacturing value added per capita and as a share of GDP was lower than the developing country average (see Figure 2.6).

The only non-oil state to exceed the developing country average was Tunisia. This was also true of the share of manufacturing in the economy (see Figure 2.7).

Figure 2.7 provides data on the share of manufacturing value added in GDP. It shows that the share in Arab countries was, on average, lower than in the developing country group. It also shows that between 1995 and 2005, the share of manufacturing value added declined in Algeria, Bahrain, Kuwait, Lebanon, Qatar, Sudan, and Tunisia.

There is a wide if not total consensus on many of the causes of the limited nature of industrialization in the Arab world.[39] The main causes of poor performance are fast population growth, low productivity, the lack of political and institutional reforms, large and inefficient public sectors, inefficient and inequitable educational systems, underdeveloped financial markets, restrictive foreign trade policies, and inappropriate trade policies. Another significant factor has been the low level of technological absorption capacity. This meant that educated labor was often unemployed or emigrated because the demand for its services within the region was limited. Imports of technology and investments from outside were relatively small and this was seldom due to a lack of funds. This was, in turn, due to the lack of depth of the industrialization process and the fact that the region was not participating in global specialization.[40] Output grew more as a result of increased inputs rather than greater efficiency in their use, something that

---

[38] Calculated from World Trade Organization. *International Trade Statistics 2006*, Geneva: WTO, 2006. 123, 128.

[39] Rivlin, Paul. *Economic Policy and Performance in the Arab World*. Boulder: Lynne Rienner, 2001. 13–28.

[40] Noland, Marcus and Howard Pack. *The Arab Economies in a Changing World*. Washington, D.C.: Peterson Institute for International Economics, 2007. 179–81.

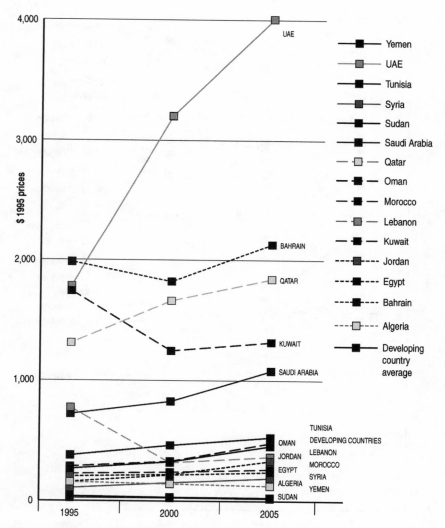

Figure 2.6. Manufacturing Value Added per Capita, 1995–2005. *Source:* UNIDO, Online Data Access, unido.org.index.php?id=4849.

ultimately limited the growth of employment. The lack of political and institutional change has been examined extensively in the Arab Human Development Reports. They have pointed to the lack of clear demarcation lines between the public and private sectors and the widespread lobbying of policy makers for private gain (rent-seeking) that generate distortions, inefficiency, and even disincentives to healthy economic activity such as investment in

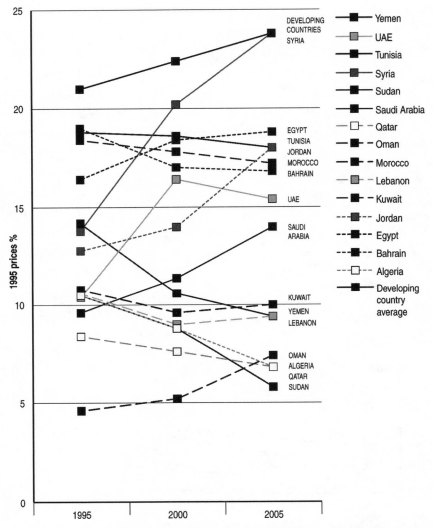

Figure 2.7. The Share of Manufacturing Value Added in GDP, 1995–2005. *Source:* UNIDO, Online Data Access, unido.org.index.php?id=4849.

manufacturing. The lack of a free press means that the public and private sectors and the relations between them are not subject to scrutiny and this makes correction harder to achieve. The fact that the public sector is so large and inefficient not only crowds out credit for the private sector but imposes large costs on the state budget.

Government intervention also prevents the private sector from developing: starting a new business, clearing goods through customs, and other bureaucratic procedures require much more time in most of the Arab world than they do in East Asia, Eastern Europe, or Central Asia. Furthermore, many Arab countries have large military budgets and are involved in conflicts within the region. Although conscription reduces unemployment, it also reduces productivity and impedes reforms in the labor market and elsewhere.[41]

One of the consequences of the lack of industrialization is that Arab countries have relatively little to sell. In 2005, intraregional sales accounted for only 10 percent of total exports in the Middle East and North Africa compared with 51 percent in Asia, and 73 percent in the European Union.[42] In that year, the Arab world relied on imports from outside the region for 92 percent of total imports while only 8 percent came from within the region.[43]

Much of Arab industrialization in the 1950s, 1960s, and early 1970s was carried out on the basis of import substitution. The emphasis was on basic, capital-intensive industries such as iron and steel and resulted in fast growth. Ultimately, however, the industries created in the Arab socialist states and later in the Gulf could not be centrally controlled by the governments that founded them. Companies were not run to make profits but were run with socioeconomic objectives in mind, including the provision of employment. Hence the creation of one million new jobs during Egypt's first five-year plan in the early 1960s was hailed as a great success. The state provided subsidies during the period of expansion but could not afford to do so when economic growth slowed. The costs of the subsidies mounted as public sector employment increased.

The planning of industrialization was weak. In the socialist countries it followed the Soviet model, but the Arab states lacked the means and the will to push the development process forward as Stalin had in the 1930s. One of the main consequences was that linkages to agriculture were weak and industrialization did not have beneficial effects throughout the economy. There was a severe lack of trained local personnel to run and maintain the new industries and so reliance on foreign sources was endemic. In the Arab

---

[41] Abed, George T. and Hamid R. Davoodi. *Challenges of Growth and Globalization in the Middle East and North Africa.* Washington, D.C.: IMF, 2003. http://www.imf.org/external/pubs/ft/med/2003/eng.abed.htm.

[42] World Trade Organisation. *International Trade Statistics 2006.* 38. http://www.wto.org/english/res_e/statis_e/its2006_e/its06_byregion_e.pdf.

[43] *Middle East Economic Survey.* Nicosia: Middle East Petroleum and Economic Publications, XLIX no. 3, 21. 16, January 2006.

socialist states, Soviet advisors were dominant; in the Gulf, it was Western advisors who fulfilled that function. The training of local personnel was slow and the consequences are still being felt.

For many years, governments in the region followed an inward-looking economic policy that relied on public investment to lead economic growth. Since public enterprises were considered to be the main instrument of growth, most governments did not focus on creating a business environment conducive to private sector activity. Through state-owned firms, governments invested directly in manufacturing capacity, financial institutions, and infrastructure, and dominated commercial activities. In oil-producing countries, investments were financed by the high oil revenues of the 1970s and 1980s, and in non–oil-producing countries, by inflows of capital and remittances.

From the 1980s, most Middle East governments encouraged or permitted the growth of a private sector that was carefully protected from external and internal competition. They erected high trade barriers around the companies in this sector, subsidized their interest rates, favored them through procurement policies and allowed them a high degree of market concentration. The larger state-owned firms that coexisted with their smaller private counterparts also benefited greatly from this strategy. Although liberalization programs and trade agreements meant that tariffs and quotas on imports were reduced in the late 1990s, they remained high in many Arab countries. Customs procedures and other forms of red tape took the place of tariffs and quotas as the main obstacles to imports. In 2000, the simple average tariff in the Middle East and North Africa was 19.4 percent, compared with 10.7 percent in East Asia and the Pacific, and 13.4 percent in South America and the Caribbean.[44] Restrictions on imports made inputs expensive. This discouraged exports and limited the region's ability to take advantage of globalization.

The result has been economies with large public sectors, private sectors protected by high tariffs, and, in most countries, smaller, informal private sectors that have emerged in a gray area outside government confines or between the public and private sectors. The informal sector mainly comprises small and medium-sized enterprises and other firms that want to escape high taxes and costly regulations, or that have been crowded out by state-owned enterprises. Initially this economic strategy was successful. Fueled by oil revenues, it was often possible for economies to remain closed to competition and still deliver improvements in living standards. In the

[44] World Bank. *Middle East and North Africa Region, Economic Prospects and Developments. 2007,* Table 5.1, p. 98. http://www.worldbank.org.

1960s and early 1970s, the rate of growth of GDP per worker was relatively high. By the 1980s, the approach no longer worked; it failed to generate economic growth, employment, or increases in the standard of living.[45] The performance of the private sector has also been disappointing. The desire of various governments to influence the direction and structure of economic activity, along with their distrust of private companies, resulted in a highly controlled business environment with a mass of regulations and restrictions. Although the informal private sector has often generated a large portion of the region's growth and employment, it has had little access to formal sector markets, sources of finance, or government support programs to help it expand.

The net results were deteriorating productivity, a large and inefficient public enterprise sector, and underdeveloped financial markets. The fall in the productivity of overall investments discouraged the private sector. The rate of growth of GDP per worker declined and in some cases became negative in the years after the 1970s. Egypt's share of world trade has not grown during the last thirty years.[46]

In the Gulf Cooperation Council states (Bahrain, Kuwait, Oman, Qatar, Saudi Arabia, and the UAE), oil revenues financed investment in many unproductive projects and permitted large-scale public-sector employment. These developments interfered with the growth of the private sector and made it harder for these economies to diversify away from oil. This, in turn, limited employment growth and resulted in the paradoxical coincidence of wealth and unemployment. In other states in the region, poor institutional quality – in terms of large and inefficient bureaucracies, corruption, and inappropriate laws – has impeded growth.[47] Another important factor that has hindered growth has been armed conflict in the region.[48] The Arab states spend a disproportionate share of their income on the military: in 2006, defense spending came to about $62 billion. This was 5.3 percent of world military spending, but Arab states had only an estimated 1.9 percent of world GDP.[49]

---

[45] Cassing, James H., Samih Fawzy, Denis Gallagher, and Hanaa Kheir-El-Din. "Enhancing Egypt's Exports" in Hoekman, Bernard M. and Jamal Zarrouk (eds.), *Catching up with the Competition: Trade Policy Challenges and Options for the Middle East and North Africa.* Ann Arbor: University of Michigan Press, 2000. 208–9.

[46] Ibid. 208–9.

[47] Hakura, Dalia S. *Growth in the Middle East and North Africa.* IMF Working Paper, no. 04/54, 2004. 19. http://www.imf.org.

[48] Elbadawi, Ibrahim A. 2005 (2006). Reviving Growth in the Arab World. *Economic Development and Cultural Change* 53 No. 54: 293–326.

[49] Stockholm International Peace Research Institute. *SIPRI Yearbook 2006.* Oxford: Oxford University Press, 2006. 336, 342.

Savings rates have been low because the high proportion of children in the population meant that the dependency ratio per household was high. This limited the amount of income that remained after consumption. The low incomes of state employees (with the exception of the Gulf States) also acted as a constraint. The lack of development of financial markets meant that savings instruments were limited. Low savings rates were one of the causes of low investment rates: over the last twenty years, governments have reduced their involvement in the economy and have reduced public sector investment. The private sector has not made up for these cuts and so, in many countries in the region, total investment levels are lower than they were twenty years ago.[50] Overvalued exchange rates coupled with taxes and nontariff barriers on imports have restricted exports because the latter are often reliant on imports, given the "shallowness" of the economy.

Agriculture

In many Arab countries, agriculture remains the largest employer and the largest sector in terms of share of GDP. In the region as a whole it accounts for about 12 percent of GDP; just over 30 percent of the population live in rural areas and nearly 34 percent of the labor force work in agriculture. The region is the driest in the world and this is a major constraint on agriculture, as is the variation in rainfall that results in droughts in some parts of the region on a regular basis. As a result, the region imports more than one-half of its food and agro-industrial needs. Agricultural production rose much faster in the period 2000–05 than it did in the 1990s mainly because of the quantity of rainfall (see Table 2.4). Per capita production growth was more modest and so imports grew.

Figure 2.8 shows that exports more than doubled in current dollar terms. This was the result of increased sales both between countries in the region and to other parts of the world, mainly Europe. Between 1990 and 2004, although imports grew slowly, the food trade deficit fell by only 4.5 percent. Given its natural resource base, there is economic logic in importing food and having a negative balance of trade in foodstuffs and agriculture. However, the deficit has to be funded and this requires exports of non-agricultural goods.

---

[50] Ikram, Khalid. *The Egyptian Economy 1952–2000*. Abingdon, Oxon: Routledge, 2006. 82; Rivlin, Paul. *Economic Policy and Performance in the Arab World*. Boulder, Colo.: Lynne Rienner, 2001.119–20, 128–9.

Table 2.4. *Indices of agricultural production,* 1990–2005 (1980 = 100)

	1990	2000	2005
Cereals	134.4	140.0	188.0
Fruit	150.6	177.7	237.3
Vegetables	137.7	146.6	221.9
Population	133.4	171.8	184.1

* Arab League except Comoros, Djibouti, and Mauritania.

Source: Calculated from http://www.fao.org.

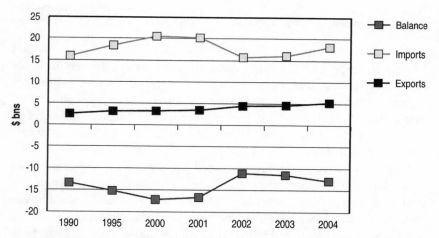

Figure 2.8. Food Trade, 1990–2004. *Source:* Food and Agriculture Organization.

Rents: Oil and Gas

The Middle East is unique, in that a large proportion of income is not derived from production carried out inside the economy. This income is referred to as *rent,* and it takes several forms. The first is income from the sale of oil and gas. The cost of the labor and capital inputs required to produce oil in the Middle East is low compared with the price at which it is sold. The excess of income over those costs is rent. The cost of producing oil in the lowest-cost oil fields in Saudi Arabia is about $2/barrel or less. A sale price of $20/barrel therefore yields up to $18 (80 percent) in rent; a sale price of $70/barrel yields up to $68, or 97 percent. In other parts of the region, costs are higher, and so the rent is lower, but remains significant.

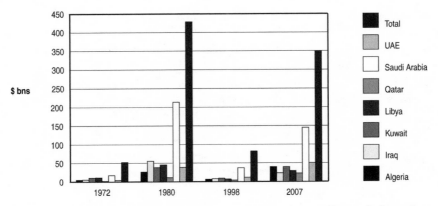

Figure 2.9. Arab OPEC Export Revenues, 1972–2007. *Sources:* Energy Information Agency, Department of Energy, OPEC Revenues Fact Sheet, January 2006, and author's calculations.

Another important characteristic of oil is that its price is very unstable and has been increasingly determined by international market conditions.[51] Figure 2.9 shows that in 2007, despite the sharp rise in international oil prices since 1999, the real value of oil revenues of the Arab members of Organization of the Petroleum Exporting Countries, or OPEC, was 19 percent lower than at the peak of 1980.

Figure 2.10 shows what has happened to oil export revenues on a per capita basis, in constant prices. In all the countries listed, oil income per capita rose sharply in the period 1972–80. In 1980–98, it declined sharply in all the countries. Since then there has been a large increase, but in 2007 oil income per capita remained much lower than in the peak year of 1980, both because prices were lower in constant terms and because the population had increased.

Political Rents

Some of the poorer Arab states received large financial flows from abroad that were essential for ensuring their economic stability. These funds came from the oil-rich states of the Arab world and from governments outside the region. The best example of the rentier state was Jordan; other significant recipients were Egypt and Syria. Aid was bilateral and multilateral, civilian

---

[51] Rivlin, Paul. "Arab Economies and Political Stability" in Rivlin, Paul and Shmuel Even, *Political Stability in Arab States: Economic Causes and Consequences.* Tel Aviv: The Jaffee Center for Strategic Studies, 2004.

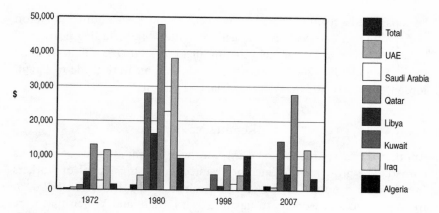

Figure 2.10. Arab OPEC Export Revenues per Capita, 1972–2007. *Sources:* Energy Information Agency, Department of Energy, OPEC Revenues Fact Sheet, January 2006, and author's calculations.

and military, and it took the form of loans, grants, and debt write-offs. Between 1973 and 1989, the poorer states received an estimated $55 billion in aid from Arab countries and multinational bodies.[52] Foreign aid declined from the mid-1980s for several reasons. First, Arab oil income declined, so there was less to give. Second, donors expressed dissatisfaction with the use to which the assistance was put, and cut their allocations. Third, Western countries and multilateral bodies tied aid to economic reforms, the success of which reduced the need for external assistance.

In the Middle East, aid given on a concessional basis (i.e., with reduced interest rates or grace periods for repayment) represented a greater share of total aid than in any other developing region. In 1999, 38 percent of long-term debt in the Middle East was concessional compared to 19 percent on average for developing countries. In Egypt it came to 86 percent, Jordan 54 percent, Syria 93 percent, and Yemen 92 percent.[53] In 1999, 57 percent of long-term net resource flows to the Middle East (excluding Turkey) was from public sector bodies, compared with 17.2 percent for all developing countries. This was due to the very low level of private sector inflows into the region: only $1 billion in 1999, compared with $219 billion for all developing countries. Aid and the rescheduling or cancellation of foreign debt can also

---

[52] Boogaerde, Pierre van den. *Financial Assistance from Arab Countries and Arab Regional Institutions*, Occasional Paper no. 87, 1991. Washington, D.C.: International Monetary Fund, 1991.

[53] World Bank. *Global Development Finance 2001*. Washington, D.C.: World Bank, 2001.

be considered a form of rent.[54] Between 1979 and 1999, about $60 billion of Arab foreign debt was rescheduled or written off, including nearly $28 billion of Egyptian foreign debt that in turn included U.S. military debt.[55] In the period 1999–2002, grants worth $6.8 billion were made to Egypt, Jordan, Morocco, Sudan, Syria, Tunisia, and Yemen.[56]

Remittances

Another major source of rental incomes was the remittances of workers abroad. The growth of oil income resulted in the movement of workers from poorer countries to the oil-rich Arab states. In the period 1973–89, the remittances of workers to Egypt, Syria, Jordan, and Yemen that were registered in balance of payments data came to about $60 billion. Morocco and Tunisia received about $24 billion from emigrants in Western Europe.[57] These funds helped to cover part of the large deficits on trade in goods and services. In the period 1990–98, remittances to Egypt, Jordan, Yemen, and Oman (the latter were minimal) came to about $58 billion. Those to Morocco and Tunisia totaled $23 billion. Given the growth of these economies, remittances declined in relative importance, but remained a large absolute source of income that was not earned inside the economy. Total registered remittances received in the Middle East between 1973 and 1998 came to about $165 billion, or $6.6 billion a year. That was equal to nearly 5 percent of the recipient states' GDP in 1990. In the period 1999–2005, remittances received by the recipient group Egypt, Jordan, Morocco, Sudan, Tunisia, and Yemen came to $81 billion.[58]

Conclusions

Demographic trends have provided the countries of the Middle East with a gift that will last for some years into the future. This takes the form of a larger share of those of working age in the total population than before. More people support and will support fewer children and elderly people, provided

---

[54] Easterly, William. *The Elusive Quest for Growth.* Cambridge, Mass: MIT Press, 2001. 123–37.

[55] World Bank. *Global Development Finance*, 2001.

[56] Rivlin, Paul and Shmuel Even. *Political Stability in Arab States: Economic Causes and Consequences.* Tel Aviv: Jaffee Center for Strategic Studies, 2004. 14. http://www.inss.org.il.

[57] Mattione, Richard. *OPEC's Investments and the International Financial System.* Washington, D.C.: Brookings Institute, 1985. 12.

[58] IMF. *Balance of Payments Yearbook 2004.* Washington, D.C.: IMF, 2004 and *Balance of Payments Yearbook 2006.* Washington, D.C.: IMF, 2006.

that they can find work. Although economic growth rates have accelerated in recent years, this has largely been due to the increase in oil prices. There is much evidence that these revenues are being used more carefully than in the past, given the growth of the population that is vital if financial and economic crises in the oil-rich states are to be avoided. The problem is that even with demographic transition, the scale of unemployment, both open and concealed (overemployment in the public sector or in the semiformal economy) is so great that much faster economic growth and structural change are needed. The governments of the region have been slow to adjust to the pressures on the labor market, even though they pose a threat to social, economic, and political stability. The reasons for this conservatism are the subject of Chapter 3.

THREE

The Constraints of History

Differences and Commonalities

The eight economies examined in this book are very different. Saudi Arabia and Iraq are rich in oil and gas, but have very different levels of income largely because of the devastating effect of wars on the latter. Tunisia has led the Arab world in terms of industrialization and has the highest per capita income of the non-oil states. Jordan has among the best educational and other human development indices. It has also moved a long way toward a liberalized economy and has, in recent years, dramatically increased its industrial exports. Egypt is the largest country demographically but despite reforms, it remains very poor. Morocco stabilized its economy before Egypt and is further ahead in terms of demographic transition but has high illiteracy rates and poverty levels. The Palestinian economy has much human capital but, even within the limits of autonomy, developed a destructively corrupt regime. Its economy has been badly affected by years of conflict and the legacy of occupation. Syria's economy is frozen in the past: economic reforms have been limited and security considerations remain dominant. The decline in its oil revenues is a major threat to economic stability because the non-oil sector has been so badly neglected.

Despite these and other differences, there are a number of factors that these and other Arab economies have in common. The first is that they are all, with the possible exception of the Palestinians, experiencing demographic transition. The phases of the transition vary: it is much more advanced in North Africa than in the Gulf. Transition has meant that a demographic gift has emerged: the share of the working-age population to total population is increasing. As a result, the burden of supporting the young and old has fallen. Governments in the region may not have been fully aware of the enormous scale of the demographic pressures that they face: they certainly

36

have not rushed ahead with programs designed to profit from it while it lasts. As a result, the mechanisms that maintained human welfare and even contributed to rising human development indices have come under threat. One consequence is that although the share of the population living in poverty did not change significantly, the absolute number rose from 40 million in 1987 to 52 million in 2001.[1]

The growth of the working-age population has led to the second factor: the rapid growth of the labor force. The labor force is currently growing by about 3.6 percent a year, adding some three million new workers to the labor market. Given that there are high levels of unemployment in all countries in the region, this presents a formidable challenge.

The third factor is that all the governments that faced economic crises introduced stabilization and structural reform programs. These reforms were usually carried out with the help and support of the International Monetary Fund (IMF) and the World Bank. When oil revenues fell in the 1980s and 1990s, the Gulf States also introduced reforms, although they did not seek IMF or World Bank assistance. Even Syria has avoided balance of payments and fiscal crises by instituting limited reforms without IMF or World Bank assistance.

The fourth factor is that despite reforms, economic growth has not been fast enough or of the right kind to provide employment for all those coming into the job market. As a result, in countries as different as oil-rich Saudi Arabia, reform-minded Jordan, and industrially strong Tunisia, unemployment is high and has been so for many years. This is true for all the other countries in the region. The rapid rise in oil income since 2000 has resulted in faster economic growth in some countries and an acceleration of employment growth, but overall levels of unemployment remain high.

Why Did Imbalances Persist?

Many explanations have been put forward for the economic problems faced by Arab countries along with suggestions on how to solve them. These have come from the IMF and the World Bank, with the latter being more nuanced following widespread criticism of the original Washington Consensus.[2] They have also come from bodies within the region, such as the

---

[1] Iqbal, Farrukh. *Sustaining Gains in Poverty Reduction and Human Development in the Middle East and North Africa.* Washington D.C.: The World Bank, 2006. xix.

[2] Rivlin, Paul. *Economic Policy and Performance in the Arab World.* Boulder, Colo.: Lynne Rienner, 2001. 199–207.

Economic Research Forum (ERF) for the Arab countries, Iran, and Turkey, and the Egyptian Center for Economic Studies, both located in Cairo. The Arab Human Development Reports, issued by the United Nations Development Program and written by Arab social scientists, have been the most outspoken, calling for political as well as economic reform.

The reasons for the failure to deepen or widen economic reform are at the center of our concerns. If the absence of political reforms can be simplistically explained as a desire by those in authority not to relinquish power, the failure to introduce more economic reforms is more puzzling. Economic failure can also threaten the power structure and bring down the regime; reform can therefore be a way of avoiding this. There are, however, two objections to this line of reasoning. The first is that Arab governments have not been brought down because of economic discontent. There have been riots, assassinations, and even, in the case of Algeria, a civil war, but these events did not bring down regimes. The second objection is that economic reform cannot be separated from political reform. In much of the world, with the notable exceptions of China and Vietnam, they have gone together. The unwillingness to introduce more radical reforms may be because rulers fear that economic reforms will alter the balance of political power away from the state.

The Arab Human Development Reports examined the relationship between political and economic reform in the Middle East. They highlighted a number of issues that previous literature largely avoided. First they raised serious questions about the relationship between Arab political systems and economic performance. They also made explicit comparisons between Arab countries and other parts of the world, something that political correctness had prevented or limited. According to *The Arab Human Development Report 2002*, during the 1980s and 1990s, growth of per capita income in the Arab world at an annual average of 0.5 percent was lower than in any other region, except Sub-Saharan Africa. Labor productivity in Arab nations was low, and declined, from one-third of the North American level in 1960 to 19 percent by 1990. If the annual growth rate of 0.5 percent continued, it would take the average Arab citizen 140 years to double his income. Other, fast-growing regions would achieve this level in less than ten years. The total gross domestic product of the Arab world – $531 billion – was less than that of Spain and one in five Arabs lived on less than two dollars a day. In 2002, unemployment in the Arab region was estimated at 15 percent of the labor force. This was the highest rate in the world. All this was despite huge investments made in social and economic infrastructure made possible by oil wealth and foreign aid.[3] Human welfare measures have been less worrying. Life expectancy in the region has increased by 15 years, mortality rates of children under age 5 have fallen by two-thirds, and adult literacy has almost doubled, but these achievements are under threat.

The Arab Human Development Report 2002 also introduced the Alternative Human Development Index (AHDI). This was based on an expanded version of the Human Development Index designed by Amartya Sen. During the 1990s, Sen's index helped to widen the debate about development, from a purely economic to a socioeconomic one by gathering statistics measuring human development such as life expectancy, literacy, schooling, and per capita income. The Arab Human Development Report's (AHDR) authors expanded Sen's index, by adding data on lifelong knowledge acquisition, especially regarding information technology, women's access to societal power, and measures of human freedom. The world's highest AHDI score was for Sweden (ranked first), the United States ranked eleven, and Turkey came in at sixty-seven, ahead of all other Middle East states. Iraq was the second lowest at 111, ahead of Congo. The rest of the Arab world was between the highest, Jordan at 68 and Sudan at 105.

Governance has long been recognized as a key issue in economic development. The main issues are the processes by which governments are chosen, monitored, and replaced, the capacities of government, and the respect citizens have for government. The report states that Arab governments were below the world average on all indicators of institutional quality, except for that of the rule of law. Improvements in political institutions were seen as conditions for economic development in line with much of the literature on new institutional economics and political economy. It stated that much needed to be done to provide people in the region with the political voice, social choices, and economic opportunities that they need for a better future. It outlined the challenges faced by Arab countries in strengthening personal and institutional freedoms and boosting broad-based citizen participation in political and economic affairs. The way forward involved promoting good governance based on expanding human capabilities, choices, opportunities, and freedoms, and empowering women and those most marginalized in society.

The main causes for the weak state of Arab development were explained in terms of deficits of freedom, women's empowerment, and human

---

[3] United Nations Development Program, Regional Bureau for Arab States. *Arab Human Development Report 2002*. New York: UN, 2002. 4, 85.

capability/knowledge deficit in relation to income. The report called for the democratization of the Arab world, not only as an end in itself but also to improve economic management. It showed, at least implicitly, what the cost of bad government was. Second, it made international comparisons and warned Arabs that they were falling behind. Finally, despite its lip service to the Palestinian or Arab cause in the struggle with Israel, it tried to place the focus on developments in Arab countries. This meant ceasing to blame outsiders (principally Israel and the United States) for all the woes in the region. These are controversial matters, especially in Middle East studies. An interview with the report's lead author was very revealing. After acknowledging the Arab view that the conflict with Israel was a major cause of economic backwardness, he stated that reform initiated *within* the Arab world would be the only guarantee of sustainable progress. Reform imposed from outside would be met by skepticism by Arabs who feel that the West is biased in the Arab–Israel conflict.[4] How likely is reform from within? The report does not deal with this vital issue and so the reader is left wondering how the region can improve its economy if governments are both so dysfunctional but also so enduring. Another intriguing question is: Why are dysfunctional governments so enduring?

One way to answer this set of questions is by means of comparison. Perhaps there is something missing in Arab countries that caused development elsewhere. Or perhaps it is the presence of some factor or factors in the region that has limited or prevented development. The doyen of Middle East economic historians Charles Issawi wrote a number of papers comparing the Middle East with other regions, but he did so at a time when sensitivity about comparisons was less than it became. He also made serious critiques of Arab economic performance, policies, and attitudes that are often ignored in contemporary Middle East studies.[5] Within the economics profession, comparisons and other methodologies amenable to measurement have been used extensively. Conventional economics tends to examine how things should be done and leave to others – historians, political scientists, or political economists – why or why they are not done. The World Bank has gone a long way in recognizing the factors at work. One explanation given for the lack of sufficient change is that in most of the region the economic crisis was not usually severe enough. In Jordan, the depth of crisis did result in radical changes. Another explanation is that either there

---

[4] *Al Ahram Weekly online.* 11–17 July 2002. http://www.weekly.ahram.org.eg.
[5] For example, "The Japanese Model and the Middle East," in Issawi, Charles. *The Middle East Economy: Decline and Recovery.* Princeton: Markus Wiener Publishers, 1995. 165–84.

was a lack of power among those interest groups that might have lobbied for change or those that benefited from the status quo were too power-ful.[6] Chapter 8 shows how the textile and clothing sectors in Morocco have developed two networks that correspond to these definitions. Understanding economic policy therefore requires an examination of the distribution of power and how it developed over time.

There is literature that throws light on the political economy of the region, but much remains to be done in terms of integrating historical and economic analysis. Economic historians and economists have begun to break down barriers with other disciplines but in the Middle East, political sensitivity remains a potent obstacle to understanding and action. The authors of the AHDR were constrained both by lack of data and by a lack of cooperation from officials in the region. The 2002 report explained the political issues behind many economic problems but did not answer the question of how those issues will be tackled in the political environment that has prevailed in the Arab world for so long. The two following reports took the analysis further. The third report placed the blame for the lack of political freedom in the region on "the convergence of political, social, and cultural structures that have suppressed or eliminated organized social and political forces capable of turning the crisis of authoritarian and totalitarian regimes to their advantage. The elimination of such forces has led to the loss of any real forward momentum." The flaw was not cultural but political.[7] Which forces were missing? The most obvious was a middle class, independent of the state: we will return to this later.

Why were governments so dysfunctional but so enduring? Why did regimes so different in their nature and in their levels of economic achievement as those in Syria, Saudi Arabia, and Tunisia have much in common when it came to policy making? Recent literature on economic history and economic development provides elements of an explanation.

Schools of Thought

There are several schools of thought among economic historians and economists about long-term economic development, although, as will be

[6] Nabli, Mustapha, Jennifer Keller, Claudia Nassif, and Carlos Silva-Jauregui. *The Political Economy of Industrial Policy in the Middle East and North Africa*. ECES Conference Paper, Cairo, 2005. 21–2. http://www.worldbank.org.
[7] United Nations Development Program. *Arab Human Development Report 2004*. New York: UN, 2005. 128.

seen, it is difficult to classify the explanations given. The first places emphasis on geographic factors, including climate. Wittfogel showed that human civilization developed in the river valleys of semitropical zones; he called them "hydraulic societies." In the Middle East there were two such valleys: the Nile and the Euphrates. The civilizations that developed in those regions (and elsewhere) needed central authority to survive. They needed to control irrigation from the river to lands around it and regulate life in the valley. The first postal and secret police forces known were developed thousands of years ago in those regions. It is very significant that geography dictated strong government. That has been a central feature of the political economy of the Middle East ever since. In all that we will have to say about Islam, we should remember that the strong state preceded it.[8] The main feature of the hydraulic society was that the leaders were holders of "despotic state power and not private owners or entrepreneurs." Land was owned by the state. In such a system, the state was stronger than the society and one of the main ways in which it maintained its strength was to *attach itself to the country's main belief system* or religion. Wittfogel's ideas, based on Marx and Weber, have been disputed, but whether they are accepted or rejected as *the* explanation for long-term developments, the links among geography, politics, belief systems, ideologies, religion, and economics that he noted are significant.

Hydraulic Despotism

The Arab Empire and Islam were preceded by other empires in Egypt and Mesopotamia. These were hydraulic states whose economic activities were based on the use of river water. This had to be controlled and monitored and these activities required a central authority. According to Wittfogel, a strong state developed in these areas because of the need to organize and control societies relying on natural irrigation systems. They therefore created bureaucracies to manage systems. Wittfogel stated that the state was stronger than society in those areas: land ownership, capitalism, and the gentry were bureaucratically controlled. In regions where there was hydraulic despotism, those that might have contested the attempts of masters of hydraulic power from attaining absolute power failed. This was because they lacked "the proprietary and organizational strength that in Greek and Roman antiquity, as

---

[8] Wittfogel, Karl. *Oriental Despotism: A Comparative Study of Total Power.* New Haven and London: Yale University Press, 1957. 49.

well as in Medieval Europe, bulwarked non-government forces of society."[9] In the hydraulic state, the government maintained a monopoly over fast locomotion, which was interlocked with an intelligence system and thus became a formidable weapon of social control.[10]

There were also very significant effects on the development of private property. Hydraulic states denied property owners or landowners the right to dispose of their property among their heirs at will. Their inheritance laws favored a more or less equal division of property in estate of a deceased person, something that helped to fragment the ownership of wealth periodically. Islam retained these laws and so the holders of *waqfs* (family endowments) kept their land undivided, because they were ultimately to serve religious and charitable purposes. While the family *waqf* temporarily benefited the grantee and his descendants, it was neither a secure nor a free form of property. Athough less frequently singled out for confiscation than other kinds of property, the family *waqfs* might be seized if the state chose. The *waqfs* were taxed, and their beneficiaries were never able to consolidate their power through a nationwide political organization.[11] This can be contrasted with the signing in England of the Magna Charter in 1215 C.E. The Charter contained a clause that effectively recognized the right of the barons, as a group, to coerce the king. In thirteenth-century England, the barons were also ensuring the perpetuation of their property rights by primogeniture and entail.[12] It reflected a plurality of political power far greater than that prevailing in the Middle East at that time.

In the Middle East, the pre-Islamic inheritance was a strong one. In Egypt, the Pharaoh was a god or son of a god. In Mesopotamia the pattern was more complex, but in effect the ruler had divine authority. In Islam, Mohammed was neither Allah nor his son: he was the Prophet. Although the caliphates were not theocracies, the caliph was strong enough to prevent the emergence of an Islamic church separate from the state.[13]

The Role of Geography

The most outspoken advocate of the role of geography in economic development is Jeffrey Sachs. According to Sachs, the most obvious and important

[9] Ibid. 55–7.
[10] Ibid. 84–5.
[11] Ibid. 84–6.
[12] Ibid. 84.
[13] Ibid. 93–7.

geographical fact about the Middle East is that it is largely a desert.[14] This is in strong contrast to largely temperate Europe. Second, the Middle East strides Africa, Asia, and Europe and is therefore a trading center. A third factor that, since the beginning of the twentieth century, has been far more important is the region's reserves of oil and gas that are the largest in the world. This has given it immense geo-political importance. The Mediterranean and the Middle East have also marked the boundary between Islam and Christianity. The border between the two shifted over time as the relative strengths of the two regions changed. Sachs suggests that the geographic factors that differentiated the two regions were more significant than cultural or religious ones.

Islam developed in the desert and those who spread the religion in the seventh and eighth centuries used technology developed in that region. The food production, camel transport, and other methods were suitable for like regions in North Africa and Central Asia. Early Islam also entered Europe but only held areas in the south. The Ottomans, who had a temperate base in Anatolia, were more successful in the Balkans and in Central Europe. Temperate regions have emerged with major advantages for economic development. They have much more wood and coal, which were the main fuels. They also have climates that are less propitious for disease and more suitable for food production. The dependence of populations on limited or even single sources of water was much more prevalent in the Middle East than in Europe. This meant that people in the Middle East were more exposed to water-borne infection. Making use of the advantages of colder climate regions required technological development: the development of metal ploughs for heavy earth and forest clearing as well as housing that could support the population in the cold. When these technologies were available, the advantages of the north began to outweigh those of the south that had sustained some of the earliest civilizations on earth. The Middle East had oil while Europe did not, but this did not change the tide. The role of oil is examined later in the chapter.

The boundary between Christianity and Islam shifted continuously since the foundation of Islam in the seventh century. The period of Arab expansion following the death of the Prophet was from 623 to about 1200 C.E. The Ottoman expansion was in the period 1200 to 1500 C.E. Between 1500 and 1700, there was a stalemate between the Ottomans and Europe and this was followed by European expansion until the collapse of the Ottoman Empire

---

[14] Sachs, Jeffrey. "Long-Term Perspectives in the Economic Development of the Middle East." *The Economic Quarterly* 48, no. 3 (2001). Tel Aviv: Am Oved. Hebrew. 417–40.

at the end of World War I. According to Sachs, the reason for these changes was the balance of long-term demographic, geo-political, and economic factors. Until about 900, the Middle East had a larger population than Europe and in line with its role as a trading center, it was more urbanized. Between 900 and 1500, Europe's population expanded faster than that of the Middle East as its agricultural technology came into play and the Middle East felt the constraints imposed by the desert. The same change occurred in urbanization as Europe overtook the Middle East in both the scale and number of urban settlements. Europe also gained from the expansion of its trade with India and the Far East, using trade routes via the Cape of Good Hope that circumvented the Middle East. Following the fall of Vienna in 1683, the Ottoman Empire lost territory to Europe. Europe began to benefit from the industrial revolution that left most of the Middle East behind to this day. The Ottoman Empire lacked the resources to finance its military operations directed to defend its frontier in Eastern Europe and to maintain internal order. It went into debt and ultimately went bankrupt while Europeans were its main creditors. This occurred despite numerous reforms designed to modernize the Empire, such as the Tanzimat of 1839–76. Egypt and other parts of the Empire were gradually taken over by the British or the French and were opened to international trade. The Western powers hardly invested in the educational system (see Chapter 6) and this placed these countries at a severe disadvantage when they gained their independence.

Factor Endowments

Closely related to the geography school of thought is the factor endowments school, the most prominent proponents of which were Engerman and Sokoloff. This school of thought suggests that different areas of the world attracted certain types of human capital because of their natural resource base. The differences between the pattern of development in North and South America can partly be explained by climatic, soil, and other geographic differences that made Central America more suitable for plantation farming and the northern region of the United States and Canada more suitable for grain farming. These products required different agricultural systems including labor intensities and social organization.[15] Tropical areas

---

[15] Engerman, Stanley L., and Kenneth L. Sokoloff. *Factor Endowments, Inequality, and Paths of Development among New World Economies*, National Bureau of Economic Research, Working Paper 9259, 2002.

were better suited to labor-intensive plantation production. More temperate areas required extensive cultivation with lower ratios of labor to land.
The classic examples were the Southern states versus the Northern states of
the United States. Geography dictated the kind of agriculture that would
be profitable and thus the human skills required. This dictated or influenced migration patterns (slaves were taken to the Southern states and
the Caribbean) while in the Northern states they were much less important. The factor endowments school shows that the natural resource base –
mainly soils and climate – determined the political institutions. In the small-
holder settlements that typified the Northern states of the United States
and Canada, wealth and income were much more equally distributed than
in slave societies in American's South, the Caribbean, and parts of South
America. Wittfogel's work can also be understood in terms of factor endowments: geography determined institutions that in turn determined the pattern of economic development.

Factor Endowments and Colonialism

Acemoglu, Johnson, and Robinson extended the work of Engerman and
Sokoloff on the role of factor endowments. They showed how large income
gaps developed between different areas and the factor endowments school
suggests that this was the result of the institutions that were created in those
areas. The areas that created legal and other systems to protect property
rights were those that were able to industrialize. Those that did not were
unable to. Central in their thesis is the role of European colonialists. Societies
that had low death rates among European settlers were better able to trans-
plant European institutions than those that had higher death rates.[16] Much
depended on the country of origin of the settlers and the kind of institutions
that they were transplanting. A significant number of English settlers in New
England emigrated in protest at the existing order in their country of origin.
They wanted to create a new society; those that set up slave economies in the
Caribbean had other things in mind. In the Middle East in the nineteenth
and twentieth centuries when Britain and France took over much of the
Ottoman Empire, there was, with the exception of Algeria, no large move of
settlers. There was, therefore, no serious attempt by the Western powers to

---

[16] Acemoglu, Daron, Simon Johnson, and James A. Robinson. "The Colonial Origins of
Comparative Development," *American Economic Review* 91, no. 5 (2001) 1369–1401.

implant Western institutions, although the Arab enlightenment of the late nineteenth century tried to move in that direction.[17]

Late nineteenth-century Egypt, like the Southern states of the United States, was a cotton producer par excellence. The cotton economy needed large numbers of cheap laborers supervised by relatively few skilled managers. Unlike the United States, Egypt had an ancient civilization with a tradition of strong central government, something that continued despite changes in rulers (Arab, Ottoman, Mamluk, British, and Egyptian). European colonial powers did not need to import slaves to work in Egypt; the labor force already existed and was organized. This limited the need for the British to impose new institutions on the area when they took control of the country.

The Western powers exploited the Middle East for its natural resources and markets, its geography (the best example is the Suez Canal), and later for its oil. Oil led to the close relationship between leading Arabian tribes and the British. It explains the way in which states were created for them by the British and how oil revenues flowed into the coffers of the rulers and from there to the state treasury. The political economy of the Gulf can only be understood if the role of oil is taken into account and this is a geographical factor. Sachs asserts that geographical factors are much more important in explaining the problems of economic development in the Middle East than cultural or religious ones. It is to these that we now turn.

Culture

Temin defines *culture* as denoting the distinctive attitudes and actions that differentiate groups of people. It is the result of and expressed through religion, language, institutions, and history. The attributes that make up culture change slowly, but they can and do change over time.[18] The founder of the culture school was Weber. He ascribed the Industrial Revolution to the dominance of Protestantism in Northern Europe, where it began. Protestantism, especially its Calvinist version, defined and advocated a set of values that were conducive to business relations. It did this by affirming a belief in predestination. This suggested that what one did in life would not lead to salvation because those who were to be saved had already been

---

[17] Hourani, Albert. *Arab Thought in the Liberal Age 1789–1939.* London: Oxford University Press, 1962. 183–4, 267–8.

[18] Temin, Peter. "Is Culture Kosher?" *Journal of Economic History* 57, no. 2 (1997), 267–82.

chosen. Motivation was provided by the fact that the chosen were likely to be those who were good, defined according to Calvinist criteria as hard working, serious, and thrifty with money and time.[19] The Catholic areas of Europe industrialized later and this was because the culture was less effective in encouraging work and savings. This view has been the subject of much controversy but it has not been abandoned. Landes and others have suggested that Islam was bad for economic development and implicitly make use of Weber's argument.

Landes claims that culture makes almost all the difference. Examining the economic success of the Chinese in East and Southeast Asia, the Lebanese in West Africa, Indians in East Africa, and other expatriate minorities led Landes to conclude that the values and attitudes that these groups took from their origin explains their business success. The lack of economic development of their home base at the time that they or their parents emigrated was because of institutions that prevented the economy from working and that was the incentive to emigrate.[20]

Culturally derived attitudes have a long legacy and evolve in complex ways. They can adapt or partly adapt to new circumstances and do not always replace older ones. Hence Egypt's Five Year Plan for 1978–82 noted that many Egyptians saw a contradiction between a socialist society and the lack of civil authority and efficiency. The emphasis on consumption and interclass mobility are, however, capitalist. The result of this mix of values is a society that lacks discipline, supervision, makes false promises, and offers freedom with responsibility.[21]

Institutions

Greif has compared the ways in which European and Middle East traders performed in the late Middle Ages. He found that European culture encouraged impersonal trade while Middle Eastern culture encouraged trade between members of extended families or closely connected communities. The two groups were in competition and the Europeans won out and gradually

---

[19] Landes, David. *The Wealth and Poverty of Nations*. New York: W. W. Norton, 1999, Chapters 4 and 12.

[20] Landes, David. "Culture Makes Almost All the Difference" in Harrison, Lawrence E., and Samuel P. Huntington (eds.), *Culture Matters*. New York: Basic Books, 2000. 2–13.

[21] Quoted in Ikram, Khalid. *The Egyptian Economy, 1952–2000, Performance, Policies, and Issues*. London and New York: Routledge, 2006. 50.

came to dominate Mediterranean trade.[22] The societal organization of the late medieval Middle East traders resembles modern collectivist societies whereas that of the late medieval Europeans resembles modern individualist society. The Middle East traders (Jews who had absorbed the dominant Islamic cultural values of the region in which they lived) considered themselves members of the same people. Their loyalty was to the *umma* and their membership meant that they were mutually responsible for each other. The fact that the group examined by Greif was made up of Jews who had moved from Iraq to Tunisia reinforced this. They "retained social ties that enabled them to transmit information that enabled them to maintain collectivist equilibrium." The collectivist culture encouraged them to retain business affiliations within this network.[23] The Middle East traders made great efforts to share information so as to maintain their trading network. Their primary concern was to discover if any of them, acting as an agent, tricked another and thus caused him a loss. The knowledge that if they acted dishonestly they would be revealed to the community was a strong incentive to behave honestly. Remaining honest was a way of staying in business, because in most circumstances it would not pay to cheat.

The European Christians, represented in Greif's work by Genoese traders, had an individualistic culture. They maintained as much secrecy about their business relations as they could; they did not restrict their choice of agents to members of their family or others with whom they had personal connections. In the absence of a network that would inform them of an agent's misconduct, they were forced to develop impersonal systems of enforcement, the most important of which was the legal system. This was, over time, to prove invaluable for the development of trade and the economy. The difference in values played a role in determining institutions that in turn influenced economic development over hundreds of years. How did cultural differences manifest themselves in the way trading was carried out? Apart from the development of legal systems mentioned earlier, the Genoese developed bills-of-lading as a method of documenting obligations and transactions; the Middle East traders did not. The Genoese were more likely than the Middle Eastern traders to be economically upwardly mobile,

---

[22] Greif, Avner. *Institutions and the Path to the Modern Economy*. Cambridge: Cambridge University Press, 2006.
[23] Ibid. 309–10.

to experience greater division of labor, and to develop the legal system. This is what happened in Europe with profound, long-term economic consequences. The belief system generated institutions that permitted economic growth. Either the absence of these institutions or their weakness was a cause of economic problems in the Middle East.[24] Lydon has noted that Islamic law placed much greater faith in verbal rather than written documentation. This was despite the Muslim emphasis on literacy and the advances of the Golden Age. The lack of faith that Islamic courts had in paper may well have prevented the growth of joint stock companies and other commercial developments.[25]

The distinction between culture and institutions is hard to make because in some respects it is artificial. Furthermore, some writers have emphasized factors that are both institutional and cultural. Mokyr, for example, noted the importance of institutions and hard work, initiative, and frugality.[26]

Religion

Rodinson argued that Islam does not explain economic problems in the Muslim world. This is because Islam has not been adopted in an overall way, and choices have always been made as to what aspects of the faith to implement. Rodinson, a Marxist, explained economic weakness as the result of material conditions that Muslims faced.[27] Much more recently, Nolan and Pack, orthodox economists, have also argued that Islam is not the cause of economic problems in the Arab world largely because it has not been adopted and therefore does not act as a constraint. They surveyed econometric attempts to assess the influence of Islam on economic growth and concluded that it was not significant. They did, however, note that Islam may well have exerted negative, indirect influences. Islam, along with other factors, may have influenced the way in which institutions in the region developed and these may have negatively influenced economic

---

[24] Greif, Avner. "Cultural Beliefs and the Organization of Society: A Historical and Theoretical Reflection on Collectivist and Individualist Society." *The Journal of Political Economy* 102, Issue 5 (1994). 912–50.

[25] Lydon, Ghislaine. "A 'Paper Economy of Faith' without Faith in Paper: A Contribution to Understanding 'the Roots of Islamic Institutional Stagnation.'" *Journal of Economic Behavior and Organization* 68, November 2008. 329–51.

[26] Mokyr, Joel. *The Gifts of Athena.* Princeton and Oxford: Princeton University Press, 2002. 285.

[27] Rodinson, Maxime. *Islam and Capitalism.* London: Allen Lane, 1974. 76–117.

growth.[28] Econometric studies, such as those surveyed by Nolan and Pack, are dismissed by Platteau. He points out that it is possible to identify factors that militate against economic growth in most religions. Furthermore, the effect of religion is hard to estimate because it is endogenous. Rather than preventing growth directly, a culture or religion may develop in a particular direction because of the lack of economic growth. It is almost impossible to find variables that influence culture or religion without somehow affecting economic growth. As a result, econometric tests based on cross-sectional analysis tell us little. The other major weakness of cross-sectional testing is that very crude measures are used because of the poor quality of the data available. Islam is not homogenous nor was it in the past.[29]

There are those who view successful economic development as a special condition that requires explanation and view the lack of such success as the norm. Viewed historically, this is correct: many societies existed with minimal economic progress for hundreds of years and the Arab world is not exceptional in this regard. Hence, Jones calls Europe's experience of economic growth the miracle that requires explanation. One of the factors that he uses to explain Europe's success is that it consisted of many countries. It could therefore be thought of as a decentralized system compared to the Arab and Islamic (and Chinese) Empires.[30] Kindleberger noted how success, or to use his term "primacy," moved from one country to another. Between the years 1500 to 1900, economic primacy moved from Italy to Portugal and Spain, to the Low Countries, to France, to Britain, to Germany, and then to the United States, and then Japan.[31]

Kuran also rejected the idea that Islam, or the culture associated with it, was the sole or direct cause of weak economic performance in the region. Rather it was the use made of it that had negative effects. Economic weaknesses were therefore due to political factors, but these were reinforced by unwillingness in Muslim society to encourage or engage in public discourse, for fear that this might lead to disunity. Kuran stated that one way in which Islamic jurisprudence hindered economic growth was its emphasis on the need for unity. Muslim jurists did not want to do anything to encourage

[28] Nolan, Marcus, and Howard Pack. *The Arab Economies in a Changing World.* Washington D.C.: The Peterson Institute, 2007. 144.

[29] Platteau, Jean-Philippe. "Religion, Politics, and Development: Lessons from the Lands of Islam." *Journal of Economic Behavior and Organization,* forthcoming.

[30] Jones, Eric L. *The European Miracle: Environments, Economies, and the Geopolitics in the History of Europe and Asia.* Cambridge: Cambridge University Press, 1987. 104–49.

[31] Kindleberger, Charles P. *World Economic Primacy: 1500 to 1900.* New York, Oxford: Oxford University Press, 1996.

factionalism and so they did not create or recognize the concept of incorporation, or what later became known as private companies or legal entities. Those services that had large set-up costs were supplied through the *waqf*, which was a form of unincorporated trust. It absorbed the resources that might have stimulated or called for incorporation and generated a constituency that had vested interests in its preservation. Muslim rulers lacked incentives to make changes in the direction of incorporation. Private merchants were unable to generate sufficient political power to reform the legal system until modern times.[32] In addition to the problems of incorporation, Islamic law inheritance was based on detailed specifications in the Koran and was therefore hard to challenge. These laws were designed to protect the family and meant that assets had to be divided between family members on death. This led to the division of land when it was inheritable, business, and other assets. This was true until the reforms of the nineteenth century.[33] The fact that in modern times the Islamic legal system was changed suggests that culture can be changed, if the legal system is considered part of culture. It requires powerful interest groups to make it happen and this is essentially a political matter.

Kuran uses the idea of preference falsification to explain the weakness of economic development in the Islamic world. When people refrain from expressing their views (in particular, their desire for change), then they make it easier for existing structures to continue. The reason why they refrain from expressing their views is that they may suffer punishment if they call for change. This may be because the state will act against them, public opinion is hostile, or they may be threatened by individuals or groups. Islam may not be the block to change, but conservative views put forward in the name of Islam may be durable because of public affection for it, which makes it dangerous to propose change. Preference falsification corrupts public debate by extinguishing it: if new ideas are never expressed, then society's new members never get to hear about them. This further reinforces the status quo. If sufficiently large numbers of people fear the consequences of expressing dissenting ideas, then the resulting social pressure will keep others from speaking honestly: this will cause preference falsification to spread and an equilibrium will be established under which the status quo

---

[32] Kuran, Timur. "The Absence of the Corporation in Islamic Law: Origins and Perspectives," *American Journal of Comparative Law* 53, July 2005. 785–834; Kuran, Timur. "Islam and Underdevelopment: An Old Puzzle Revisited," *Journal of Institutional and Theoretical Economics* 153 (1997), 41–71.

[33] Kuran, Timur. "The Islamic Commercial Crisis: Institutional Roots of Economic Underdevelopment in the Middle East," *Journal of Economic History* 63 (2003), 414–46.

will be reinforced by the lack of opposing ideas. This equilibrium could and did last for generations. Preference falsification was not only due to fear of the regime but also to the identity of the regime and Islam.[34] Kuran differentiates this from the political explanation put forward by Rodinson because it puts the emphasis on the individual's perception and reaction to the institutions, environment, and prevalent opinions. Islam had a role in the creation and maintenance of perceptions and beliefs. Lewis showed how the education system failed to encourage curiosity, judgment, and critical thinking and encouraged learning by rote.[35]

Greif noted that in the early Muslim world, legitimacy resulted from being close to the Prophet. Later it came from maintaining a strict or pure interpretation of Islam. The Muslim jurist al-Mawardi stated that a caliph should not be obeyed if he contradicted Islam. Hundreds of years later, adherence to Shari'a remained a source of legitimacy. The constitution of the Egyptian monarchy, established in 1922, declared Shari'a to be a source of law. In 1971, the constitution of the Arab Republic of Egypt declared it to be a socialist and democratic state and that Shari'a was the principal source of legislation. In Europe, by way of contrast, legitimacy increasingly derived from the state and corporations. In the late medieval period, the church in Europe lost its bid to become the ultimate source of legitimacy governing economic, social, and political affairs. Unlike Islam, it was not there at the foundation of what became Europe's polity. Christianity came to the Roman Empire, which had its own laws and traditions of secular conduct. It had to fight for its place and this resulted in conflicts, splits, and wars.[36]

Kuran suggests that there is a two-way relationship between cultural and material factors. He also rejects absolutist explanations that either culture or materialistic factors is the sole explanation for the region's woes. Rodinson showed how the Islamic ban on paying interest was rarely obeyed and suggested that this was proof of the insignificance of cultural–religious factors in the economic development of the Islamic world. By implication, materialistic factors were the explanation in Rodinson's and other Marxist works. Kuran suggests that Islam did have a negative influence due to indirect

---

[34] Kuran, Timur. "Islam and Underdevelopment: An Old Puzzle Revisited," *Journal of Institutional and Theoretical Economics* 153 (1997), 41–71.

[35] Lewis, Bernard. *Islam in History.* Chicago and La Salle, Ill.: Open Court, 1993. 354–7.

[36] Greif, Avner. *Institutions and the Path to the Modern Economy,* 149–50. In 2004, there was a debate about whether to include a specific reference to Christianity in the proposed European Constitution. After much discussion, a compromise agreement included a reference to Europe's cultural, religious, and humanist inheritance.

effects on long-term economic development, even though its precepts were often ignored. Because of the restrictions on incorporation and the nature of inheritance laws, the Middle East failed to create companies of significant size. This restricted the level of economic activity within the region and also left it unable to compete with European joint-stock companies. Over time these factors had cumulative effects and resulted in the poor growth performance noted in Chapter 2. The loss of competitiveness was not only the result of these organizational factors; it was also because of the lack of technological, educational, and even military power.[37]

Both North and Lal suggest that societies can continue for hundreds of years in what economists call *suboptimal equilibria*, with institutions that maintain stability but prevent growth largely because it suits key interest groups. The most important of these was the state and one of the reasons why it was able to continuously underperform was that other sections of society were weak. It was these groups that pushed for change elsewhere. Most obvious was the political weakness of the middle class.

Platteau, using historical rather than econometric analysis, concludes that Islam was the handmaiden of politics. Religion was not the cause of economic failure in the Middle East: instead, it was the use made of it that was the problem. In his words there is a "complex interaction and feedback between culture and institutional change." In Western Europe, institutional and ideological changes reinforced each other in a manner that was beneficial for economic development. In the Islamic world, economic development and social progress were hindered by despotism and the lack of a revolutionary idea that would attract enough people to cause political change.[38]

Long-Term Stagnation

Theoretical background on how institutions are created and develop has been supplied by North. Institutions are, from an economic point of view, limits that men create to organize economic and social activity, to maintain order, and to reduce uncertainty. There are formal institutions and informal ones. The evolution of institutions is incremental.[39] Hundreds of years can

[37] Kuran, Timur. "Explaining the Economic Trajectories of Civilizations: Musings on the Systemic Approach," *Journal of Economic Behavior and Organization*, forthcoming.

[38] Platteau, Jean-Philippe. 60.

[39] North, Douglass. *Institutions, Institutional Change, and Economic Performance*. Cambridge: Cambridge University Press, 1990.

pass without sufficient change occurring to permit economic development. One well-documented example of institutional stability blocking social and economic development was the persistence of the caste system in India.

Lal explains the persistence of the caste system, which lasted for a thousand years until the twentieth century, in the following way.[40] The ancient Hindus tried to overcome a series of chronic social and economic problems by creating a unique institution: the caste system. When the caste system began, there was a severe shortage of labor and this persisted for much of India's history since then. To retain labor in agriculture and prevent it from being conscripted into armies or forcefully removed for other purposes, the caste system was developed. In effect, it made it impossible for people to leave the villages or change professions. Despite, or perhaps because, India was divided into many warring factions, the caste system provided a vital element of stability and a supply of agricultural labor. In the harsh environment dominated by the monsoon, agriculture was thus maintained throughout the country despite the ravages of war. Lal called this the "Hindu Equilibrium."

The Middle Class

The economic and political weakness of the Arab middle class has been a key feature in the development of the region for hundreds of years. Issawi noted the difference between the major political influence of the Hansa merchants of Northern Europe between the thirteenth and sixteenth centuries and the limited influence of the Karimi merchants of the Indian Ocean area between the twelfth and sixteenth centuries.[41] There have been exceptions, the most obvious of which is Lebanon. Of the countries examined in this book, Egypt during the period of Taalat Harb, Morocco, and Syria provide temporary and partial examples. Tignor showed how sections of the bourgeoisie planned to change Egypt's economy by introducing modern industry, banking, and other services. They were a small group and faced opposition from the landowning elite (although they had their origins in that group) and from others. The fact that a significant number of them were foreigners weakened them politically at a time of rising nationalism. This group was expelled from the country after the revolution of 1952 with the loss of their skills,

---

[40] Lal, Deepak. *The Hindu Equilibrium: Cultural Stability and Economic Stagnation, India c. 1500–AD 1980.* Oxford: Clarendon Press, 1988. 309–15.

[41] Issawi, Charles. "The Adaptation of Islam to Contemporary Economic Realities," in *The Middle East Economy: Decline and Recovery.* Princeton: Markus Wiener Publishers, 1995. 192.

capital, and international connections.[42] Hansen also stated that large and middle-sized landowners who were subject to expropriation after the 1952 revolution were not merely a feudal class who prevented progress, but they were also entrepreneurial. Their destruction may have been harmful to agriculture, economic growth, and even to the distribution of income.[43]

In Morocco, a group of prominent families, who had their origins in Fez, played a dominant role in the economy. They could be called the old elite because of their long-standing connections to the court. Using these connections, they were able to gain monopolies over the import and export of certain goods and won public procurement contracts. In the late 1980s a new group rose to prominence, taking advantage of the liberalization of the economy. This group pushed for the end of the traditional privileges that had been granted to the "Fez elite"; they also demanded reform of business practices and called for Morocco to adopt international standards in taxation and regulation (see Chapter 8).

In Syria, the merchants of Aleppo invested in mechanizing agriculture. The sharecropping system provided peasants with incentives to work in estates and landlords had incentives to invest in physical capital. Much of this was brought to a halt by Syria's membership in the United Arab Republic with Egypt in 1958. This was followed by the implementation of agrarian reforms that were the result of political rather than economic factors. In 1961, a group of conservative business leaders, together with members of the armed forces, staged a military coup that resulted in the denationalization of a number of companies and raised the ceiling on land ownership. In 1963, however, the Ba'ath staged a coup and the nationalization program was renewed.[44]

The development of the middle class in the Arab world contrasts strongly with that in Europe, especially west and northwest Europe. In the development of late medieval Europe, the structures that substituted for an effective state were not tribal or family based. In the cities of Northern Italy and in other urban centers where commerce developed, the main social institutions were self-governed, interest-based organizations set up to benefit their members. The most famous of these were the guilds. Greif disputes North's assertion that market expansion and economic development required a

[42] Tignor, Robert L. *State, Private Enterprise, and Economic Change in Egypt, 1918–1952.* Princeton, N.J.: Princeton University Press, 1984. 243–53.
[43] Hansen, Bent. *Egypt and Turkey: The Political Economy of Poverty, Equity, and Growth.* Oxford: Oxford University Press, 1991. 534.
[44] Springborg, Robert. "The Arab Bourgeoisie: A Revisionist Interpretation," *Arab Studies Quarterly* 15, no. 1 (1993). 13–39.

strong state. Private institutions were the hallmark of the expansion of trade in late medieval Europe. This distribution/pattern of political power was the result of several factors. First, the Holy Roman Empire was a partly decentralized one and in 1356 it became a constitutional monarchy. This reflected the plurality of political power. Second, the church had weakened social structures based on clans and tribes and had contributed to the development of individualism. Furthermore, the church itself had limited powers. In this environment Europeans were able to draw on Roman and Germanic legal traditions to create a corporate culture.[45]

The rise of the European cities in the tenth to twelfth centuries was the result of a breakdown of the feudal order in rural areas and a desire to move to areas where people could improve their lot. The towns provided this space; the environment was more innovative and less controlled than in the countryside. Not only peasants but also lesser feudal nobility, merchants, and artisans migrated. According to Cippola, the towns became centers of power of the triumphant bourgeoisie following long political struggles and with big differences among Italy, Germany, England, and Eastern Europe. This had major economic implications. The new class had new patterns of consumption and the income to fund them. Given the hostility of the rural and still feudal world, the urban population felt the need for new types of organization. In the feudal system, organization was vertical from the king to the lord, vassal, and serf. In the towns, a horizontal system emerged among equal citizens. The guilds were the most important. The towns became the source of radical changes in values, relations, administration, education, production, and trade that were to transform the economy of Europe.[46] The middle class were at the center of this.

In contrast, Muslim society was based on tribes, families, and clans. Corporations did not emerge, as Greif says, "endogenously" nor were they recognized as legal entities. Merchants and guilds could not intervene in the political process to advance their interests. There was no urban autonomy in the Muslim world as there was among the cities and city-states of Europe. Society was not organized along corporate lines to represent the interests of classes or particular groups. As has been said, there was very little contact between the traders and the government. Traders preferred it that way because governments were so venal. As trade was discouraged by the laws governing incorporation, over time the social standing of the merchant

---

[45] Greif, Avner. *Institutions and the Path to the Modern Economy: Lessons from Medieval Trade.* 388–91.

[46] Cippola, Carlo M. *Before the Industrial Revolution.* London: Routledge, 1993. 117–22.

class deteriorated. This facilitated the spread of antimercantile ideologies, which, in turn, made it harder for merchants to get legal changes that would encourage trade.[47]

Given that these factors, with their origin hundreds of years ago, cannot be quantified, how far do they provide an explanation for the current state of Arab economies? Greif gives a number of theoretical reasons why they do. As the division of labor is a condition for long-run economic growth, institutions that provide formal enforcement of exchange make economic development possible. Individualism reinforces these institutions, enabling the economy to capture efficiency gains. Individualism also reduces social pressure to conform to social norms and corporations are better able to mobilize resources and diversify risks than families. This encouraged risk taking, initiative, and organizational and technological changes. Corporations set up to further the interests of their owners are institutionally dynamic; those that succeed continue and flourish. Those that do not tend to disappear.[48]

In the 1970s and 1980s, as state-owned sectors of the economy buckled under the strains of overemployment and low productivity, governments had to find other ways to generate revenues. In most Arab states they turned to the private sector and encouraged its expansion. Permission was given to private-sector entrepreneurs to operate with or within sectors run by the state. In a situation in which resources were scarce and the government played a central role in controlling the economy, rent-seeking (lobbying of policy makers for private gain) became an important activity.

Sadowski analyzed the relationship between business people and bureaucrats in government in the liberalization of Egyptian agriculture in the 1980s. Both sides felt that the other was indispensable. Business people have gained influence through political parties and lobbies to such an extent that they could not be ignored.[49] The rise of the middle class has been a result of changes in state policy, most notably the shift away from public-sector domination of the economy toward a liberalized system. Both Marxists and liberals have claimed that these new forces have captured the state. An alternative view was that new forces were created by economic policy

---

[47] Kuran, Timur. "The Islamic Commercial Crisis: Institutional Roots of Economic Underdevelopment in the Middle East." 39.

[48] Greif, Avner. *Institutions and the Path to the Modern Economy: Lessons from Medieval Trade.* 398.

[49] Sadowski, Yahya M. *Political Vegetables.* Washington, D.C.: Brookings Institution, 1991. 139.

change.[50] The near-collapse of the landowning class resulted in economic losses.[51]

It is significant that the regimes that came to power with the end of Western colonialism in the middle of the twentieth century often made the political and economic position of middle classes even weaker. This was true in all the countries that experienced Arab socialism and nationalized assets and expelled or expropriated the assets of minority populations. Insofar as entrepreneurship was associated with the middle class, the weakness of the latter had negative effects on the economy. In political terms it meant that one of the forces that might have challenged the regime did not exist on a scale that would provide a threat or alternative source of leadership. In many respects, the regimes that rule in the Arab world today continue a tradition of centralization that has existed in the region for hundreds if not thousands of years.

Policies favoring economic growth are likely when class conflict and ethnic tensions are absent. When the middle class has a large share of the national income and there is a high degree of ethnic harmony, then a middle-class consensus exists. When there is a middle-class consensus, better institutions, faster and more stable economic growth are likely. According to Easterly, middle-class consensus explained the difference between North and South America's development and it helps to explain development successes and failures elsewhere.[52]

Conclusions

The arguments put forward in this chapter suggest that history and geography play a role in determining the state of the economy. However, it is the political system and the values surrounding it that are most significant. The states of the Middle East have always had strong central rule, either under the Arab or Ottoman Empires, under the British and French, or since independence. The strength of this rule has been reflected in its willingness and ability to use force rather than in the extent that it represents the people. As a result, Arab rulers have tended to operate outside or above society rather than within it. As they have hardly ever permitted democratic opposition, many have relied on Islam as a source of inspiration, welfare, and alternative

---

[50] Richards and Waterbury. 34.
[51] Ibid. 403.
[52] Easterly, William. "The Middle Class Consensus and Economic Development." *Journal of Economic Growth* 6, no. 4 (2001). 317–36.

values. As there is no platform for debate, there is no way to get consensus and as a result governments have found it hard to get things done in the civilian sphere. Radical change is avoided and reforms are usually slow and partial. This has meant that the opportunities offered by demographic transition – to the extent that they have been appreciated – are in danger of being lost.

FOUR

Comparative Economics

The Arab World, East Asia, and Latin America

Introduction

The economic development of the Arab world during the last fifty years contrasts sharply with that of East Asia and has in some respects paralleled that of Latin America. In 1960, per capita income levels in nine poorer Arab states (the non-oil-rich states plus Iraq) were about 17 percent higher than those in East Asia. Incomes in South America were 40 percent higher than in the Arab nine and about 60 percent higher than in East Asia. Since then, a huge gap in favor of East Asia has developed. Despite differences of opinion about how East Asia developed, there is an agreement about some of the causes. An examination of the causes of success in East Asia and some of the problems facing countries in Latin America will throw light on the problems of development in the Arab world. Figure 4.1 shows that since 1980, gross domestic product (GDP) per capita growth in fifteen Latin American countries has paralleled that in fifteen Arab states, while that in the eight East Asian countries accelerated much more rapidly. In the nine Arab states the pattern of growth was similar but the level of income was much lower than in the Latin American group. The increase in the value of oil production had a much larger effect on Arab economies than on those in any other part of the world.

Figures 4.2 to 4.4 provide details of the growth of national income, population, and national income per capita since 1960. Figure 4.2 shows that East Asia's achievement was fast and consistent economic growth. The crisis of the late 1990s was reflected in the slight reduction in the growth rate in 2000–04, but it still averaged more than 8 percent. Latin America experienced fast growth in the 1960s and 1970s but there was a sharp decline in the 1980s and the recovery since then was not to earlier rates. The Middle East and North Africa (MENA) experienced the slowest growth of the three

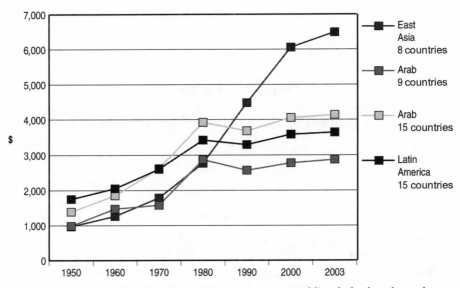

Figure 4.1. GDP per Capita, 1950–2003. *Source:* Angus Maddison's database located at http://www.ggdc.net/maddison/.

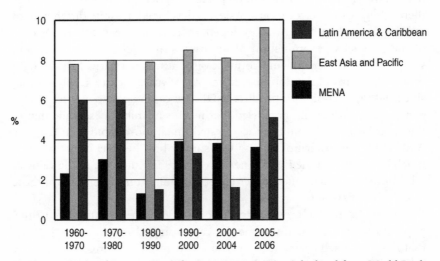

Figure 4.2. National Income Growth, 1960–2006. *Source:* Calculated from World Bank World Development Report 1980, 1990; World Development Indicators 2006, UN World Population Prospects: the 2006 Revision; World Development Report 2008; and author's calculations.

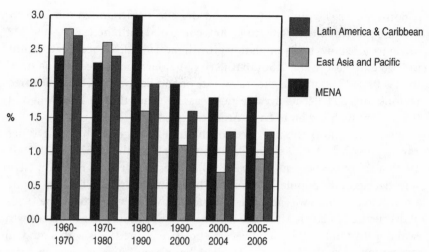

Figure 4.3. Population Growth, 1960–2006. *Source:* Calculated from World Bank World Development Report 1980, 1990; World Development Indicators 2006, UN World Population Prospects: the 2006 Revision; World Development Report 2008; and author's calculations.

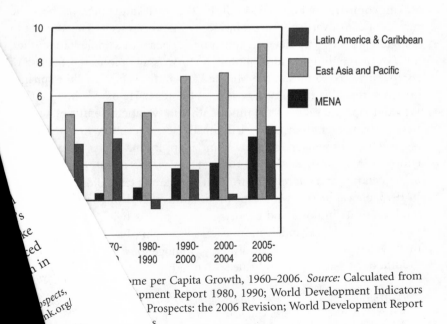

me per Capita Growth, 1960–2006. *Source:* Calculated from
pment Report 1980, 1990; World Development Indicators
Prospects: the 2006 Revision; World Development Report
s.

regions, although rising oil prices and the effects of reforms did help to increase growth in the 1990s and 2000s compared with the 1980s.

Figure 4.3 shows how population growth rates in MENA accelerated until the 1980s. In East Asia and South America, they have been decelerating since the 1960s. MENA still has the fastest rate of population growth of the three regions: In 2000–04, its average rate was 2.5 times that in East Asia and 0.5 percent higher than in Latin America.

Figure 4.4 shows the net effect of the trends described here. GDP per capita growth in East Asia accelerated throughout the period 1960–2004 (with a fall of 0.6 percent in the 1980s) as a result of rapid growth of GDP and decelerating population growth. In Latin America, GDP per capita growth in the 1980s was negative and after recovering modestly in the 1990s it decelerated in 2000–04. The MENA pattern was more consistent. Growth was negative in the 1960s and became positive in the 1970s with a gradual expansion since then. Since 2004, there have been improvements in Latin America and MENA.[1]

The Arab States, East Asia, and Latin America

Making comparisons between Middle East countries and others has been the subject of controversy because it has sometimes been seen as an attempt to denigrate Islam.[2] This view has constrained debate in Middle East studies, but not in economics and economic history. Issawi pioneered the use of comparative economics in the Middle East, and it is partly in the spirit of his work that this methodology is adopted here. He asked the question: Why did Japan develop in the nineteenth and twentieth centuries and not Egypt? His answer was as follows. In the nineteenth century, Egypt, in many respects had a stronger economy than Japan. By the 1830s, thanks to the efforts of Muhammed Ali, the ruler of Egypt, the country had a better understanding and interest in European science and technology than Japan. In 1913, per capita gross domestic product was slightly higher in Egypt and the level of its imports and exports per capita was twice as high. Egypt railway network was much more extensive. Egypt, like Japan and unli many Arab states, was ethnically very homogenous. It had experien thousands of years of central rule and although that had broken dow

---

[1] *The Economist.* 18 August 2007; World Bank. *2007 Economic Developments and Pr Middle East and North Africa Region* located at http://siteresources.worldba INTMENA/Resources/EDP_2007_REPORT_Aug7.pdf. pp. 1–2.

[2] Owen, Roger. "The Uses and Abuses of Comparison." *Al-Ahram Weekly Online,* 566 (27 December 2001–2 January 2002).

the eighteenth century it was restored by Muhammed Ali in the nineteenth. Egypt had an agricultural surplus: between 1821 and 1900, farm output per acre rose nearly twice as fast as the rural population. It had an excellent internal navigation system consisting of the Nile River and its branches and canals. Even the dominant northerly wind direction was favorable, enabling boats to sail upstream and float downstream. The centralized government was able to extract the agricultural surplus: Muhammed Ali's tax system was similar to the Soviet one with low prices paid to farmers and higher prices charged to urban dwellers and in export markets. Finally, in 1800, Egypt's capital, Cairo, had a population of 200,000 and 10 percent of its population was urban, an important precondition for economic development.

According to Issawi, Japan had a number of advantages compared with Egypt. Its long shore line made coastal navigation possible and saved the costs of much railway development in the early stages of industrialization. Its location protected it from much, although not all, foreign intervention at least until the 1850s, in strong contrast to Egypt. This meant that its military costs were much lower than Muhammed Ali's or those of the Ottoman Empire as a whole. Japan had unique social cohesion, highly developed human resources (measured by literacy rates), what Issawi calls an early orientation toward economic growth, and much curiosity about the rest of the world, especially the developed West. (Muhammed Ali's interest in bringing European science and technology to Egypt was the exception rather than the rule in the Middle East). Japan also had very good economic leadership.[3] Issawi emphasizes the importance of Japan's social cohesion, what Ibn Khaldun called *asabiyya*. According to Issawi, Ibn Khaldun was prepared to see what "many Anglo-Saxon scientists are still not prepared to see, that *asabiyya* is the foundation of a country's greatness and prosperity...."[4] The implications of this are examined in Chapter 13. More recently, the Arab Human Development Reports have made extensive comparisons between Arab economic performance and that of other countries.[5]

---

[3] Issawi, Charles. "The Japanese Model and the Middle East," in *The Middle East Economy: Decline and Recovery*. Princeton: Markus Wiener, 1995. 165–84.

[4] Issawi, Charles. "The Japanese Model and the Middle East." 173; Issawi, Charles. "Why Japan" in Ibrahim, I. (ed.), *Arab Resources: The Transformation of a Society*. Washington, D.C.: Centre for Contemporary Arab Studies, 1983; Issawi, Charles. 1989. "The Middle East in the World Context: A Historical View." In *The Middle East Economy: Decline and Recovery*, ed. Charles Issawi, 1–30. Princeton: Markus Wiener Publishers.

[5] United Nations Development Program, Regional Bureau for the Arab States. *Arab Human Development Report 2002*. New York: UN, 2002.

Kuran has provided another powerful argument for comparative economics. He suggests that looking at the problems of one region without comparison limits vision and understanding. Those who stand on Mount Catherine in Sinai, Egypt's highest point, may feel that they are at the peak of the world, even though Mount Everest is three times higher. Individual horizons are limited, in this case by the shape of the earth and its size. A wider vision may enable us to capture the truth more accurately.[6]

There are two objections to the methodology of comparative economics. What might be called the unsophisticated objection is that conditions in East Asia and the Arab states were so different that comparison is invalid. After World War II, certain key conditions in the two regions were similar. Both regions gained their independence from colonialist powers by the early 1950s and both regions benefited from inflows of capital from abroad, East Asia mainly from the United States, the Middle East from the United States, the Soviet Union, and later from oil-rich Arab states. Economic conditions, measured by per capita national income were also similar. Figure 5.5 compares GDP per capita in South Korea and Egypt. The South Korean figure was $185; the Egyptian figure, $151. These figures should be treated with caution, given problems of using exchange rates that are not purchasing power parity rates, but they do provide a general guide. The role of initial conditions, beyond the level of income, is examined in Chapter 5, in the section "The Role of Initial Conditions in Egypt and South Korea." In policy terms, Egypt, South Korea, and Taiwan all launched industrialization programs in the early 1960s. Although these were not their first attempts to industrialize, they had certain features in common, including the use of import substitution (IS).

Industrialization

In 1990, MENA accounted for 1 percent of world industrial output; in 2002 it reached 1.37 percent. Latin America and the Caribbean accounted for 5.26 percent and 4.95 percent, respectively. East and Southeast Asia, including China, accounted for 7.17 percent and 14.42 percent, respectively. East and Southeast Asia, excluding China, accounted for 4.99 percent and 7.84 percent, respectively. In 1990, Latin America and the Caribbean – dominated by Mexico and Brazil – was the largest industrial producer in the

---

[6] Kuran, Timur. "Explaining the Economic Trajectories of Civilizations: Musings on the Systemic Approach," 2007. www.usc.edu/schools/college/crcc/private/ierc/conference_registration/papers/Kuran.pdf. p. 11.

Table 4.1. *Exports of manufactured goods, 2000–2005*

	2000		2005		
	$ billions	Share of world (percent)	$ billions	Share of world (percent)	2000–2005 growth (percent)
World	4,699	100.0	7,311	100.0	55.6
Asia	1,396	29.7	2,310	31.6	65.4
Middle East	61	1.3	139	1.9	127.9
Arab states	28	0.6	95	1.3	239.3
Arab states excluding Saudi Arabia and UAE	5	0.1	22	0.3	340.0
Central and South America	70	1.5	124	1.7	77.1

Source: World Trade Organization, International Trade Statistics, 2006 (Geneva: WTO, 2006).

developing world. By 2002, it had been overtaken by East and Southeast Asia excluding China and by China alone. MENA was the third largest industrial region.[7] These trends were also reflected in exports of manufactured goods, which are in many respects one of the causes as well as consequences of industrial growth. Between 2000 and 2005, the share of Arab states in world exports in manufactured goods rose from 0.6 percent to 1.3 percent (see Table 4.1). If Saudi Arabia and the UAE are excluded, then the growth was the fastest in the world, but the volume was very small.

East Asia

The conventional explanation of the rapid development of East Asia is that it was made possible by free market policies. Private domestic demand and rapidly growing human capital were the main sources of growth. High levels of investment were made possible by high levels of savings. Although agriculture became relatively less important, it experienced rapid growth and productivity improvements. Nevertheless, in its 1993 report, *The East Asian Miracle*, the World Bank stated that governments had intervened. They had targeted and subsidized credits to selected industries, protected local markets, made public investments in applied research, set export targets

---

[7] United Nations Industrial Development Organization. *Industrial Development Report 2005*. 130. http://www.unido.org.

for specific firms and industries, provided export marketing institutions, and shared information between the public and private sectors.[8] The story of East Asia's success was therefore more than just the application of free markets.

Investment in education helped to ensure technical progress, and thus economic growth. When markets for labor, capital, and technology are free, it is easier to both start and close down firms and this promotes the spread of knowledge and accelerates technological change. The role of the state in East Asia was, in the conventional story, like that in England at the beginning of the Industrial Revolution: it made industrialization possible by removing barriers to growth that had been inherited from the feudal system. Hence, those countries that removed the barriers to free markets, including those to international trade, would grow while those that did not would stagnate. The role of the state was to remove the barriers, enabling the market – private-sector entrepreneurs – to step in, and following Adam Smith's invisible hand, act in their own interest, thus producing growth. Public and private interests were synonymous.

Although this may have happened in early nineteenth-century England, it was not the story of East Asian development. After 1945, in a very different world, Taiwan and South Korea, among others in Southeast and East Asia, moved along different paths. Before examining how they developed, it is worthwhile to look at some of the objections to the conventional or neoclassical model of East Asian development.

At the theoretical level, the conventional story ignores demand, as does much neoclassical theory. The demand for factors of production and for products is assumed and does not form part of the analysis: full employment is taken as a given. Second, perfect competition and information are assumed, although we know that this is only a theoretical construct that seldom, if ever, exists. These are not merely theoretical squabbles; they are key assumptions in the neoclassical model. The implications for policy making are serious. Empirically, the evidence for total factor productivity (TFP) growth as the motor for growth is shaky. Annual increases in East Asian TFP fell from 2.6 percent in 1960–73 to 1.3 percent in 1973–87. This was true of all other developing regions of the world except South Asia.[9] Conventional analysis suggests that the decline in TFP growth was due to distortions, lack of competition, and lack of integration in the world economy. In fact, the

---

[8] World Bank. *The East Asian Miracle*. New York: Oxford University Press, 1993. 5–6.
[9] World Bank figures quoted by Singh, A. "How Did East Asia Grow So Fast: Slow Progress Towards an Analytical Consensus." *UNCTAD Discussion Paper* 97 (1998).

period 1973–87 was one of increasing integration and fewer distortions in many developing countries. It was also one of much greater volatility in oil prices.

An alternative model may therefore provide a better explanation. Verdoorn's Law suggests that the faster production grows, the faster productivity increases, and that the slower growth of world demand in the period 1973–87 resulted from the increase in oil prices, the collapse of the Bretton Woods system, and the slowdown of economic growth in the Organisation for Economic Co-operation and Development (OECD) countries. Slow demand growth resulted in slower output growth and thus slower TFP growth. This is a Keynesian explanation because it puts demand at the center.[10] Young suggested that most economic growth in East Asia was explained by the rapid expansion of factor inputs. This meant more labor, either in the form of more work or longer hours worked, and capital. Given the large increase in labor supply and investment there is little to explain in *The East Asian Miracle*.[11] The implication is that a slowdown in the rate of growth of inputs would lead to a slowdown in output growth. This would happen with new capital embodying new technologies or by managerial/organizational change leading to higher productivity: the level of investment is therefore crucial.

The view that the addition of large amounts of labor and capital to the production process is not an achievement is based on the long-term view that its effectiveness runs out in time, if only because the resources cease to be available or because diminishing returns set in. The experience of the Soviet Union is often cited in this regard.[12] There, huge quantities of labor and capital were added in the 1930s and as a result economic growth was rapid. By the 1950s and 1960s, this was no longer possible and growth slowed and eventually the economy went into crisis. It should be noted that in the case of South Korea and Taiwan, the likelihood that technological progress could replace the mere addition of factors of production as the motor of growth is greater than it was in the former Soviet Union because a system of incentives existed. The market was in place; in the Soviet Union it was not. Nelson rejects the view that the "Asian Miracle" was just a matter of increased inputs. To use the increased inputs, entrepreneurs and managers

[10] Young, A. "Lessons from the East Asian: A Contrarian View." *European Economic Review* 38, no. 3/4 (1994).

[11] Rodrik, Dani. "King Kong Meets Godzilla." Center for Economic Policy Research Discussion Paper 944 (1994).

[12] Krugman, Paul. "The Myth of Asia's Miracle." *Foreign Affairs* 73, no. 6 (1994).

had to acquire new skills, methods of organization, and marketing. The latter was essential for the export effort that was so successful.[13]

Industrial Policy

The debate about growth in East Asia also hinged around policy issues. The most controversial issue in the debate has been that of industrial policy. Industrial policy in East Asia has been interpreted as an attempt to create competitive advantages through government intervention.[14] It involved policies designed to help industry as a whole and measures aimed to assist specific sectors. These included IS, export promotion, loans, grants, subsidized interest rates, privileged access to credit and foreign exchange, the provision of infrastructure, and services by the government as well as other measures.

The East Asian Miracle was dismissive of industrial policy. Defining it as an attempt to change industrial structure, the World Bank concluded that the structure that resulted from industrial policy was similar to that which would have been created by the market, more or less on its own. This implies that governments were able to calculate which sectors, industries, or firms would succeed; in other words to pick winners![15] The criticism that intervention resulted in the same structure that the market would have created on the basis of comparative costs means that industrial policy cannot win, whether it succeeds or not. If it succeeds, then it has done no better than the market and the implication is that there was no point in intervention. If it fails, then it did less well than the market would have done and the economy would have been better off without it. The key assumption is that the market would have taken the economy to the same or to a better point than intervention did. This has been questioned by a number of economists who have developed models of endogenous economic growth that emphasize the imperfect nature of information, increasing returns to scale, and conclude that growth processes have no single explanation.[16]

Critics of the Report also point out that industrial policy should be seen in a much wider context. One of its aims was to protect the balance of

---

[13] Nelson, Richard R. *Technology, Institutions, and Economic Growth.* Cambridge: Cambridge University Press, 2005. 39–64.

[14] Singh. 14.

[15] Ibid.

[16] Amsden, Alice H. "Why Isn't the Whole World Experimenting with the East Asian Model to Development?: Review of *The East Asian Miracle.*" *World Development* 22, 4 (1994), 627–33.

payments (this was an explicit aim in Japan). In so doing, many sectors of the economy were helped, not just those that were the focus of industrial policy. Another important implication about the controversy over industrial policy is that if it was not effective in East Asia, where there were competent bureaucracies to implement it, then it is less likely to be effective in other countries that lack such administrative strengths.[17]

South Korea sought to create competitive advantages where none existed; the South Korean steel industry was an example of this. In the 1960s, a team of advisors from the World Bank suggested that the creation of an integrated steel mill in South Korea was premature and that it was not economically feasible. The industry was capital intensive, a resource that South Korea lacked at the time; costs were sensitive to scale and the South Korean market was small. Furthermore, it lacked raw materials. Its nearest substantial market, Japan, had an efficient industry. Finally, South Korea lacked the skills needed in the steel-making process. These factors constituted a lack of comparative advantage. Yet by 1986, the Pohang Iron and Steel Company Ltd. (POSCO) had become one of the lowest-cost steel producers in the world and in that year entered into a joint venture with United States Steel (USX) to modernize the latter's Pittsburg, California, plant. POSCO supplied capital, training, and technology for its U.S. partner.[18] What was the role of the government in POSCO's success? First, it was a state-owned company. Assistance was received in the form of capital and up-to-date technology from Japan under the latter's reparations scheme for South Korea. Second, the government subsidized the development of the infrastructure; provided POSCO with long-term, low-interest loans in foreign currency to buy imports of machinery; and subsidized loans for building purposes. Water supply facilities, roads, and rent subsidies were not high enough to account for all of POSCO's early profitability.[19]

The successful application of industrial policy in the private sector is demonstrated by the South Korean automobile sector. In 1962, the first state-owned car plant was established in cooperation with the Japanese company Nissan. Tight controls were imposed on imports of finished vehicles. Components were allowed in duty-free and tax exemptions were provided for local products. In 1965, the plan was transferred to the private sector and a new technology agreement was signed with Toyota of Japan.

---

[17] Singh. 13.

[18] Amsden, Alice H. *Asia's Next Giant: South Korea and Late Industrialization.* New York: Oxford University Press, 1989. 191–2.

[19] Ibid. 127.

This provided for a minimum domestic content of 50 percent and this was rigorously enforced. During the 1970s, the industry was chosen as one that was to receive a major push. Three companies were identified as primary producers, each being part of a large conglomerate. In 1974, a detailed plan for the industry was issued, which forced the three domestic producers to cooperate in the production of standardized parts and components. The ministry of trade and industry was empowered to select certain items for special promotion. Once government-set prices and quality standards for that item were met, imports were banned, thus guaranteeing local producers the whole of the domestic market in return for their investment and meeting of standards. Then, export targets were introduced. Exports of vehicles were subsidized and sales were made at prices below costs. Domestic sales subsidized exports. In response to the 1980 oil price rise, the government forced one producer out of the industry and compensated it by giving it a monopoly in light trucks. Then it forced the other two companies to choose between automobile and power equipment production so as to bring to an end what it saw as counterproductive rivalry. To ensure economies of scale, the government prevented companies from entering the market, and until the late 1980s, virtually banned vehicle imports.[20]

In Taiwan, the government manipulated market forces to achieve its economic objectives. In the early 1950s, the chief economic planner of the Taiwan government, despite advice to the contrary from other more conventional economists, decided that Taiwan should develop a textile industry. This was to be done by providing companies with an assured local market and guaranteed supplies of raw materials. An assured local market meant that competing imports had to be restricted or banned altogether, at least temporarily. Having provided inducements for entrepreneurs to invest in the industry, the government then exposed these new firms to the rigors of the market, making export quotas dependent on quality and price checks. Gradually protection was reduced, and only then were incentives shifted to exports. Later, the state was able to enforce the creation of a free market, an indication of its autonomy vis-à-vis cartels or oligopolies.[21] The importance of sequencing should be noted here: imports were restricted before exports were encouraged. Exports were only deemed feasible after the creation of a domestic industry. Developing countries today are, in effect, being called

---

[20] Wade, Robert. *Governing the Market: Economic Theory and the Role of Government in East Asian Industrialization.* Princeton: Princeton University Press, 1990. 309–12.

[21] Evans, Peter. "The State as Problem and Solution: Predation, Embedded Autonomy, and Structural Change" in Haggard, Stephen and Robert Kaufman (eds.), *The Politics of Economy Adjustment.* Princeton: Princeton University Press, 1992. 164.

upon to skip the first stage and concentrate on exporting. Restrictions on imports were also designed to protect the balance of payments and were, during crucial periods, successful in doing so.

More recently, the Taiwan government permitted imports of video cassette recorders, or VCRs, in response to the failure of local companies to produce internationally competitive models.[22] Competition policies in South Korea and in Japan were designed to create dynamic efficiency, or the highest possible long-term productivity growth rate. This was done by acting on the firm and industry level, sometimes restricting competition and sometimes encouraging it. The policies followed were highly pragmatic and were altered to meet changing circumstances.[23] An effective state was important in all the models of economic growth in East Asia, including those that emphasized the role of market forces. It is therefore necessary to examine the state more closely.

The Hard State in South Korea and Taiwan

The concept of the soft state was developed by Gunnar Myrdal in the 1960s in his *Asian Drama: An Inquiry into the Poverty of Nations*, which dealt with the problems of development in South Asia. The soft state was defined as one that demanded very little of its citizens.[24] The East Asian states have been called "hard states" because they have been effective in carrying out their economic objectives. Soft states register demands by different groups but are unable to do much more. Hard states not only resist private demands but enforce their will. To use one of the favored terms among political scientists, these are states that *penetrate* their societies, regulate social relations, extract resources, and then use them effectively.[25]

In the 1930s and 1940s, Taiwan and South Korea experienced massive dislocation in war, were threatened from outside, and suffered (and benefited) from colonization. These factors provided symbols for unity and incentive for the leadership to succeed. The same was true for Japan in the second half of the nineteenth century.[26] These changes were, according to

---

[22] Wade. 207–8.

[23] Amsden, Alice H. and Ajit Singh. "The Optimal Degree of Competition and Dynamic Efficiency in Japan and Korea," *European Economic Review* 38 (1994), 941–51.

[24] Myrdal, Gunnar. *Asian Drama: An Inquiry into the Poverty of Nations*, vol. II. New York: Pantheon, Random House, 1968. 895–6.

[25] Migdal, Joel S. *Strong Societies and Weak States*. Princeton: Princeton University Press, 1988. 4.

[26] Wade. 328.

Migdal, preconditions for the creation of strong states with a concentration of social control in the hands of the government. War or revolution swept away existing systems of social control, enabling new regimes to mobilize the country behind programs designed to stimulate economic development.[27]

A second factor present in so-called hard states was independent and skilled bureaucracy that was successfully isolated from excessive politicization or association with private-sector interest groups.[28] These factors were, however, present in other countries that did not experience such fast rates of economic growth. India provides an excellent example of a merit-based, professional civil service, with highly selective entry, but this did not guarantee fast growth. Conversely, South Korea and Taiwan were not immune to corruption.[29] When the regime interprets its survival in terms of the need to provide economic results, then it has motivation. When it has both political power and an effective bureaucracy to implement its policies, then it has capacity. The combination of these factors is the key component of a "hard," or effective, state.

Taiwan

In Taiwan, GNP grew by an annual average of 8.8 percent between 1953 and 1986. The population grew by 2.6 percent and GNP per capita by 6.2 percent.[30] In 1985, Taiwan had a GNP of $74 billion and GNP per capita of $3,297; by 1995, in current prices, it had risen to $235 billion and $12,439, respectively. In 2006, GDP was estimated at $346 billion and GDP per capita at $15,193.[31]

Taiwan has had strong and effective central government since it came into being in 1949. The origins of the ruling Nationalist Party lay in the Chinese mainland where its predecessor overthrew the dynasty that had ruled China for 250 years. It also faced the task of consolidating a huge country that had been ruled by local warlords. This took many years of fighting against the warlords, communists, and the Japanese. The leader of the mainland Nationalists Sun Yat-sen believed that in view of the history of foreign

---

[27] Migdal. 262, 269–71.
[28] Wade. 338–9; World Bank, "The East Asian Miracle: A World Bank Policy Research Report." Washington, D.C.: IBRD, 1993. Chapter 4.
[29] Rodrik. 32–3.
[30] Wade. 38.
[31] Sponsored section by Republic of China Government, *Foreign Affairs*, September/ October 1996; CIA World Factbook. https://www.cia.gov/library/publications/the-world-factbook/geos/tw.html#Econ.

domination over China, a strong state was the only way in which the Chinese would be able to develop the country. His economic philosophy involved a mix of private and public activity, market and government guidance.

As a result of the defeat of China in the opium wars of the mid-nineteenth century, Sun Yat-sen was suspicious of capitalists, even Chinese capitalists. Having examined Bismarck's Germany, Meiji's Japan, and the USSR's New Economic Policy of the early 1920s for guidance in the construction of a Chinese development model, Sun advocated a form of market socialism. These models suggested to him that state ownership of key sectors was feasible and could form the basis of an industrialization program for China. Although there would be a role for private capital, it would be subject to limitations. In agriculture, private ownership would be permitted but landlordism would be banned. These ideas, which formed Sun's "Three Principles of the People," were followed after his death in 1925 until the defeat of the Nationalists on the mainland in 1949.[32]

The Communist victory resulted in the Nationalist leadership retreating to Taiwan, from where they ruled on the basis of their claim to power over all of China, of which Taiwan was a province. The nationalist leaders, led by Chiang Kai-shek, were not native Taiwanese; they were almost foreigners and thus had to find ways to legitimize their rule. This was done by force and by emphasis on the threat to Taiwan from the Communists on the mainland, but there was another significant aspect to this effort that is of relevance for other countries. In the early 1950s, the nationalist leadership concluded that its future control over Taiwan would depend on economic development.[33] It had an economic philosophy, that of Sun Yat-sen, that could be used as the basis for economic policy.

Nationalist economic policy in Taiwan also took into account the factors that, in the opinion of the leadership, had led to their defeat on the mainland. Among the economic factors were the rebellion of agricultural tenants against exploitative landlords; labor unions that ran out of control; bankers and financiers who failed to maintain control over credits and the money supply, thus feeding hyperinflation; and the close association between the government and vested interests.[34] The nationalists in Taiwan were determined to learn the lessons of history: This they felt would ensure their control over the island and prevent conditions that might result in a successful Communist invasion.

[32] Wade. 257–8.
[33] Ibid. 246.
[34] Ibid. 260.

The Taiwanese government was quite explicit about both the importance of private property and the limits of its role. It was also clear about the need for equality in landownership and restrictions on private capital where appropriate for the national interest. The fourth four-year plan, issued in 1965, stated that the government must be involved in all sectors of the economy but that it would not adopt a controlled economic system, or even central planning.[35]

South Korea

South Korea, like Taiwan, has experienced rapid economic growth since 1960 and has been a member of the OECD since 1996. Between 1960 and 1985, GDP per capita rose by an annual average of 3.5 percent and in 2005, GDP was $788 billion and GDP per capita $16,315.[36]

From 1392 until overthrown by the Japanese in 1910 Korea was ruled by the Yi Dynasty. The extraordinary longevity and stability of this dynasty was a result of the equilibrium between different social forces in the country – something that helped to maintain political stability, but could not respond effectively to the foreign challenges that faced Korea in the twentieth century. The Yi in Korea relied on the Ming Dynasty and then on the Qing Dynasty in China to supply luxury goods and to help suppress a peasant uprising in 1894. In 1910, Japan formally annexed Korea after declaring it a protectorate, and Japan's rule continued until 1945.[37] The Japanese abolished slavery, codified civil law, and introduced a tax system based on cash payments rather than those in kind. They created an independent court system and separated the judiciary from the executive branch of government.[38] They also reformed the landownership system and taxed landlords who collected rents from their tenants. Although the system was highly exploitative, it introduced market relations in agriculture.

The Japanese legacy left Korea at the mercy of outside powers in 1945. The period between the end of World War II and the outbreak of the Korean War in 1950 was one in which the country was polarized between right and left, with the USSR and the United States taking increasing interest in the country as the Cold War intensified. The United States backed the Korea

---

[35] Ibid. 261.
[36] World Bank. *The East Asian Miracle.* Oxford and New York: Oxford University Press, 1993. 3.
[37] Amsden. 29–31; World Bank, Republic of Korea Data Profile. http://devdata.worldbank. org/external/CPProfile.asp?CCODE=KOR&PTYPE=CP.
[38] Ibid. 32.

Democratic Party, which safeguarded remnants of the feudal dynasty. U.S. forces stationed in Korea relied on the same Korean civil servants who had served the Japanese. The United States also extended the land reforms that the Japanese introduced. This helped to further reduce the power, influence, and wealth of the landlords; it encouraged funds to move from speculation in land to investment in manufacturing; and it led to an increase in food production. Finally, it helped to develop the South Korean army that by 1953, when the war ended, numbered 600,000.

The period of the first republic, 1948–60, was one in which sales of confiscated Japanese property and United States' aid provided a gravy train of benefits for those with political connections to the regime. They were also provided with subsidized loans and were allowed to import commodities in scarce supply. This did permit industrialization and rapid economic growth, but it was not sustainable, and in 1959 the economy went into recession. In April 1960, there was a student revolt that spread and the army refused to heed the call by the very unpopular president Syngman Rhee to intervene. Rhee was removed from power and the general elections that followed were won by a party very similar to the one that had been ousted in the revolt. In 1961, a military coup brought General Park Chung-hee to power. The military's main claim to power was its claim that it would bring about economic growth.

The United States, South Korea's main aid donor, favored policies aimed at stabilizing the economy as a precondition for economic growth. The military government realized that only growth would provide stability.[39] Park Chung-hee, who ruled South Korea until his assassination in 1979, was influenced by the writings and actions of the Meiji reform in Japan, Sun Yat-sen's modernization of China, the policies of Mustafa Kemal Atatürk in Turkey, and Gamal Abdel Nasser in Egypt. He placed the need for economic growth at the center of his policy prescription.[40] Within one hundred days of assuming power, the military government announced that it would launch a five-year plan. The emphasis of policy was on large-scale enterprises and long-term planning, but the latter would not be allowed to stifle private enterprise.

The military government was able to play a dominant, almost entrepreneurial role in the economy because of the weakness of other social classes. The working class was small and the capitalists relied on the state for

---

[39] Amsden. 49.

[40] Park C. H. *Our Nation's Path: Ideology for Social Reconstruction.* Seoul: Dong-A. 1962. 224, quoted by Amsden, ibid. 49.

finance and other forms of assistance. One month after the 1961 coup, a law against illicit wealth accumulation was passed and a number of profiteers were arrested. They were threatened with the confiscation of their assets, but the threat was not carried out. Instead they were allowed to play a central role in the economy by promising to invest sums in industry equal to those that they were alleged to have gained through corruption under the previous regime. In this way an alliance was formed between industrialists and the military government that was to form the backbone of the investment boom that followed.[41] Land reform had dissolved the aristocracy and peasants who were, or had recently become, small holders were atomized, and did not form a homogeneous social class. The military government was influenced by a powerful student movement that had played a major part in the downfall of Rhee's regime and continued to act as a watchdog helping to keep the military government honest.[42] The presence of the U.S. occupation forces pushed the Korean military toward a policy of accelerating economic development, to reduce reliance on United States' aid.

Both South Korea and Taiwan benefited in a more general sense from their strategic relationship with the United States. As allies of the United States in the struggle against communism in Asia, they received large amounts of economic aid that helped them to maintain healthy balance of payments. During the Vietnam War (1965–75), the United States bought agricultural and industrial goods from them for its war effort and it used these countries as rest and recreation centers for its troops. In addition, companies from these countries won large construction contracts in Vietnam. This massive, localized form of demand assisted the two countries in expanding their industry and developing their economies. The United States was also willing to overlook for political reasons the very restrictive trade practices that both South Korea and Taiwan adopted. This was a price that it was willing to pay for their support.

In the 1960s and 1970s, international trade grew much faster than in the following two decades: countries entering international markets in the earlier period therefore had much greater room for maneuver than those that are now trying to follow suit. In the 1950s the volume of world trade doubled. In the 1960s, it increased by nearly 130 percent. In the 1970s, however, it rose by only 63 percent and in the 1980s by 49 percent. In the period 1990–99, it grew by 45 percent and in 2000–05 by 109 percent.[43]

---

[41] Amsden. 72.
[42] Ibid. 52.
[43] Calculated from GATT, *International Trade 1994* and World Trade Organization, *International Trade Statistics 2006*. http://www.wto.org/english/res_e/statis_e/its2006_e/appendix_e/a06.xls.

The conclusions that can be drawn from the experience of South Korea and Taiwan are of two kinds. The first relates to the types of policies followed and the second to the reasons why those policies were followed. The policies followed in South Korea and Taiwan were not identical, and if Japan and the other fast-growing economies of Southeast Asia are included in this analysis, then the policy mix becomes even more heterogeneous. There are, nevertheless, some common themes.

Investment in human capital and infrastructure increased the private sector rate of return on investment, and thus promoted economic growth. Economic policy was pragmatic and adaptive; it was adapted as circumstances changed and as the economy developed. Policies were designed to complement or enhance markets rather than replace them; they neither abandoned the market nor were slaves to it. Policy interventions were designed to fill in where there were market imperfections; investment in real estate was discouraged and so more resources were available for other sectors.[44] Exports were encouraged after IS was successfully used to create domestic competitive advantages. Exports were encouraged through effective microeconomic policies and interventions and systems of cooperation rather than just through macroeconomic adjustments.

Both the World Bank and its critics agree on the importance of strong, effective, and inclusive leadership by government. The state in South Korea and Taiwan, as well as elsewhere in Southeast Asia, was strong and often led by virtual dictators. It used its powers to develop the economy and had effective civil services to implement its policies. These policies were intended to yield widespread benefits, and although income distribution became less equal over time, it remained much more equitable than in many other developing countries.[45]

Initial conditions were built on; they were not considered a given or immutable external factor. South Korea even subsidized school meals and uniforms. Between 1960 and 1989, the share of government spending devoted to education rose from 11 percent to 20 percent.[46] The importance of equality as a policy goal was reflected in the emphasis placed on primary education.[47]

Strong and effective government did not mean that there was no corruption or favoritism. In South Korea, large business corporations performed

---

[44] Stiglitz, Joseph E. "Some Lessons from the East Asian Miracle." *The World Bank Research Observer* 11, no. 2 (1992). 151–77.
[45] Wade. 180; World Bank. 43–7.
[46] World Bank, Figure 1.3. 31.
[47] World Bank, "The Evolving Role of the World Bank: The East Asian Miracle." (undated). (Washington, D.C.: World Bank).

well. They did this as a result of the very extensive and effective policies adopted by the government designed to push exports.[48]

Discipline in South Korea and its absence elsewhere was due to differences in the nature of state power rather than in differential abilities among policy makers.[49] According to the World Bank, in each of the high-performing Asian economies new leaders faced an urgent need to establish their political viability before economic takeoff. The Republic of Korea was threatened by invasion from the North, Taiwan from China, and Thailand from Vietnam and Cambodia. In Indonesia, Malaysia, Singapore, and Thailand, leaders faced formidable communist threats. In addition, those in Indonesia, Korea, and Taiwan, having taken power, needed to prove their ability to govern. Others in Malaysia and Singapore had to contend with ethnic diversity and issues of political representation. Even in Japan, leaders had to earn public confidence after the debacle of World War II. In all cases, leaders needed to answer a basic question: Why should they rather than others lead their countries? They hoped that rapid, widely shared improvement in economic welfare would bring legitimacy.[50]

South Korea and Taiwan had a common inheritance. They had effective bureaucracies, their traditional agrarian elites were wiped out after World War II, and industrialists were, as a group, unorganized and reliant on the state for capital. External resources (U.S. aid) were channeled to the state, but the ideological environment forced them to rely on private capital. This was despite the fact that the position of the state in U.S.-occupied Korea and Japan had been enhanced.[51]

Although the 1998 Asian economic crisis revealed institutional weaknesses such as the excessive closeness of the public and private sectors in South Korea, measures were taken to restore growth and they worked. In 2006, the World Bank noted that the assumptions of traditional theory had to be abandoned. New growth, trade, and economic geography theories all abandoned the assumption of constant returns to scale and emphasized scale economies. The latter meant that production costs fall as output rises or product development costs decline as new products are introduced. Economic growth occurs when scale economies are exploited through specialization and innovation. This is reflected in the international integration of markets for goods, services, finance, and technology. These factors can

---

[48] Amsden. 146–7.
[49] Ibid. 147.
[50] World Bank. 157.
[51] Evans.161–2; Wade, Robert. 80.

feed back into more scale economies through the concentration of production in successful areas (countries or regions) and provide the incentives for acquiring more skills. The fact that a larger share of international export growth is the result of new product development rather than increases in the volume of existing products suggests that entrepreneurship and ideas (or the development of new technology) play a central role in industrial development.[52] Knowledge has become the central factor exhibiting increasing returns.

Latin America

The most important factors in the development of modern Latin America were the Spanish and Portuguese conquests of the sixteenth century. These were largely carried out by individuals contracted by the Spanish or Portuguese state, and facilitated by the weakness of those who were to be conquered. Under a system of *capitulaciones* or concessions, the state ceded prerogatives to the individual and in return he fulfilled certain obligations. (This was in marked contrast to the Middle East: see next section.) The most important reward granted by the state in Spain was land; in Latin America it was the *encomienda*, or native population, that was entrusted to a *conquistador* (conqueror). He ensured that the natives converted to Catholicism and he maintained law and order. Where possible, an economic surplus was obtained from the local labor force, but in most of the continent the level of development was so low that this was impossible. The solution for the conquistadors was to impose slavery, something that destroyed much of the native population. The surplus was remitted to Europe, partly for the throne but mainly for the conquistadors. In areas controlled by the Spanish, a small colonial class controlled the surviving native population and the search for gold and silver dominated all activity. In areas controlled by the Portuguese – Brazil – tropical agriculture involving investment and cooperation among the colonialists was established. The relationship between the conquistadors and the crown was marked by conflict, mainly over the amount of gold and silver to be remitted to the crown. The provincial authorities and the local landowning elites clashed with the Spanish king: in 1546 the Peruvian viceroy was removed from office. Despite the clashes, the provincial governments were able to extract huge amounts of gold and silver and transport it

---

[52] Gill, Indermit, and Homi Kharas. *An East Asian Renaissance.* Washington, D.C.: The World Bank, 2007. 7–27.

to Spain. The cost to the crown was considerable: in the sixteenth century, its royalties were only 20 percent of mining output.[53]

Because slaves were not paid, the labor costs of production were minimal and so the profit or potential profit of the plantation owners was high. As a result, the import of slaves and the expansion of the plantation agriculture on which they worked resulted in a very unequal distribution of income. This contrasted with the British colonies of North America where Native Americans were expelled from their land and colonialists from Europe took their place. The failure of the nineteenth-century Latin American economy to grow has been explained by the extreme inequality of its income distribution. This was also in strong contrast with the experience of the North American economy.[54] The power of the landed elites limited the ability of the authorities to impose taxation and define property rights clearly. This was also true of the experience of the former British colonies in the Caribbean. Both the capitalists and the workers were weak compared to the feudal landowning class. The power of the landowners in Latin America was reinforced by the growing British influence in the region. The British wanted to buy agricultural products and sell industrial ones and were able to sign treaties enabling them to do so. This helped to create export markets for landowners, and the domestic markets of the capitalists in urban areas who owned manufacturing industry were limited.

The internal balance of power began to change as international economic conditions changed. With the international slump that developed at the end of the 1920s and the Great Depression of the 1930s, demand for Latin American goods on world markets fell. Given the decline in export revenues, the countries of the region had to increase production of goods at home that they previously imported and could no longer finance. Import substitution industries were therefore created. The rise of the industrial sector increased the economic and political power of both the labor unions and the capitalists. This was reinforced by World War II, during which far fewer manufactured goods were available on world markets. Labor and capital were represented by political parties and the military whose influence increased as that of the landowners declined. The expansion of industry meant urbanization and the towns came to dominate the continent's

---

[53] Furtado, Celso. *Economic Development of Latin America*. Cambridge: Cambridge University Press, 1970. 8–11.

[54] Engerman Stanley L. and Kenneth L. Sokoloff. "Factor Endowments, Inequality, and the Paths of Development among New World Economies," *National Bureau of Economic Research Working Paper*. no. 9259 (2002). http://www.nber.org/papers/w9259.

political life. Government bureaucracies also expanded and, like the military, became powerful interest groups. Mexico's Institutional Revolutionary Party (PRI) was an example of the alliance of owners of capital and workers against owners of land and foreign interests and it ruled Mexico for seventy years until 2000. The Peronist party of Argentina has a very similar complexion. The military frequently toppled civilian regimes, in alliance with other groups.

The period 1925–80 was one of relatively fast economic growth based on import substitution, and contrasts strongly with the lost century (1820–1900) when there was very little growth. Urban groups had a mutual interest in protection but were often in conflicts over distributional issues. As a result, social democratic governments that tried to change the distribution of income were often blocked by military interventions. The resulting instability meant that civilian governments had strong incentives to make short-term improvements and few, if any, long-term ones. This led to populist policies being adopted that caused large budget deficits, high or even hyperinflation, balance-of-payments problems, and foreign debt crises. To make matters worse, exchange rates were frequently fixed, leading to deterioration of competitiveness and worsening foreign accounts. By the 1980s, financial crises affected many countries in the region. The collapse of communism in Eastern Europe and the USSR led many to question the socialist model while the success of market-oriented policies in East and Southeast Asia reinforced the pressure for change. The 1980s and 1990s were years in which democracy was restored in many countries and economic liberalization implemented.[55]

Economic liberalization consisted of fiscal reforms, exchange rate adjustment, and the reduction of external tariffs. Privatization and labor reforms have occurred but have not been as common. Not all was smooth sailing: In Argentina, many of the privatization proceeds were pocketed by officials and taken out of the country. Later, Argentina partially reneged on its foreign debt but in recent years its economy has experienced recovery from a very deep crisis. The overall level of liberalization has varied by country. Since 2004 there has been an acceleration of economic growth, partly because of the rise in international prices of commodities that dominate Latin America exports. Living standards have risen and inflation has been low. There is also evidence of the growth of what might be called a lower middle class: among the main beneficiaries of growth have been sections of the working

[55] Rodriguez, Francisco. "The Political Economy of Latin American Growth." (undated). www.gdnet.org/pdf/322_F.Rodriguez.PDF. 4–8.

class whose incomes have risen. Not all the benefits of growth have been funneled to the rich.[56]

A number of conclusions can be drawn about Latin American development. The first is that in the 1980s, as the region dismantled its import substitution system, the developed economies found ways of increasing trade protection. Like the Arab states, Latin America found exporting manufactured goods much harder than the East and South Asian countries that started earlier. Second, the fiscal base in most countries of the region was so weak that development efforts resulted in monetary expansion, inflation, and foreign debt. In the 1980s and 1990s, there were echoes of this in the Middle East when debt crises on a smaller scale occurred. The private sector (both import substitution and export industries) has been very dependent on governmental financial support and infrastructure investment. Privatization has benefited a narrow section of the population that acquired state assets and this reinforced income and wealth inequality. It has not resulted in enhanced productivity. Latin American industry, like that in the Middle East, has exhibited little endogenous technological progress.[57]

The Arab World

One of the most important themes in the economic history of the Arab world has been the role of the state. Although central to most of what has happened in the region, its role has been considered to be negative in many respects. An examination of the role of the state shows how the economy developed.

For much of the history of the region since the Prophet, land was largely owned by the state. Inheritance laws made the accumulation of property (of all kinds) difficult and this prevented the development of groups that could threaten the ruler on a basis of economic interests. There were, of course, challenges during the period of the Arab Empire (seventh to sixteenth centuries C.E.): Ashtor described slave revolts that were put down or accommodated but these did not lead to economic pluralism; they ended with the state being dominant. Under the Arab Empire, the Ottoman Empire, and in the period of Arab Independence, the state was dominant; society or civil society was weak. This was a very different pattern from that in Europe. The way in which class relations and property developed in the Arab world

---

[56] *The Economist*, 18 August 2007. 19–21.
[57] Bulmer-Thomas, Victor. *The Economic History of Latin America since Independence.* Cambridge: Cambridge University Press, 1994. 420–8.

is an important explanation of current socioeconomic problems in the region.

Its strength did not mean that the state could do what it wanted. In fact, its relations with the rest of society were such that its effectiveness was and is very limited. In countries that have tried to reform their economies and place greater reliance on the private sector, the problematic history of state–private sector relations (e.g., nationalizations in the 1950s and 1960s) has had to be overcome.

The Rise of the Islamic State

Islam's success in Arabia was because of the appeal that it had as a native religion rather than as an imported one, such as Judaism and Christianity, and the fact that it offered a source of wealth to its followers. This came from booty: the conquest of new territories that were often much richer than the region in which Islam developed.[58] According to Crone and Cook, Mohammed's success lay in his ability to integrate religious insights taken from Judaism and with "a religious articulation of the ethnic identity of his Arab followers."[59] Booty and conquest were to provide a means for consolidating and maintaining the empire after the death of the Prophet.

The state and Islam were identical in the world that Mohammed founded. There was no separation of power between them as in the Roman Empire or Christian Europe. They were both created simultaneously by Mohammed, who was both the Prophet and head of state. Hence, the idea that the ruler was implementing God's will and therefore could not be opposed; something that persisted in medieval and Ottoman periods.[60] Mohammed's support came from two groups that had initially rejected him: the Bedouin tribes of Arabia and the urban merchants in Mecca and Medina.[61] The tribes combined individual ownership of herds with collective use of land: there was no significant private agrarian property in Northern Arabia or Central Asia. Urban merchants did own land in and around the cities and continued to do so even later. When the empire expanded, newly conquered lands were distributed among the faithful. When more land was conquered after the death of Mohammed, Bedouin traditions asserted themselves in new forms.

---

[58] McNeill, W. H. *The Rise of the West*. Chicago: Chicago University Press, 1963. 424.

[59] Crone, Patricia and Michael Cook. *Hagarism: The Making of the Islamic World*. Cambridge: Cambridge University Press, 1977. 77.

[60] Lewis, Bernard. *Islam in History*, Chicago and La Salle, Ill.: Open Court, 1993. 262–3.

[61] Lewis, Bernard. *The Arabs in History*. London and New York: Hutchinson's University Library, 1950. 29.

Royal and other estates belonging to the Byzantine and Persian Empires that fell to the Arabs were appropriated by the Islamic community, or Umma, headed by the caliph. Infidels who accepted a negotiated surrender were allowed to retain their land, provided that they paid tribute. Arab soldiers were granted leases on confiscated lands or could buy land outside Arabia.[62]

The founder of the Arab empire, Omar (634–44 C.E.), who was the second successor to Mohammed, conceived an Arab military class that would rule and a working class of non-Arabs and non-Muslims. The ruling class would be supported by taxes paid by all the subjects of the state. This system lasted for four generations until non-Arab converts to Islam began to claim the same rights as the Arab Muslims.[63] The rise of feudalism in the Arab Empire and later in the Ottoman Empire resulted from the need of the state to finance the army and its military leadership.

The Umayyads

The Umayyad Dynasty was established in Damascus in 660 C.E. Its founder Umayya ibn Abd Shams Mu'awiya established his regime on the basis of an alliance between the Kalbi Arab tribes and the semi-feudalist and official elite in Syria. The semi-feudal regime was based on agrarian tribute. Although the land belonged to the state, feudal lords used it with the support of the bureaucratic and security authorities. Non-Arabs formed the peasant class and their tribute benefited a mainly Arab military and official ruling class. The elite gradually integrated themselves into existing official and semi-feudal elites that were the inheritors of the Sassanian, Byzantine, and Pharaonic regimes. A small commercial sector and tiny slave sector also existed but under the Umayyads, commerce did not develop significantly.[64] The treatment of non-Arab populations and other groups led to revolts in parts of the empire and eventually led to the overthrow of the Umayyads in 750 C.E. and their replacement by the Abbasids. Their capital was Samara and later Baghdad, and their dynasty placed greater emphasis on Islamic rather than Arab symbols. The Umayyads continued to rule in Spain, where the flowering of Islamic civilization – the Golden Age – was as dramatic as anywhere in the empire.

---

[62] Anderson, Perry. *Lineages of the Absolutist State.* London: New Left Books, 1974. 497.
[63] Ashtor, Eliyahu. *A Social and Economic History of the Near East in the Middle Ages.* London: Collins, 1976. 22–3.
[64] Ayubi, Nazih. *Overstating the Arab State: Politics and Society in the Middle East.* London and New York: I. B. Tauris, 1996. 73.

The Abbasids

The new dynasty set about expanding the state bureaucracy. Ministerial posts were created and the security apparatus – police, prisons – was expanded. It also improved the irrigation system, land reclamation, and the tax collection.[65] Achievements were based on an open internal and external trading system, made possible by the peace that the empire provided.[66] Artisan and industrial production flourished: sugar, glass, paper, textiles, carpets, and chemicals were among the sectors. There was a scientific renaissance that resulted in advances in chemistry, biology, astronomy, medicine, mathematics, and mechanics.[67]

It was during the reign of the first Abbasid caliph that a bourgeois class began to play a significant role. It took one hundred years for it to gain political influence but its economic role was not strong enough to transform the economy or lay down the seeds of capitalism. The level of capital accumulation was not strong enough for the bourgeoisie to gain control of industry. Industries were controlled by the state rather than by traders who exported their products in the way that fourteenth-century Florentine capitalists did. The emerging mercantile class declined rapidly after a vigorous start, and its demise was the result of its symbiotic reliance on the state and the shrinkage of markets resulting from the secession of peripheral regimes from the empire. As a result economic activity declined in scale, reverting to semi-feudal modes in both industry and agriculture.[68]

There were a number of reasons why capitalism failed to develop in the Arab Empire. First, the rulers were engaged in trade and acted to protect their monopolies. As they had a monopoly of force, they occupied the space that in Europe was reserved for the bourgeoisie. The second was the lack of security from arbitrary tax impositions. The system of landownership was significant. The tradition of public ownership of land in the Middle East was an ancient one. Omar II, the second Umayyad caliph (717–20 C.E.), decided that conquered land would not be distributed to the soldiers. Instead the semi-feudal systems of ownership (peasants, semi-feudal owner-farmers, and officials) would be retained and the owners would pay a land tax to fund the army. By the mid-eighth century, a *kharaj* or fairly uniform land tax was payable by all cultivators, regardless of their faith, to the caliph. All

[65] Ibid. 62.
[66] Ashtor. 71.
[67] Ayubi. 63.
[68] Ibid. 63.

land in conquered countries belonged to the caliph and those who used it paid rent to the ruler. This became a "legal canon" in the Umayyad and Abassid Empires and in the Islamic political systems that followed them: the Ottoman Empire and the Safavid Empire in Persia.[69]

During the period 1000–1250 C.E., the mercantile class did not seek to gain political power because it was, in Goitein's words, the "standard-bearer" of Islam and the attitude of Muslim religion toward the state was "thoroughly negative." Religious Muslims did not oppose the state; they tried to have as little to do with it as possible. As a result, the state was left in the hands of barbarian soldiers, whose misrule, along with the decline of trade in the Mediterranean, led to the downfall of the mercantile class and the empire as a whole. The middle class developed Muslim religious law, which was the "backbone and very essence of Islam."[70] Shari'a, Islamic religious law, was all-embracing and covered all aspects of life. It was formally accepted by the Abbasids but its implementation was affected by varying interpretations. The caliph had near total power to "complete" Shari'a in matters affecting the state, especially war, politics, taxation, and crime. In Anderson's words, "There was a permanent gulf between juridical theory and legal practice in classical Islam, the inevitable expression of the contradiction between a secular polity and a religious community in a civilization that lacked any distinction between Church and State."[71] The diversity of religious interpretations within the empire meant that no lucid or precise legal order emerged. As a result, landownership was characterized by ambiguity and improvisation.[72]

Water resources also remained publicly owned. The state thus became the extractor of the agricultural surplus and its disburser in the form of salaries for soldiers and public officials. Taxation was therefore at the center of state–society relations. When private ownership of land was permitted, crop sharing – whereby the owner rents the land in return for a share of its product – was prevented, thus limiting the emergence of private, capitalistic investment.[73] Tax farmers acted as intermediaries in tenth-century Baghdad under the Abbasids, leading to what has been called military feudalism, a system that spread geographically and was adopted by the Ottomans. Landownership remained overwhelmingly public. Private land, like other forms of private property, was subject to Islamic inheritance law, which

---

[69] Anderson, op cit. 497.

[70] Goitein, S. D. *Studies in Islamic History and Institutions*. Leiden: E. J. Brill, 1966. 217–42.

[71] Anderson. 498.

[72] Ibid. 499.

[73] Ayubi. 73.

impeded capital accumulation among merchants and prevented the emergence of landed gentry. The key relationship in rural areas was between the peasant and the state, not between the peasant and the *muqta* (tax official), who was in charge of agricultural land holdings.[74] There was, therefore, no one or no group to challenge the ruler on an economic basis. As a result, the separation of power that existed in Europe and was symbolized (or expanded?) in the Magna Carta of 1215 did not occur in the Middle East. Eliyahu Ashtor concluded that "for three hundred years the Near East bourgeoisie tried to resist the feudal lords and . . . the struggle between these two classes was one of the leitmotivs of Oriental history."[75] The word *feudal* should be used with care in the Middle East, given its specifically European connotations. The granting of land was less common during that time and was often replaced by the right to collect taxes for the use of land. The feudal lords were therefore often mere tax collectors.[76]

If the bourgeoisie were heroes of economic growth, then the feudal lords were its enemy, and from the economic point of view, the wrong side won. In Western Europe the bourgeoisie triumphed after a struggle that took hundreds of years (the Magna Carta was the first time in modern history that a king signed away any of his powers, even nominal, and can be considered the first phase of this process). This suggests that the development of economic classes and the consequent shift in the balance of political power between them was one of the major factors determining the course of economic history.

What were the consequences of the onset of feudalism in the Arab Empire? Its central feature was the granting of land by the state to soldiers on a non-inheritable basis. This led directly to the decline of agriculture. The agricultural achievements of the Golden Age of Islam from the seventh to the fourteenth centuries were considerable; new crops were imported from outside the region, new irrigation techniques were introduced, and new cropping patterns were developed.[77] The onset of feudalism led to the abandonment or destruction of much that had been achieved. Agriculture had been the largest sector in the economy and so its decline was a major factor in the empire's decline.

The second consequence was the loss of freedom. In the pre-feudal period crucial freedoms existed, at least for the bourgeoisie; Cahen points out that

[74] Ibid. 75.
[75] Ashtor. 114.
[76] Lewis, Bernard. *The Middle East.* London: Phoenix, 1996. 201–2.
[77] Watson, Andrew M. "The Arab Agricultural Revolution and Its Diffusion, 700–1100." *Journal of Economic History* XXXIV (1974), 8–36.

price fixing was limited apparently because of the influence of the merchants.[78] Furthermore, local rulers in the decentralized empire often encouraged scientific research and freethinking among selected elite. Although the masses were cut off from many of these developments, this did not prevent the achievements of the Golden Age but it may have limited its duration. The loss of freedom and the increased emphasis on learning by rote, the rise of dogma, and the ossification of religion rapidly sealed its fate.

There is a paradox in the relations among the ruler, government, and the individual or society in Islam. The ruler was both a secular leader and the religious one. As such he could do no wrong and Muslims were called on to obey him in the name of Allah (see next section). Yet he and his administration were often despised. Among the explanations that can be offered was the fact that after the first four so-called righteous caliphs, in the Umayyad and Abbasid Dynasties, they followed caliphs who had no special religious fervor, with the exception of Omar II, who ruled for less than four years. According to Goitein, "Although their rule was based on being the Prophet's cousins and true successors, most of them displayed a mode of behavior which was the opposite of sanctity, while the senseless luxury of the court was made possible only through ruthless oppression of the common people."[79] The development of Islamic law, lore, and thought during Umayyad rule generated tensions between men of religion and the rulers. Finally, the Abbasids employed foreign barbarian mercenaries as guards and troops after less than one hundred years of taking power. Government, from then on, was in the hands of foreigners who were regarded as inferior to Muslims.

The notion of public opinion or acceptance of a leader by the majority of the public was an alien one in Islam. The emphasis of much Islamic thought was that the leader should be accepted once he had been appointed whether he had gained rule by inheritance, usurpation, or by other means. The twelfth-century jurist and theologian Al Ghazali's injunction was to obey the ruler so as not to break the central rule of Islam: unity.[80] Although the caliph rules in the name of Allah, contact with him or his government is to be avoided. Hence the saying attributed to the Abbasid caliph, al-Ma'mun, "Happy is the man who has a large home, a beautiful wife, sufficient means – and neither knows us or is known by us."[81]

[78] Cahen, Claude. "Economy, Society, Institutions" in P. M. Holt, Ann K. S. Lambton, and Bernard Lewis (eds.), *The Cambridge History of Islam*. Cambridge: Cambridge University Press, 1970. 529.

[79] Goitein. 210–11.

[80] Ibid. 203.

[81] Ibid. 206.

A unique feature of the Arab and Ottoman Empires was the use of slaves as rulers. The best example was the Mamluks who were prominent from the ninth to the eleventh centuries. The liberated slave owed his loyalty to the ruler who had freed him rather than to the population that he administered. This system was condemned by Ibn Khaldun as immoral; Lal concluded that it inhibited economic development and led to a "disjunction between state and society – and between central military power and local economic power."[82] The Mamluks were not the only outsiders brought in to rule. In 1801, Muhammed Ali, an Albanian general, was sent by the Ottoman Sultan to fill the vacuum resulting from the collapse of Napoleon's forces in Egypt. He established a dynasty that lasted until 1952.

Ashtor noted the difference between Middle Eastern and European feudalism. European feudalism sprang from personal dependence and subordination, whereas Middle Eastern feudalism was a means of securing payment for soldiers. In the Middle East there were frequent changes in the fiefdom and fealty was of little importance. In the Middle East, knights owed their allegiance to the sultan and so decentralization was avoided. Although knights belonging to the lower ranks committed their fiefs to more powerful lords against a fee to be deducted from their income, no hierarchy developed as in Europe. The introduction of feudalism came at different stages: in Europe it developed in conditions of what Ashtor calls a "contracting economy sunk to the lowest ebb of primitive self sufficient economic units"; in the Middle East it was superimposed on a precapitalistic economy.[83]

Lewis noted that in much of the Middle East, physical conditions made irrigation essential. This required centralized systems of investment, allocation, and control, and also encouraged large land holdings. These were of several kinds. The first was the equivalent of freehold or private ownership and was found in and around cities in the Ottoman Empire. In the countryside, under the early caliphs, land was usually owned by the state and granted to individuals for their lifetime. The recipient paid a tithe to the state that he financed by collections from the peasants working his land. This system was replaced by the delegation of fiscal rights of the state rather than the land itself. These grants were not heritable or alienable. Unlike the European lord, the Middle East landlord often did not reside in the area of his grant. He did not dispense justice locally and had no rights over the

[82] Cook, M. "Islam: a Comment" in Baechler, J. et al. (eds.), *Europe and the Rise of Capitalism.* Oxford: Blackwell, 1988, 133; Lal, Deepak. *Unintended Consequences: The Impact of Factor Endowments, Culture, and Politics on Long-Run Economic Performance,* Cambridge Mass.: MIT Press, 1998. 61.

[83] Ashtor quoted in Issawi, Charles. *The Arab World's Legacy.* Princeton: The Darwin Press Inc., 1981. 116.

inhabitants of his area other than to collect taxes. In general, Muslim rulers did all they could to prevent the emergence of a hereditary landowning class; their aim was to maintain a situation in which all power, authority, and wealth derived from the state. The import of Mamluk slaves was part of this process.[84]

Military rulers handed out land to soldiers, instituting a semi-feudal system that continued for hundreds of years. The results in terms of agricultural production have already been referred to; what was equally serious for the economy was the decline of the bourgeoisie. This had important implications for industrialization and the development of services such as banking and foreign trade. The expansion of feudalism meant that private property came under ever-increasing threat. This was one of the central contrasts with Europe.[85]

Ibn Khaldun and the Tribal State

Another mode of production was the nomadist state. This was analyzed by Ibn Khaldun, in the fourteenth and fifteenth centuries, who described the conflict between nomadic warriors and urban-agricultural societies. The nomads despised agriculture and crafts (according to Ayubi, the Arabic word for "craft" or "profession" is derived from the same root as *imitihan* or humiliation), but they were tempted by what settled populations could produce and took them over by force. Nomads who settled became softened by luxury, and then other nomads, who had retained their military prowess, would invade and replace them. In this way a cycle of rule came into being with alternating periods of conflict and peace. In this system, production was not emphasized: political power was not derived from productive relations but from "a sense of group solidarity leading to the domination and acquisition of privilege and ready wealth." According to Al-Jabiri, this model can be generalized to most phases of the history of the Islamic state and to the modern Arab world. Circulation and consumption were more important than investment and production and helped give rise to a rentier mentality.[86]

North asks why institutions that are favorable for economic growth did not develop in certain kinds of society. Three factors are relevant in considering the Arab world. In tribal societies deviance and innovation are

---

[84] Lewis, Bernard. *The Middle East*. 200–4; Lewis, Bernard. *The Arabs in History*. 155.
[85] Landes, David. *The Wealth and Poverty of Nations*. New York: W. W. Norton, 1999. 34.
[86] Ayubi. 49, 42–3.

considered a threat to group survival. In a regional economy with bazaar or *suq* trading, the lack of political institutions meant that legal structures and courts to enforce contracts did not develop and therefore voluntary organizations did not evolve to insure against hazards and uncertainties. As a result, intensive bargaining, the development of clientization, and high measurement costs persist. These are very inefficient. Finally, in the long-distance caravan trade, tribal chiefs found it profitable to protect merchant caravans but they lacked the military power and political structure to extend, develop, and enforce property rights.

The collapse of the empire and the end of the Abbasid Dynasty can partly be explained in terms of the tensions between regions. Revolts resulted in the division of the empire between different rulers. Many of the conflicts during the Abbasid period were socioeconomic in nature: revolts against the state were because of the burden of supporting both the central state and semi-feudal rulers in the periphery. The bourgeoisie suffered from their close connections to a weakened state and the decline in the size of markets resulting from the secession of the peripheries. One response of the caliphs was to raise armies among the Turkic minorities, who were in many ways autonomous from the society and only loyal to their political masters. By using autonomous armies to maintain their rule, the caliphs and those who followed them helped to make the state autonomous from society. These outsiders were eventually to take over the empire and reinforce the outside nature of the state and its ability, as political scientists call it, to penetrate or mobilize the society. This was the origin of the distinction between a "fierce" state and a "strong" state made by Ayubi.

Conclusions

The experiences of the three regions examined here were so different that comparison is a dangerous task. At any date chosen, they had different natural resource bases, and the balance between indigenous populations and colonialists varied. Their human capital base, measured by the level of education, was also different. Another difference was their attitude to the past and to those who had colonized them. In the Middle East and East Asia, the colonists left and indigenous populations gained their independence, largely in the second half of the twentieth century. In Latin America, millions of migrants followed the original Spanish and Portuguese colonists and were absorbed into the population following liberation struggles against the Europeans. Many in the Arab world, free of direct European rule, remained preoccupied with struggles against the West and measured proposals for economic change as to whether they would benefit the West (Europe, the United States, and sometimes Israel) rather than if they would benefit them. The world was often seen as a zero-sum game: if they won, we lost. The fundamental economic proposition that both sides could win was denied. This was in strong contrast to the attitudes adopted by governments and others in East Asia, where the appalling crimes inflicted on them by the Japanese were set aside in order to concentrate on the present and the future.

FIVE

Egypt

The Submerged Giant?

Egypt is the largest Arab country in demographic terms and has one of the largest economies in the region. Economic conditions in Egypt are harsh, with 2006 gross domestic product (GDP) per capita of US$1,350.[1] Egypt's political influence within the Arab world and in the Middle East as a whole is considerable. As a result, the economic policies that it follows are something of a weathervane for Arab countries.

Decision making has been gradual, with a move away from socialism dating back to the 1970s. Despite this, the economy remains centrally run; the public sector is large and the private sector is reliant on the state. Behind all economic decisions there is the need to take into account annual population growth of more than one million. As a result, Egypt has failed to overcome many of the socioeconomic problems that it faced at the time of the 1952 revolution.[2]

Demographic Trends

In 2005, Egypt's population was estimated at 74 million, some 24 percent of the Arab world's population.[3] In demographic terms, it was the third largest country in the Middle East after Turkey and Iran. The rate of population growth in Egypt has fallen as it experienced demographic transition. Despite this, the absolute annual increase in the population currently

---

[1] World Bank. *Egypt Data at a Glance.* 30 October 2007. http://devdata.worldbank.org/AAG/egy_aag.pdf.

[2] El-Ghonemy, M. Riad. *Egypt in the Twenty-First Century.* London and New York: Routledge Curzon, 2003. 73–111.

[3] Population Division of the Department of Economic and Social Affairs of the United Nations Secretariat. *World Population Prospects: The 2004 Revision* and *World Urbanization Prospects: The 2003 Revision.* http://esa.un.org/unpp.

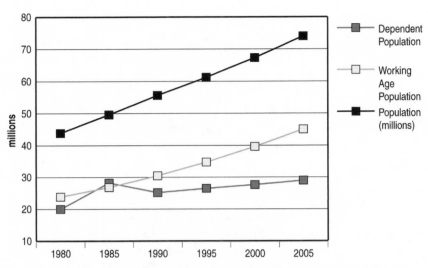

Figure 5.1. Egypt: Population Growth and Demographic Transition, 1980–2005. *Source:* Population Division of the Department of Economic and Social Affairs of the United Nations Secretariat, World Population Prospects: The 2004 Revision and World Urbanization Prospects: The 2003 Revision, http://esa.un.org/unpp.

exceeds one million and the number of people reaching working age and entering the labor market each year may be as high as 900,000. The increase in female participation in the labor force has been a major factor behind the decline in fertility, but it has also increased pressures in the job market. The challenge for the economy, in terms of generating new jobs, is therefore formidable.

Data on the Egyptian population and its development is problematic, with different sources using varying definitions and methodologies. United Nations (UN) data, revised in 2004, is given in Figures 5.1 and 5.2. It includes the approximately two million Egyptians living outside the country. The U.S. Bureau of Census and Egypt's Central Agency for Public Mobilization and Statistics (CAMPAS) data also include Egyptians living abroad. The Egyptian population census only includes those actually residing in the country.

In the period 1980–2000, the population increased by 23.4 million or 53 percent. For the period 2000–20, it is forecast to grow by 22 million or 41 percent on the basis of the UN's medium variant assumptions about fertility rates. This is despite the fall in the growth rate from 2.2 percent to 1.4 percent annually. Between 1995 and 2005, the population rose by almost

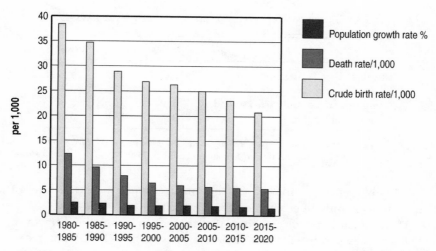

Figure 5.2. Egypt: Demographic Trends, 1980/85–2015/20. *Source:* Population Division of the Department of Economic and Social Affairs of the United Nations Secretariat, World Population Prospects: The 2004 Revision and World Urbanization Prospects: The 2003 Revision, http://esa.un.org/unpp.

21 percent, the working-age population by 30 percent, and the dependent population by just under 9 percent (see Figure 5.1).

Figure 5.2 provides explanations for the changes noted. The crude birthrate has fallen continuously, largely because of reductions in fertility. The sharp fall in the death rate because of improvements in health meant that the balance between the birth and death rates – the population growth rate – declined more slowly than the birthrate. Life expectancy increased, which meant the share of the elderly in total population rose. Infant mortality also declined from 115 deaths per 1,000 live births at the beginning of the 1980s to 65 deaths per 1,000 at the end of the 1990s. Part of the decline in infant mortality was because of the fall in fertility rates and the increased period of time between births that resulted.[4]

The balance is expected to change over the next twenty years: birthrates are expected to continue decelerating while death rates will remain fairly stable. Because the size of the population has increased, the lower population growth rate will barely affect the absolute numbers added to the population each year. In the period 1980–5, the average annual addition to the population was 1.2 million. In 2000–05, it is forecast at 1.4 million – a

[4] Cochrane, Susan H. and Ernest E. Massiah. *Egypt: Recent Changes in Population Growth, Their Causes, and Consequences.* Washington, D.C.: World Bank Working Paper, 1995. 6–7.

Table 5.1. *Egypt: Fertility rates by female educational level, 1986–1995*

	1986–90	1990–92	1993–95
Uneducated	5.69	5.03	4.57
Incomplete primacy	4.74	3.98	3.72
Complete primary and partial secondary	3.68	3.01	3.07
Secondary and above	2.99	2.91	3.00

Source: Courbage, Youssef. *New Demographic Scenarios in the Mediterranean Region.* Paris: National Institute of Demographic Studies, 1999, 53.

fall of only 1.3 percent. In 2015–20, the annual absolute increase is forecast at 1.3 million, only 14 percent less than in 1980–5.

The estimates in Table 5.1 show that the rate of population growth in 2000 was 1.89 percent. Egypt's official statistics agency, CAMPAS, forecast a growth rate of 1.9 percent. Furthermore, official figures issued in March 2001 showed that actual growth was 2.1 percent. This meant that between the end of 1999 and the end of 2000 the population increased from 65.21 million to 66.55 million. If growth had been as CAMPAS forecast, the population would have been 66.45 million at the end of 2000 or 100,000 less. If the growth rate was 1.82 percent, as suggested by the UN, then it would have been 66.40 million at the end of 2000, 150,000 less. According to the National Center for Population, the faster than expected rate of population growth was because of a cutback in the government's family planning program and a rise in poverty. This suggests that poor families believed that they could earn more by sending their children to work in the informal labor market.[5] The implication is that because of these incentives, they had more children. As is shown later, economic hardship has also been used to explain the opposite: the fall in fertility.

Why did fertility rates fall? One explanation, given for the period 1985–92, was government policy. Since Nasser, governments in Egypt have adopted policies to reduce the population growth rate. These changed over time, with the emphasis moving from supply to demand factors and back. The policies adopted by Mubarak's governments have all been carefully designed to take religious sensitivities into account.[6]

Another explanation suggests that the real causes for the fertility decline, although facilitated by the extension of family planning services, were social

[5] Hammond, Andrew. Reuters, 15 May 2001. http://archives.his.com/populations-new/msg02003.html.
[6] Gilbar, Gad. *Population Dilemmas in the Middle East.* London: Frank Cass, 1997. 113–36.

and economic changes. The most important of these was the sharp fall in real wages that began in the mid-1980s.[7] Evidence suggesting socioeconomic rather than direct political causation is the fact that fertility among educated women, especially those with higher education, increased between 1986 and 1995, while that of the less educated and presumably poorer, fell (see Table 5.1). Fertility among uneducated women fell by 20 percent, while that of women with incomplete primary education declined by almost 22 percent. Those with complete primary and partial secondary education had a near 17 percent decrease and those with secondary and higher education had a 0.3 percent rise. Between 1990–2 and 1993–5, the two categories of better-educated women experienced increases of 2 percent and 3 percent, respectively. These were changes over a short period and may not reflect longer trends, but within the periods examined, the correlation between levels of female education and changes in fertility rates is clear.

The current fertility rate is well above the level that would result in stabilization of the population. Fertility rates are higher in Upper Egypt, especially in poor, rural regions. One-third of the total population, and one-half of the poor, live in Upper Egypt. It is also the area with the highest infant mortality rates, 36 percent above the national average. The fall in fertility has not translated into a lower absolute number of births. This is because the number of women of reproductive age (aged 15–49) increased, from 25.7 percent of the total population in 1986 to 26.5 percent in 1996 and was forecast to go on rising until 2005 at least. Between 2000 and 2005 their number rose by two million (see Table 5.2).

In 1976, women accounted for 7.3 percent of the labor force aged 15 and older. Ten years later this had increased to 9.1 percent; and in 1996, it reached 13.4 percent.[8] This is part of a trend that is evident in much of the Arab world and is of great significance. Women increasingly went to work outside the home and so they did not have as many children. This was in part because the cost of maintaining children rose while welfare benefits were reduced under the impact of economic stabilization programs. It was also because of the need to maintain the real income of the family at a time when real earnings were falling. Women went to work to increase total family income; they had fewer children to increase income per family member.

---

[7] Fargues, Philippe. "State Policies and the Birth Rate in Egypt: from Socialism to Liberalism." *Population and Development* 23, no. 1 (1997), 115–38.

[8] United Nations. *Egypt Human Development Report, 2000–2001.* 97. http://www.undp.org.eg.

Table 5.2. *Egypt: Number of women of reproductive age,*
1976–2010

	Number (thousands)	Share of population (%)
1976	8,140	21.0
1986	15,247	25.7
1996	16,059	26.5
2000	16,672	26.3
2005	18,626	27.0
2010	17,769	24.0

Source: Courbage, Youssef. New Demographic Scenarios in the Mediterranean Region. Paris: National Institute of Demographic Studies, 1999. 53.

Courbage suggests that female employment increased to compensate for the fall in rental incomes (earned from the sale of oil and minerals) throughout the Arab world. The process began in Morocco when income from phosphates collapsed in 1975. To supplement its income, the government increased taxation and encouraged women to work outside of the home. In the years after 1975 – more as a result of real economic incentives rather than just government propaganda – Moroccan women increasingly participated in the labor force and the demographic transition gathered momentum. As rental incomes (especially from oil) fell elsewhere in the Arab world in the 1980s and 1990s, the same patterns became apparent.[9] This was also true for Egypt when rental incomes declined in the 1980s.

Demographic Growth and the Labor Force

Despite the deceleration in the rate of growth of the population, a change in the age structure has resulted in an increase in the working-age population. This phenomenon presents opportunities as well as serious challenges for the labor market.[10]

Table 5.3 shows that the aged 15 to 24 cohort increased by 41 percent between 1976 and 1983 while the total population rose by 16 percent. In the period 1983–91, the size of the cohort rose by 6.9 percent while total

---

[9] Courbage, Youssef. "Economic and Political Issues of Fertility Transition in the Arab World: Answers and Open Questions." *Population and Environment* 20, no. 4 (1999), 353–80.

[10] Yousef, Tarik M. *Macroeconomic Aspects of the New Demography in the Middle East and North Africa* 2002. 5–8. http://www.worldbank.org.

Table 5.3. *Egypt: Labor market entry age cohort, 1976–2010*
(aged 15–19, 20–24, thousands)

	Males	Females	Total	Total, both cohorts
1976				
Aged 15–19	2,142	1,849	3,994	7,075
Aged 20–24	1,522	1,562	3,084	
1983				
Aged 15–19	2,619	2,465	5,084	9,897
Aged 20–24	2,840	1,973	4,813	
1991				
Aged 15–19	2,617	2,964	5,581	10,499
Aged 20–24	2,643	2,275	4,939	
2000				
Aged 15–19	3,945	3,670	7,615	14,285
Aged 20–24	3,479	3,191	6,670	
2005				
Aged 15–19	3,798	3,562	7,360	14,934
Aged 20–24	3,921	3,653	7,574	
2010				
Aged 15–19	3,328	3,179	6,507	13,834
Aged 20–24	3,779	3,548	7,327	

Source: UN Demographic Yearbook 1982. New York: United Nations, 1984; UN Demographic Yearbook 1985. New York: United Nations, 1987; UN Demographic Yearbook 1993. New York: United Nations, 1995; "U.S. Census Bureau, Summary Demographic Data for Egypt." www.census.gov.

population rose by 20 percent. This downward trend came to an end between 1991 and 2000 when the cohort increased by 35 percent and the population by 22 percent. Between 2000 and 2005, the size of the aged 15 to 24 cohort is forecast to increase by 650,000 (or 4.6 percent). The absolute number is forecast to decline between 2005 and 2010.

It should be noted that entry into the labor market does not only occur at the completion of school or college education. There was also a large number who dropped out from school, with children usually going to work in the informal urban sector or in agriculture. If dropouts are included, then in 1999/2000 the total number of job-seekers was 896,000.[11] The dropout rate was correlated with poverty levels, with more children from poorer homes

[11] Radwan, Samir. "Employment and Unemployment Rates in Egypt: Conventional Problems, Unconventional Remedies." Cairo: The Egyptian Center for Economic Studies, Working Paper No. 70. (2002). 3.

failing to complete their education and fewer of them going to school at all.[12] In 2000–05 the number entering the labor market annually was estimated at an average of 1.523 million, with 245,000 leaving, giving a net addition of 1.278 million. In 2005–10 it is forecast at 1.472 million with 243,000 quitting, giving a net addition of 1.229 million. In 2020–5, 1.395 million entrants and 502,000 quitting will give a net addition of 893,000.[13]

Unemployment

In 1995, unemployment was estimated at 10.8 percent of the labor force, with the rate among females at 23.6 percent and among males at 7.2 percent. The underestimation of female participation rates and underreporting of the employment of individuals younger than 15 and older than 60 meant that the overall rate was probably nearer 15 percent. Unemployment was much higher among those with intermediate educational levels than among the illiterate or low educational level populations. In 1995, 33.3 percent of those with intermediate educational levels were unemployed compared with 0.4 percent of illiterates, 0.6 percent among those with reading and writing skill levels only. Those with advanced intermediate levels of education had a 19.4 percent unemployment rate and among those with university education, 11.8 percent.[14]

Why was unemployment higher among those with more education than among those with less? Those with basic skills either found work or they left the labor market. Those with higher skills had a harder time finding work but if they could not, they remained in the market. There were two reasons why the better educated were not in demand. The first was the structure of the economy and the second was the nature of their education and skills. Between 1988 and 1998, unemployment increased from 890,000 to 1.72 million or from 5.4 percent to 7.9 percent of the labor force.[15] In September 2005, unemployment was officially estimated at 12 percent.[16] To halve the rate of unemployment by 2015, it has been estimated that employment

[12] El-Kogali, Safaa E. and El Daw A. Sulim. "Poverty, Human Capital, and Gender: A Comparative Study of Yemen and Egypt." Cairo: Economic Research Forum, Working Paper 0123 (2003). 8–10.

[13] El-Kogali and Sulim. 8–10.

[14] Radwan, Samir. *Towards Full Employment: Egypt into the 21st Century.* Cairo: The Egyptian Center for Economic Studies. 1997. 6–10.

[15] Assaad, Ragui. *The Transformation of the Egyptian Labor Market, 1988–1998.* Cairo: Economic Research Forum for the Arab Countries, Iran, and Turkey, 2000. 4.

[16] IMF. Arab Republic of Egypt: 2006 Article IV Consultation-Staff Report. Country Report no. 06/153. 7. http://www.imf.org/external/pubs/ft/scr/2006/cr06253.pdf.

Table 5.4. *Egypt: Employment by sector, 1988–1998*

	1988		1998		1988–98
	No. (000s)	%	No. (000s)	%	Growth %
Government	2,974	19.0	4,794	23.9	61.2
State-owned enterprises	1,294	8.6	1,043	5.2	−19.4
Total state sector	4,323	27.6	5,837	29.1	35.0
Agriculture	6,643	42.4	7,817	39.0	17.7
Private sector, nonagricultural	4,707	30.0	6,377	31.8	35.5
Of which: manufacturing, mining, utilities	883	5.3	1,339	6.7	51.6
Total	15,673	100.0	20,031	100.0	27.8

Source: Assaad, Ragui. "The Transformation of the Egyptian Labor Market, 1988–1998." Cairo: The Economic Research Forum for the Arab Countries, Iran, and Turkey, 2000. 14.

growth will have to increase from an actual rate of 1.4 percent a year in 1973–94 to 3.6 percent in 2002–15.[17]

Employment

Where will the jobs come from? Where have they been created in recent years? Table 5.4 gives the breakdown of employment by sector in 1988 and 1998. Agriculture was the largest single sector supplying an extra 1.2 million jobs. Next came the private, nonagricultural sector where employment increased by 1.7 million. The share of the state in total employment increased despite the liberalization and privatization programs. The fall of employment in state-owned enterprises was more than outweighed by an increase in that of the civil service. This sector includes manufacturing, mining, and utilities, where the increase was 450,000 or just more than 9 percent of the total increase in employment in the economy.

The Egyptian bureaucracy has expanded rapidly since independence. For instance, in the period 1988–98 alone, and despite reforms, the civil service grew rapidly from 2.974 million to 4.794 million while employment in the rest of the public sector fell from 1.349 million to 1.043 million.[18]

[17] Dhonte, Pierre, Rina Bhattacharya, and Tarik Yousef. "Demographic Transition in the Middle East: Implications for Growth, Employment, and Housing." Washington, D.C.: International Monetary Fund, Working Paper WP/00/41 (2000). 7.

[18] Rivlin, Paul. *The Dynamics of Economic Policy Making in Egypt.* New York: Praeger, 1985. 21; Assaad. Table A11. 54.

Table 5.5. *Egypt: GDP and investment, 1961–2006*
(real growth, annual average, %)

	GDP	GDP/Capita	Gross fixed capital formation/GDP
1961–70	5.4	3.0	14.7
1971–80	6.6	4.3	19.6
1981–90	5.6	3.0	27.8
1991–2000	3.9	1.8	19.9
2001–04	3.5	1.3	17.9
2004/5–2005/6	5.25p	3.3	18.0

p = preliminary figures.
Source: IMF, Staff Report Egypt, July 2006; IMF: Arab Republic of Egypt
Selected Issues, July 2005.

Education

Egypt's education system is biased toward higher education and toward males. The return on the educational investments has been low despite the fact that the education system has raised literacy. In 1992–3, the dropout rate at the primary school level was 15.7 percent. At the preparatory level, in the following year, 1994–5, it was 12.9 percent. These two statistics suggest that there were opportunity costs for sending children to school; for poorer families there were potential earnings losses. A significant number of children found work; if they did not they would remain in school. This work was, by definition, unskilled. This fact is in line with one of the findings in surveys of the unemployed in Egypt and other Arab countries: the illiterate and unskilled categories of workers experienced lower unemployment rates than those with more skills.[19] The lack of demand for skilled workers was because of the nature of economic growth and the shallowness of industrialization.

Economic Growth and Structural Change

Economic growth is subject to long cyclical swings and has decelerated during the forty years to 2004, as shown in Table 5.5. The projected figures for 2004/5–2005/6 show a modest improvement but are not as high as those in the 1970s and 1980s.

---

[19] Galal, Ahmed. *The Paradox of Education and Unemployment in Egypt.* Cairo: The Egyptian Center for Economic Studies, March 2002. 4–5.

In the period 1961–75, the state played a dominant role in the economy, using import substitution as the backbone of its policies. The government invested heavily in industry and social services, and the private sector played a very limited role. The emphasis of government policy was on quantitative targets, like those used in the Soviet Union, and exports were directed to the East, communist block, that had low-quality requirements.

The period 1975–85 brought many changes. The Infitah (economic opening) policy implemented by President Sadat (see next section) resulted in partial liberalization of the foreign trade and exchange-rate systems. The revenues of the Suez Canal were restored after the canal was reopened and petroleum earnings rose. Between 1975 and 1985, these two sources of income rose from 3.5 percent to 12.5 percent of GDP. Tourism and remittance revenues also rose. As a result, GDP increased but most of the increase was a result of rents rather than domestic production. The government used the rise in revenues to increase spending on subsidies and wages. The rise in the government deficit resulted in a growth of the internal debt and thus of interest payments. Oil prices collapsed in the mid-1980s and this reduced Egypt's income from oil exports and workers' remittances. Fiscal deficits of 15 percent of GDP became untenable and the monetary policy that accompanied them resulted in inflation of 20 percent a year. Exports stagnated and large current accounts accumulated. This worsened the already burdensome foreign debt.

In 1992, Egypt implemented a stabilization program that reduced the budget deficit, cut the rate of inflation, and improved the current account of the balance of payments. Economic growth was, however, slower in 1991–2000 than it had been in the previous thirty years.

There are a series of legacies that contribute both positively and negatively to the economy's current position and to its ability to generate employment. These are the legacies of Nasser, Sadat, and the policies followed by Mubarak in recent years.

Nasser's Legacy: Centralization

In the period 1960–5, the economy grew by an average annual rate of 5.5 percent, although this figure was partly inflated by the growth of civil service and public-sector payrolls. A massive employment drive led to the creation of one million jobs. A total of 1.7 billion Egyptian pounds was invested, of which between 25 percent and 28 percent went into industry. About 94 percent of planned investment was carried out, although industrial investment fell 10 percent below target, electricity 22 percent, and housing

20 percent. The Achilles heel was the balance of payments. Imports rose much faster than had been planned, and exports grew much more slowly. Instead of falling by 6 percent between 1960–1 and 1964–5, imports rose by 80 percent, mainly because agriculture failed to grow as planned and because imports of intermediate goods for industry were much higher than expected. As a result, there was a balance-of-payments crisis as early as 1962. However, the 5.5 percent annual GDP growth rate was 1.5 percent lower than the planned rate. Agricultural production increased by 3.3 percent, as compared with a planned rate of 5.1 percent. All other sectors, with the exception of electricity and construction, also fell behind their target growth rates.

There were three main problems with the policies adopted under the First Five-Year Plan. First, the key policy adopted was one that had been implemented since the 1930s: import substitution. Its main weakness was that it reduced imports of one kind, only to increase those of another. The new industries developed in the 1960s were designed to supply local markets; they lacked the economies of scale and the marketing expertise needed for export. Most significantly, they required imports, but were not able to finance them through exports.

The second problem was the reliance on private-sector investment at a time when private-sector activity was strongly discouraged. In the final analysis, this meant that the plan was doomed. It could have been saved had the public sector been able to raise the funds instead, but there was no mechanism in place for this, and no adjustments were made to the plan to allow for the radical changes in ownership that occurred. The First Five-Year Plan (1960/61–1964/65) stated that 55 percent of locally funded investment was to come from the private sector. The forecast for private-sector savings was unrealistic, even in more harmonious conditions than those of Egypt in the late 1950s and early 1960s. The implied marginal savings rate for households in the First Five-Year Plan was 16 percent, as compared with an actual rate of 3 percent in 1959–60. There was virtually no discussion in the plan of how the savings rate was to be increased so radically. The failure of the private sector to mobilize its share in investment in the first year of the plan was one of the factors that provoked the nationalization measures of 1961. In 1959, laws were enacted that forced joint stock companies to invest 5 percent of their net distribution to stockholders in state banks and to limit profit distribution to 10 percent of the nominal value of company shares. This caused a collapse of share prices on the stock market. In February 1960, two major Egyptian banks were nationalized; one of them, the Misr Bank, owned much of the country's textile industry that thus fell into the hands of the state. In July 1961, a year after the First Five-Year Plan was launched, the remaining banks, as well as insurance companies, shipping companies, heavy and basic industries, were nationalized. Many firms were forced to sell 50 percent of their shares to the public sector. Public utilities, foreign trade, and the Alexandria Cotton Exchange were also nationalized. The plans and the nationalization had different origins. This was part of a more serious problem – the separation of planning from the policy-making system. In July 1961, the Finance Minister was abroad when he heard of the nationalization, something he said occurred without any reference to the planning framework.[20]

The third major problem was, ironically, a result of the achievements. The employment drive that created one million jobs resulted in the public sector and the civil services becoming dumping grounds for graduates who had received guarantees of employment. The massive expansion of public-sector employment had serious, negative effects on the efficiency of various enterprises, but managers of companies who had protected markets and a guaranteed source of raw material had few incentives to protest. Nor did the repressive political environment encourage debate, let alone protest.

Egyptian planners sought progress on all fronts. They wanted heavy industry and an increasing supply of consumer goods. They designed import substitution projects that were expected to increase exports in only a few years. They planned to reach full employment and efficiency, to finance the Aswan High Dam project, and to invest in massive horizontal expansion in agriculture. The economy, however, could not meet all these demands within the limited period allocated in the plan, and, by 1964–5, it came to a standstill. The Five-Year Plan had no proposals for the production of machinery or other capital goods.[21] This was despite the fact that the regime talked about industrial policy in very comprehensive terms and aimed to manufacture everything "from the needle to the rocket."[22]

Sadat's Legacy: Growth of Rental Income and Partial Liberalization

Between 1970 and 1980, the economy grew mainly as a result of large increases in foreign exchange income from oil, the Suez Canal, tourism revenues, and workers' remittances. These sources of income had equaled

[20] The late Abdul Moneim Kaissouni was interviewed by the author in 1980.
[21] Mabro, Robert and Samir Radwan. *The Industrialization of Egypt.* Oxford: Oxford University Press, 1976. 105–6.
[22] Waterbury, John. *The Egypt of Nasser and Sadat.* Princeton: Princeton University Press, 1983. 81.

3 percent of GDP in 1970 and rose to 24 percent in 1980.[23] The share of rental income in GDP continued to grow until the mid-1980s. This led to a real appreciation of the exchange rate, which in turn encouraged the development of non-internationally traded sectors of the economy such as housing, infrastructure, and other services at the expense of non-oil tradeables, such as textiles, agricultural goods, and other industrial products. The rapid growth of the economy enabled the government to spend money on the badly neglected infrastructure. It also permitted improvements in nutrition, life expectancy, educational enrollment, electrification, housing, and other services, all of which contributed to an increase in welfare.

The weakness in this pattern of development was that reliance on imports rather than on domestic production increased. Between 1974 and 1980, GDP rose by 81 percent but GDP excluding rental sectors rose by 47 percent.[24] Thus 34 percent of growth was due to sources of income that were unstable and largely determined abroad. The state benefited from the boom, in that much of the foreign income went to the treasury and it therefore became a major supporter of investment and welfare. This could not, however, be sustained when, in the 1980s, these sources of income fell. As a result, large budget deficits developed.

In 1975, Egypt began discussions with the International Monetary Fund (IMF) on an aid package. A letter of intent was signed in 1976, but reductions in food subsidies, which were part of the agreement with the IMF, resulted in major riots in January 1977. These riots have affected Egyptian policy making ever since. The government has been unwilling to take steps that would reduce the living standards of the poor, especially in urban areas. They also made it impossible for the government to implement the reforms contained in the agreement. In 1978, an agreement was reached with the IMF for an Extended Fund Facility for a three-year period. This enabled Egypt to obtain an additional $650 million from the Gulf Organization for the Development of Egypt (GODE). Then in response to the September 1978 Camp David agreement with Israel, the Gulf States stopped all concessional loans to Egypt. Western donors took their place. With increasing oil revenues, Suez Canal tolls, tourism receipts, and workers' remittances, Egypt did not need to implement IMF-based measures, which called for budget cuts, austerity, and structural reforms. At the same time it lagged behind on interest payments on foreign debt. In January 1981, Egypt's

---

[23] Rivlin. 166. Table 8.1.
[24] Ibid. 166. Table 8.2.

non-Arab creditors agreed to provide an additional $3 billion of concessional loans and grants.

In 1981, Egypt's foreign debt equaled about $30 billion and its servicing cost $2.9 billion a year, $1.3 billion in repayments of principal, and $1.6 billion in interest. Debt servicing consumed 28 percent of total foreign-exchange earnings. During the period 1980–4, Egypt's oil revenues fell by 36 percent and its other main foreign currency earnings were stagnant. From 1981 to 1986, the total value of exports of goods and services declined by 11 percent. In June 1986, the foreign debt equaled $46.3 billion. Although debt servicing increased more slowly in the first half of the 1980s than in the 1970s, military debt rose rapidly after the 1979 peace treaty with Israel. In 1989, the debt-service ratio reached 32 percent and total debt equaled 117 percent of GNP.

Sadat's legacy was an unreformed public sector and a liberalized foreign-trade sector. During his years in power, rental incomes increased rapidly but so did foreign indebtedness. Sadat began the process of restoring private property to the position it had been in before the sequestration, confiscation, and nationalization carried out by Nasser. It was, however, accompanied by much corruption and the deepening of what is now called crony capitalism. The motivation behind the opening of the economy in the early 1979s was much more modest than its rather grandiose billing suggested. In fact the *infitah* was an opportunistic tactic intended to facilitate the inflow of Arab funds rather than a strategy for fundamental economic change.[25] It was not, therefore, accompanied by reforms that would stimulate growth in the rest of the economy.[26]

Mubarak: The Hesitant Reformer

In 1981 Husni Mubarak succeeded Anwar Sadat following his assassination. Few economic reforms with long-term effects were introduced in the 1980s, but by 1990 change had become unavoidable. The Gulf War of 1991 provided the opportunity to introduce radical reforms and incentives for the international community to reduce Egypt's debt burden. The government was able to sell the reforms at home as being a necessary part of Egypt's international commitments. In May 1991, Egypt and the IMF agreed on a $372 million standby loan. The government increased energy prices, reduced

---

[25] Ikram, Khalid. *The Egyptian Economy, 1952–2000, Performance, Policies, and Issues.* London and New York: Routledge, 2006. 1819.
[26] Rivlin. 165–77.

subsidies, unified the exchange rate, increased interest rates, partially liberalized foreign trade, reduced the growth of credit, reformed the tax system, and cut government spending and the budget deficit. The Paris Club of official international creditors agreed to write off $10.1 billion of Egyptian debt by mid-1994. This equaled 50 percent of the amount owed to Egypt's main creditors. The World Bank agreed to lend Egypt $300 million and the African Development Bank agreed to lend $250 million. A $400 million social fund was also created with foreign assistance to help cover the social costs of structural change and to compensate workers laid off as a result of privatization.

During the Gulf War in the spring of 1991, the United States wrote off nearly $7 billion of military debt that had cost Egypt about $700 million a year to service. The Gulf Arab states also wrote off about $6 billion, none of which was being serviced. The main result of the 1991 program was a large reduction in the budget deficit. This permitted a deceleration in monetary growth that in turn helped to reduce inflationary pressures. The reduction in inflation was a considerable achievement given the increases in government-administered prices that occurred between 1991 and 1993. Many commodities were removed from price controls, and prices of other goods produced by monopolies were increased to levels closer to those abroad. The dispersion of import tariffs was reduced; almost all export quotas were abolished, as were many nontariff barriers to trade. A securities market law was introduced to improve the functioning of the stock exchange. The public sector was restructured: seventeen diversified holding companies were set up, each with financial autonomy. The government ceased providing investment funding and credit guarantees for public-sector firms. The aim of this reform was to prepare companies for privatization. As well as this, it improved the environment for private-sector business: numerous controls and licensing requirements were either abolished or simplified, although many others remained in force, especially at the local level.

The budget deficit was sharply reduced from 20 percent of GDP in the fiscal year (FY) 1991 to 1.6 percent in FY 1995. Excluding interest payments, the change was even more dramatic: from a deficit of 12.8 percent in FY 1991 to a surplus of 8.4 percent in FY 1995.[27] Interest payments on domestic debt rose as treasury bills were sold to cover much of the budget deficit.

---

[27] World Bank. *Trends in Developing Countries 1996.* Washington, D.C.: World Bank, 1996. 155; United Nations, *International Trade Statistics Yearbook 2002*, Vol. 1. New York: UN, 2004.

To stabilize the economy, attract funds from abroad, and encourage saving, interest rates were sharply increased in 1991. This meant high interest payments on the treasury bills issued: in 1994 they reached the equivalent of 11.3 percent of GDP. By 1995, they had fallen to 7 percent as a result of lower domestic interest rates and debt stocks that, in turn, were made possible by the decline in the budget deficit.[28]

Another achievement was a major improvement in the balance of payments. The current account (which measures the gap between payments and receipts for trade in goods and services and movements of income in and out of the country) improved, moving from a deficit of $1.3 billion in 1989 to a surplus of $1.9 billion in 1991. This was the result of the slowdown in the economy because of the Gulf crisis and the deflationary impact of the 1991 measures. There was also an increase in remittances as a result of higher interest rates on Egyptian pound deposits and the easing of controls on the movement of capital. Furthermore, the Paris Club agreement reduced the debt-servicing burden; the amount due in 1991 was $7.9 billion; in 1992 it was $3.9 billion. Only with the announcement of a more comprehensive privatization program in 1996 did economic growth accelerate.

These measures provided Egypt with much-needed financial stability. The balance-of-payments deficit fell to a level that could be financed with ease; the budget deficit was cut sharply, reducing the need for much internal borrowing by the government and thus releasing, at least potentially, resources for investment by the private sector. Inflation was brought under control: from 1990 to 1993 it averaged 16.7 percent a year; from 1997 to 2000 it averaged 5.4 percent.

Nevertheless, the economy responded slowly. Between 1991 and 2000 the economic growth rate averaged 3.9 percent a year and in 2001–04 it averaged 3.5 percent. Why was the response slow and only temporary? The main reason was the weakness of the two main productive sectors: industry and agriculture. There is a broad consensus among economists that industrialization is the solution to Egypt's economic problems. According to the Economic Research Forum for the Arab World, Iran, and Turkey, manufacturing will become the leading sector if the economy becomes more outward looking. This will enable it to make full use of human resources and generate employment, as was done in East Asia. Egypt's industrial sector has received a major share of public and private investment but only accounts for 14 percent of employment. In 2002, exports accounted for only 10 percent of output. This was because of the effects of import substitution,

---

[28] World Bank, *Trends in Developing Countries.* 155.

Table 5.6. *Egypt: The structure of merchandise exports, 1990–2002 (%)*

	1990	1996	1999	2002
Agriculture	16.3	8.8	10.9	10.1
Mining and quarrying	19.3	25.1	10.2	10.0
Manufacturing	64.4	66.1	78.9	79.9
Textiles	28.1	19.5	18.5	8.9
Chemicals	15.3	25.1	37.5	43.6
Food, beverages, and tobacco	2.9	6.0	5.9	5.4
Other*	0.0	0.0	0.0	6.5
Value of total exports ($m)	2,582	3,535	3,501	6,160.7

* This category excludes metals and metal products; it is not a residual.
Source: UN. International Trade Statistics Yearbook, 1999, Vol. 1. New York: UN, 2000; Yearbook 2002, Vol. 1. New York: UN, 2004.

weaknesses in education and training (despite large national investments in higher education), and the weaknesses of links between science/technology and industry. It also resulted from the lack of incentives for firms to improve product quality and management and to adopt technological improvements or seek export markets. Manufactured exports increased from $1.3 billion in 1992 to $4.9 billion in 2003. As imports of manufactured goods rose from $3.9 billion to $10.9 billion during the same period, the deficit on trade in manufactured goods increased sharply from $2.6 billion to $7.9 billion.[29] Since the mid-1980s, international economic conditions have been much less favorable for the development of exports by new entrants onto international markets than they were in the 1960s and 1970s when the East Asian tigers began their rapid growth phase. International markets were growing less quickly, have been more saturated with goods from competitors, and were in part more protected against imports. For Egypt to get a foothold in export markets in these conditions was not easy even if it was better prepared in terms of basic socioeconomic variables, suitable policies, effective administration, and dedicated economic leadership.

Table 5.6 shows that between 1990 and 2002, the share of manufacturing in exports rose from 64 percent to 80 percent. In 2003, just more than half of manufactured exports were textiles and chemicals, the latter being

[29] Handoussa, Heba. "A Balance Sheet of Reform in Two Decades" in el-Mikawy, Noha and Heba Handoussa (eds.), *Institutional Reform and Economic Development in Egypt*. Cairo: American University Press, 2002. 96–97; UN, *International Trade Statistics Yearbook*, 1999. Vol. 1. New York: UN, 2000; "International Bank for Reconstruction and Development and International Finance Corporation." *Country Assistance Strategy for the Arab Republic of Egypt for the Period FY06–FY08*. 2005. Report No. 32190-EG.

mainly by-products of petroleum refining. The range of products exported was narrow and the share of other manufactured exports suggests that the economy was not diversified and did not build much new export capacity beyond traditional products and petrochemicals and related products. These policies had been designed to boost domestic production by limiting imports; in such a framework, exports were not a priority. Policies were gradually reformed in the 1980s and 1990s but remained largely in force until the reforms of 2004.

In 1997, the nominal rate of protection was estimated at 24.6 percent. The effective rate, which applied to value added, was 30.5 percent. Despite reforms, rates of protection were highly dispersed and so their effect between products and industries was far from neutral. The effect of the tariff system was to pull resources away from sectors that were more productive to less productive ones. Resources were also drawn away from labor-intensive industries to capital-intensive ones. This limited employment creation as well as exports. The furniture industry was the most highly subsidized, "benefiting" from an 80-plus percent effective rate of protection. In contrast, cotton-ginning exports were effectively taxed at a rate of 11 percent. The result was that in 1997, exports were subject to an average tariff rate of 19.7 percent. Even with duty drawbacks this was a burden, particularly so for nontraditional exporters who were in effect being taxed out of existence. The need for imports that were subject to taxes and other restrictions limited the extent of exports and industrialization. In addition, there were nontariff barriers such as port charges, both explicit, such as fees, and implicit, such as the costs of delays.[30] These added considerable costs to exporting and were significantly higher than in other Mediterranean countries with which Egypt competed on European agricultural markets.

At least three interests were at work to maintain restrictions or taxes on imports. First, government revenues from tariffs on imports were significant. Second, domestic producers were a lobby or interest group that the government had to face. Third, the government was always under pressure to maintain employment levels. The removal of import substitution meant reducing employment now in the hope that more employment would be created in the future. What was not understood was that more employment might be created through policy reforms than would be destroyed.

---

[30] Cassing, James H., Samih Fawzy, Denis Gallagher, and Hanaa Kheir-El-Din. "Enhancing Egypt's Exports" in Hoekman, Bernard M. and Jamal Zarrouk (eds.), *Catching up with the Competition: Trade Policy Challenges and Options for the Middle East and North Africa.* Ann Arbor: University of Michigan Press, 2000. 208–9.

Recent Trends

An important aspect of structural change in the Egyptian economy has been the declining role of oil. In the late 1960s and 1970s economic growth was largely a function of changes in the real price of oil, the fruit of oil export revenues, remittances by Egyptian workers in the Gulf, economic aid from the oil-rich Arab states, investments, and Arab tourism. In the early 1980s, more than 20 percent of Egypt's labor force worked abroad. By 2005, this share had fallen to about 7 percent; remittances by Egyptian workers fell from 14 percent of GDP in 1979 to about 3 percent in 2005. Between 1979 and 2003, foreign direct investment fell from almost 7 percent of GDP to less than 1 percent, although it rose to 4 percent in 2005. Official aid fell from 19 percent of GDP in 1975 to less than 2 percent in 2005 and net oil exports declined from more than 20 percent in 1980 to about 3 percent.[31]

In many respects Egypt's economic performance has deteriorated over the last three decades. In the period 1971–80, real GDP rose by an annual average rate of 6.6 percent and GDP per worker by 4.5 percent. In 1981–90, GDP increased by 5.6 percent annually and GDP per worker by 1.3 percent. In 1991–2000, the increases were 3.9 percent and 2.3 percent while in 2001–04 they were 3.5 percent and 1.3 percent.[32] Table 5.5 suggests that there was an improvement in 2004/5 and 2005/6. There is a strong cyclical pattern in Egypt's growth experience. The high but uneven growth in employment since 1980 explains the differences between cyclical fluctuations and the long-run decline in GDP growth. The rapid growth of employment and labor-force growth in the 1980s was in turn because of the demographic boom of the 1960s and 1970s, when the population increased by more than 2 percent a year. Egypt also experienced an investment boom in the 1970s and 1980s. The deceleration in the growth of output per worker is due both to lower investment and to lower efficiency, the latter measured by total factor productivity.[33]

Over the last twenty years there have been many changes in economic policy, and real incomes have increased, but in terms of structural change there have been a number of worrying trends. First, the share of domestic savings as a share of national income has fallen. Domestic savings were supplemented by those of Egyptians working abroad (the total is defined as national savings). Nevertheless, the total was significantly lower in 2003

---

[31] World Bank. *Economic Developments and Prospects*, 2006. 11. http://www.worldbank.org.
[32] IMF. *Arab Republic of Egypt: Selected Issues*, Country Report No. 05/179, 2005. 15.
[33] Ibid. 20.

than it was ten years earlier. Second, although in recent years exports have grown, they took a lower share of GDP in 2003 than a decade earlier. On a more positive note, the share of manufacturing industry increased from 13.2 percent in 1993 to 18.9 percent in 2003, although part of this was accounted for by petroleum-related activities. Despite the efforts at liberalization, government spending (including the net acquisition of financial assets) fell from 39.5 percent of GDP in fiscal year 2003 to 35.5 percent in fiscal year 2007.[34]

In 2001–02, the economic growth rate decelerated to an average of 3.3 percent as a result of a series of factors. The overvaluation of the Egyptian pound encouraged imports and discouraged exports, resulting in a shortage of foreign exchange. The high interest rates that supported the high exchange rate discouraged investment in productive (tradeable) sectors. As the economy became less and less competitive, more funds went into property investments (untradeable) and consumption. This was encouraged by the large-scale release of land for private investment and public investment in low-return desert reclamation schemes. The effects of the Palestinian *intifada* against Israel were felt in the Egyptian tourist market and were reinforced by the major terrorist attacks in the United States on September 11, 2001. The downturn in the international economy hurt Suez Canal revenues and oil revenues declined.[35] Growth continued to be slow in the first half of 2003.[36]

The fiscal deficit has grown in recent years as a result of large infrastructure spending (including that on the New Valley) coupled with weak tax revenues resulting from the low level of economic activity. Public-sector wages have risen, as have allocations for new jobs – a result of the weakness of the rest of the economy and its inability to generate sufficient new employment.[37]

Table 5.7 shows that the current account of the balance of payments was in surplus in 2002/3 to 2005/6. The emergence of a continuous surplus began in 2000. This represented a major change: throughout the period 1965–2000, the balance of payments suffered severe structural weakness and in recent years deficits were recorded on the current account.[38] The

[34] IMF. Arab Republic of Egypt: Selected Issues Report No. 07/381. 28. http://www.imf.org/external/pubs/ft/scr/2007/cr07381.pdf.

[35] Economist Intelligence Unit. *Country Report: Egypt, February 2003.* London: Economist Intelligence Unit, 2003. 8–12, 23.

[36] Economic Research Forum for the Arab Countries, Iran, and Turkey, *Egypt Country Profile, 2004.* Chapter 1. 22.

[37] IMF. *Arab Republic of Egypt, 2005.* Article IV, Consultation-Staff Report, Country Report 05/177. June 2005. 14.

[38] Ikram. 117–18.

Table 5.7. *Egypt: The balance-of-payments current account,*
2002/3–2005/6 ($ mns)

	2002/3	2003/4	2004/5	2005/6*
Current account	1,943	3,418	2,894	1,752
Trade account	−6,615	−7,523	−10,377	−11,986
Exports	8,205	10,453	13,833	18,455
Oil exports	3,161	3,910	5,299	10,222
Imports	14,820	17,975	24,193	30,441
Service balance	4,949	7,318	7,842	8,191
Transfers	3,609	3,934	5,428	5,547

* Preliminary figures.
Source: Central Bank of Egypt, *External Position of the Egyptian Economy,*
no. 6 (October 2004), no. 10 (December 2005), no. 14 (September 2006).

surpluses recorded in the 2000s were because of an increase in the surplus on the service account and a rise in transfers. Although exports rose, the trade deficit increased because imports rose faster than exports. As a result, Egypt had a large and increasing trade deficit that was covered by surpluses on services and transfers.

In July 2004, President Mubarak installed a new technocratic government to accelerate economic reforms. The new prime minister, Ahmed Nazif, was a technocrat, much younger and more business-minded than his predecessor, and the new minister of industry and foreign trade, Rashid Mohamed Rashid, was one of the few senior Egyptians with international business experience. The new government quickly introduced a series of changes in economic policy. These included unification of the exchange-rate system, reductions in import tariffs (the average weighted tariff was reduced from 14.6 percent to 9.1 percent), reductions in the number of tariff bands, and abolition of import fees and surcharges. There were reductions in the subsidies on fuel and electricity; tax and public expenditure reforms were announced. Reforms were announced for the banking sector and the government declared that most state-owned firms would be privatized, including those operating in what had been off-limit sectors. Between July 2004 and March 2005, seventeen nonfinancial firms were sold, generating $400 million.[39]

---

[39] IMF. *Arab Republic of Egypt, 2005* Article IV, Consultation-Staff Report, Country Report 05/177. June 2005.

The Qualified Industrial Zones

One of the most sensitive issues in Egyptian politics is that of relations with the rest of the world, particularly with the United States and Israel.[40] There are two main schools of thought regarding international economic policy in Egypt. The first is the Nasserist or socialist view, namely that the United States is an imperialist power, now dominating the international economy through globalization. Israel is an extension of U.S. power, oppressing the Palestinians, and so Egypt should have nothing to do with either. Many Islamists come to similar conclusions from a very different perspective. The second school of thought is the view held by members of the private sector and other technocrats who see Egypt's integration into the international economy as the only long-term hope for the country. Some of them, along with a very small number of intellectuals and others, want to improve relations with Israel partly for economic reasons and also in the hope that this will help to end the Israeli–Palestinian conflict. The government maneuvers within this context and its exact position can best be identified from what it does rather than from what it announces.

On 14 December 2004, the Egyptian and Israeli ministers of industry and the U.S. trade representative signed an agreement to create eight Qualified Industrial Zones (QIZs) in Egypt. The agreement permits goods made in Egypt with a specified minimum Israeli content to enter the United States duty free. Because there is no free trade agreement between Egypt and the United States, Egyptian exports to the United States are currently subject to duties and other restrictions. The QIZ agreement will make it possible to expand industrial exports and create thousands of jobs – two vital needs of the Egyptian economy.

The QIZs are located in the Greater Cairo area, in Alexandria, and in Port Said on the Suez Canal. For goods to have duty-free access to U.S. markets, they will have to contain a minimum 11.7 percent Israeli share in the value added for the factory concerned, measured on a quarterly basis. The method of calculation is designed to encourage a wide range of activities. An investment fund has been set up in London by groups interested in investing in the new zones.

---

[40] On the tendency to confuse economic and national security and foreign policy issues in Egypt and other Arab countries, see Waterbury, John. "The State and Transition in the Middle East and North Africa" in Nemat, Shafar (ed.), *Prospects for the Middle East and North Africa: From Boom to Bust and Back*. London: Macmillan, 1999. 159–77.

Negotiations on the Egyptian–Israeli agreement lasted several months, but its completion and the timing of the signing ceremony were highly political. For Egypt, the considerations were complex: much of Egyptian public opinion was and remains extremely hostile to Israel, as is the media, which is under the direct or indirect control of the government. The Egyptian public – including those who will benefit from the creation of new jobs – continues to perceive Israel as the enemy. Many Egyptians believe that economic cooperation with Israel is a zero-sum game: whatever Israel gains, Egypt (and the Palestinians and the Arabs, in general) lose. Accordingly, cooperation with Israel should be avoided. Trade between the two countries has reflected this disposition.

The signing of the agreement indicates that the government was convinced of the economic gains: Egypt desperately needs jobs, investment, and income, and the agreement with Israel offered all these. Moreover, the agreement strengthens Egypt's position in the United States, where there have been calls to reduce the military and economic aid given to Cairo. Furthermore, it protects Egypt's markets in the United States that were threatened by the end of the multilateral multi-fibre arrangement that would have resulted in the imposition of 35 percent tariffs in place of the quota system that guaranteed it limited access.[41]

President Mubarak and his ministers have seen how QIZs have benefited Jordan (see Chapter 7). The United States is encouraging other Middle East countries to produce goods jointly with Israel. Egypt's decision about QIZs is also part of a broader trade picture. Negotiations with the United States on a free-trade agreement have stalled: Egypt has doubts about the ability of its weak industrial sector to compete with American imports and fears the loss of revenues from import duties. The advantage of the QIZ agreement is that it promotes exports in a way that does not threaten local industry but rather encourages it. The disputes within Egypt therefore tend to be over which areas will benefit from QIZ status and whether companies will move to them. In 2005, it was reported that 15,000 jobs had been created in Egypt as a result of the trilateral agreement.[42] Egyptian apparel exports to the United States rose from $422 million in 2004 to $444 million in 2005, an increase of only 5.3 percent. According to official Egyptian sources, without QIZs, Egyptian garment exports to the United States would have actually decreased in 2005 under the pressure of Chinese competition. In

---

[41] Yadav, Vikash. "The Political Economy of the Egyptian-Israeli QIZ Trade Agreement." *Middle East Review of International Affairs* 11, no. 1 (March 2007), 1. http://meria.idc.ac.il.
[42] Israel Radio. 16 December 2005.

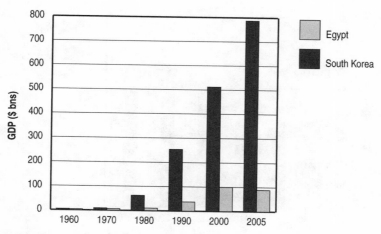

Figure 5.3. Egypt and South Korea: GDP, 1960–2005. *Source:* International Financial Statistics Yearbook 1987 and 1995, World Bank, Data and Statistics Series.

2004, Egyptian exports of textiles, textile products, and garments were $563 million. In 2005, they increased by nearly 9 percent to $613 million and in 2006 they rose by 31 percent to $806 million.[43] During the first nine months of 2006, Egyptian apparel exports to the United States reached $464 million, 46 percent higher than in the same period in 2005. In 2005, ninety-three Egyptian garment exporters participated in QIZs. In 2006, their number rose to 160.[44]

The Role of Initial Conditions in Egypt and South Korea

This section examines the role of initial or basic conditions using Egypt and South Korea as examples. Three sets of basic conditions favoring economic development were present in East Asia, but were largely absent in the Arab world. The first was that between 1970 and 1990 the deceleration in demographic growth and the onset of demographic transition occurred in East Asia while in the Arab world it accelerated. This is shown in Figures 2.2 and 2.3. During the 1960s, a transition to lower population growth took place in South Korea and Taiwan and over time this reduced pressure to generate employment. Figures 5.3, 5.4, and 5.5 summarize the development

[43] U.S. Census Bureau. Foreign Trade Statistics. http://www.census.gov/foreign-trade/statistics/country/sreport/country.txt.

[44] Emerging Textiles.com. 21 November 2006. http://www.emergingtextiles.com/?q=art&s=061121Egypt&r=free&n.

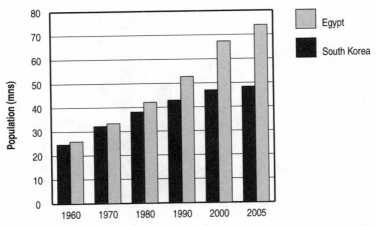

Figure 5.4. Egypt and South Korea: Population, 1960–2005. *Source:* International Financial Statistics Yearbook 1987 and 1995, World Bank, Data and Statistics Series.

of national income and population growth in the period 1960–85 in Egypt and South Korea.

In 1960, the Korea crude birthrate was 43 per 1,000 and the death rate 14 per 1,000. By 1970, the birthrate had fallen by 25 percent to 30 per 1,000 and the death rate by 36 percent to 9 per 1,000. These trends continued in the 1970s and 1980s, and by 1991, the birthrate was 16 per 1,000 and the death rate was 6 per 1,000. Egypt did not experience such demographic transition in the 1960s and the progress that did come in the 1970s and 1980s was much slower. In 1960, it had a crude birthrate of 44 per 1,000 and

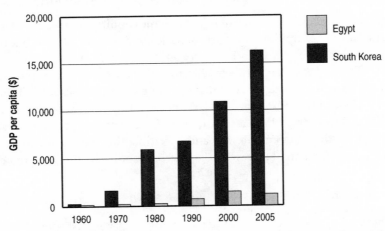

Figure 5.5. Egypt and South Korea: GDP per Capita, 1960–2005. *Source:* International Financial Statistics Yearbook 1987 and 1995, World Bank, Data and Statistics Series.

a crude death rate of 19 per 1,000. In 1970, the birthrate was 40 per 1,000 and the death rate 17 per 1,000. As a result, the population growth rate in the 1960s and 1970s remained unchanged at about 2.5 percent.[45] In the 1980s, Egypt's population increased by more than 2.4 percent annually.[46] In contrast, South Korea's population grew by only 1.1 percent.[47]

Demographic transition also reduced the burden of education and health services and permitted resources to be allocated to improving the quality of those services, which in turn yielded further economic benefits. The economic benefits of transition in East Asia were large. According to the World Bank, in 1975 South Korea saved 0.6 percent of GNP by having a growth rate of school-age population that was lower than Kenya's; by 1988–9, the saving was 2.8 percent. The savings in other East Asian countries were also considerable. Despite this, Korea increased its spending on education from 2 percent of GNP in 1960 to 3.6 percent in 1989.[48]

The second basic condition was greater equality in the distribution of income, wealth, and land at the beginning of the period of modern industrialization in East Asia than in the Middle East or Latin America. In 1960, the Gini coefficient for the distribution of income in South Korea was 0.34 while that for Egypt was 0.42. In the same year, the Gini coefficient for land distribution in South Korea was 0.39 while in Egypt it was 0.67.[49] In Latin America, the Gini coefficient for the distribution of household per capita income in 1960 was 52.8 (in 1992 it was 54.8).[50] (The closer the Gini coefficient is to zero the greater the level of equality.)

The distribution of land was also much more equal in East Asia. In South Korea the reform of landownership was radical although the regimes were not revolutionary. In the 1930s, 3 percent of farm households owned two-thirds of the land. By the 1940s, less than 7 percent of the rural population was landless and by the late 1940s there were few landless wage earners. The land reforms dissolved the landed aristocracy.[51] In Egypt, between 1952 and 1961, during the major agrarian reforms of the Free Officers movement,

[45] World Bank. *World Development Report 1981–82*. Washington, D.C.: World Bank, 1981; *World Development Report 1993*. New York: Oxford University Press, 1993.
[46] Amin, Galal. *Egypt's Economic Predicament*. Leiden: E. J. Brill, 1995. 28.
[47] World Bank. *The East Asian Miracle*. Oxford and New York: Oxford University Press, 1993. 40.
[48] Ibid. 195, 198.
[49] Rodrik, Dani. "King Kong Meets Godzilla: The World Bank and the East Asian Miracle." Discussion Paper. No. 944. London: Center for Economic Policy Research, 1994. Table 2.
[50] World Bank. *Inequality in Latin America and the Caribbean: Breaking with History*. 2003. Table A18, 416. http://www.worldbank.org.
[51] Amsden, Alice. *Asia's Next Giant: South Korea and Late Industrialization*. New York: Oxford University Press, 1989. 28, 52, 203.

14 percent of total cultivable land was redistributed with property rights transferred to only 10 percent of the population. Each family received one hectare. Two-thirds of the tenants and nearly all of the landless wage earners were excluded from the reforms although excluded tenants were given security of tenure and paid low, fixed rents in real terms until the liberalization of the 1990s. The ceiling for landownership was fixed at 42 hectares.[52] For as long as there have been records, land distribution in Latin America was the most unequal in the world. Reforms have had very limited effect and in the mid-1970s and 1980s the Gini coefficient for land distribution ranged from a low of 0.58 in Mexico to a high of 0.73 in Brazil. In Uruguay it was 0.71 and in Chile 0.63.[53]

The third factor was higher and rising literacy rates in East Asia compared to the Arab world. In 1960, adult literacy in Egypt was 20 percent, in Morocco 17 percent, and in Jordan 32 percent. In Iraq it was only 15 percent! In South Korea it was 71 percent, in the Philippines 72 percent, in Taiwan 54 percent. By 1999, Egypt's literacy rate had risen to 55 percent, Morocco's to 48 percent, and Jordan's to 79 percent. The rates in East Asia were more than 95 percent.[54] Furthermore, relatively high literacy rates improved. Between 1960 and 1989, the share of government spending devoted to education rose from 11 percent to 20 percent.[55] The importance of equality as a policy goal was reflected in the emphasis placed on primary education.[56] In 1960, the primary school enrollment ratio was 94 percent and the literacy rate was 71 percent. Both of these were significantly higher than were predicted on the basis of South Korea's national income level.[57] In educational terms, initial conditions were better in South Korea where primary school enrollment in 1960 was 96 percent, compared to 66 percent in Egypt (see Table 5.8). The two Latin American countries in Table 5.8 have relatively good figures for 1960 for primary net enrollment and literacy but have progressed more slowly than Malaysia and South Korea since then.

---

[52] El-Ghonemy, M. Riad. *Affluence and Poverty in the Middle East.* London: Routledge, 1998. 160.

[53] Herrara, Marianna. "Land Tenure Development and Policy Making in Latin America." Organization of American States, 2005. 2. http://www.oas.org/dsd/Documents/LTDpolicysummary_LATIN%20AMERICA.pdf.

[54] World Bank. *World Development Report 1978.* New York: Oxford University Press, 1978. *World Development Report 1979.* New York: Oxford University Press, 1979. *World Development Report 2002.* New York: Oxford University Press, 2002.

[55] World Bank. *East Asian Miracle.* Figure 1.3. 31.

[56] World Bank. *The Evolving Role of the World Bank.* Washington, D.C.: World Bank, 1995. 6.

[57] Rodrik. 4–5. Tables 1 and 2.

Table 5.8. *Educational achievements in selected Arab, East Asian, and Latin American countries, 1960–2004*

	Primary net enrollment*				Literacy rate[†]			
	1960	1978	1991	2004	1960	1976	1991	2004
Egypt	66	74	84	94	26	44	47	71
Morocco	47	72	56	94	14	28	39	52
Syria	65	89	91	98	30	58	65	80
Tunisia	66	100	94	97	16	62	65[‡]	74
Malaysia	96	94	n.a.	93	53	60	81	89
South Korea	94	111	100	100	71	93	95[‡§]	98
Brazil	95	88	85	97	61	76	82	89
Mexico	80	116	98	100	66	82	87	91

* Number enrolled in primary school as percent of total relevant age group.

[†] Percent of population older than age 15.

[‡] 1994.

§ 95 percent or more.

Source: World Bank: World Development Reports, 1981 and 1996, World Development Indicators, 2006; UNDP: Human Development Report 2006.

Between 1960 and 2004, primary school enrollment rates improved in Egypt, and the literacy rate more than doubled. Despite that, in 2004, almost one-third of the population older than 15 was illiterate. The main obstacle to increasing the literacy rate in Egypt was the rate of growth of population although there was also evidence of declining effectiveness of Egyptian education.[58] In Morocco the situation was, in some respects, worse: primary net enrollment rates rose faster than in Egypt, but literacy rates remained very high, with almost 50 percent of the population older than 15 illiterate in 2004. Syria's record, both for enrollment and literacy, was better than Egypt's or Morocco's, but even there 20 percent of the population older than 15 was illiterate in 2004.

Another important aspect of literacy is the difference between the sexes. In 2006, male literacy (of those aged 15 or older) in the MENA was 81 percent; female literacy was 61 percent. In East Asia and the Pacific the figures were 95 percent and 87 percent, respectively, and in Latin America and the Caribbean, 91 percent and 89 percent, respectively. MENA was therefore not only behind in male and female literacy but the gender gap

---

[58] Fergany, Nader. *Egypt 2012 Education and Employment.* Economic Research Forum for the Arab Countries, Iran, and Turkey, 1995. 2. http://www.erg.org.eg.

was 20 percent compared with 7 percent in East Asia and the Pacific and 2 percent in Latin America and the Caribbean.[59]

The economic policies implemented from the 1960s in East Asia were very successful in achieving growth although there has been much debate about how they worked. The countries of East Asia maintained stable macroeconomic conditions in the early phases of their rapid industrialization in the 1960s and 1970s. This included low inflation and the avoidance of significant budget deficits. Conservative and sustainable fiscal policies were organized so that the rewards from growth were shared equitably. This, together with the relative equality of initial conditions, meant that governments were not under pressure to subsidize basic commodities or other goods. This was in strong contrast to the Arab world, where oil-rich and poor countries have all used subsidies on a large scale. One of the benefits of the policies followed in much of East Asia was the minimization of price distortions. Financial development and liberalization in East Asia maximized domestic savings and meant that economies in the region were less dependent on inflows of funds from abroad in the early stages of their development. In 1971–90, the average real interest rate of deposits in South Korea was 1.88 percent while in Egypt it was −6.32 percent.[60] Negative interest rates in Egypt discouraged savings in local currency and encouraged the dollarization of the economy.[61]

Another crucial ingredient in East Asia's success was the quality of government. There were several aspects to this, first of which was the commitment of the political leadership to economic growth. In the aftermath of World War II, East Asian governments sought legitimacy through economic achievements. Economic conditions were harsh, so improvements were easy to see and generated political popularity and stability. Closely connected was the existence of a competent bureaucracy that was able to manage intricate development strategies. Third, the bureaucracy was isolated from political pressures of lobbyists and other interest groups including politicians.[62] A very different pattern prevailed in much of the Arab world, where among other things, the state was bigger (accounting for a larger share of national income) and parliamentary, press, and judicial oversight were weaker because they were largely under state control.[63]

---

[59] World Bank. *World Development Indicators 2007*. http://www.worldbank.org.

[60] The standard deviations were 5.86 percent for South Korea and 3.52 percent for Egypt. World Bank. *The East Asian Miracle*. 206.

[61] Rivlin. 119.

[62] World Bank. *The East Asian Miracle*. 167–81.

[63] El-Ghonemy. 112–23.

The East Asian economies were opened up in stages, firms were provided with incentives to export, and those that received government assistance were penalized if they failed to meet quotas. This only happened after a phase of import substitution that let firms learn and achieve economies of scale, among other factors. The pragmatic nature of economic policy was because there was very little ideology or ideological change in East Asian policies. In Egypt, Iraq, Syria, and Tunisia (as well as in Yemen) there was a strong socialist phase that was also mirrored in some of the monarchies such as Jordan and Morocco. During the socialist phase the private sector was either eliminated or seriously weakened and as a result, when socialism was abandoned, it was unable to fill the economic space left by retreating governments.[64]

The 1950s were largely a lost decade for South Korea. They were years of war and when it ended, the very corrupt regime under Syngman Rhee put limited emphasis on development. Both economies grew in the 1950s, but the pattern of growth was less stable and the rate slower than in the 1960s.

In Egypt, by contrast, the 1950s were productive: a new regime came to power that swept away the monarchy. It recognized the need for the state to play a central role in the economy and introduced major land-reform programs. It invested in industry, created a planning framework, and took over foreign assets in stages. By the late 1950s, President Nasser had nationalized the Suez Canal and other foreign property. In 1960, he introduced a five-year plan for the whole country modeled on Soviet experience and then nationalized major sectors of the economy. Egypt was, in 1961, at the height of its Arab socialist phase. The regime was trying to mobilize the economy for a huge development effort and in many respects, to break with the past. The 1950s would seem, at first sight, to have been an auspicious prelude to the Egyptian industrialization drive of the 1960s but, as will be shown, this is too superficial a view. As in South Korea, growth was the order of the day. The method chosen was import substitution (IS) industrialization.

The more sophisticated objection to the use of the comparative method is based on one of the conclusions of recent economic analysis. It is that initial conditions are one of the determinants of the growth pattern. As they are given at the moment of comparison it is unfair to compare regions. However, the purpose of comparison is not to lay blame but to work out solutions. If it is found that, for example, lower literacy rates in one

---

[64] Yusuf, Shahid. "The East Asian Miracle at the Millennium" in Stiglitz, Joseph E. and Shahid Yusuf (eds.), *Rethinking the East Asian Miracle*. New York: Oxford University Press and the World Bank, 2001. 1–55.

region held it back, then a solution may be in hand if more is invested in education.

The absence of large inequalities in the distribution of income meant that the government did not have to deal with wealthy and thus powerful vested interests in agriculture or industry. Policy makers were therefore insulated from pressures to follow the interests of particular sectors and were able to plan and implement policies designed to maximize the growth of the economy as a whole. Administrative reforms were undertaken without outside interference and economic regulations were generated in the technocratic elite with politicians, especially President Park in South Korea, acting to prevent vested interests from interfering. Given relatively equal distributions of income in South Korea and Taiwan, governments were not under pressure to redistribute income.[65] They were also less concerned about the consequences of growth on distribution than would otherwise have been the case. It should be noted that this equality was in large part the result of external factors rather than deliberate decisions in South Korea and Taiwan. Between 1945 and 1953, war and revolution resulted in the redistribution of wealth in both countries.[66]

Another initial condition, much like the economic historian W. W. Rostow's precondition for takeoff, was strong growth in agricultural production.[67] South Korean agricultural production rose by an annual average of 4.5 percent in the 1960s and by 5 percent in the period 1970–7. By contrast, that in Egypt rose by an annual average of 2.9 percent in the 1960s and by 3.1 percent in the period 1970–7.[68] The importance of these factors has been recognized by both the World Bank and its critics in the debate about growth in East Asia.[69]

There is one other factor that played a crucial role in South Korea but was absent in Egypt: the quality of leadership. The leadership of the East Asian states gave priority to economic growth while that in Egypt did not. The former were more determined and by the start of the 1960s had

---

[65] Rodrik, Dani. "Getting Interventions Right: How South Korea and Taiwan Grew Rich." *Economic Policy* 20 (1995), 55–107.

[66] Perkins, Dwight H. "There Are at Least Three Models of East Asian Development." *World Development* 22, no. 4. (1994), 655–61.

[67] Rostow, W. W. *The Stages of Economic Growth*. Cambridge: Cambridge University Press, 1960.

[68] World Bank. *World Development Report 1979*.

[69] *East Asian Miracle* (see note 47); and Rodrik, Dani, King Kong Meets Godzilla. The World Bank and the East Asian Miracle. 9–10. Discussion Paper no. 944, London: Centre for Economic Policy Research, 1994.

disengaged themselves or had been significantly disengaged from regional military struggles. The opposite was true of the Arab world: Egypt increased its defense spending during the period of the First Five-Year Plan in the early 1960s and its leadership was preoccupied with noneconomic developments inside and outside the country. Conflict and a preoccupation with conflict remain uppermost in the public mind in the Middle East and in that of the leadership.

The Egyptian regime failed to create an effective civil service or give economic issues an absolute priority. The first can be seen as part of the second. The regime did not see economic success as vital to its own survival. This is not to say that Nasser and others in the leadership did not want the best for their people: their concern for them was demonstrated in their unwillingness to impose burdens. The net effect of their policies was, however, to leave the country in severe difficulties in the mid-1960s, even before the Six-Day War broke out. To understand this it is worthwhile looking at the political context in which the regime was operating.

The question remains: Why did Nasser abandon his industrialization drive in the mid-1960s and allow defense spending to rise? Why did he not devote much more attention to raising the finances needed to cover the balance of payments? Ayubi, using a wide range of Arab and non-Arab sources, has outlined some of the reasons why Arab states have not concentrated their efforts on economic issues, why they might be called "fierce" rather than "hard."[70] Those parts of his analysis that relate to economic development are highly relevant here, although they are referred to in order to suggest lines for future research rather than provide a complete or even definitive answer.

Both the Arabist and Islamic movements historically gave relatively little weight to the issue of the state; they regarded national borders, populations, rights, and markets as artificial or superficial. Since the nineteenth century, according to Ayubi, the Arabs have been concerned with the manifestations of power but have paid much less attention to its social, economic, and intellectual manifestations within the state.[71] Organizational reforms failed to transform the attitudes of individuals in Arab countries toward political authority and so the modern state failed to be appreciated as a manifestation of general will or public ethics. In many respects, the state remained alien to

---

[70] Ayubi, Nazih N. *Overstating the Arab State.* London: I. B. Tauris, 1995.
[71] Ibid. 9–10.

society and its achievements paled compared with the nationalist, pan-Arab, Arab Socialist, or later religious ideals.

The first and uncontroversial conclusion that can be drawn from this comparative analysis is the importance of initial conditions. From the 1960s, positive demographic trends, high and rising educational levels, and strong industrial and agricultural growth were present in South Korea and in Taiwan. The absence of these initial conditions in Egypt may, in itself, be a sufficient explanation for the failure of the economy to take off or move into sustained growth.

The second and more controversial conclusion relates to factors identified in the so-called endogenous growth models as being crucial for economic development. These emphasize imperfect information, increasing returns to scale, and other factors, and lead to the conclusion that there is no single explanation for economic growth. The new growth models stress the link between macroeconomic variables and their microeconomic foundations, the institutions that support them. Savings, for example, are a function of the financial and business systems that exist in an economy. During the 1960s and 1970s, all the banks in South Korea and Taiwan were in the public sector. The implication for other countries is that the institutions that served growth so well in East Asia need to be analyzed along with the performance of the economy in macroeconomic terms.[72]

What are the implications of this analysis for policy makers in the Middle East today? First is that until initial conditions exist, a country cannot successfully embark on an industrialization drive. It needs to concentrate its efforts on education, health, and income equality and only then can move toward investment in industry. This may, however, be too literal an interpretation of history. In 1960, the South Korean population growth rate was high and the transition to lower growth rates only came during the 1960s, which suggests that efforts to industrialize can go on at the same time that initial conditions are being improved. Governments can and should act to improve initial conditions.

The second implication is more worrisome. There is a growing realization that the "East Asian Miracle" was achieved as a result of government intervention in support of the market (or to use Wade's phrase, by "governing the market") and that this involved a very selective use of IS. The IS policies

---

[72] el-Mikawy, Noha. "State/Society and Executive/Legislative Relations" in el-Mikawy, Noha and Heba Handoussa (eds.), *Institutional Reform and Economic Development in Egypt.* Cairo: American University Press, 2002. 24–5.

followed in East Asia had two aims. First, they were designed to create local markets for domestic producers during their infant stage. This is the infant industries argument. Second, they were designed to protect the balance of payments. A more controversial point is that IS preceded and then coexisted with export promotion. Boosting exports is traditionally recommended and that means reducing or eliminating import controls. The fact that in the early phase of industrialization South Korea and other countries in East Asia promoted their exports while restricting imports is an uncomfortable fact for many economists. In this respect, there was an important difference between the policies followed in East Asia and those followed in Egypt and other Arab countries, both in the 1960s and in the period since then.

The implication for the policies now being followed in non-oil Arab countries is serious. They are being urged to open their economies to imports and to rely on exports as the engine of growth. The experience of South Korea and Taiwan was that export growth followed IS and even coincided with it. The East Asian states had the administrative capacity as well as the political will to supervise firms and regulate their exports so as to ensure quality and quantity control. This occurred in a very different international economic climate from that which has prevailed since the mid-1980s, when non-oil Arab states have undergone IMF-style stabilization programs. It is doubtful whether these Arab states, even if they wanted and had the capacity to, would be permitted by the IMF, the European Union, and the World Trade Organization to develop policies akin to those used in East Asia thirty years ago.

Egypt has benefited from demographic transition and from the potentially low dependence ratio made possible by the so-called demographic gift. Despite this, the demographic and labor-force challenges are enormous. The economy's performance has been uneven. Growth accelerated in the second half of the 1990s but fell to a slower rate in 2001–02 than in the first half of the 1990s. The nature of the growth process was also problematic; it was not employment-intensive enough to absorb all those entering the labor market. Furthermore, it did not demand skilled labor on a sufficient scale to absorb those completing school and college. Nor did it provide incentives for education that could help transform the quality of the labor force and thereby increase its productivity.

In view of the success of the measures taken in 1991, 1996, and 2004, why did Egypt not go further in reforming the economy? The answer is that radical reforms were seen, on balance, as a threat to the stability of the regime. The legacy of the past weighed heavily on the regime and the public sector. As a result of the central role of the Nile in the economy, the state has had a central role since pharaonic times. More recently, this has been reinforced by rental incomes from Suez Canal tolls, oil revenues, workers' remittances, and foreign aid, most of which accrue to the government. Populism and Nasser's corporatist experiment reduced (or even extinguished) the middle class's ability to mobilize, organize, and make their voice heard. Channels of mediation between the people and the state were also severely weakened. Private entrepreneurs had to rely on family connections and on lobbying the state via personal patronage rather than through collective organizations.[73]

Egypt's economy has paid a heavy price for maintaining the regime in power. Close links between favored businesspeople, the military, senior military officers, and politicians, combined with a vast bureaucracy, provide a system of patronage while stifling much private initiative and political freedom. The system was inward looking, feeding off rents that were the result of monopolies and oligopolies generated by government policies.

Organized political activities outside government control were seen as a threat and were treated accordingly. The amount of freedom granted to political parties in Egypt, while greater than in some of the other Arab states, is still very limited. This means that the electorate is not offered real alternatives and the government is not subject to effective scrutiny.

Conclusions

Despite the fact that Egypt is experiencing demographic transition, the scale of population growth is huge. The economy has struggled to create enough jobs for the numbers coming into the labor market and meet the subsidies bill for those basic commodities still supplied to the poor. The economy has moved a long way from the socialism of Nasser's era. Sadat's policies liberalized the foreign sector while Mubarak has tackled reform of the domestic economy. The pace of change has been slow and fitful, allowing the growth of the population to weigh down even more heavily than the benefits of change. Furthermore, as under Sadat, those benefits have not been evenly spread, leading a political discontent that is funneled into the Islamic opposition. Distributional issues contrast strongly with the experience of South Korea. Their greater equality in the distribution

---

[73] Henry, Clement M. and Robert Springborg. *Globalization and the Politics of Development in the Middle East.* Cambridge: Cambridge University Press, 2001. 155.

of land, wealth, and income in the early 1960s meant that the government could concentrate on growth rather than distribution. The demographic slowdown in South Korea meant that the poor were far fewer in number and the need to create jobs was much smaller than in Egypt. This suggests that Egypt will have to "run to stand still" or at best "run in order to walk" for many years.

SIX

Iraq

After Destruction

Introduction

Five years after the 2003 war, Iraq's prospects for reconstruction and development are bleak. The country is plagued by terrorism that is resulting in the deaths of hundreds of people every week. The three main communities, the Shi'ites, Kurds, and Sunni, have had a very hard time agreeing on political structures that would hold the country together. In this dangerous and confused environment, oil production is much lower than planned, thus limiting the main source of government income. One of the issues dividing the communities is the allocation of oil wealth. Virtually all of Iraq's oil resources are in the Kurdish north of the country, the economy of which is thriving, or in the Shi'ite south. The Sunni, who constitute about 35 percent of the population and who ruled the country under the Ba'ath, lost power in 2003 when the United States invaded Iraq. They are now fighting, if not for control, then at least for a share of the oil wealth as well as a share of political power.

Iraq suffers from a number of problems that have their origins in the first half of the twentieth century. The first is the polarization between social classes and ethnic groups: primarily those among the Shi'a, Sunni, and Kurds. The second is closely related: the polarization of the rulers from the ruled, something that reached its horrific apogee under Saddam Hussein and is currently manifested in the tensions between American occupation forces and many Iraqis. Third is the pattern of investment, most notably the failure to invest in agriculture and industry. Fourth is the continued and even intensified reliance on oil as the major source of income.

Two other factors had major impacts on the economy. The first was the Ba'athist regime that, between 1980 and 2003, centralized power in the hands of one man. Second was Saddam Hussein's decisions to attack Iran in 1980 and to invade Kuwait in 1990, wars that brought ruin on Iraq and made the economy even more dependent on oil and thus on the international economic system. These wars and their effects negated everything that the struggle for independence, Arab Socialism, and the Ba'ath party claimed to stand for.

There has been considerable continuity in economic policy between the colonial and independent periods and therefore this chapter covers a longer period of history than the others. Developments since 1980 have reinforced these patterns in an entirely negative way. This chapter concludes with an analysis of the situation following the U.S.-led invasion of 2003, and shows that the economic legacy has imposed severe constraints on future development.

The Colonial Inheritance

In the early nineteenth century the effects of floods dominated the area that became Iraq; the salinity of river water increased and there were severe problems of silt and plagues. There was widespread insecurity with corrupt, Ottoman-appointed Sunni governors ruling over a largely Shi'a population. During the second half of the nineteenth century, change came with the opening of the Suez Canal and the expansion of demand for Iraqi agricultural production. As a result, the cultivation of land increased. The tribal system of landownership and control came under pressure from urban interests and from stronger central government. Private ownership, mainly in the form of very large estates, began to replace tribal ownership. This encouraged the expansion of agriculture and the development of systems to protect against salinity that had spread in irrigated areas, but productivity was low and yields fell. Despite these developments, the Ottoman authorities favored tribal rulers over the working class and integration of the middle class into the ruling establishment was very limited. In consequence, feudal landownership patterns were largely maintained. In 1858, the Ottoman Land Code confirmed the existing distribution of land, which resulted from the granting of land-use rights to tribal sheiks, city merchants, and Kurdish village heads in the north of the country. This effectively denied millions of peasants access to the land that they and their ancestors had used for centuries. Five large landowners possessed 4 percent of the total land area while 70 percent of the farming population owned 3 percent of the land. Clan heads, chiefs of smaller tribes and city traders, held the remaining 93 percent.[1]

[1] El-Ghonemy, M. Riad. *Affluence and Poverty in the Middle East.* London: Routledge, 1998. 33.

In 1869–71, the Ottoman governor attempted to reform landownership by applying ownership ceilings and giving compensation to those whose land was taken. However, these measures failed and in 1880 and 1891, the reforms were suspended and a new extra-legal class of land, in which ownership and usufruct belonged to the state, was created. Those who used the land became tax-paying tenants. Following World War I, the British continued this system. In 1958, 3,400 landowners held 68 percent of the land and there were only 168,000 registered landowners. Millions remained landless.[2] At the beginning of the twentieth century, agricultural output increased and population growth accelerated. Prior to World War I, the Turks, Germans, and British began to invest in railways and the oil industry. The war caused much damage and was followed by British rule and the establishment of the Mandate in 1922. This was done in the face of widespread local opposition that was put down with the use of force. In 1921, the British established the modern state of Iraq: the Hashemite, Faisal, was made king. Railways were built linking Iraq to Syria and thus extending the network to Turkey and even Germany. Basra's port was expanded and aviation and telecommunications links with the rest of the world developed.

Agricultural development policies favored the elite. The British based their power on the close links with sheiks, and the landlord-dominated parliament did little to change the landownership system. There were, therefore, few incentives to improve productivity. Increased use of irrigation did, however, make more land available: the cultivable area increased from 900,000 acres in 1913 to 4 million acres in 1943. Wheat output doubled between 1928 and 1938. Public investment, funded by oil revenues, favored the creation of dams to solve irrigation problems. This increased the supply of irrigated land but reinforced the inequitable distribution system.[3] Only after the revolution of 1958 were radical changes in land distribution made.[4]

Iraq's oil income rose sharply after the end of World War II, from $6 million in 1945 to $105 million in 1951, following the introduction of a 50:50 profit-sharing agreement with Western oil companies. By 1958, Iraq's oil income had reached $224 million.[5] In 1950, the Development Board, consisting of foreign advisors and Iraqis, was set up to control the

---

[2] Issawi, Charles. *An Economic History of the Middle East and North Africa*. London: Methuen, 1982. 147–8.

[3] Alnasrawi, A. *The Economy of Iraq: Oil, Wars, Destruction of Development, and Prospects, 1950–2000*. Westport, Conn. and London: Greenwood Press, 1994. 17–33.

[4] Mahdi, Kamil A. "Iraq's Agrarian System: Issues of Policy and Performance" in Mahdi, Kamil A. (ed.), *Iraq's Economic Predicament*. Reading: Ithaca, 2002. 321–3.

[5] Owen, Roger and Sevket Pamuk. *A History of the Middle East Economies in the Twentieth Century*. Cambridge: I. B. Tauris, 1998. 162.

spending of these revenues, but its powers were curtailed with the creation of the Ministry of Development in 1953. The board allocated large sums for irrigation projects that did little to benefit the life of ordinary Iraqis. In 1956, an increase in allocations for health, welfare, and drinking water was implemented.

The British hardly invested in education. In 1920, there were only 10,000 children in school in Iraq; in 1937 there were 110,000.[6] By 1940–5, an average of only 20 percent of children were in school and the dropout rate was 90 percent. This meant that only 2 percent of Iraqi schoolchildren completed primary school.[7] This was a key area in which independent Iraq was to break with its past: it gave priority to education and by 1980 there were considerable achievements.

Demographic Trends

Table 6.1 shows how rapidly the population grew between 1950 and 2005. Between 1950 and 1980 population growth accelerated; since the early 1990s,

Table 6.1. *Iraq: Population and dependency ratios, 1950–2005*

	Population (millions)	Working-age population	Dependent population	Dependency ratio*
1950	5.34	2.99	2.35	78
1960	7.33	3.73	3.6	96
1970	10.11	5.00	10.11	102
1980	14.09	7.04	7.05	100
1985	16.29	8.33	7.96	96
1990	18.52	9.69	8.83	91
1995	21.63	11.55	10.08	97
2000	25.01	13.65	11.36	84
2005	28.81	15.60	13.21	79

* The total dependency ratio is the ratio of the sum of the population aged 0–14 and that aged 65 and older to the population aged 15–64. This is expressed as number of dependents per 100 persons of working age (aged 15–64).

Source: Population Division of the Department of Economic and Social Affairs of the United Nations Secretariat. *World Population Prospects: The 2004 Revision* and *World Urbanization Prospects: The 2003 Revision.* http://esa.un.org/unpp. Based on medium variant forecast.

[6] Issawi, Charles. Iraq: "A Study in Aborted Development" in *The Middle East Economy: Decline and Recovery.* Princeton: Markus Wiener, 1995. 154.

[7] El-Ghonemy 37.

Table 6.2. *Iraq: Demographic trends, 1980–2005*

	1980–85	1985–90	1990–95	1995–2000	2000–2005*
Annual population growth (000s)	439	445	623	689	747
Population growth (%)	2.90	2.56	3.11	2.95	2.71
Crude birthrate/1,000	39.8	39.6	39.0	38.3	35.3
Crude death rate/1,000	8.3	6.9	9.6	10.0	9.7
Total fertility rate	6.35	6.15	5.70	5.37	4.83
Life expectancy at birth: males (years)	60.6	63.6	58.0	57.3	57.3
Life expectancy at birth: females (years)	63.7	66.7	61.1	60.4	60.4
Infant mortality/1,000 births	60.4	47.9	73.1	94.3	94.3

* Medium variant forecast.

Source: Population Division of the Department of Economic and Social Affairs of the United Nations Secretariat. World Population Prospects: The 2004 Revision and World Urbanization Prospects: The 2003 Revision. http://esa.un.org/unpp.

there has been a slowdown in the growth rate. From the 1950s, death rates fell as a result of improved health, sanitation, and nutrition. As this was accompanied by high birthrates it led to an acceleration of the population growth rate. By the 1980s, the availability and use of contraception had increased and fertility rates fell. The increase in the female labor-force participation rate, resulting from the draft of men into the army because of the war in 1980–8, reinforced these trends. The absence of hundreds of thousands of men at war also had its effect on population growth. In 1990, Iraq invaded Kuwait and the war that followed in 1991 resulted in a socioeconomic calamity. Incomes fell, unemployment rose, and personal security deteriorated. As a result, fertility rates fell although they remained very high by international standards.

According to the United Nations, in the period 1995–2005 the population grew by 33 percent. The population of working age rose by 35 percent and the working population by 31 percent (these figures are estimates and were not checked by census). Since 2003, the resident population has fallen by two million as Iraqis have left for Jordan, Syria, and other countries to escape the conflict at home.

Table 6.2 shows how, between 1980–5 and 2000–05, the absolute annual increase in the population rose by 70 percent. This was despite the slowdown in the population growth rate from 1990–5. In the last twenty years Iraq was almost unique in the Middle East: the crude birthrate hardly fell while the death rate rose. The latter is also reflected in the decline in life expectancy at birth. The male rate fell as a result of huge losses in the war against Iran and both male and female life expectancy, as well as infant mortality, were affected by economic deterioration after the 1991 war.

The effects of the 1991 war and the sanctions that followed wiped out improvements in health and infant mortality recorded in the 1970s and 1980s. The infant mortality rate doubled between 1985–90 and 1995–2000. Although there was an improvement in the second half of the 1990s, the rate remained substantially higher than in the early 1980s. A similar trend was apparent for life expectation at birth. It increased in the late 1980s, part of a long-term trend, but fell in the early 1990s as nutrition, economic, and health conditions deteriorated before partially recovering to almost its 1985–90 level in the second half of the 1990s.

The effects of war are also apparent from the data on the sex composition of the population in 2000. The share of females in the total population exceeded that of males in the 25 and older age-group. The Iran–Iraq War resulted in the death of hundreds of thousands of Iraqi soldiers. The 1991 war resulted in the death of between 50,000 and 150,000 soldiers and between 11,000 and 25,000 civilians. In addition, between 20,000 and 100,000 civilians were killed by the Ba'athist regime in the uprising that followed the war in the south of the country; 15,000 to 30,000 Kurds were killed at the same time.[8] Despite the deprivations that the population has suffered in the last twenty years, Iraq has high fertility and birthrates. Like other countries in the region, its population is very young: in 2000, more than 46 percent of the population was below age 15. The labor force grew by 3 percent a year between 1980 and 2001 compared with a population growth rate of 2.9 percent.[9] These rates pose formidable challenges regarding the provision of public services and employment. United Nations (UN)–World Bank figures indicate annual population growth rates of 2.8 percent between 2001 and 2002 and 3.1 percent between 2002 and 2004. This means that the UN and the World Bank expected improvements in socioeconomic conditions to result in an *acceleration* of the demographic growth rate.[10] The exit of hundreds of thousands of Iraqis since the 2003 war puts these estimates in doubt. Emigration reduced demographic and labor market pressures. Many

---

[8] Alnasrawi, Abbas. *Iraq's Burdens: Oil, Sanctions, and Underdevelopment*. Westport, Conn.: Greenwood Press, 2002. 68.

[9] World Bank. *World Development Indicators, 2003*. Washington, D.C.: World Bank, 2003. 39, 43.

[10] World Bank. *Interim Strategy Note of the World Bank Group for Iraq*, Report No. 27602. 14 January 2004. 4. http://www.worldbank.org.

Table 6.3. *Iraq: Employment by sector, May 2004 (%)*

	Male	Female	All
Agriculture	13	33	17
Manufacturing	7	7	7
Construction	12	1	10
Wholesale, retail, and repairs	23	5	20
Transport, storage, and communications	12	1	10
Public administration and defense	18	16	18
Education	4	30	8
Health and social work	2	4	2

Source: UNDP. Iraq Living Conditions Survey 2004 Vols. II and III. Baghdad: Central Organization for Statistics and Information Technology, Ministry of Planning and Development Cooperation, 2005, Vol. II, 127.

emigrants fled to Jordan and Syria and it is not clear how long they will stay. Increased stability and prosperity at home may draw them back and that will have an impact on the labor market and on the demand for social services. If those who leave are the more mobile, then their return will be a net gain as Iraq recovers some of its more productive labor force.

The Labor Force

In 2005, according to official estimates, the labor force was 6.7 million. The population of working age was 16.4 million and so the labor-force participation rate was 41 percent, low by international standards, but similar to that of neighboring countries. Of the 6.7 million in the labor force, 6 million were estimated to be at work and 700,000 unemployed.

Table 6.3 shows the pattern of employment in 2004 by sector. The leading sector was wholesale, retail, and repairs closely followed by government, including defense. The next largest was agriculture. Then followed education, and only in fifth place was manufacturing.

The World Bank estimated unemployment in 2006 at 30 percent, with more than 50 percent of young males without work. With the disbanding of the Iraqi army after 2003, the civilian labor force increased by up to one million. Labor-force growth of 2.4 percent means that two hundred thousand people are added to the labor force each year, assuming no immigration.[11]

---

[11] World Bank, *Rebuilding Iraq: Economic Reform and Transition*, Report No. 35141-IQ. 2006. 31. http://www.worldbank.org.

If, as has been proposed, state-owned companies are privatized with consequent job losses, then the need to create employment will be even greater. Furthermore, if the private sector, as well as the public sector, is unable to compete with imports then there will be even more job losses.

Agriculture

The 1958 revolution brought about a large change in the landownership pattern and in other aspects of agriculture. In 1957, 1.7 percent of landowners held 63 percent of the land. Thirty-three people owned 9.8 percent, and eight people owned 4.43 percent of Iraq's 8 million hectares. At the same time, 84 percent of landowners owned only 15.3 percent of the land.[12] Between 1958 and 1977, large amounts of privately owned land were nationalized and distributed to former tenants. Large-scale investment in irrigation and land reclamation did not prevent a fall in the agricultural area, especially in regions that had been subject to land reform. This was because of the government's failure to manage the estates or provide machinery and other services that had been previously provided by private-sector landowners. Some 335,000 farmers were reported to have received land under the reforms by 1971, but because of land consolidation and other factors, only 231,000 retained their land. These figures confirm the decline in the sector. By 1979, the problem of landlessness that had prevailed throughout the century had been overcome: there were some eight hundred thousand agricultural landholdings, compared with five hundred thousand in 1971. There were, however, a large number of small absentee landlords. There was also a tendency for agricultural land and labor to be lost and to be used for other purposes. As agriculture developed it became more reliant on imports but failed to develop links with industry. Its products were not sold to and processed by industry on anything like the scale that was expected. As a result of price controls, the misallocation of investment, and mismanagement, agricultural production was limited. Agriculture had developed in the 1960s partly because it had been able to mobilize family labor for work on the farm. The increase in oil revenues in the 1970s resulted in large spending on industry and other urban sectors. This pulled labor out of agriculture at a time when agricultural prices were kept down by government controls.[13]

---

[12] Food and Agriculture Organization. *Special Report: FAO/WFP Crop, Food Supply, and Nutrition Assessment Mission to Iraq.* 23 September 2003. http://www.fao.org.
[13] Mahdi. 335.

Table 6.4. *Iraq: Agricultural production, 1961–2005 (1989–91 = 100)*

	1961	1971	1981	1991	2001	2005
Production	49.9	70.4	78.8	78.1	78.0	87.1
Production/capita	121.8	125.5	101.4	75.7	57.0	57.2

Source: Food and Agriculture Organization, FAOSTATS. http://www.fao.org.

In the late 1960s, the Ba'athist regime introduced land-reform measures that were much more radical than those in Egypt, but it was far less effective implementing them. Agricultural production fell as a result of the chaos that prevailed in rural areas. By 1963, only 40 percent of expropriated land had been reallocated and the government then halted the reforms. In 1970, a law was introduced that limited landownership drastically: unlike the 1958 law, it did not include compensation to expropriated landlords. As a result of this law, the amount of land held by the state rose by 6.5 million acres to 9 million acres or about 64 percent of the agricultural area of Iraq.[14]

Agricultural production increased by 56 percent between 1961 and 2001 but between 1981 and 2001 it was stagnant (see Table 6.4). Until 1970, agriculture was the largest employer in Iraq. In 2000, it accounted for more than 9 percent of all employment and directly supported more than two million people. Between 1961 and 2001, the population increased 3.3-fold and agricultural output per capita fell by 53 percent. There was no significant increase in agricultural output in the 1970s, a period of rapid growth in the economy as a whole and one in which Iraq was not at war. Food production patterns were similar to those of agriculture, both in terms of total output and output per capita. Cereal production was much weaker, with output per capita in 2001 at just 20 percent of its 1961 level.

In 1979, Saddam Hussein introduced a liberalization and privatization program in agriculture. This involved reducing the number of agricultural collectives and cooperatives, relaxing the ceilings on land holding, and allowing private lessees to obtain usufruct rights from the state. More funds were made available to the private sector rather than to the public sector. Members of the urban middle class invested in agriculture on the basis of their connections with the regime. Vegetable and fruit production soared between 1979 and 1982, as did fodder production.[15] In 1983, the introduction

[14] Springborg, Robert. "Iraqi's *Intifada*: Agrarian Transformation and the Growth of the Private Sector." *Middle East Journal* 40, no. 1 (1986). 33–53.
[15] Richards, Alan and John Waterbury. *A Political Economy of the Middle East.* Boulder, Colo.: Westview, 1996. 255.

of Law No. 35 led to the leasing of 6 million dunams (or 1.48 million acres) of land to the private sector, mainly to entrepreneurs rather than farming families. In the early 1980s, agriculture was feeling the effects of war: men were being conscripted with consequent disruption; their replacement by thousands of workers from Egypt failed to boost output.

In 2003, cereal production was estimated at 4.12 million tons (2.55 million tons of wheat, 1.32 million tons of barley, 125,000 of maize, and 125,000 of milled rice). This was 22 percent more than the 2002 level. Despite this, planned cereal imports for the period July 2003–June 2004 were forecast at 3.44 million tons.[16] The 2003 war did not affect agriculture in the north of the country, but there were delays in the planting of industrial crops in the center and the south. Maize and rice production were affected by the reduction in water supply because of electricity shortages, and also by a lack of fertilizers and plant protection chemicals.

Despite the favorable trends in cereal production in recent years, sanctions and three years of severe drought (1999–2001) had major effects on the population. In 2004, about 55 percent of the population was classified by the UN as poor and lacked the means to buy food sold on the open market. The Public Distribution System (PDS), operated under the Oil for Food program (OFF), provided food for the whole population. Since April 1997, virtually all Iraqis have received a monthly ration on the payment of $0.18 per person/ration in the center and south of the country and $0.36 in the north. This has prevented starvation, but not malnutrition. Since the end of the war in 2003 the population has remained entirely reliant on OFF. By 1990–2, 1.2 million or 7 percent of the population were classified as undernourished. In 1999–2001, the number had increased to 6.2 million, or 27 percent of the population.[17] In 2005, as a result of mismanagement, war, population growth, and weather conditions, agricultural production per capita was half its 1981 level (see Table 6.4).

Manufacturing Industry

The development of manufacturing industry in modern Iraq has gone through a number of stages. In 1952, the first phase of import substitution began, with the emphasis on increasing output and generating employment.

---

[16] Al-Khudayri, Tariq. "Iraq's Manufacturing Industry: Status and Prospects for Rehabilitation and Reform" in Mahdi, Kamil A. (ed.), *Iraq's Economic Predicament*. Reading: Ithaca, 2002. 201–33.

[17] Food and Agriculture Organization. *State of Food and Agriculture, 2004*. Table A.2. http://www.fao.org.

In 1958, central planning was added to the tools used by the government. In 1963, more than 75 percent of output in large industrial firms was in the private sector. The nationalizations of 1964 meant that 60 percent of output and half of employment in large industrial firms were transferred to the public sector. In 1964, twenty-seven major manufacturing plants were nationalized. By 1968, state intervention and central planning were both in place. In the 1970s, the increase in oil wealth enabled Iraq to invest $14 billion in the heavy-industry sector, including oil.

By 1972, just less than 75 percent of output in larger firms was in the public sector. Smaller companies were concentrated in the private sector and between 1972 and 1982, their output increased faster than that of the public sector.[18] During the 1970s, there was a huge growth of oil income that went to the state and an increase in the centralization of political power by the Ba'ath party. Between 1972 and 1975, the oil industry was nationalized.

Between 1980 and 1988, the war with Iran resulted in damage to large industrial installations and the loss of export markets because of disruptions to shipping. Skilled labor was taken out of industry due to conscription and huge casualties meant that much of the workforce was permanently lost. In 1987–8, a shortage of government revenue led to partial privatization. The government hoped that privatization would enable it to attract funds from abroad, given Western preferences for a more liberalized economy. In 1988, the import of inputs for industry was liberalized and private-sector activity was permitted in more sectors. The ceilings for capital invested in private companies were also raised. In 1989, this was followed by increases in tax exemptions. In the summer of 1990, Iraq's invasion of Kuwait was followed by the imposition of UN sanctions and as a result the level of industrial activity fell sharply.[19]

Table 6.5 gives a breakdown of the structure of industrial output. The chemical sector was the largest, dominated by petroleum refining, which accounted for 25 percent of industrial output in 1980 and in 1994. Table 6.5 also shows how the volume and value of production of output in industry collapsed between 1990 and 1994.

The fact that manufacturing value added rose between 1980 and 1985 while value added per capita output fell suggests that more people were employed in industry. It should be noted that the figures for value added

[18] Issawi. 143–64.

[19] Alnasrawi, A. *The Economy of Iraq: Oil, Wars, Destruction of Development and Prospects, 1950–2000.* Westport, Conn. and London: Greenwood Press, 1994. 152.

Table 6.5. *Iraq: Industrial value added and output, 1980–1994*
($ millions, current prices)

	1980	1985	1990	1994
Value added:				
Food	382	661	570	85
Textiles	330	383	480	49
Wood and furniture	11	1,415	1	
Paper and paper products	77	85	128	28
Chemicals	703	1,490	1,460	245
Of which petroleum refining and related products	432	908	892	146
Nonmetallic minerals	212	601	589	104
Metal and engineering	357	441	379	94
Total value added	2,072	3,675	3,621	561
Total industrial output	5,155	n.a.	n.a.	1,387

Source: UNIDO, Industrial Development Global Report, 1996.

per capita apply to manufacturing industry, while those for value added are for all industry.

In 2000, the state-owned sector included 102 enterprises, most of which were classified as large. Their workforce accounted for 33 percent of the total in industry. Some 57 percent of industrial workers were employed in small-scale, private-sector firms where the average number of employees per firm was two.

The Allocation of Oil Revenues and Their Effects

The increase in oil revenues from the 1950s had major effects on the economy. By the 1970s, it made possible economic, social, and military expenditures on a massive scale. The leaders of the 1958 coup condemned the old regime for favoring the feudal class and the British. The Arab nationalism favored by the new regime provided a basis for policy in its first five years, but by 1963 the leaders had lost direction. Between the mid-1960s and the mid-1980s, Nasser's Egypt was the model for the Iraqi leadership and this meant nationalization among other things.

As will be seen, oil revenues were used in an increasingly wasteful and then ruinous manner. This was possible because, as in other oil-rich countries in the Middle East, oil revenues accrued to the government. After the nationalization of the oil industry even more funds went to the state. The government became the motor for economic growth, and allocations at

Table 6.6. *Iraq: Oil revenues, development allocations, and actual spending, 1951–1980 ($ bn)*

| | 100.6 | | |
Oil revenues	Planned spending	Actual spending	Actual/planned
Agriculture	10.35	4.96	48%
Industry	18.88	12.43	66%
Other sectors	38.18	25.91	68%
Total	67.40	43.14	64%

Source: Calculated from Alnasrawi, 2002. 57–59.

both the macro and micro levels inevitably became politicized. This severely limited the emergence of decentralized wealth creation in the private sector that might have provided the economic basis for more pluralistic political development over time. As the political system became more tyrannical, the misuse of funds increased. During the period from 1930 to 1958, the small-scale and weak private sector had an element of independence but this was lost with the socialist policies and the regime of terror that was to follow.

Between 1951 and 1980, 67 percent of oil revenues were allocated and 43 percent were actually spent. Only 11 percent of spending went on agriculture and 29 percent on industry (see Table 6.6).

Table 6.6 shows that in the period 1951–80, revenues exceeded allocations by about $57 billion. In the period 1981–3, the opposite pattern prevailed. A total of $4.5 billion was allocated to agriculture, $10.5 billion to industry, and $46.6 billion to other sectors. Total development allocations therefore came to $61.6 billion while oil revenues equaled $29.4 billion.[20] Two points should be made about this. The first is that agriculture remained the lowest priority. The second is that the allocations had no relationship to the country's main source of income. This period marked the end of economic planning in Iraq at least insofar as published information is concerned.

Table 6.7 shows how dominant mining (mainly oil) was in the economy in 1975 and 1980 and how small a share agriculture took. In the early 1980s, oil production fell, and between 1981 and 1986 international oil prices fell by more than 50 percent. This led to the sharp fall in the share of the oil sector in gross domestic product (GDP) and to a 40 percent fall in the

---

[20] Alnasrawi; Rivlin, Paul. "Iraq's Economy: What's Left?" *Tel Aviv Notes* no. 65 (2 February 2003. 70–103; UN/World Bank, Joint Iraq Needs Assessment, October 2003, Annex 1.

Table 6.7. *Iraq: The sectoral composition of GDP, 1975–2005 (%)*

	1975	1980	1985	2000	2005
Oil and mining	56.7	61.7	23.2	83.9	67.7
Agriculture	7.4	4.7	14.4	5.4	
Manufacturing	5.9	4.5	10.0	0.9	1.5*
Construction	2.3	7.3	9.4		21.0[†]
Other sectors	27.5	21.8	43.0		

* 2004.
[†] Services, 2004.
Source: UN. Proceedings of an Expert Group Meeting on Assessment of Economic and Social Developments in the ESCWA Region During the Last 25 Years and Priorities for the Next Decade. New York: UN, 1999, and World Bank, 2006.

volume of GDP. The increase in the share of non-oil sectors did not reflect increases in output: they only reflected decreases in oil revenues.

The economic policies of the Ba'ath were similar to those of its military predecessors: it maintained the system of central planning but the expansion of oil revenues made economic growth much easier to attain. In the 1970s as the oil boom took hold, Iraq suffered from shortages of skilled labor, stagnant agriculture, inflation, and increasing reliance on imports, especially of food. It lacked administrators and managers as well as those with the technical knowledge to carry out the investment projects that were being developed. The economy became increasingly dependent on oil revenues, which played a dominant role in the state budget and the balance of payments.

The Costs of Conflict

In the 1970s Iraq accumulated foreign assets as a result of balance-of-payments surpluses and loans from Arab states. This enabled it, at least initially, to finance the war with Iran without cutting private consumption. In 1983, however, oil revenues collapsed as a result of war damage and lower international prices. Iraq was forced to cut its imports and restrain consumption. The conscription of hundreds of thousands of men, particularly in 1984, meant that the economy became reliant on imported labor, mainly from Egypt. Foreign workers remitted funds home with adverse effects on the balance of payments. In 1970, there were 62,000 in the armed forces, or nearly 3 percent of the labor force; by 1988, there were 1 million people, 21 percent of the labor force. Military spending rose from less than $1 billion

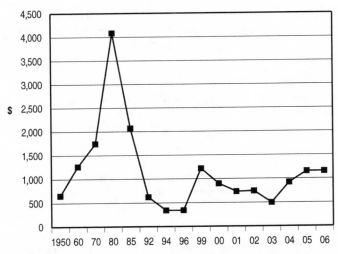

Figure 6.1. Iraq: GDP per Capita, 1950–2006. *Sources:* 1950–1999: Alnasrawi, 2002; 2000–05: IMF, Country Report No. 06/301; August 2006; IMF Country Report No. 07/115 March 2007; and author's calculations.

in 1970 to $19.8 billion in 1980. In 1984, it peaked at $25.9 billion, which was more than three times its oil revenue and equal to 60 percent of GDP.

The 1982–8 war caused losses to Iraq worth some $450 billion. This included damage to the infrastructure ($91 billion) and losses of oil revenues ($192 billion), interest on reserves that were consumed by the war ($79 billion), and potential foreign reserves because of massive defense imports ($80 billion). By 1990, Iraq had a foreign debt of $86 billion. It conceded that its debt was $42 billion (excluding interest payments), claiming that funds received from Arab states during the war were grants. It had begun the war with virtually no debt and $46 billion of foreign exchange reserves.[21] The regime was able to buy "guns and butter" and to avoid hard choices between economic priorities. It expanded the role of the public sector in agriculture and took over foreign and domestic trade, but in the mid-1980s it scaled down its role in agriculture and in the second half of the 1980s, started privatizing. Between 1980 and 1990, Iraq's GDP rose from $53 billion to $77 billion in current prices and exchange rates. The real increase was about 9 percent but the population rose from 13.2 million to 18.9 million and so real GDP per head fell by 24 percent (see Figure 6.1).

Since the 1950s, the Iraqi economy has lost its international competitive advantage. What was once a country with a broad resource base, a variety of

[21] Alnasrawi. 70–1.

economic sectors, and a skilled labor force has become an extreme rentier state. The dominance of the public sector, restrictions on the private sector, and capricious political and bureaucratic interventions have played havoc with the economy. Oil wealth has been squandered on war and on high consumption levels among those in and close to the regime. It also resulted in an overvalued exchange rate that further discouraged economic activity outside the oil sector.

On 6 August 1990, the UN Security Council passed Resolution 661 that imposed economic sanctions on Iraq. It banned imports from Iraq and Kuwait and banned exports to Iraq except for medical and food supplies. All Iraqi funds held abroad were frozen, as were all financial transactions with Iraq. Later that month, maritime and air blockades of Iraq were added. Within a very short period the effects were felt: on 12 August 1990, Saddam Hussein called on the Iraqi people to reduce their consumption of food and clothing. On September 1, 1990, the government introduced food rationing, providing 1,270 calories per person per day, equal to only 37 percent of the average intake in 1987–9. Iraq has had food rationing ever since. Food prices rocketed and shortages resulted in malnutrition, rising infant mortality rates, and other signs of deteriorating public health. Iraq's oil exports collapsed following the invasion of Kuwait. Although Iraq had control of Kuwait's oil fields it could not export Kuwaiti production either.

If the losses from the Iran–Iraq War and the 1991 Gulf War, compensation claims, the effects of sanctions, and foreign debt increases are added together, the total exceeds $780 billion. This is some twenty-eight times the size of Iraq's GDP in 2001 and fifty-eight times its current level of oil revenues. If Iraq had been able to sell two million barrels a day of oil at the prices then prevailing, between 1981 and 1986 it would have earned an additional $60 billion and between 1991 and 1997, an additional $8 billion a year. This total of $128 billion should be added to the losses listed here, giving a total of $908 billion. The 2003 war resulted in much less physical damage to the economy than in 1991, but the level of economic activity was disrupted and oil production and exports were hit. A very crude estimate of physical damage, production losses, and oil income losses is $20 billion. This brings the total war-related losses incurred between 1980 and 2003 to $928 billion.

Figure 6.1 shows how GDP per capita, measured in constant prices, fell during the Iran–Iraq War and again after the 1990 invasion of Kuwait. Part of the fall after 1980 was because of lower prices for Iraqi oil on international markets. Another factor was the reduction in the volume of production and exports due to the war. The third factor that came into effect from

August 1990 was international sanctions that limited the amount that Iraq could sell.

Iraqi oil production peaked in 1980 and only in 1999 did it return to near that level. In 2002, Iraqi oil production averaged 2.014 millions of barrels a day. This was 13 percent lower than in 2001. The main reason for the decline was Iraq's disagreement with the UN Sanctions Committee over the pricing of oil exports under the OFF program. Iraq's State Oil Marketing Organization wanted to underprice the oil it sold under the program so that it could impose a surcharge that oil purchasers would pay to the government. In this way the Iraqi regime hoped to divert funds from the UN program to its treasury. The UN rejected Iraqi moves and, as a result, oil sales and revenues fell by almost 50 percent in April 2001. They did not fully recover until October, as a result of Iraq reversing its policy. In March 2003, prior to the Second Gulf War, Iraqi output was estimated at 2.3 million barrels a day.

The 2003 War and Its Aftermath

On 16 May 2003, the United States created the Coalition Provisional Authority (CPA). This agency was given the power to rule Iraq until an Iraqi government was formed. Since then it has issued orders, regulations, memoranda, and budgets for 2003 and for 2004.

On May 22, 2003, the UN Security Council adopted Resolution No. 1483 on Iraq. This ended trade restrictions on Iraq and permitted exports, imports, and financial and other transactions with it, excluding sales of arms. The resolution granted wide interim governing powers to the United States and its coalition partners, including a role for a UN special representative working with this provisional authority, and lifting sanctions imposed almost thirteen years earlier following the invasion of Kuwait. A week later, the U.S. Treasury Department lifted most U.S. sanctions on Iraq, in accordance with UN Security Council Resolution 1483. For more than a decade since Iraq's invasion of Kuwait in 1990, the United States had maintained unilateral economic sanctions against Iraq. These banned the import and export of goods or services from Iraq, with the exception of those within the framework of the UN's OFF program.

In October 2003, a donor's conference was held in Madrid to raise funds for the reconstruction of Iraq in cooperation with the UN, the World Bank, the IMF, the Iraqi Governing Council, and the CPA. It followed the publication of the UN/World Bank needs assessment report. A total of $13 billion was pledged in addition to the $20 billion pledged by the United States.

Reconstruction

The UN and the World Bank estimated that in the period 2004–07, a total of $36 billion would be needed to reconstruct fourteen non-oil sectors and the United States estimated that rehabilitating the oil sector and providing security would cost an additional $19 billion.[22] The chances for successful reconstruction in Iraq depend first on an end to the current conflict inside the country, second on the political system that evolves with the end of direct U.S. rule, and third on the success of the economic policies that are implemented. At the time of this writing, the first condition has not been met. With regard to the second, an Iraqi government exists but has had many problems functioning. The third – the economic factor – is discussed next.

The Oil Sector

Iraq has the world's second largest reserves of oil. In 2001, they totaled 112.5 billion barrels, or 10.7 percent of the world total. They accounted for 16.4 percent of Middle East oil reserves and 13.7 percent of those in OPEC.[23] Only twenty-four of Iraq's seventy-three oil fields were in operation in 2002. Lack of maintenance, overpumping, and water-injection had caused damage that will lead to falls in production in the future. In late 2002, Iraq's oil-sector infrastructure was in bad condition, and production was declining by 100,000 barrels a day per year. Increasing oil production will require massive repairs and reconstruction, costing billions of dollars and taking months if not years to implement. The costs of repairing existing oil export installations alone has been estimated at about $5 billion, while restoring oil production to pre-1990 levels would cost an additional $5 billion, plus $3 billion per year in annual operating costs.[24]

Iraq's export infrastructure has been badly damaged in two wars. A rapid increase in oil exports will not be possible given the limitations of Iraq's production and export facilities. The World Bank–UN Working Group believes it will take Iraq between eighteen months and three years to return

---

[22] World Bank. "Interim Strategy Note of the World Bank Group for Iraq" (14 January 2004). 11. http://www.worldbank.org.

[23] Calculated from British Petroleum. "Statistical Review of World Energy, 2003." http://www.bp.com.

[24] Council for Foreign Relations and James Baker III Institute, Rice University. "Guiding Principles for US Post Conflict Policy in Iraq" (2003). http://www.cfr.org/content/publications/attachments/Post-War_Iraq.pdf.

to its pre-1990 production level of 3.5 million barrels a day. Some $20 billion will be needed to restore the pre-1990 electricity capacity. Iraq has previously stated a desire to expand its oil production capacity to six million barrels a day. This is geologically possible but would take a number of years and cost tens of billions of dollars.

Between April and December 2003, production rose from 180,000 barrels a day to 1.8 million barrels a day. In 2004, the CPA allocated $2.1 billion for the oil sector. It increased further to 2.5 million barrels a day in March 2004 but fell to 2.3 million barrels a day in April 2004. In the first half of 2005, it had fallen to 1.9 million barrels a day as a result of terror attacks and the inability of the oil ministry to implement reconstruction projects.

The potential for Iraq's oil sector is huge. Of Iraq's seventy-four discovered and evaluated oil fields, only fifteen have been developed. Iraq's western desert is considered to be highly prospective but has yet to be seriously explored.

Basic Needs

Iraq has huge basic needs. In 2003, in the aftermath of the war, there were an estimated 1.7 million disabled people (nearly 7 percent of the population) as a result of conflict, imprisonment, torture, illness, and old age. One million women (8 percent of the female population) were heads of households; huge numbers of girls dropped out of school to work at home and thus release their mothers to work outside the home. This had major, negative effects on literacy rates. Some 70 percent of families in Iraq had a disadvantaged or vulnerable member. Between 270,000 and 650,000 people were internally displaced and there were 3–4 million Iraqis living abroad.[25]

According to the CPA, the basic needs of the Iraqi people were to be met from the proceeds of the OFF program. This would consume funds that were badly needed for reconstruction of the economy, something that would enable agricultural and industrial production to increase and might lower the price of nonrationed items. It would also increase the demand for labor and thus generate incomes among a population currently suffering 50–70 percent unemployment.[26] This was something of a trap: if funds were consumed providing rationed food then there would be less for reconstruction and the dynamic of growth would be delayed. This suggests that Iraq

---

[25] UN/World Bank Working Paper. *Livelihoods, Employment, and Reintegration* (October 2003). 25.

[26] *International Herald Tribune.* 13 October 2003.

needs large-scale aid, as the United States and the UN/World Bank have suggested.

Liberalization and Privatization

In September 2003, the CPA made a major policy announcement: Foreigners would be allowed to invest in all sectors of the economy except oil. They would also be allowed to lease land for forty-year periods. Income tax and corporate tax were set at 15 percent maximum; a reconstruction tariff was introduced at 5 percent for two years on all imports except food, medicine, books, and other humanitarian items. The aim of the reforms was to introduce a market economy after thirty years of state control.[27] In October 2003, a new currency was introduced.

Currently the public sector plays a central role in the Iraqi economy. Public-sector employment at the end of 2003 was estimated at 1.3–1.5 million or about 20 percent of the labor force. There are 500,000 workers in 200 state-owned enterprises.[28] Moves to privatize state-owned companies raise a number of crucial issues.

The first is who is able and willing to buy Iraqi enterprises? Is there anyone in Iraq capable of buying privatized assets? If there are, will these be the types of insider takeovers/buyouts that occurred in the 1990s in Russia? If not, will vital sectors of the Iraqi economy be bought out by foreigners? Can Iraq create a decentralized economy that is not dominated by the state? Will the fact that oil plays such a large role mean that either the state or foreign oil companies become dominant? Should Iraq have a "shock therapy" as experienced in Russia and East Europe in the 1990s or should it undergo a more gentle process? Will the "creation" of a strong private sector be a new model for the Arab world, where the private sector is either very weak or tied to the state?

In 2003 the Iraqi minister for trade stated his opposition to radical U.S. plans to privatize the economy. He stated that the economy had been subject to too many "experiments" under the Ba'ath. Privatization and subsidy cuts would result in increases in unemployment and rises in prices.[29]

The reduction of import duties to 5 percent and the ending of other controls on imports have resulted in a flood of imports. Insofar as these

---

[27] *Ha'aretz.* 30 September 2003.
[28] *International Herald Tribune.* 13 October 2003; UN/World Bank Working Paper. *Livelihoods, Employment, and Reintegration* (2003). http://iraq.undg.org/uploads/doc/ LIVELIHOODS%20final%20sector%20report%2016%20October.pdf. 25.
[29] *International Herald Tribune.* 13 October 2003.

increased the supply of a wide range of goods and services needed by the economy, this may be a good thing. The problem is that local industry, handicapped by the factors analyzed here, will find it hard to compete.

Foreign Debt

In 2003, Iraq's foreign debt was estimated at $383 billion. This was made up of $127 billion in loans, including $47 billion in accrued interest, $199 billion in reparations, and $57 billion in contractual obligations.[30] If Iraq has to pay interest at 5 percent on the loans then it will have an annual bill of $6.4 billion, about half of its current oil income. Moratoriums on interest payments and partial debt write-off are therefore prerequisites for economic progress.

The Economy since 2003

The economic recovery in Iraq in 2004 was dominated by oil, which accounted for 75 percent of GDP and 97 percent of exports and government revenues. Oil production in that year was 54 percent higher than in 2003, reflecting both a recovery from the war and the continuing effects of terrorism. The northern oil fields were much more affected by terrorism than those in the south. At the end of 2004 and the beginning of 2005 the activities of the oil ministry, crucial to the rehabilitation of the sector, were slowed by political uncertainties as to who would be appointed minister. In 2004, revenues rose sharply to $20 billion compared with $7.5 billion in 2003, as a result of the increase in production and the rise in prices. This enabled the government to increase payments to civil servants, soldiers, and the police, thereby helping to fund a boom in consumption. As the economy moved from the rigid controls of the Ba'athist regime to a U.S.-advocated free-trade system, imports increased rapidly.[31]

Domestic oil product prices were much lower than world levels, implying a subsidy of some $7 billion or nearly 35 percent of GDP. The government has announced its intention to increase domestic prices over the coming years. The economy has also benefited from large-scale U.S. spending both on the military and on civilian reconstruction. As a result of postwar reconstruction, Iraq's balance of payments experienced large deficits. In 2004 and

---

[30] Looney, Robert. "Bean Counting in Baghdad: Debt, Reparations, Reconstruction, and Resources." *Middle East Review of International Affairs Journal* 7, no. 3 (2003). 61.

[31] *Financial Times.* 15 April 2005.

2005, the current account deficit was $10 billion.[32] Partly as a result of the very low base in 2003, the economy grew by about 20 percent in 2004, but in 2005, because of terrorism and the deteriorating state of the oil industry's infrastructure, it grew by only about 10 percent. Growth decelerated further in 2006 to an estimated 3 percent as a result of conflict and the inability to increase oil production significantly. Between October 2005 and October 2006, consumer prices rose by 53 percent as a result of the reduction in government subsidies on oil products and increases in the prices charged by many producers and importers as a result of the security situation in the country.[33] Economic growth decelerated further in 2006 to an estimated 3 percent. This was due to the continued level of violence. The exit of skilled and other workers and the inability to increase oil production all played their role in dampening economic activity. Inflation remained very high at about 65 percent, because of shortages of key commodities and rising security costs. The security situation prevented much investment, and that in turn reduced government spending below planned levels. As a result, the state budget balance improved.[34]

Conclusions

An end to internal armed conflict is a precondition for economic progress. If the government can obtain more support among Iraqis then it may be able to tackle the country's economic problems. To do this requires increasing oil production and exports to finance the development of the non-oil sector. Ultimately, Iraq needs to reduce its overwhelming reliance on oil revenues by developing agriculture and industry and thereby provide new sources of employment, income, and output. It should learn a lesson from neighboring countries such as Saudi Arabia that have huge oil resources but increasing unemployment. Achieving these changes, in the face of foreign competition, will not be easy, especially if controls on imports are excluded. Encouragement of the private sector will limit state domination of the economy such as occurred under the Ba'ath.

[32] IMF. *Country Report, Iraq,* 04/325, September 2004; *MENA Economic Development and Prospects 2005.* 16.

[33] United Nations Economic and Social Commission for West Asia. *Estimates and Forecasts for GDP Growth in the ESCWA Region 2006–2007,* E/ESCWA/EAD/2007 Technical Material. Document No. 2. (4 January 2007). 2, 8; IMF Country Report, Iraq, no. 07/115. March 2007. 5.

[34] IMF. *Iraq: Third and Fourth Reviews Under the Stand-By Arrangement, Financing Assurances Review, and Requests for Extension of the Arrangements and For Waiver of Nonobservance of a Performance Criterion-Staff Report,* 2007. Country Report No. 01/115. 5.

Iraq has a combination of assets that other Arab states lack: oil, fertile land, water, and an educated labor force. All these could be put to good use if the politics of the country were different. At present it is hard to envisage the required level of political stability: only when it is achieved can the serious economic legacy be tackled.

SEVEN

Jordan

From Rents to Markets?

Jordan, more than any other Arab economy, is trying to wean itself off reliance on economic rents. The reorientation of the economy has brought about a dramatic increase in exports but, despite large investments in education and welfare, it suffers from high unemployment rates especially among the young and the better educated.

The economy moved from stagnation and crisis in the late 1980s to relatively fast growth that has exceeded that of the population in recent years. This was achieved by orthodox economic reforms, changes in Jordan's political stance, and the slowing of demographic growth. The period 1980–90 was marked by a decline in the share of rents in the economy. In recent years, the success of Jordan's economic reforms and its political realignment has also resulted in an increase in U.S. aid with positive implications for the state budget and the balance of payments. Jordan also benefited indirectly from the aftermath of the 2003 war in Iraq and the rise in oil revenues in the Gulf States although by 2005, there was evidence that these effects were receding.

Demography

Jordan has one of the fastest growing populations in the world, due to both natural growth and periods of net immigration. In 1950, the population was about 500,000; by 2000 it had recorded an almost tenfold increase. The total fertility rate (number of children per woman) declined from an annual average of 6.77 in 1980–5 to 3.53 in 2000–05, still a high figure by international standards. When accompanied by falling death rates, it meant that population growth remained fast. Fertility rates declined because of improved health and the use of family planning. Better education led to a later age of marriage for women but this contributed less to lowering

155

Table 7.1. *Jordan: Population and dependency ratios, 1950–2005*

	Population (millions)	Working-age population	Dependent population	Dependency ratio*
1950	0.47	0.23	0.24	102
1960	0.87	0.46	0.41	94
1970	1.62	0.83	0.79	96
1980	2.23	1.06	1.17	111
1990	3.25	1.63	1.62	100
2000	4.97	2.73	2.24	78
2005	5.70	3.31	2.39	68

* The total dependency ratio is the ratio of the sum of the population aged 0–14 and that aged 65+ to the population aged 15–64. This is expressed as number of dependents per 100 persons of working age (aged 15–64).

Source: Population Division of the Department of Economic and Social Affairs of the United Nations Secretariat. *World Population Prospects: The 2004 Revision* and *World Urbanization Prospects: The 2003 Revision.* http://esa.un.org/unpp.

fertility rates than in other parts of the region. In 1994–7, the total fertility rate among illiterate women was 4.59 children. Among women with primary school education it was 4.54; those with secondary education 4.53. Among women with higher education it was 3.66, almost twice as high as among the equivalent group of women in Morocco or Tunisia.[1] Table 7.1 gives estimates of the population for the period 1980–2005 and shows that in that quarter century the population increased by more than 150 percent. In the period 1995–2005, the population rose by 75 percent, the population of working age by 103 percent, and the dependent population by almost 48 percent.

Table 7.2 shows that the population growth rate declined steadily between 1980–5 and 2000–05, the result of a 53 percent fall in the death rate accompanied by a 30 percent fall in the birthrate. The subperiod 1990–5 was an exception: the acceleration of the population growth rate was due to the return home of thousands of Jordanians who had been working in the Gulf until the Iraqi invasion of Kuwait in 1990.

In the period after 1973, thousands of Jordanians went to work in the Gulf States where demand for labor rose after the increase in oil prices and revenues. When oil revenues fell in the mid-1980s, emigration declined,

---

[1] Courbage, Youssef. *New Demographic Scenarios in the Mediterranean Region.* (1999). http://www.ined.fr.

Table 7.2. *Jordan: Demographic trends, 1980–2005 (annual rates of change %)*

	Population growth	Crude birthrate per 1,000 of population	Crude death rate per 1,000 of population
1980–1985	3.92	42.3	8.9
1985–1990	3.69	38.8	7.1
1995–1990	5.52	34.4	5.8
2000–1995	2.96	32.6	4.6
2000–2005	2.74	27.8	4.2

Source: Population Nations Secretariat. *World Population Prospects: The 2004 Revision and World Urbanization Prospects: The 2003 Revision.* http://esa.un.org/unpp. Division of the Department of Economic and Social Affairs of the United Nations. 2005.

and in the early 1990s many returned home. In recent years, as the economy has grown, foreign workers – mainly from Egypt and Syria – have come in thousands to work in Jordan. Since 2000, there has also been an influx of Palestinians from the West Bank escaping the conflict with Israel. Demographic transition has resulted in rapid growth of the working-age population (2.9 percent annually) and a fall in the dependency ratio (the ratio of the young and elderly to the working-age population).[2] This has provided Jordan with a demographic gift.

The Labor Market

Between 1990 and 2003, Jordan had the fastest labor-force growth rate in the world: an annual average of 6 percent.[3] In 2005, the total population was estimated at 5.7 million, while that of working age (aged 15–64) was 3.6 million. Given a labor-force participation rate of about 38 percent, the labor force was estimated at 1.44 million. The annual addition to the working-age population has been estimated at almost 100,000.[4]

The reason for the rapid increase in the labor force is the growth of the working-age population. The other factor behind growth was the increase in the female participation rates that rose from 14.8 percent in 1980 to 17.7 percent in 1990 and then to 30.3 percent in 2003 (see Table 2.3). Meanwhile the male rate fell between 1980 and 1990 but had recovered by 2003. Increased female participation rates may have affected male rates. Low

[2] Kanaan, Taher H. and Marwan A. Kardooh. *Employment and the Labour Market in Jordan.* (2002). 4–5. http://www/worldbank.org.
[3] World Bank. *World Development Indicators, 2005.* http://www.worldbank.org.
[4] Courbage.

Table 7.3. *Jordan: The sectoral and nationality breakdown of nonagricultural employment, 2000–2004*

	2000		2004	
	Total	Jordanians	Total	Jordanians
Mining and quarrying	9,065	8,738	7,017	6,582
Manufacturing	126,229	110,768	166,973	131,202
Electricity, gas, and water	14,174	14,153	13,950	13,948
Construction	23,378	17,050	24,627	17,009
Wholesale and retail trade	160,283	145,199	224,120	212,549
Hotels and restaurants	28,144	20,280	38,171	29,836
Transport, storage, and communication	30,920	29,192	30,410	28,639
Finance	19,582	19,466	17,966	17,781
Real estate	29,440	27,154	34,724	33,210
Public administration	74,026	70,590	77,843	73,743
Education	123,821	122,635	143,478	141,979
Health and social work	42,430	41,595	48,849	47,758
Other services	20,401	18,857	23,408	21,382
Total	701,900	645,676	851,897	776,434

Source: Jordan: Department of Statistics. www.dos.gov.jo.

female participation rates plus the increase in the working-age population, means that the labor force will go on rising at an accelerating rate. The current increase of 40,000 to 50,000 new job-seekers a year represents a 4-percent rise, a major challenge for the economy.

Jordan has one of the best records of educational investment and literacy in the Arab world. The average number of years of schooling for those aged 15 and older rose from 2.3 years in 1960 to 6.9 years in 2000.[5] Between 1985 and 2004, the number of students registered in higher education institutions rose from 25,000 to 150,000. The influence of increased education is reflected in female employment patterns more than in male ones. Two-thirds of the total employed have secondary education or less; one-third have post-secondary education. Among women, two-thirds of those employed have postsecondary education; among men the share is only 25 percent.[6]

Jordan has imported workers from Egypt and Syria who are often cheaper to employ than Jordanians. According to the official data in Table 7.3, there were nearly 56,000 foreigners working outside agriculture or 7 percent of

[5] Forum Euro-Méditerranéen des Instituts Economiques (Femise). *Jordan Country Profile, The Road Ahead from Jordan.* 92. http://www.femise.org/PDF/cp/cp-jordan-0508.pdf.
[6] Ibid. 90.

the nonagricultural labor force. It is likely that the share in agriculture was higher, given the demand for cheap labor there.

Table 7.3 also shows the sectoral pattern of employment in 2000 and 2004. It shows that total employment in sectors other than agriculture rose by 21 percent while for Jordanian citizens it rose by 202 percent. The total increase in employment was more than 150,000 or 37,500 a year. These figures suggest that during the years 2000–04, nonagricultural employment grew by only about 37 percent of the rate that was required to prevent a rise in unemployment. If we assume that employment in agriculture grew at the same rate (62,000 × 5 percent), then another 3,100 jobs were created annually, giving a total employment rise of about 43,000, or about 40 percent of the rise needed to contain unemployment. During the period 2000–04 the economy grew by an annual average rate of 5 percent. These figures imply that the economy will have to grow much faster to generate enough jobs to prevent unemployment rising let alone reduce it.

As has been shown, unemployment remains a major problem. In 2002, the unemployment rate was 15.3 percent (196,000).[7] In 2003, it was 14.5 percent and in the first half of 2004 it fell to 12.5 percent.[8] In the first half of 2005, the rate rose to 15.7 percent.[9] These high rates prevailed despite fast economic growth and suggest that growth was not fast enough and was not of the right kind to reduce unemployment. In 2005, unemployment among those aged 15–19 was almost 39 percent, while among those aged 20–24, it was nearly 29 percent. The rates of unemployment for women were much higher than those for men.

Characteristics of the Economy

In 2006, Jordan had an estimated gross domestic product (GDP) of $14.3 billion and GDP per capita of $2,441.[10] The service sector was the largest, accounting for 21 percent of GDP of which government services accounted for about 17 percent. Next came transport and communications followed by manufacturing.

---

[7] Kardoosh, Marwan A. and Riad al Khouri, *Qualifying Industrial Zones and Sustainable Development in Jordan.* 2004. 23. http://www.erf.org.eg.

[8] IMF, *Jordan Post-Program Monitoring Discussions-Staff Report.* 2005. 6.

[9] World Bank. *Jordan Quarterly 2006.* Washington, D.C.: World Bank, 2006.

[10] IMF: Jordan: *Fifth Post-Program Monitoring Discussions-Staff Report*; and *Press Release on the Executive Board Consideration,* Country Report No. 07/284. 17. http://www.imf.org/external/pubs/ft/scr/2007/cr07284.pdf; data from Table 6.1.

For many years, the economy was characterized by extreme reliance on external sources of income. In 1986, some 276,000 Jordanians, or about 10 percent of the population worked abroad. Foreign aid, mainly from Arab countries, was a major source of support for the balance of payments and for the government budget. The country's largest commodity exports were minerals and their prices were determined on international markets, with relatively little value added inside the economy. When international or regional conditions changed, the economy was exposed to sudden shocks. Agriculture and manufacturing were relatively small sectors: in 2000, they accounted for 2 percent and 13.3 percent of GDP, respectively.[11]

Jordan's geo-political position has had major effects on its economic development. Located between Israel, the Palestinian Territories (in July 1988, it ceded its claim to the West Bank), Syria, and Iraq, Jordan has, at different times, felt threatened on all sides. By siding with Saddam Hussein in 1990, the late King Hussein lost the support of the United States for some years and this increased Jordan's isolation. The 1994 peace treaty with Israel was an attempt to break out of this isolation, improve relations with the United States, and benefit from economic links with Israel. Jordan's internal structure is also a source of concern, if not instability. It has a large population of Palestinian origin (possibly a majority), 1.78 million of whom were classified by the United Nations Relief and Works Agency (UNRWA) as refugees.[12]

Table 7.4 covers the period 1993 to 2002 and reveals a number of economic trends that are a cause for concern. First, private consumption rose from 72 percent of GDP in 1993 to nearly 109 percent in 2006. The share of investment in GDP declined sharply between 1993 and 2003, with a partial recovery by 2006. Jordan experienced something that a number of other Arab states went through: stabilization, liberalization, recession, and a fall in private investment. Between 1993 and 2003, there was the fall in the share in exports although this was less unhealthy than appears at first glance because the fall in the total was accompanied by structural change in what was exported. Public spending was stable, despite the emphasis on liberalization. Finally, there was a reduction in the excess of imports over exports from 30.6 percent of GDP in 1993 to 22.3 percent in 2003. The rapid increase in oil prices in recent years has widened this gap.

---

[11] IMF. *Jordan Selected Issues and Statistical Appendix, 2004.* 168. http://www.imf.org.
[12] Fargues, Philippe. 2006. *International Migration in the Arab Region: Trends and Policies.* Beirut: UN Secretariat, Department of Economic and Social Affairs, Population Division 2006. 4.

Table 7.4. *Jordan: Macroeconomic indicators, 1993–2006 (shares in GDP %, current prices)*

	1993	1998	2003	2006 estimated
Private consumption	71.9	73.3	78.3	108.7
Government consumption	22.1	24.4	23.2	20.7
Gross fixed capital formation	36.6	21.2	20.6	27.6
Of which: public	6.3	6.0	8.8	7.3
Of which: other	30.3	15.8	12.1	20.3
Exports	50.5	44.8	45.0	36.4
Imports	81.1	56.3	67.3	65.0

Sources: IMF. International Financial Statistics Yearbook, 2005, 2006; IMF. Jordan: Selected Issues and Statistical Appendix, May 2004 and IMF. Jordan: Fifth Post-Program Monitoring Discussions-Staff Report; and Press Release on the Executive Board Consideration, Country Report no. 07/284.

The Jordanian private sector has tended to invest in real estate and construction while foreign investment has been largely in the so-called Qualified Industrial Zones (QIZs; see section Qualified Industrial Zones) and in privatized companies. Neither of these has generated jobs for Jordanians on a significant scale. Investments in tourism have been of limited effectiveness in generating employment because of regional instability.[13]

Another significant feature of the economy is the very small average size of firms. In 2001–03, firms with one to four employees accounted for 90 percent of those in an official survey (that excluded those working at home or in the street). They accounted for 190,500 workers, 41 percent of private-sector employment outside agriculture, and 25 percent of total nonagricultural employment. Firms with five to nineteen employees accounted for 8 percent of those surveyed. In the manufacturing sector, 17.5 percent of firms had one to four employees and 29 percent had five to nineteen employees. Thus almost half the firms in manufacturing had fewer than twenty employees.[14] This is an indication of the relatively low state of industrial development.

The Crisis of the 1980s and Its Solution

From 1973 until the mid-1980s, the economy grew rapidly, fueled by foreign aid, loans, and the remittances of Jordanian workers abroad as well as exports of minerals. The fall in international oil prices brought about a recession in

[13] Femise. *Jordan Country Profile.* 90.
[14] Ibid. 95.

Table 7.5. *Jordan: The balance of payments, 2000–2006 ($ millions)*

	2000	2001	2002	2003	2004	2005	2006 preliminary
Current account	59.4	−4.1	361.4	1,179	−17.9	−2,260	−1,933
Trade balance	−2,174.4	−2007.0	−1730.8	−1996.3	−3,370	−5,016	−5,028
Workers' remittances	1,660.5	1,810.1	1,921.4	1,781.0	1,819	1,871	2,161
Grants	410.8	465.5	511.3	1,406.5	1,334.1	751.9	n.a.
Foreign direct investment	814.8	137.7	74.5	424	651	1,531.9	3,121
Exports of goods	1,899.3	2294.4	2770.0	3,081.6	3,883.9	4,301.4	1,198
Imports of goods	4,033.7	4,301.5	4,500.9	5,077.9	7,261.1	9,317.3	10,226

n.a. = not available.

Source: IMF. Balance of Payments Yearbook 2006; UN. International Trade Statistics. 1990. Vol. 1. UN: New York, 1992; 2004. Vol. 1. UN: New York, 2004; IMF. Jordan Post-Program Monitoring Discussions-Staff Report. 2007. http://www.imf.org/external/pubs/ft/scr/2007/cr07284.pdf.

the Gulf States that resulted in a reduction of aid and a fall in remittances. The deterioration in Jordan's finances made it harder to borrow abroad, which further worsened the balance of payments. As a result, the economy experienced a sharp slowdown in growth, from annual averages of 11.9 percent in 1973–9 and 9.9 percent in 1980–5 to −1.2 percent in 1985–9.[15] This led, among other things, to a large increase in unemployment from 4.8 percent in 1983 to 18.8 percent in 1991.[16]

As a result, the budget deficit rose, the balance-of-payments current account deficit worsened, and foreign and internal debt increased (see Figure 7.1 and Table 7.5). In 1989, Jordan turned to the International Monetary Fund (IMF) and requested support. The removal of subsidies on some basic foods and price rises resulting from a 50-percent nominal devaluation led to riots. This did not prevent the IMF stabilization program from being implemented, but did result in political reforms designed to make the economic medicine easier to swallow.[17] The crisis resulted in a fall in GDP and an even sharper fall in GDP per head, higher unemployment, and a large increase in poverty. In 1986–7, some 3 percent of the population was below the poverty line; in 1992 the figure had risen to 14.4 percent.[18]

[15] World Bank. *Peace and the Jordanian Economy*, Washington, D.C.: World Bank, 1994. 8.
[16] Abdel Jaber, Tayseer. *Key Long-Term Development Issues in Jordan*. Working paper 199522. Cairo: Economic Research Forum.
[17] Economist Intelligence Unit (EIU). *Jordan Country Profile, 2005*. London: EIU, 2005. 5–6.
[18] IMF. *Jordan. Selected Issues and Statistical Appendix*. Country Report No. 04/121. May 2004. 12. http://www.imf.org/external/pubs/ft/scr/2004/cr04121.pdf.

The Iraqi invasion of Kuwait in the summer of 1990 and the war against Iraq in early 1991 had major effects on the Jordanian economy. Initially Jordan lost its markets in Iraq; however the return of Jordanians from the Gulf generated an influx of labor and capital. After the war, Jordan's role in the reconstruction of and supply of goods to Iraq increased. These developments led to optimism that investment would grow and that unemployment would fall. In fact, investments by returning Jordanians did increase but they failed to lead to a reduction in unemployment because they were mainly in real estate and not in manufacturing. The 1994 peace treaty with Israel also led to hopes of an influx of foreign aid that would carry the economy forward and reduce unemployment. This, too, did happen on a significant scale, at least initially.[19]

Foreign Debt and the Balance of Payments

Jordan's foreign debt increased more than fourfold in the 1980s, and by the end of the decade could no longer be financed. The rise in the foreign debt was the result of government borrowing from foreign commercial banks to maintain the rapid economic growth of the 1970s, which had, in turn, been sustained by remittances of Jordanians working in the Gulf and grants for oil-rich Arab states. The government responded with more restrictive economic policies and discussions with lenders on rescheduling foreign debt. In 1989 an agreement was reached with the Paris Club of official creditors and other bilateral creditors on rescheduling. Negotiations were completed with commercial banks on rescheduling debt and the option of converting debt at a discount. Four further rescheduling agreements were signed between 1992 and 1999, resulting in $5 billion of foreign debt being rescheduled with longer maturity dates and lower interest payments.[20]

Between 1990 and 1996, Jordan had current account deficits averaging $420 million a year. In 1997–9, the current account moved into surplus, averaging about $150 million a year. This was also a period in which foreign investment rose as a result of the creation of QIZs. Table 7.5 gives details of the current account of the balance of payments for the period 2000–06. The table shows that Jordan had a large trade deficit, financed largely by workers remittances and grants from abroad. When financial inflows were low, the current account went into deficit and this was financed by borrowing abroad. Since 2001, Jordan's balance of payments has been relatively healthy as a

[19] Blue Carroll, Katherine. *Business as Usual? Economic Reforms in Jordan.* Lanham, Md.: Lexington Books, 2003. 57–79.
[20] IMF. Jordan. *Selected Issues and Statistical Appendix.* May 2004. 65–6.

Table 7.6. *Jordan: Foreign debt, 1980–2005 ($ millions)*

	1980	1988	1990	2000	2005
Total debt	1,867	5,759	8,333	7,355	7,696
– Short term debt	485	331	1,037	710	582
Total debt service/exports of goods and services (%)	8.4	30.9	20.4	12.6	6.5
Total debt/GNI* (%)	46.6	100.3	219.0	85.6	58.8

* GNI = gross national income.
Source: World Bank. Global Finance Development 2005. Vol. II; 2006 Vol. II; 2007 Vol. II.

result of inflows of remittances and foreign aid. Between 2000 and 2006, merchandise exports increased 2.7-fold, a remarkable achievement, but imports rose slightly faster and from a much larger base, so the trade deficit increased by $2.9 billion. Without the inflow of remittances and grants from abroad, Jordan's external account would collapse.

Between 1990 and 2000, foreign debt declined as a result of rescheduling and improvements in the balance of payments at the end of the decade. Servicing the debt accounted for a peak of almost 31 percent of exports in 1988 and this was more than halved by 2000 and halved again by 2005 (see Table 7.6).

In recent years, the financing of the balance of payments has been eased by the availability of foreign aid: U.S. assistance to Jordan has increased significantly since the Gulf crisis in 1991. In 1994 and 1995, the United States waived around $700 million in debt relief to the kingdom. In 1997, the U.S. Congress increased aid to Jordan significantly to reach the present level of $150 million in economic aid and $75 million in military aid. In 1999 and 2000, as part of the Wye agreement, Congress allocated an additional $200 million in military assistance and $100 million in economic assistance.[21] In 2003, the United States gave Jordan an additional $700 million to help it cope with the effects of the war of that year.[22]

The State Budget

Figure 7.1 shows the main trends in the state budget since 1984. It reveals how Jordan moved from budget deficits to surpluses between the 1980s and the early 1990s and has moved back into deficits since then. It also

---

[21] Website of the Jordanian Embassy in Washington, D.C. *US Assistance to Jordan*. 17 October 2007. http://www.jordanembassyus.org/new/aboutjordan/uj1.shtml.
[22] USAID. *Budget*. http://www.usaid.gov/policy/budget/cbj2006/ane/jo.html.

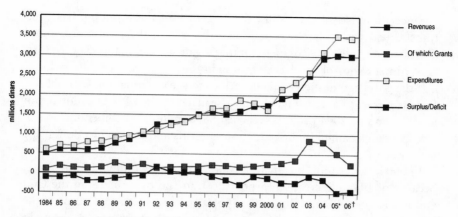

Figure 7.1. Jordan: The State Budget, 1984–2006. *Source:* IMF, Government Finan-
cial Statistics 1994 and 2004; IMF, Jordan Post-Program Monitoring Discussions-Staff
Report 2005; 2006 Budget Speech.
* Official estimate. † Budget.

shows how the role of grants from abroad declined in the 1990s and then
rose sharply until 2003. Since 2003, there has been a sharp deterioration
in the budget with the emergence of the largest deficits in nominal terms
experienced in twenty years.

In 1989, in response to the crisis facing the economy, the government
introduced a stabilization package: the dinar was devalued by 50 percent,
the foreign exchange market was liberalized, austerity measures were implemented to cut government spending, and structural reforms were begun in
trade, agriculture, and in the public sector. These were not easy measures to
undertake: in 1989, a 30-percent rise in fuel prices resulted in riots in Ma'an.
These measures were introduced with the backing of the IMF and the World
Bank, so those bodies became a lightening rod for public discontent.[23] In
1989 the living standards of the poor were badly hit: GDP fell in real terms
by 13 percent and inflation reached 25 percent. Between 1987 and 1993, per
capita income fell by 37 percent from $2,237 to $1,404, as earnings fell and
unemployment rose. The share of the population living below the poverty
line grew from 3 percent in 1986–7 to 14.4 percent in 1992 and to 11.7
percent in 1997. GDP growth averaged 5.2 percent a year in 1993–5, 2.8
percent in 1996–9, and 5.1 percent in 2000–04.[24]

---

[23] Economist Intelligence Unit (EIU). *Jordan Country Profile, 2005.* London: EIU, 2005. 25.
[24] IMF, *Jordan: Selected Issues and Statistical Appendix.* Report No. 04/121. May 2004. 12–13;
World Bank, *Jordan Quarterly Update.* First Quarter 2005. 9–10.

Since the crisis of the 1980s, the structure of the economy has been transformed with a large reduction in the role of the public sector and liberalization of the environment for the private sector and foreign investors. Government controls on basic commodity prices were gradually reduced and the government increased allocations to the poor via the National Aid Fund to help compensate them for the rise in living costs. Privatization began in 1998, and by 2004 proceeds reached $800 million. The liberalization of foreign trade resulted in the reduction in tariffs and a simplification in the tariff system.

In 2004, the economy grew by 7.5 percent, nearly double its 2003 rate, because of a large increase in exports to Iraq and other states in the Gulf and to the United States. In 2003, exports accounted for 45 percent of the increase in GDP, in 2004 for 84 percent. The growth of exports was the main cause of the rise in output in the manufacturing sector of 14 percent in 2004, compared to 4.4 percent in 2003. The rise in exports had positive effects on the transport and communications sectors and even on construction.[25]

These positive trends carried on into 2005, although there were signs of overheating. The trade balance deteriorated as a result of the growth of imports, in part because of the rise in international oil prices. This was financed by a rise in remittances and transfers from abroad, which suggests that rents were becoming more important, just as the economy was becoming more productive as a result of the rise in manufactured output and exports.[26] The manufacturing sector increased production by 11.8 percent in the first half of 2005 – a slowdown compared with the 14.5 percent recorded in the first half of 2004. This slowdown was the result of reduced Iraqi demand for Jordanian exports. GDP increased by 7.5 percent in the first half of 2005.[27]

In his presentation of the 2006 budget, the finance minister pointed to a number of structural imbalances in the economy. These stemmed from the gap between resources available (supply) and the population (demand) and were manifested in balance-of-payments deficits, budget deficits, poverty, and unemployment. Interest payments on high levels of foreign debt, the result of past balance-of-payments deficits, consumed resources badly needed for other uses. The minister noted how dependent the budget was on foreign aid. In 2004, foreign aid covered 26 percent of

---

[25] World Bank, *Jordan Quarterly Update.* First Quarter 2005. 9–10.
[26] Ibid. 9.
[27] Ibid. 8–9.

spending, in 2005 an estimated 32 percent. The willingness of donors to continue supplying aid to Jordan was subject to the implementation of reforms that imply a reduction in reliance on aid and to political considerations that were outside the government's control. Despite reductions, subsidies accounted for 24 percent of public spending in 2005. Much of the benefit of these subsidies (including fuel subsidies) went to the richer sections of the community and to foreigners. The problems of unemployment and poverty meant that there were inadequate resources for investment. The minister also noted how exposed the economy was to external influences.[28] In 2005–06, this was manifest in the rise in the price of oil that increased Jordan's import bill and worsened its trade deficit.

The Development of the Business Community

During the hundreds of years of Ottoman rule until 1917, Transjordan had a subsistence economy with no significant indigenous business community. In the late Ottoman period, thanks to legal reforms and the construction of the Hijaz railway that began in 1900 between Damascus and Medina, merchants from Syria and Palestine settled in the region.

After the First World War, the British created a free-trade zone in areas that they controlled: Palestine, Transjordan, and Iraq. The import of British goods was favored over the development of local manufacturing. This discouraged local traders from making long-term investments in manufacturing. To retain the loyalty of the trading class, the British diverted business in their direction: in the late 1930s and early 1940s, they enforced regulations, which meant that all imports to Palestine had to go through Jordan. The British sold import licenses to Jordanians, some of whom resold them illegally to Palestinians.[29] Wartime restrictions and production licenses further hampered the trading class, but it earned rents by selling imports of goods in scarce supply.

Prior to Jordan's independence in 1946, the Emir Abdullah maintained close contact with the country's merchants. In exchange for his interventions with the British-controlled bureaucracy, the merchants met shortfalls in the palace budget. Following independence, Jordan's small market size, high transport costs, limited natural resources, and lack of a capital market made the development of the infrastructure and industrialization difficult.

---

[28] Ministry of Finance. *Budget Speech 2006.* 21 December 2005. Amman. 2–3. http://eng. mof.gov.jo/english/inside1.asp.

[29] Blue Carroll. Footnote 3.

The government therefore offered merchants incentives to invest in the form of monopolies, tax breaks, and exemptions from customs and other fees.

During Israel's 1948 War for Independence, Jordan conquered the West Bank and incorporated it into its territory. Its merchant class swelled considerably as a result of the conquest and the Palestinians, who came to dominate it, were made Jordanian citizens. The merchant class as a whole was perceived to be less loyal to the kingdom than residents of the East Bank, the original citizens of the state. As income gaps widened during the war, the government took on the role of the protector of the mass of the population against traders who had become rich as a result of wartime conditions. The East Bank elite saw the state as the motor for growth, in part because it provided an alternative power focus to that of the Palestinian-dominated private sector. The aim of policy makers was to help the East Bank catch up with the more industrialized West Bank. As a result, investment in the West Bank was restricted, and by 1959, the East Bank had 36 percent of Jordan's industry. The government received economic aid from abroad that helped to finance East Bank industrialization. Even more aid was received after the 1967 war, in which Israel occupied the West Bank.[30] After 1967, a growth in the number of Palestinian merchants who fled from the West Bank reinforced the distinction between the largely Palestinian business class and the dominantly East Bank state apparatus. This happened again in 1991 with the return of Jordanians of Palestinian origin from the Gulf. The differences between the Jordanians of Palestinian and East Bank origin made economic reform and privatization a highly political issue in a way that did not apply in other Arab countries.[31]

The availability of rents reinforced the strength of the government. By the mid-1970s, half of the labor force was employed by the government, in either a civilian or military capacity.[32] Officials became unwilling to devolve power to the private sector and King Hussein had to take into account Jordan's political and social fabric when making economic decisions. This meant maintaining a balance between the Palestinian population – who comprised a trading class as well as refugees in camps – as well as East Bankers who dominated the bureaucracy and the army.

[30]   Ibid. 25–51.
[31]   Moore, Pete W. *Doing Business in the Middle East: Politics and Economic Crises in Jordan and Kuwait.* Cambridge and New York: Cambridge University Press, 2004. 179.
[32]   Owen, Roger and Sevket Pamuk. *A History of the Middle East Economies in the Twentieth Century.* London: I. B. Tauris, 1998. 192.

The economic crisis of the 1980s reduced the government's ability to finance the development process. It therefore turned to the private sector to restart economic growth. One advantage of this strategy was that it received the strong support of the IMF, the World Bank, and Western countries. The private sector was not strong enough to take over this role with ease. Only in cooperation with the government could it undertake the investments that would bring economic growth.

King Abdullah's Economic Priorities

Since coming to power in February 1999, King Abdullah has given priority to economic issues with the intention of achieving two aims. The first was to strengthen the economy, increase employment, and reduce poverty, all of which threatened social and political stability. The second aim was political: to position Jordan closer to the United States and the global economy. The peace treaty signed with Israel in 1994 repaired much of the damage done to relations with the United States by Jordan's support for Iraq in the 1991 war.[33] In 2005 the Jordanian government issued a document, *The National Agenda 2006–2015*, which set out economic and other targets to be achieved by 2017 and provided a serious critique of the current state of the economy. This was done against the background of rapid economic growth and suggests that the government is realistic in understanding Jordan's weaknesses. The document stated that Jordan, one of the smallest and poorest economies in the Middle East, was failing to provide employment for the annual increase in the number of job-seekers. In its words: "With the current population growth rate and the economic status quo, unemployment rates could well exceed 20 percent and could account for more than half a million unemployed in the coming ten to fifteen years."[34] It also listed a series of failings in a similar vein to those made by the IMF and the World Bank. The growth of small and medium enterprises was constrained by limited access to finance and by bureaucracy as well as by the quality of the workforce. Government programs in support of this sector were limited, uncoordinated, and demonstrated little understanding of businesses' needs; the tax system hindered the private business sector as did high electricity tariffs and information and communication technology access costs; the

---

[33] Bank, Andre and Oliver Schlumberger. "Jordan: Between Regime Survival and Economic Reform" in Volker Perthes (ed.), *Arab Elites Negotiating the Politics of Change.* Boulder, Colo.: Lynne Rienner, 2004. 50.

[34] Prime Minister's Office. *National Agenda 2006–2015*, Amman: Prime Minister's Office, 2005. 5.

government remains the largest employer in Jordan and controls much of the economy either directly or indirectly, a situation that has led to high levels of government spending and debt. There were also large inequalities in the provision of health, education, and other services to different regions and sections of the population. The main aims of the National Agenda are to achieve GDP growth of 7.2 percent and to create 600,000 jobs to reduce unemployment from 12.5 percent to 6.8 percent in the period 2006–15.[35]

King Abdullah has pushed reform but has encountered opposition among those that support him. This was because economic reforms such as subsidy cuts, privatization, and administrative reforms undermined some of the interests of groups that support the monarchy. One solution was to control the privatization program so that the government could maintain control of the economy and prevent unemployment rising. Given that the East Bank population had been given jobs in the public sector, as opposed to Palestinians, this was a sensitive political issue as well as a socioeconomic one. The answer was to sell public companies to strategic investors who had close ties to the palace and were often past or present members of the security establishment.[36]

Qualified Industrial Zones

In 1996, the U.S. Congress passed legislation aimed at encouraging business links between Arab countries and Israel. Under this legislation, the United States extended the benefits already available to Israeli companies in the U.S. market under the U.S.–Israel Free Trade Agreement of 1975. The benefits of free access were offered to companies located in QIZs. The main conditions applied were that 35 percent of the "appraised value" of the product entering the United States must originate in the West Bank, the Gaza Strip, a QIZ in Jordan, or Israel. One-third of the 35 percent (11.7 percent) must come from Jordan: high-tech products must include a minimum 7 percent Israeli content; for other products the minimum is 8 percent. The remainder of the 35 percent value-added requirement may come from the West Bank, the Gaza Strip, and a QIZ in Jordan, Israel, or the United States. The appraised value is the price paid by the U.S. buyer plus other costs such as packaging. Shipping, insurance, and freight are not included.

---

[35] Ibid. 5–7.
[36] Choucair, Julia. "Illusive Reform: Jordan's Stubborn Stability." Carnegie Paper No. 76. December 2006. 15–16. http://www.carnegieendowment.org/files/cp76_choucair_final.pdf.

The Agreement was signed in 1997 and since their inauguration the QIZs brought about a huge increase in Jordanian exports to the United States: from $2.4 million in 1998 to $930 million in 2004. In 2007 they were estimated at almost $1.33 billion of which 70 percent came from the QIZs.[37] During the early years, the bulk of these exports were garments and they represented a huge increase in the total exports of that sector. Their growth was also a major step in the diversification and growth of output in the economy. By the first half of 2005, garments accounted for 20 percent of exports; food and beverages 12 percent; chemicals and other manufactured goods, excluding clothing, came to 35 percent.

In the first half of 2005, total employment in the QIZs was 50,569 of which 19,216 (38 percent) was Jordanian. Furthermore, it has been estimated that for every five jobs generated in the QIZs, one additional job has been created outside them. As a result, an additional 10,114 jobs have therefore been created. Although the employment of foreigners has also increased outside the QIZs, it is assumed that the employment gain accrued mainly to Jordanians. The total increase in employment of Jordanians over these eight years as a result of the QIZs was therefore 29,330, an average annual rise was 3,666, or nearly 7 percent of the annual increase in the labor force.[38] More than 60 percent of the jobs created in the QIZs were taken by foreigners, brought in either because they had skills lacking in Jordan or because they were cheaper than Jordanians or because it was also possible to obtain more compliant labor outside the kingdom. There have been reports of sweatshop conditions in some plants.[39] Given the scale of imported labor, it would seem that cheap labor accounted for the majority.

Agriculture

The problems faced by the imbalance between resources and population growth are most graphically illustrated in agriculture, especially in food production. The total arable land area in Jordan is only about 400,000 hectares, less than one-tenth of a hectare per capita. Renewable fresh water resources are scarce, at about 750 million cubic meters per year, an average

---

[37] Embassy of the United States, Amman, Jordan. Press Release: *QIZs Provide an Engine for Export-Led Growth in Jordan.* 13 March 2008. http://amman.usembassy.gov/user/NewsDetail.aspx?NewsId=1379.

[38] Kardoosh and al Khouri. 20. http://www.erf.org.eg; *Jordan Economic Monitor.* February 2006. 4–6.

[39] *New York Times.* 3 May 2006.

Table 7.7. *Jordan: Agricultural and food production indices, 1990–2004*
(1999–2001 = 100)

	Agricultural production	Agricultural production/capita	Food production	Food production/capita
1990	82.4	127.6	81.2	125.8
1995	113.1	134.2	111.1	131.7
2000	111.4	111.5	111.2	111.2
2001	100.0	97.2	100.2	97.4
2002	137.4	129.9	136.9	129.4
2003	117.3	108.0	117.2	107.9
2004	118.1	106.0	118.2	106.1

Source: http://www.fao.org.

of 170 m³ per capita for all uses. Around 80 percent of the cultivated area is rain fed.

The quantity of rainfall and its distribution over the cultivation season has a strong influence on agricultural production, affecting not only output in rain-fed lands, pasture, and livestock but also irrigated land as a result of its impact on dams, groundwater, and water-storage sources. Despite its small contribution to GDP, agriculture remains an important sector of the economy. It is the base for integrated rural development, a source of income and employment for the rural sector that accounts for 30 percent of the population and for the semidesert or nomad population. Agriculture also generates activity in other sectors, especially industry and services.

Table 7.7 gives an indication of the problems faced in agriculture. Although between 1990 and 2004 total agricultural production rose by 43 percent, output per capita fell by 17 percent. Food production followed the same trends. Agriculture could not keep up with the increase in the

Table 7.8. *Jordan: Wheat production, consumption, and trade, 1980–2005*

	1980	1985	1990	1995	2000	2005
Production (tons)	133,535	62,827	82,970	58,457	29,150	33,154
Harvested area (hectares)	133,182	94,827	57,306	40,555	27,000	24,418
Yield (kg/ha)	1,003	666	1,446	1,441	1,080	
Imports (tons)	162,913	376,908	610,985	335,435	584,064	794,415*

* 2004.

Source: 1980–2000: Asian Wheat Producing Countries: Jordan. www.fao.org/ag/agp/agpc/doc/field/ wheat/asia/jordan.htm; 2005: FAOSTAT.

population and, as a result, imports of foodstuffs rose from $639 million in 1990 to $710 million in 2000 and to $1.045 billion in 2004.[40]

The largest food import is wheat. Since 1980, as a result of falling production and increased demand because of the rise in the population, the quantity imported has risen sharply. This is illustrated in Table 7.8.

Conclusions

Jordan has successfully carried out many of the reforms demanded by the IMF and the World Bank. It has continued to lead the Arab world in key human development indices in health and education. The development of QIZs has resulted in the generation of millions of dollars of industrial exports. All this has been achieved despite Jordan's geo-strategic position located between hostile or potentially hostile neighbors.

Although the reforms have resulted in an acceleration of economic growth, they have not yet had a significant effect on unemployment. The QIZs have created more jobs for foreigners than for Jordanians. Furthermore, the economy remains dangerously reliant on foreign aid and on other rental incomes from abroad. A regional downturn in the level of economic activity would hit Jordan's economy as it has in the past. This is ironic given how much Jordan has done to increase its economic ties outside the Middle East, with the United States, the European Union, and Japan.

Jordan has devoted larger shares of its budget to education and health than many other countries in the region. As a result it has among the best human development indices in the Middle East. Nevertheless, this has not prevented the emergence and persistence of poverty although it has helped to limit its intensity. Improvements in demographic trends have occurred but these will take years to affect the numbers entering the labor force. This is the main reason why unemployment remains persistently high.

[40] Food and Agriculture Organization. *FAOSTAT.* http://faostat.fao.org.

EIGHT

Morocco

Reforms That Did Not Cure

Morocco is a country of sharp contrasts. Although it has among the most impressive demographic trends in the Arab world, it suffers from mass poverty and high rates of unemployment and illiteracy. The economic reforms that Morocco has undertaken since the 1980s, with the backing of the IMF and the World Bank, have improved its finances but the economy still suffers from slower growth than the average for developing countries. The instability of growth resulting from large fluctuations in agricultural production remains a serious problem. It has more political freedom than most Arab countries, but this has not provided a pluralistic basis for economic development.

Demographic Trends

Between 1980–5 and 2000–05, Morocco's population growth rate fell from 2.56 percent to 1.48 percent a year, one of the lowest growth rates in the Arab world. In 2005, the Moroccan population was estimated at almost 31.5 million and the annual increase in the population is about four hundred and fifty thousand a year (see Tables 8.1 and 8.2).

The move toward having smaller families, the key factor in demographic transition, was dramatic and continues to be. In 1979–80, the average number of births per woman was 5.6; by 2003–04 it had fallen to 2.5. The gap between rural and urban averages continued but in rural areas the decline in the number of births per woman was most dramatic. In 1979–80, it was 6.6 and by 2003–04 it was three. In urban areas in 1979–80 it was 4.5 and in 2003–04 the average was 2.1. The fall in fertility rates was because of an increase in average age of marriage and in the use of contraceptives by

Table 8.1. *Morocco: Population and dependency ratios, 1950–2005*

	Population (millions)	Working-age population	Dependent population	Dependency ratio*
1950	8.95	4.72	4.23	90
1960	11.63	6.11	5.52	90
1970	15.31	7.39	7.92	107
1980	19.58	10.44	9.14	87
1985	22.19	12.13	10.16	84
1990	24.69	13.99	10.70	77
1995	27.00	15.71	11.29	72
2000	29.23	17.78	11.45	62
2005	31.45	19.67	11.78	55

* The total dependency ratio is the ratio of the sum of the population aged 0–14 and that aged 65+ to the population aged 15–64. This is expressed as number of dependents per 100 persons of working age (15–64).

Source: Population Division of the Department of Economic and Social Affairs of the United Nations Secretariat. *World Population Prospects: The 2004 Revision* and *World Urbanization Prospects: The 2003 Revision.* http://esa.un.org/unpp.

married women. The proportion of women aged 15–19 who were married fell from 21 percent in 1980 to 11 percent in 2004. During the same period, the proportion aged 20–24 who were married fell from 64 percent to 34 percent. The use of contraceptives among married women of reproductive age rose from 19 percent to 64 percent. The increase in the age of marriage was related to improved education among girls and women. Despite

Table 8.2. *Morocco: Demographic trends, 1980–2005*

	Population growth (% annual average)	Total fertility rate (births per woman)	Birthrate of per 1,000 population	Death rate of per 1,000 population
1980–5	2.56	5.40	36.9	10.9
1985–90	2.14	4.45	31.6	8.7
1990–5	1.79	3.66	27.3	7.1
1995–2000	1.59	3.00	24.2	6.2
2000–05	1.48	2.76	23.3	5.8

Source: UN Population Division: World Population Prospects: The 2004 Revision Population Database. www.esa.un.org.

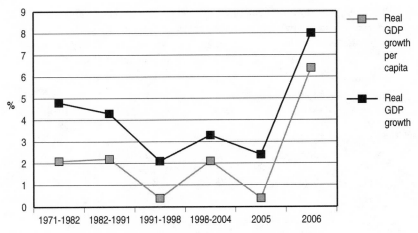

Figure 8.1. Morocco: Economic Growth, 1971–2006. *Source:* World Bank. Kingdom of Morocco Country Economic Memorandum, Vol. II, 2006. International Monetary Fund. International Financial Statistics Yearbook 2002. World Bank. Kingdom of Morocco, Country Economic Memorandum, 2006. IMF. Morocco: 2007 Article IV Consultation-Staff Report; Staff Statement; Public Information Notice on the Executive Board Discussion; and Statement by the Executive Director for Morocco, Country Report 07/323.

unemployment, more women entered the labor force – a factor limiting family size.[1]

The sharp fall in the death rate was a factor that contributed to the growth of the population and the increase in the number of elderly people added to the pressure on social services. Between 1995 and 2005, the total population rose by almost 16.5 percent, the working-age population by 25 percent, and the dependent population by 4.3 percent.

Economic Development and Structural Change

Figure 8.1 shows how economic growth decelerated between 1971 and 1998–2004. The slowdown in demographic growth mitigated the effect on income per capita growth but did not outweigh it. The sharp upturn in growth in 2006 was because of good harvests made possible by plentiful rains. The structure of the economy has changed little over the last twenty-five years. The primary sector, which includes mining and agriculture, has accounted for about 16 percent of GDP since the 1970s, with agriculture increasingly important and mining decreasingly so. Manufacturing has remained within

---

[1] Ayad, Mohamed, and Farzaneh Roudi. *Fertility Decline and Reproductive Health in Morocco: New DHS Figures.* 10.5.2006–10 MAY 2006?. http://www.prb.org/Articles/2006/FertilityDeclineandReproductiveHealthinMoroccoNewDHSFigures.aspx.

the 16–19 percent share of GDP with an increase in the importance of textiles and leather as a result of their export performance until 1995. Since then, those subsectors have been in decline. The construction sector stagnated from 1975 to 1996. The share of the service sector has also remained stable, although within it, tourism has increased in importance.

Morocco has followed the stabilization and structural change policies recommended by the IMF and the World Bank in the early 1980s. The aim was to reduce large budget deficits and the expansion of inflationary credit used to finance them. Stabilization programs reduced both total demand and that of the public sector. The IMF advocated raising interest rates to real levels (i.e., above the rate of inflation) to encourage savings and reverse capital flight and restrictions on domestic credit and money creation. These measures were designed to strengthen the balance of payments. The IMF also placed emphasis on the liberalization of foreign trade and the need to devalue the exchange rate so as to encourage exports and discourage imports.

The economic reforms resulted in much greater economic and financial stability than was experienced in the 1970s, but the rate of growth has been neither fast nor stable. The slowdown in the rate of growth was largely caused by a fall in agricultural value added (as a result of severe drought) and the failure of the nonagricultural sector – industry and services – to compensate. Another reason was that stabilization policies resulted in a 20 percent real overvaluation of the dirham between 1990 and 2000. This made Moroccan exports more expensive on foreign markets and imports cheaper at home, both of which had negative effects on growth. In 2001, there was a corrective devaluation that helped to restore competitiveness.

In the 1970s, when minerals played a large role in the economy, fluctuations in the international price of phosphates had major effects. Since then minerals have played a smaller role but fluctuations in agricultural production have meant that volatility in GDP growth rates has continued. There has been an improvement in recent years, as a result of better harvests, and in the period 1999–2004, GDP growth averaged 3.5 percent, although in 2005 it was estimated at only 1.5 percent, once again as a result of drought.[2]

One of the main aims of reforms in the 1980s was to reduce the economy's reliance on phosphates thereby reducing exposure to volatile international

[2] IMF. *International Financial Statistics* (IFS), *2002 Yearbook*; IFS, May 2004; World Bank, *Memorandum of the President of the International Bank for Reconstruction and Development and the International Finance Corporation to the Executive Directors of the World Bank Group for the Kingdom of Morocco*, 1994. 5. World Bank, *Kingdom of Morocco Poverty Update, 2001*, 1. 16. World Bank, Kingdom of Morocco, *Country Economic Memorandum, 2006*. 2.

commodity markets. In this respect there was a significant improvement. In the 1980s, manufacturing output rose by an annual average of 4.1 percent, a considerable achievement, given that this was the decade of restructuring and it compared well with other countries undergoing similar processes.[3] Since then the performance has been less impressive. Between 1992 and 2002, industrial output rose by an annual average of only 3.3 percent. In 1992 only 9.6 percent of industrial production came from the modern sectors of machinery, transport equipment, electronics, office, measuring, and optical equipment. Ten years later this situation had hardly changed.[4]

The reform program was successful in reducing inflation and improving the balance of payments and the external debt. In the period 1980–3, the consumer price index rose by an annual average of 9.7 percent. In 1984–7 it rose by 7.9 percent and in 1988–92 by 6.6 percent. In 1993–5 it averaged 5.4 percent and in 1996–7, 2.0 percent. Inflation was even lower in 1999–2003, averaging 1.4 percent a year.[5]

Although the reforms made it possible to borrow abroad with greater ease and on more favorable terms, they also reduced the amount of government investment that was financed by foreign borrowing. The other main change was the increase in manufacturing exports that occurred as a result of the removal of many distortions in the economy. These reforms also encouraged emigrants to remit funds home through the banking system, thus benefiting the balance of payments. There was also a strong increase in tourism revenues in the 1980s. The diversification of exports and sources of foreign finance helped to insulate the economy from the effects of fluctuating phosphate prices and those of droughts. An improvement in the current and capital accounts continued at least until 1995. As a result of the economic reforms of the 1980s, subsequent debt rescheduling, and slow economic growth in the 1990s, Morocco's foreign debt fell from $25 billion in 1990 to $17.7 billion in 2004. At the same time, the debt–service ratio (debt servicing/exports) rose from 21.5 percent to 14 percent.[6]

Manufacturing output growth has been weak.[7] This meant that job creation was limited and Morocco largely missed out on the boom in third-world manufacturing exports that transformed the economies of South Korea, Taiwan, Mexico, China, and India. Although the rate of economic

---

[3] Richards, Alan and John Waterbury. *A Political Economy of the Middle East.* Boulder, Colo.: Westview, 1996. 238.

[4] IMF. *Morocco Statistical Appendix, 2004,* Report No. 04/163. 20.

[5] Calculated from IMF, *International Financial Statistics,* August 1998 and IMF, *Morocco Statistical Appendix,* 2004. Report No. 04/163. 11.

[6] World Bank. *Global Development Finance 2006.* Vol. II. Washington, D.C.: World Bank, 2006. 364.

[7] World Bank. *Kingdom of Morocco Poverty Update, 2001.* 1. 16.

growth was faster than that of the population, it was not fast enough to generate sufficient new jobs to reduce unemployment. Other macroeconomic issues remain: in recent years, the fiscal deficit equaled 5–6 percent of GDP, which has led to the expansion of government debt. The balance of payments is threatened by the reliance on food imports (see next section) and by the slow growth of exports.

More positively, the reduction in government investment that has been going on since the early 1980s has, since the mid-1990s, been accompanied by a rise in private-sector investment. As a result, total investment as a share of GDP increased from about 20 percent in 1995 to about 25 percent in 2004. Despite this, until 2003 investment was lower than the developing country average.

According to the World Bank, most of Morocco's economic growth was because of increases in inputs of labor and capital rather than improved productivity. In fact, factor productivity has been negative since the early 1990s and was largely due to the weak performance of agriculture. If agriculture is excluded, then the picture is brighter, with an increase in the contribution of total factor productivity (a residual that measures the efficiency with which labor and capital were used together) since the early 1990s.

Nonagricultural growth in the 1970s was impressive but was based on increases in inputs of labor and capital that could not be sustained. Productivity declined as a result of inefficient public investment. In the 1980s, nonagricultural growth decelerated, but productivity rose. One explanation was that as the investment boom of the 1970s ended, capacity utilization improved and employers became more selective in hiring labor. As a result, employment growth outside agriculture decelerated and urban unemployment rose from 12.7 percent in 1982 to 17.3 percent in 1991. During the 1990s, there were droughts that affected agricultural production but the rest of the economy fared better. Investment and employment growth were weak. In recent years, investment has increased, but employment growth has continued to decelerate. The recent improvement in productivity suggests that economic reforms have benefited the economy in terms of greater efficiency but not, at least yet, in terms of employment.[8]

The World Bank has reached some important conclusions regarding Morocco's weak growth performance: it is not because of financial constraints at the macro level; nor is it because of a lack of human capital, despite the fact that illiteracy remains high. In fact the returns to education were low and there is evidence that they have declined. This is

---

[8] World Bank. Kingdom of Morocco, *Country Economic Memorandum* (CEM), Vol. II, Report No. 32948-MOR. 2006. 12. Washington, D.C.: The World Bank, 2006.

consistent with high unemployment. Demand for highly skilled labor is missing and very few engineers are employed in the average manufacturing plant. The World Bank also concluded that the quality of governance was not a significant constraint. Compared with the rest of the world, Morocco's governance performance is average; compared with the rest of the Middle East it is above average. Macroeconomic risks or instability, as have been shown, are no longer constraints. The World Bank concluded that the constraint preventing an acceleration of the growth rate is in the combination of other government and market failures that prevent the diversification of production and restrict investment. These prevent structural change and thus limit economic growth. Government failures include a rigid labor code that results in high redundancy payments and payroll cost. Increased rights to strike, minimum wage regulations, and controls over the number of hours worked all discourage investment. The fixed exchange-rate system has resulted in a loss of competitiveness. The loss of revenues from import duties has been matched by increased revenues from direct taxes on individuals and firms. The updating of tax brackets has been slow, pushing relatively low earners into paying higher tax rates. The final government failure is the bias against exports in the trade regime. In 2004–05 the Overall Trade Restrictiveness Index, a measure of antiexport bias of the trade regime, was 0.51 in Morocco, 0.37 in Tunisia, and 0.20 in China. The market failures are information externalities, coordination externalities, and learning externalities. Information externalities occur when an entrepreneur identifies a new activity, especially in exports, he is bound to be copied and will thus have to share his earnings with others. If he fails, others will notice and avoid following him into the activity. In both cases, he generates information, but is not fully rewarded for it. Coordination externalities arise when the rate of return on one project depends positively on another project being put into use. One example is the construction of hotels without adequate transport infrastructure to serve them. The final externality is the lack of labor training that is prevalent in Morocco.[9] These problems exist to a greater or lesser extent in other Arab countries. Their solution requires detailed and continuous government attention.

Agriculture

Agriculture is one of the most important sectors in the economy, especially with regard to employment. In 1985 it accounted for 63 percent of the

[9] Ibid. 22–67.

labor force; in 2004 it accounted for 38 percent, when it produced about 17 percent of GDP.[10] In many respects agriculture remains the Achilles heel of the economy. As output growth failed to match that of the population, imports increased and the growth of agricultural employment was limited. The causes were both internal and external: there were not enough incentives within the economy to increase output and the Common Agricultural Policy of the European Union discouraged or limited agricultural exports to Morocco's main market.

Agriculture remains dangerously reliant on the level of rainfall. In 2002, only 16 percent of arable land was irrigated, a meager 3 percent increase over more than twenty years.[11] This affected rural income and employment levels, the number of migrants to the towns, and the rate of urban unemployment. Not only has agriculture suffered from fluctuations in output levels, but also the growth of output has failed to keep up with that of the population. In 2000–03, the average level of agricultural output per capita was 83.8 percent of its average 1989–91 level. As a result, between 1992 and 2000, the quantity of food, beverages, and tobacco imports rose by 70 percent; those of wheat alone by 39 percent. The costs of those imports rose by 100 percent and 125 percent, respectively.[12] In 1992, food accounted for 13.3 percent of the value of imports. In 1995, this rose to a peak of 17.6 percent and in 2002 it declined to 12.6 percent.[13] Average agricultural output per head in Morocco in 2000–02 was 12 percent lower than in 1989–91.[14] Figure 8.2 shows that there was an improvement in 2003–04. In 2005, there was a drought and output of cereals fell sharply (see Figure 8.3).

The share of cereal production in the total value of primary-sector output fell from one-third in 1980 to one-fifth in 2003. The shares of other products, such as fruit and livestock, expanded. Food prices have been more stable and the government successfully implemented countercyclical policies during the droughts of 1999 and 2000 with some success. The weakness of cereal production is shown in Figure 8.3. In 2005, for example, output was about 45 percent lower than in 2004. Between 2003 and 2004, the value of food imports rose by an estimated 46 percent.

[10] Ibid. 124; Food and Agriculture Organization (FAO). FAOSTAT. *Food and Agriculture Indicators: Morocco.* http://www. fao.org.
[11] Ibid.
[12] Premier Ministre. *Annuaire Statistique du Maroc.* Departement de la Prevision Economique et du Plan, Direction de la Statistique (1997). 495; the 1997 edition, pages 495 and 630; the 2000 edition, 630 (2002), 612–14.
[13] IMF. *Morocco Statistical Appendix 1998.* 52; *Morocco Statistical Appendix 2004.* 16. http://www.imf.org.
[14] FAO. *Bulletin of Statistics* 4, No. 1 (2003).

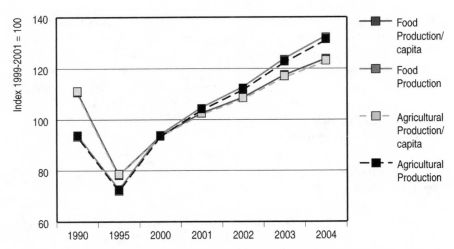

Figure 8.2. Morocco: Agriculture and Food Production Indices, 1990–2004. *Source:* Food and Agriculture Organization, Agricultural Statistics.

The Balance of Payments and the International Economic Environment

One of the main achievements of the stabilization sector of the 1980s was the improvement in the external sector. This was reflected in the balance of payments and the foreign debt, neither of which have posed problems

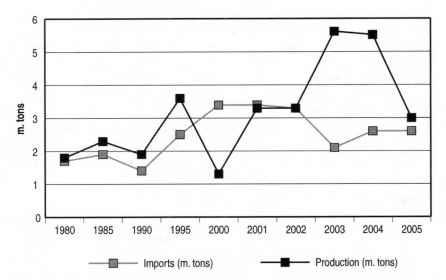

Figure 8.3. *Morocco:* Wheat Production and Imports, 1980–2005. *Source:* Food and Agriculture Organization, Agricultural Statistics.

Table 8.3. *Morocco: The balance of payments, 2001–2005 ($ millions)*

	2001	2002	2003	2004*	2005†
Exports fob	7,142	7,839	8,762	9,739	10,191
-Agriculture	1,477	1,648	1,825	1,532	1,633
-Phosphates and derived products	1,171	1,160	1,241	1,625	1,819
Imports fob	10,164	10,900	13,095	16,228	18,696
-Petroleum	1,282	1,167	963	1,639	2,157
-Food	1,363	1,374	1,194	1,534	1,745
Trade balance	−3,022	−3,061	−4,334	−6,489	−8,505
Services	1,910	1,946	2,617	3,388	3,724
-Tourism	2,583	2,646	3,225	3,920	4,267
Income	−832	−738	−790	−651	−740
Transfers	3,555	3,330	4,098	4,861	5,066
-Workers' remittances	3,261	2,877	3,612	4,218	4,459
Current account balance	1,611	1,477	1,591	1,109	−455
Foreign direct investment	2,727	452	2,302	822	1,316
Privatization receipts	2,068	0	1,471	0	1,442

* Estimate. † Projected.

Source: World Bank, Kingdom of Morocco Country Economic Memorandum, 2006. 25.

for economic management in recent years. Table 8.3 shows, however, that over the last five years Morocco's balance of payments on current account has deteriorated as a result of a large increase in the merchandise trade deficit. This had been traditionally financed by workers' remittances and tourism revenues. Although those two inflows continued to increase until 2005, they did not do so fast enough to cover the trade deficit. The latter increased because between 2000 and 2005 imports rose by 85 percent while exports rose by only 43 percent.

The Foreign Trade System

Despite the moves toward a more liberalized foreign-trade system, in 2003 Morocco had an unweighted average import tariff of 36 percent, compared with the average of 15 percent in lower middle-income countries worldwide.[15] High rates of taxes on imports mean that the loss of revenues when they are cut will be considerable. As they are high, they provide considerable protection for domestic industry and their removal will have negative effects on employment and output at least in the short term.

[15] *The Economist.* 8 April 2006. 41.

Liberalization continues, however, and in 1999–2000, taxes on imports accounted for 19.6 percent of total taxation; by 2003, they accounted for 13.3 percent.[16]

In 2002, Morocco's Association Agreement with the European Union (EU) came into force and it will be fully implemented by 2012. Morocco has also signed a free-trade agreement with the United States that will fully come into force in 2009. These agreements provide duty-free access to Moroccan markets for EU and U.S. goods with significant consequences for local producers and government revenues. In 1994, the EU took 64 percent of Morocco's exports and supplied 56 percent of its imports. In 2004, it accounted for 74 percent of Morocco's exports and supplied 56 percent of its imports. In that year the United States accounted for 4 percent of Morocco's exports and imports.[17]

In January 2005, the Multi-Fibre Arrangement[18] ended and this was followed by the liberalization in international trade in textiles. Morocco's preferential access to EU and U.S. markets ended and it began to feel the effects of competition from cheaper sources of supply in China and elsewhere. In the early 2000s, textiles and clothing accounted for 17 percent of industrial value added, 34 percent of merchandise exports, and 42 percent of industrial development. The effects were felt in the first quarter of 2005, with significant falls in exports of various clothing items.[19] Worries about Morocco's ability to compete together with rising costs of oil imports, the effects of the 2005 drought, and limited access to fishing zones because of environmental preservation agreements have resulted in pessimism about the future of the economy. This has had its effect on the level of activity that is estimated at 1.2–1.5 percent (or 3.5 percent excluding agriculture) in 2005.

---

[16] Premier Ministre. *Annuaire Statistique du Maroc,* Departement de la Prevision Economique et du Plan, Direction de la Statistique, (2002). 496–504.

[17] IMF. *Morocco: 2005 Article IV Consultation – Staff Report; Public Information Notice on the Executive Board Discussion*; and *Statement by the Executive Director for Morocco 2005.* 5. http://www.imf.org; World Bank. Kingdom of Morocco, Country Economic Memorandum, 2006. 2. 124.

[18] The Multi-Fibre Arrangement (sometimes known as the Agreement on Textiles and Clothing) governed the world trade in textiles and garments from 1974 to 2004. It enabled developed countries to impose quotas on the exports of developing countries. As a result, until 2004, the European Union could discriminate in favor of countries with which it had preferential trade agreements, such as Morocco. From 1 January 2005 when the MFA expired, it no longer could and cheaper producers such as China could and did take advantage of the market.

[19] World Bank. Kingdom of Morocco, Country Economic Memorandum, 2006. 122–7.

Emigration

Another major issue in Morocco's politics and economics is that of emigration. Mass unemployment has meant that many Moroccans want to leave for Europe where they believe that there are jobs and the possibility of higher earnings. Legal emigration to the European Union has been limited to the category of family reunion since the 1970s. As a result, illegal emigration has become a much more significant phenomenon. Moroccans are regularly drowned and others arrested and returned illegally in attempts to get to Spain by boat, and this phenomenon remains an issue of contention in Morocco's relations with the European Union. Emigration also played a part in reducing demographic pressures. In 1995, there were 1.27 million Moroccans estimated to be living in the main European countries and 105,000 Moroccans living in Libya and the Gulf States. In 2003 there were reported to be more than 2.5 million, equal to 8 percent of the population and 23 percent of the labor force.[20]

In 1968, remittances came to $400 million and increased by an annual average of 14 percent since then. In 2004, remittances by Moroccans living abroad came to $4.2 billion, equal to 8.4 percent of GDP and 26.2 percent of exports of goods and services. Their share in GDP rose sharply in the 1960s and 1970s and slowed since then. As the economy became more export oriented, their share in total exports declined until 2000. Since then, the slowdown in exports and the increase in remittances led to an increase in their share of exports.[21] The economy remains very reliant on these inflows.

Foreign Investment

Foreign direct investment has played a very limited role in the Moroccan economy, with the exception of telecommunications. The privatization of the sector and the selling of mobile phone licenses attracted large capital inflows. Foreign investment in other sectors has been restricted by bureaucracy, uncertainty about taxes, licenses, regulations, and other government controls. As a result, the creation of new jobs, manufacturing output, and exports has been limited, as has the country's integration into the international economy. In the period 2000–04, annual foreign direct investment inflows averaged $660 million a year (about 1.7 percent of GDP and

[20] World Bank. *Kingdom of Morocco Poverty Update, 2001.* 1. 5–6.
[21] Ibid. 5–6.

Table 8.4. *Morocco: Labor market trends, 1986–2004*

	Thousands			Annual growth rate %	
	1986	1995	2004	1985–90	2000–04
Labor force					
Total	8,750	10,006	11,183	3.4	2.1
Urban	3,211	4,982	5,860		
Rural	5,538	5,024	5,323		
Employment					
Total	7,751	8,510	9,887	1.0	1.7
Urban	2,712	3,870	4,727	4.0	2.2
Rural	5,039	4,640	5,160	−0.9	1.2
Unemployment					
Total	999	1,495	1,296	4.6	−1.6
Urban	499	1,111	1,133	9.3	0.2
Rural	499	384	163	−2.9	−9.1

Source: World Bank. Kingdom of Morocco Country Economic Memorandum, 2006. 124.

7.2 percent of total investment) and resulted from Morocco's privatization program.[22]

The Labor Market

As has been shown, although the Moroccan economy has undergone many of the reforms recommended by the IMF and the World Bank, it has not achieved the fast and stable rates of economic growth that would reduce unemployment. Table 8.4 shows that the labor force was estimated at 11.2 million in 2004, and the labor-force growth rate was 2.1 percent a year. This meant that almost 240,000 people entered the labor market a year. Between 1986 and 2004, the urban labor force increased by 83 percent while the rural labor force declined by 4 percent. Employment grew much more rapidly in urban than in rural areas but it did not increase as fast as the labor force. Between 1995 and 2004, rural employment rose modestly after falling sharply, largely because of the migration of rural workers to urban areas in search of work, during periods of drought. Between 1985–90 and 2000–05, employment growth in the urban sector decelerated, as a result of factors discussed earlier. In consequence, unemployment was concentrated in the towns and cities.

[22] World Bank. Kingdom of Morocco, Country Economic Memorandum (CEM), 2006. 9.

The figures in Table 8.4 show that in 2004, the unemployment rate was estimated at 11.6 percent, compared to 15 percent in 1995. Unofficially, the rates were deemed to be significantly higher: In 2001, urban unemployment was unofficially estimated at 19.5 percent; in rural areas 4.5 percent. Most of the unemployed from rural areas went to the towns in search of work and those that did not find it became urban unemployed. In the greater Casablanca region, unemployment was 21.4 percent. Among those aged 15–24, the national unemployment rate was 18.9 percent and among males in urban areas it was 35.4 percent.[23] In 2004, urban unemployment rate was 18 percent.[24]

One of the most worrying aspects about unemployment in Morocco is the fact that the average education level among the unemployed is higher than that of the labor force as a whole. The problem is particularly acute among those joining the labor force, leading to higher unemployment among young people than older ones. The fact that education achievements are higher in urban areas has resulted in a concentration of the unemployed in those areas. In 2004, the unemployment rate among urban workers with less than basic education was 11 percent while for those with secondary education it was 32 percent and for university graduates it was 35 percent. Women with higher education accounted for fewer than 10 percent of the total labor force, yet unemployment among this group accounted for 20 percent of total unemployment.

Employment is dominated by sectors that are not high value added and are subject to volatile changes because of internal or external factors. Agriculture is the largest single employer and the droughts that it suffers severely limit its employment capacity. Employment in manufacturing and its share in value added increased in the 1980s, declined in the early 1990s, and increased from the late 1990s until the effects of the end of the Multi-Fibre Arrangement began to be felt in the early 2000s. Between 1994 and 2002, total employment rose by 923,000. Agriculture provided 106,000 of these jobs (11 percent) and manufacturing only 62,000 (6.6 percent). As a result the share of manufacturing in total employment declined.[25] The fact that manufacturing contributed such a small share of total employment is in sharp contrast with the achievements of China and other countries

---

[23] World Bank. *Trade, Investment and Development in the Middle East and North Africa.* Washington, D.C.: The World Bank, 2003. 3. 136; World Bank, CEM, Morocco. 124.
[24] IMF. *Morocco Statistical Appendix 2004.* 16.
[25] IMF. *Directions of Trade Statistics Yearbook, 1998.* Washington, D.C.: IMF, 1998. *Directions of Trade Statistics Yearbook, 2005.* Washington, D.C.: IMF, 2005.

in East and Southeast Asia and reflects that fundamental weakness of the industrialization process in Morocco.

Poverty

The number of people living in poverty increased from 3.4 million in 1991 (13 percent of the population) to 5.3 million in 1998–9 (19 percent). Poverty was defined as living below a minimum level of consumption per head, equivalent to $2.50/head on a national level, in 1993 purchasing power parity terms. The economically vulnerable population – whose consumption levels were at or below 150 percent of the poverty level – increased from 9 million (35 percent of the population) to 12 million (44 percent).[26]

In the 1990s, 84 percent of the increase in poverty was due to the slow-down in economic growth while the remainder was because of changes in the distribution of income. In the period 1986–91, GDP increased by an annual average of 4.1 percent. In 1991–8, the average was only 1.9 percent. In urban areas, changes in the distribution of income among the poor damp-ened the effects of the slowdown in economic growth. In rural areas, the lack of growth combined with greater inequality in the distribution resulted in rising poverty. Thus, in 1999, 66 percent of Morocco's poor lived in rural areas that contained 44 percent of the total population. A total of 34 percent lived in urban areas that accounted for 56 percent of the total population. Another key measurement of human welfare – nutrition – showed a serious deterioration in the late 1990s. In 1990–5, an annual average of 1.5 per-cent of the population was undernourished. In 1999–2001, the share was 2.1 percent, or some 600,000 people.[27]

Human Development Indices

The UN's human development index (HDI) combines information on life expectancy, adult literacy, school enrollment, and GDP per capita. Morocco has one of the lowest indices in the Middle East, despite the fact that it has improved gradually over time. In 1990 it was 0.54 and in 2003 it was 0.63,

---

[26] World Bank. CEM, Morocco. 113–14.
[27] Safir, Nadji. "Emigration Dynamics in the Maghreb" in Appleyard, Reginald (ed.). *Emigration Dynamics in Developing Countries IV, The Arab Region*. Aldershot: Ashgate Publishing Ltd, for the UN Population Fund and the International Organization for Migration, 1999. 104; Nybery Sorensen, Ninna. *Migrant Remittances as a Development Tool: The Case of Morocco*, International Organization for Migration (IOM) Working Papers Series, No. 2. (June 2004). 5. http://www.iom.og.

an improvement of nearly 17 percent. In 2003, Morocco ranked 124th in the world. One element in the HDI is adult literacy and here Morocco's failings are apparent: in 2003, more than 49 percent of the population aged 15 and older was illiterate.[28] The Alternative Human Development Index added data on lifelong knowledge acquisition, especially regarding information technology, women's access to societal power, and measures of human freedom. When these additional criteria were added, in 2002 Morocco's HDI was ranked seventy-nine. Morocco's political freedom score was a low 0.35.[29] In the 1990s and the early 2000s, Morocco had become a less oppressive society but still faced massive socioeconomic deprivation.

The Private Sector and the State

Although Morocco never experienced a socialist phase like Tunisia and other Arab countries, the public sector (including the government, public-sector bodies, and the court) still plays a dominant role in the economy, accounting for at least 50 percent of GDP.[30] The late King Hassan, who ruled from 1961 until 1999, expanded the role of the state by buying into the private sector during the period of ostensible economic liberalization in the 1980s.[31] Through his holdings in Omnium Nord Africain (ONA), King Hassan acquired interests throughout the Moroccan economy, including shares in privatized companies. As a result of ONA shareholdings in major banks, the court has gained much control in the banking sector (including placing its people in key positions) and can allocate credit in return for political support. The private sector still maintains very close links with the court both on an individual basis and through organizations such as chambers of commerce.[32] All this limits the socioeconomic status of the business community and the political elite.[33]

---

[28] World Bank. CEM, Morocco. 161.

[29] United Nations Development Program. *Human Development Report 2005.* 220. http://hdr.undp.org/reports/global/2005.

[30] United Nations Development Program. *Arab Human Development Report, 2002.* New York: UN, 2002.

[31] Al Chaleck, Al Fadel. "Challenges to the Economy and State in the Middle East" in Perthes, Volker (coordinator), *Looking Ahead Challenges for Middle East Politics and Research.* EuroMeSco Paper No. 29, April 2004. 35. http://www.euromesco.net.

[32] Henry, Clement M. and Robert Springborg. *Globalization and the Politics of Development in the Middle East.* Cambridge: Cambridge University Press, 2001. 172–3.

[33] Dillman, Bradford. "Facing the Market." *Middle East Journal* Vol. 55, No. 2 (Spring 2001). 198–215.

King Mohammed VI, who succeeded his father in 1999, has not relinquished the extensive power that his father accumulated, even though he has widened the circle of people consulted, increased the freedom of debate in the press and elsewhere. Nor has he sold the huge economic interests owned by the court. The privatization of recent years consisted of the sale of government-owned assets. The changes that he has made have been more a matter of continuity than change: the elite remain concerned with economic development rather than political change and the monarchy remains central in all significant decision making.[34] The king and parliament continue to respond to vested interests by often blocking reform. For example, in 2000, a major educational reform was passed by parliament, but it was never implemented because of opposition from the teachers' unions and other entrenched interests.[35]

Conclusions

Morocco faces a very tough international environment that fails to complement the structural changes that it has made at home. When the IMF and the World Bank call on developing countries to make their economies more competitive both internally and externally, the assumption is that they will be given fair access to foreign markets, especially those that they do the vast majority of their trade with. This has not happened. Morocco's major trading partner – the EU – has restricted its imports of one of the main categories of goods in which Morocco and other North African states have a comparative advantage: agricultural products. Furthermore, through its common agricultural policy, the EU subsidizes exports of its own agricultural production. This is something that Morocco has, at the behest of the IMF and the World Bank, largely stopped doing. It could never afford the level of subsidy that the EU offers its producers. As a result, it has incentives to import artificially cheap agricultural goods (mainly food), with all the negative consequences for employment and the balance of payments.

The state has tried to convince foreign firms to invest, and foreign governments and international organizations to extend aid. Implicit (and perhaps explicit) in these effects has been the warning that without foreign inflows, the socioeconomic and thus political situation will deteriorate dangerously.

---

[34] Henry, Clement M. *The Mediterranean Debt Crescent.* Cairo: The American University in Cairo Press, 1997. 158–9.
[35] Zerhouni, Saloua. "Morocco: Reconciling Continuity and Change" in Perthes, Volker. *Arab Elites, Negotiating the Politics of Change.* Boulder Colo.: Lynne Rienner, 2004. 78–81.

The paradox in this situation is that as the state derives its legitimacy from its role as interlocutor in the international economy, the inequality associated with its foreign relations (e.g., implementing IMF stabilization programs) provides fuel for the opposition.[36]

The late King Hassan outflanked the private sector as he consolidated his power. The result was that economic liberalization yielded limited benefits. The inability to cope with foreign competition will threaten the economy when EU and other trade agreements come into full force and import taxes are cut.

[36] White, Gregory W. "The Mexico of Europe" in Vandewalle, Dirk. *North Africa: Development and Reform in a Changing Global Economy.* Basingstoke, England: Macmillan, 1996. 127.

NINE

Palestine

The Making and Unmaking of a State

This chapter examines the development of the Palestinian population and economy in the West Bank and Gaza. From 1948 until 1967, the West Bank was occupied by Jordan. In 1950, it was annexed and its 400,000 residents were given Jordanian citizenship. Despite this, the development of the area was neglected and most of Jordan's development was concentrated on the East Bank. The Gaza Strip was occupied by Egypt in 1948 and its development was also neglected. By 1950 it had a population of 200,000.[1] As a result, when Israel occupied these areas in 1967, it took over an economy that was very poor, with Gaza even less developed than the West Bank. There were refugee camps in both areas, occupied by those who had fled from the area that became Israel in 1948.

From 1967, the economy was characterized by increasing dependence on Israel. Israel supplied nearly all its imports and from 1970 on provided employment to an increasing number of Palestinians. Employment was both legal (with Palestinians receiving Israeli work permits and Social Security benefits) and illegal. Between 1967 and the outbreak, in 1987, of the First *Intifada* (Palestinian uprising against Israel), the economy grew faster than the population: GNP per capita in the West Bank rose from $550 in 1968 to $2,070 in 1993 in 1986 prices, while in Gaza it rose from $375 to $1,090.[2] The structure of the economy was notable for the paucity of its infrastructure and the lack of manufacturing industry. Both of these factors were largely due to Israeli policies. The effect was to leave the economy completely exposed when, during the 1990s, Israel began to close its labor market to Palestinian workers. It also meant that the role of the middle class in

---

[1] Palestine National Information Center. *Population in Palestine* (2 December 2007). http://www.pnic.gov.ps.

[2] Arnon, Arie, Israel Luski, Avia Spivak, and Jimmy Weinblatt. *The Palestinian Economy*. Leiden: Brill, 1997. 55–60.

developing the economy was severely restricted, despite the fact that the private sector was dominant. In the state-in-making – the Palestinian Authority that succeeded Israeli rule in many respects in 1994 – the business class counted for little. Those close to the leadership were granted monopolies and other benefits, something that discouraged genuine entrepreneurship. As a result, the Palestinian economy, even before it attained independence, exhibited many of the problems plaguing other Arab countries discussed in this book. These factors played an important role in the outbreak of the Second *Intifada* and pose a further serious challenge to the creation of an independent Palestinian state.

Demographic Developments

The demographic growth rate in the West Bank, and even more in Gaza, has been the fastest in the world. Despite conflict and emigration, the population of the West Bank and Gaza (excluding Israelis) rose from almost 1 million in 1967 to an estimated 3.5 million in 2005.[3] The economy, therefore, needed to grow by more than 3 percent a year just to maintain living standards. Unlike many other factors that determined per capita income and living standards, demographic growth was largely under Palestinian control.

In 1967, when the Israeli occupation began, the population of the West Bank was 586,000 and that of Gaza was 381,000. By 1993, the last year of full Israeli rule, the population of the two areas had grown by 89 percent to 1.83 million; an increase of 85 percent in the West Bank and 96 percent in Gaza. The natural increase in the population of Gaza rose to the extraordinarily high rate of 6 percent a year in 1992 and 1993, and would have been even higher had emigration not been significant.

In the period 1967–77, the crude birthrate in the West Bank was about 45 per 1,000. This declined to about 40 per 1,000 in the 1980s, but the number of women of reproductive age increased. In Gaza, the birthrate was higher and fertility rose in the late 1980s and early 1990s. Between 1968 and 1993, the population of women aged 15–49 in the West Bank rose by 93 percent and in Gaza by 83 percent, outweighing by far the effect of the decline in fertility rates. Birthrates were also affected by female participation in the labor force that was higher in the West Bank than in Gaza. That in

---

[3] Israel Central Bureau of Statistics. *Demographic Characteristics of the Arab Population in Judea, Samaria, and the Gaza Area, 1968–1993,* Publication No. 1025 (July 1996), 16; World Bank, *The Palestinian Economy and the Prospects for Its Recovery, Economic Monitoring Report to the Ad Hoc Liaison Committee, no. 1.* Washington, D.C.: World Bank, December 2005. 7.

Table 9.1. *Palestine: Population and dependency ratios, 1950–2005*

	Population (millions)	Working-age population	Dependent population	Dependency ratio*
1950	1.01	0.48	0.53	102
1960	1.10	0.57	0.53	94
1970	1.10	0.57	0.53	94
1980	1.48	0.72	0.76	104
1985	1.78	0.89	0.89	101
1990	2.15	1.08	1.07	100
1995	2.62	1.31	1.31	99
2000	3.15	1.57	1.58	101
2005	3.76	1.92	1.80	96

* The total dependency ratio is the ratio of the sum of the population aged 0–14 and that aged 65+ to the population aged 15–64. This is expressed as number of dependents per 100 persons of working age (15–64).

Source: Population Division of the Department of Economic and Social Affairs of the United Nations Secretariat. *World Population Prospects: The 2004 Revision* and *World Urbanization Prospects: The 2003 Revision.* http://esa.un.org/unpp.

turn was a function of education levels and may have been influenced by the greater religiosity of Gaza residents.[4] After 1967, mortality rates fell, largely as a result of improved health services. Infant mortality was more than halved in the following twenty years and life expectancy increased.[5] The high birthrate resulted in a young population, a large number of dependents (mainly children), and thus a lower level of income per capita than might otherwise have prevailed.

Between 1967 and 1993, net emigration from the West Bank and Gaza was 284,000, of which 174,000 were from the West Bank and 110,000 from Gaza. Emigration was particularly rapid in the period 1975–81 when the boom, fueled by high oil prices, occurred in the Gulf. In the period 1982–9, net emigration slowed. In the period 1990–2, there was a net immigration of about 26,000. Between 1967 and 1993, net emigration equaled almost 33 percent of the population increase. Without it the resident population would have risen by 1.15 million, excluding the dynamic effect of reproduction among the emigrants. In the period 1995–2005, the total population increased by 43.5 percent and the working-age population by 46.6 percent. During the same period, the dependent population grew by 37.4 percent (see Table 9.1).

[4] Arnon, Spivak, and Weinblatt. 64.
[5] Israel Central Bureau of Statistics. *Demographic Characteristics of the Arab Population in Judea & Samaria and the Gaza Area, 1968–1993.* 20–3.

Table 9.2. *Palestine: Demographic trends, 1970–2005 (annual averages)*

	Population growth rate (%)	Crude birthrate (per 1,000 population)	Crude death rate (per 1,000 population)	Total fertility rate (children per woman)
1970–5	2.72	46.6	16.8	7.73
1975–80	3.25	47.8	13.5	7.39
1980–5	3.78	44.6	9.1	7.00
1985–90	3.78	45.1	6.3	6.43
1990–5	3.84	45.6	6.9	6.46
1995–2000	3.76	41.8	5.1	5.99
2000–05	3.23	38.8	4.2	5.57

Source: Population Division of the Department of Economic and Social Affairs of the United Nations Secretariat. *World Population Prospects: The 2004 Revision* and *World Urbanization Prospects: The 2003 Revision.* http://esa.un.org/unpp.

Demographic trends in the West Bank and Gaza have been quite different from those in much of the Arab world. In the late 1970s, 1980s, and early 1990s the rate of population growth accelerated, the result not only of sharply falling death rates (which fell by more than half between 1970–5 and 1985–90), but also of increasing birthrates during part of the period. The latter reflected the gradual fall in total fertility rates during much of the period (with a reversal in the late 1980s and early 1990s) and an increase in the number of women aged 15–49. The figures in Tables 9.1 and 9.2 suggest that demographic transition has hardly begun.

Since the beginning of the Second *Intifada* in 2000, the population has continued to grow. In the period 2000–05, the average annual rate of growth was estimated at 3.2 percent. This was slower than the rate for 1995–2000 and resulted from a decline in the birthrate from 41.8 per 1,000 to 38.8 per 1,000 combined with a fall in the death rate from 5.1 per 1,000 to 4.2 per 1,000. The fall in the birthrate was related to a decline in the total fertility rate from 5.99 in 1995–2000 to 5.57 in 2000–05.[6] Since 2000, conditions in the West Bank and Gaza have been chaotic and so these figures should be treated with caution.

The very high fertility rates in the Palestinian Territories, especially Gaza, are notable for two reasons. First, they are significantly higher than in both neighboring Arab countries and among Arab citizens of Israel. Second, there

[6] Population Division of the Department of Economic and Social Affairs of the United Nations Secretariat. *World Population Prospects: The 2004 Revision; World Urbanization Prospects: The 2003 Revision.* http://www.esa.un.org/unpp; World Bank. *The Palestinian Economy and Prospects for Its Recovery, Economic Monitoring Report to the Ad Hoc Liaison Committee, Number 1,* December 2005.

is not the clear relationship between female education levels and fertility that has been noted worldwide. The Palestinian case does seem to be similar to that of Syria, which has been better documented. In Syria in the 1970s, fertility did not decline as education levels rose, because economic growth was accompanied by a lack of employment opportunities for women. Rising real wages for men limited the need for women to work outside the home. The decline in Syrian fertility rates since the early 1980s was due to the increased need for women to work outside the home. Education per se did not reduce fertility unless it was accompanied by an increase in employment. Furthermore, high fertility levels among the highly educated meant that there was little chance of the less educated being influenced to have fewer children by more successful sections of society, a factor that has been noted as having been significant elsewhere.[7]

In the Palestinian Territories, high fertility was the consequence of an early start to childbearing and very short intervals between births. Fertility rates were much higher than would have been expected given the levels of female education, infant mortality, and levels of population density (particularly in Gaza). One of the explanations for the persistently high rate is political: When the First *Intifada* began in 1987, fertility rates that had been declining, especially among more educated women in the West Bank, rose. In the 1990s, with the end of the First *Intifada* and prior to the outbreak of the second, it declined. There are several aspects to this. Many Palestinian men went to work in Israel, and women were left at home to look after the family usually from early in the morning until late in the evening, and sometimes for longer periods. The fact that men could earn much more by working in Israel than they did in agriculture at home reinforced the traditional role of women: they were not encouraged to extend their education or go to work outside the home. This created conditions that encouraged childbirth, or at least did not discourage the large numbers of births per woman that prevailed.

Many families received funds from relatives in the Gulf and large numbers who were classified as refugees received benefits from the United Nations Relief and Works Agency for Palestine Refugees in the Near East (UNRWA). In March 2006, 1.7 million people in the West Bank and Gaza were classified as refugees.[8] The prevalence of assistance, either private or public, meant

---

[7] Courbage, Youssef. "New Demographic Scenarios in the Mediterranean Region." Paris: National Institute of Demographic Studies. (Undated). http://www.ined.fr. Chapter 2, Section III.5.

[8] United Nations Relief and Works Agency (UNRWA). *Medium Term Plan 2005–2008.* http://www.un.org/unrwa/news/mtp.pdf.

that the additional costs of having children were limited. As economic conditions deteriorated, the disincentives to having children were therefore limited and this helps to explain the paradox of rising fertility rates during the First *Intifada* and the apparent stable, or near stable, rates during the Second *Intifada*. These factors make it easier to understand how population growth was related to the political struggle against Israel.[9]

During the twentieth century in much of the developing world, mortality fell much faster than fertility. As a result, the onset of demographic transition has been accompanied by fast population growth. This phenomenon was true of and in marked contrast to demographic transition in Europe, where the decline in fertility rates more closely paralleled that of mortality rates. The Arab Middle East is an extreme example of what happened in the Third World and the Palestinians, especially in Gaza, are the most extreme version of the Arab experience.[10]

Although demographic factors determine the quantity of labor, its quality is largely determined by the education system. There were major improvements in educational indicators during the period of Israeli rule. In 1970, the share of the West Bank population with thirteen or more years of education was 0.9 percent; in 1985 it reached 10 percent. The trend in Gaza was similar with a decline to 8.4 percent in 1992. Until the creation in 1994 of the Palestinian Authority, the small size of the public sector meant that employment possibilities for the better educated were limited.[11] This was one of the factors that encouraged the emigration of those with education. Those with skills left for the Gulf and for other parts of the world; those without worked in Israel.

The Labor Market

The rapid growth of the Palestinian population meant that the population of working age rose sharply. Those that found employment outside the home, or looked for work there, rose. As a result, the labor force increased. The working-age population increased from 521,000 in 1970 and to 1.90 million in 2005 (see Tables 9.1 and 9.3). The labor force rose from 147,000 in

[9] Pedersen, Jon, Sara Randall, and Marwan Khawaja (eds.). *Growing Fast: The Palestinian Population in the West Bank and the Gaza Strip*. Oslo: FAFO Institute for Applied Social Science, 2001. 118, 121; Fargues, Philippe. "Protracted National Conflict and Fertility Change: Palestinians and Israelis in the Twentieth Century." *Population and Development Review* 26, No. 3 (2000). 441–82.

[10] Pedersen, Randall, and Khawaja. 11.

[11] Arnon, Spivak, and Weinblatt. 70.

Table 9.3. *Employment of West Bank and Gaza residents, 1968–2005 (thousands)*

	Labor force	Total employment	Unemployed	Employed in West Bank and Gaza	Employed in Israel*	Employment in Israel as percentage of total
1968	146.5	135.0	19.1	130.0	5.0	3.7
1972	180.3	139.0	1.9	139.0	67.0	32.5
1975	206.7	139.0	1.9	139.0	67.0	32.5
1980	218.3	141.3	2.6	141.3	77.1	35.4
1985		153.6		153.6	89.5	34.4
1990		188.8		188.8	107.7	36.3
1993	430.6	232.1	29.0	232.1	84.0	26.6
1995	497.9	407.3	90.6	341.7	65.6	19.2
2000	695.0	596.0	100.0	479.0	116.0	19.5
2001	682.0	505.0	170.0	435.0	70.0	13.9
2002	707.0	474.0	216.0	424.0	49.0	10.3
2003	758.0	565.0	194.0	509.0	54.0	9.6
2004	790.0	578.0	212.0	527.0	50.0	8.7
2005	826.0	633.0	193.0	569.0	64.0	10.8

* Includes employment in Israeli settlements in the West Bank and Gaza.
Sources: Israel, *Central Bureau of Statistics, Publication No. 1012* (1996); *National Accounts of Judea, Samaria, and Gaza Area, 1968–1993*; and World Bank, "The Palestinian Economy and the Prospects for Its Recovery: Economic Monitoring Report to the Ad Hoc Liaison Committee," 2005; Arie Bregman, *Economic Growth in the Administered Areas 1968–1973*. Jerusalem: Bank of Israel, 1975; Arie Bregman, *Economic Growth in the Administered Territories 1974–1975*. Jerusalem: Bank of Israel, 1976; Dan Zakai, *Economic Development in Judea and Samaria 1983–1984*. Jerusalem: Bank of Israel, Research Department, 1986, Hebrew.

1968 to 826,000 in 2005, a 5.6-fold rise compared to a 3.6-fold increase in the working-age population. As in other Arab countries, the population of working age has grown faster than that of the total population. Because of emigration, this is not reflected in the population statistics as these only cover residents.

Since 1970, the reliance on employment in Israel meant that when – for security reasons – this was restricted, the economy suffered. Employment in Israel peaked in 1987, when 109,000 Palestinians were legally employed in Israel, equal to 39 percent of total Palestinian employment.[12] The trends since 1968 can be seen in Table 9.3. This shows the rapid increase from 1970 when the Israeli labor market was opened to Palestinian workers. They were attracted by the fact that there were jobs available and that those jobs

[12] Ibid. 75.

paid more than those at home. Since the late 1960s there have also been thousands of Palestinians who worked in Israel illegally.

The start of the First *Intifada* in December 1987 resulted in a fall in Palestinian employment in Israel. It ended in 1992, but terrorist attacks in Israel following the signing of the Oslo Accords led to restrictions on the movement of Palestinians into Israel (and their partial replacement by workers from the Far East and elsewhere). In the second half of 1993 approximately 315,000 were in the labor force (16 percent of the population). Of these, about 260,000 were in employment. Each Palestinian at work had to support an average of seven people. Half of the West Bank and Gaza population was less than age 15; the population became younger in the 1980s because of increasing fertility and declining child mortality. By 1995, some 66,000 Palestinians were employed in Israel and Israeli settlements in the West Bank and Gaza. This rose to a peak of 135,000 in 1999, but that represented only 12 percent of total employment. By 2002 the number had fallen to 49,000 or 9.6 percent of employment.[13] The jobs lost have not been made up elsewhere in the economy (see Table 6.3). Between 2000 and 2005, total employment increased by 37,000 of which that in the West Bank and Gaza grew by 88,000 while that in Israel fell by 52,000. The labor force rose by 131,000 and as a result unemployment increased by 94,000. (The figures do not add up because of rounding.)

By 2005, the population had reached 3.5 million, the labor force was about 790,000 (23 percent of the population) of whom 590,000 were in employment (75 percent of the labor force and 17 percent of the population). As a result, each Palestinian employed had to support an average of nearly six people.[14]

Although there have been fluctuations as a result of the Second *Intifada*, the labor force grew even faster than the working-age population because of an increase in labor force participation until 2000. Between 2001 and 2005, the labor-force participation rate fell from 40.9 percent to 38.6 percent although the labor force increased from 675,000 to 826,000, or 22 percent. Employment in Israel fell from 116,000 in 2000 to 64,000 in 2005, and that in the West Bank and Gaza fell from 435,000 to 241,000.[15] Female labor-force participation was much lower than in other Arab countries: in 2000

[13] World Bank. *The Palestinian Economy and the Prospects for Its Recovery, Economic Monitoring Report to the Ad Hoc Liaison Committee.* (2005). 9.

[14] World Bank. *West Bank and Gaza Country Economic Memorandum.* 1 Report No. 36320 WBG. Washington, D.C.: World Bank, 2006. 2.

[15] World Bank. *The Palestinian Economy and the Prospects for Its Recovery, Economic Monitoring Report to the Ad Hoc Liaison Committee.* 9.

it was only 13 percent, compared to 22 percent in Egypt and 40 percent in Morocco. (The participation rate is the ratio of the labor force to the working-age population.) The figure for Gaza was 10 percent.[16]

The Economy

Between 1968 and 1986 (the last year for which there is a single figure, rather than a range of estimates), the gross national product of the West Bank and Gaza, rose almost fivefold in real terms. As a result, GNP per capita increased by a factor of 3.38. Between 1986 and 1991, GNP rose by between 39 percent and 42 percent in real terms; GNP per capita by between 11 percent and 14 percent. The gap between GNP and GDP grew rapidly from 1968 as income earned in Israel played an increasingly important role (see Tables 8.3 and 8.4). The proportion of West Bank and Gaza income that came from abroad was significant. This rose from 3.3 percent of GDP in 1968 to 34 percent in 1986. Adding these receipts and also deducting payments made abroad from GDP gives the GNP. Then adding net transfers from abroad gives national disposable income. The latter increased by a factor of 4.1 between 1968 and 1986.

A macroeconomic overview suggests a major success story. Between 1968 and 1986, national disposable income (that includes aid from abroad), rose 3.8-fold (in real terms) in the West Bank and 4.2-fold in Gaza resulting in large increases in living standards. In fact, the economic development of the West Bank and Gaza has been much more problematic than this suggests. First, there has been a great deal of instability, especially since the mid-1980s. GDP fell in 1983, 1985, 1988, and 1991. Second, as has been pointed out, income and transfers from abroad played a much bigger role in the economy than they did in the late 1960s and 1970s, but were much more unstable than domestic production (see Table 9.4).

The volume of transfers reflects the large number of Palestinians who worked outside the West Bank and Gaza. In 1987, 109,000 worked in Israel (33 percent of the employed population in the West Bank and 45 percent in Gaza).[17] Many thousands of skilled Palestinians worked in the Gulf and in other parts of the world.

Fluctuations in GDP and GNP also reflected the political situation in the West Bank and Gaza. Between 1987 and 1992, the First *Intifada* affected every aspect of life. It resulted in continuous interruptions in the movement

---

[16] World Bank. *Long-Term Policy Options for the Palestinian Economy*. 2002. 34.
[17] World Bank. *Developing the Occupied Territories* 6. 1993. 8–12.

Table 9.4. *West Bank and Gaza: National income, 1968–1992 ($ millions, 1986 prices and exchange rates)*

	GDP	Net factor income from abroad	GNP	Net transfers from abroad	National disposable income
1968	463	4	467	146	613
1972	767	224	991	130	1,121
1975	909	284	1,193	63	1,256
1980	1,321	349	1,670	199	1,869
1985	1,350	417	1,767	103	1,870
1990	1,832	567	2,399	133	2,532
1992	2,275	743	3,018	n.a.	n.a.

Source: World Bank. *Developing the Occupied Territories, an Investment in Peace*, Vol. 2. Washington, D.C.: World Bank, 1993, 139; author's calculations.

of labor into Israel, sometimes because of strikes by the Palestinians, later because of closures by the Israelis. During the Gulf War in 1991, and again in 1993 and 1994, the West Bank and Gaza were closed and Palestinians were not allowed into Israel. Earned income fell sharply with effects throughout the economy. The *intifada* also included a boycott of goods and services from Israel. Although this was only partly effective, it did encourage moves toward Palestinian economic independence. This had hardly begun when Jordan renounced its claim to the West Bank and stopped paying the salaries of public-sector workers in the West Bank. Also the Jordanian dinar was devalued in 1988, further reducing the purchasing power of those who had income from Jordan or savings held in dinars. In the early 1990s, Israeli demand for Palestinian labor declined as immigrants from the former USSR and native Israelis were encouraged to work in the construction industry, both for security and economic reasons.

The Structure of the Economy

Changes in the structure of the economy are examined in Table 9.5. It shows that the share of agriculture declined continuously. This was due both to the growth of other sectors and to the restrictions imposed by Israel on land and water use by the Palestinians. (By 2006, Israeli settlements covered less than 3 percent of the 5,860 square kilometers of the West Bank, but their municipal areas covered up to 40 percent.)[18] Manufacturing output

[18] CIA. *Factbook*. http://www.cia/cia/publications/factbook/geos/we.html; http://www.peacenow.org.il.

Table 9.5. *Palestine: The structure of the economy: Shares of GDP, 1968–2005 (%)*

	1968	1980	1990	1995	2000	2005
Agriculture and fishing	37.0	29.8	38.2	13.0	9.2	10.6
Manufacturing	8.0*	6.4*	8.0*	18.5	13.4	14.4
Construction	5.0	18.1	15.7	6.9	6.3	8.4
Services	33.0	33.4	34.5	48.1	55.5	51.7
Public administration and defense	17.0	12.3	11.0	11.4	13.2	12.8

* Industry.
Source: 1969: Arie Bregman, *Economic Growth in the Administered Areas, 1968–1973.* Jerusalem: Bank of Israel, 1974; 1980–1990: World Bank, *Developing the Occupied Territories,* Vol. 2. Washington, D.C.: The World Bank, 1993; 1995–2005 World Bank, West Bank and Gaza Country Economic Memorandum, Volume 1, 2006, Report No. 36320WBG. http://www.worldbank.org.

grew, but not fast enough to take the place of agriculture. The service sector was large, but the decline in the share of public administration and defense after 1968 reflects differences in definitions in the sources used. In 1968, the main productive sectors, agriculture and industry, accounted for 45 percent of GDP whereas in 2005 it was only 25 percent. A decline in the share of agriculture is a feature of economies that are industrializing; in Palestine the growth of manufacturing industry was slow and its share *declined* after 1995.

Manufacturing

Although the share of manufacturing rose from 5.8 percent of GDP in 1968 to 14 percent in 2002, the depth of this development was limited: the size of enterprises remained small and their technological development slight.[19] In 1999, 73,000 were employed in manufacturing, or 12 percent of total employment.[20] The main reasons for the lack of industrialization after 1967 were Israeli restrictions and the fact that many Palestinians worked in Israel. Israeli policy was designed to protect its domestic industries from Palestinian competition. Wages were much lower in the West Bank and Gaza than in Israel and this was felt to be a real threat. Manufacturing was the most underdeveloped sector and in the early 1990s, most enterprises were small: 60 percent employed fewer than four people and only 7.5 percent

[19] Arnon, Spivak, and Weinblatt. 75; Mustafa Naquib, Fadle. "Economic and Social Commission for West Asia (ESCWA)." *Linking Aid to Development in the Current Palestinian Situation.* Beirut: ESCWA, 2004. 12.

[20] IMF: *West Bank and Gaza: Economic Performance and Reform under Conflict Conditions.* September 2003. 33.

employed more than ten people. Forty-three percent were owner-operated work shops. Little changed in the next decade: in 2002, 92 percent of firms in the manufacturing sector had fewer than ten employees.[21]

During the First *Intifada*, the investment rate was not high enough to cover depreciation; capacity utilization was low, at about 60 percent. This led to a fall in the contribution of industry to GDP. In 1987, industry accounted for 7.6 percent of GDP in the West Bank; in 1990 only 5.9 percent. In 1987 industry accounted for 13.9 percent of GDP in Gaza; in 1990, 12.2 percent. Between 1987 and 1990, industrial growth was either negative or zero. From 1991, with the easing of administrative restrictions, very slow growth restarted. Most firms were privately owned, family businesses. They were largely self-financing; bank credit was very limited. In 1991, there were 3,688 industrial enterprises in the West Bank and Gaza, 13 percent fewer than in 1987. The average monthly revenue per establishment was $10,750 in the West Bank and $5,150 in Gaza. Most firms reported that they operated in highly uncompetitive conditions: despite their existence over as long as twenty-seven years they were in an embryonic state. Competition between firms began to develop in the textile and leather industries. Industrial wages equaled about $2.8 million out of industrial revenues of $30 million. Industry in the West Bank and Gaza found it hard to recruit skilled workers because of the opportunities that, at least until 1990, existed for Palestinians in the Gulf.

The change in orientation of industry in the West Bank after 1967, from supplying Jordan to supplying Israel, was largely the result of restrictions imposed by Israel. Subcontracting in the textile, leather, and building materials industries was the way in which West Bank and Gaza firms entered the Israeli market. The main source of demand for these firms was the home market, followed by Israel (which was more important for larger firms) and finally Jordan and other Arab countries. Subcontracting for Israeli companies provided access to the relatively large Israeli market. (In the 1990s, Israel's GDP was twenty times as large as that of the West Bank and Gaza.) A lack of working capital was another important reason for continuing the relationship. Subcontractors benefited from access to Israeli technology with the advantage of higher-capacity utilization rates, higher profits, and low levels of working capital to total assets ratios, faster sales growth, and higher training allocations than other firms.

Industrial potential was not realized because of political uncertainty that resulted in low-capacity utilization and thus discouraged investment. The

[21] World Bank. *West Bank and Gaza Country Economic Memorandum*, 2006. 57.

regulatory environment was unpredictable and volatile and it restricted the free flow of goods, services, people, and information. Military restrictions limited access to new technology and machinery. Despite this, Palestinian firms had a number of significant competitive advantages. They used existing technology efficiently in manufacturing, demonstrated abilities to learn by doing, and increased the knowledge and skills of the labor force. In addition, they had detailed knowledge of local markets.

Agriculture

In the early 1960s agriculture accounted for about 40 percent of output and employment in the West Bank and Gaza. By 2000, both had shrunk to about 10 percent, largely because of increased employment in Israel. Since then the share of agriculture in employment has increased slightly as urban areas have become the centers of conflict and some Palestinians have returned to live in the villages.

The West Bank has an area of 5.86 million dunams (5,860 square kilometers). In the early 1990s, about 1.5 million dunams were cultivated and 230,000 were irrigated. Gaza has an area of 360,000 dunams of which Palestinians cultivated 165,000 dunams, two-thirds of which was irrigated. In 2006 Israel closed its civilian settlements in Gaza and as a result some 15,000 dunams of cultivated land (1 dunam equals 1,000 square meters) were added to Palestinian agriculture.[22]

The area available for agriculture has declined since 1967 due to economic and administrative factors. In the West Bank, Palestinians used 15–20 percent of water from aquifers shared with Israel. Improved technology has increased the efficiency of water use, but has not mitigated the loss of water to Palestinians. A growing number of farms in areas that lack irrigation survive because of the availability of cheap labor. Although much of this employment is not recorded, its output is. Traditionally, production was mainly for local markets with Gaza exporting citrus products to Jordan and other Arab countries since 1967. Exports have suffered from competition in Arab markets and from administrative restrictions by Israel, Jordan, and others. Production growth coupled with falling exports helped to lower prices on the domestic market. The *intifadas* also encouraged Palestinians to boycott Israeli products and switch, where possible, to Palestinian ones. This helped to stimulate production.

---

[22] World Bank. *Developing the Occupied Territories.* 4. Washington, D.C.: World Bank, 1993. xii–xvi.

Israel helped to develop Palestinian agriculture by making available much of its technology and technical expertise. Israel did not permit imports of Palestinian agricultural products until the implementation of the Paris Agreement in 1994. It also allowed Palestinians to use some of Israel's quotas to export agricultural commodities to the European Union from the mid-1990s.

Investment

After 1967, the Israeli authorities took responsibility for maintaining basic welfare and ensuring employment, but limited both taxation and government spending. They did not, however, set themselves to the task of developing the Palestinian economy. The Palestinian private sector was weak, both because it was undeveloped and because the political and economic environment did not encourage risk taking. The financial system was primitive and so savings could not easily be converted into funds that could be loaned to the private sector. The inadequacy of the financial system was one of the reasons why firms remained very small. Savings were channeled into housing: investment in construction (mainly housing) rose from 2.3 percent in the West Bank and 4.6 percent in Gaza in 1968 to about 15 percent in both areas in 1986–7. Under Israeli rule, public investment in the West Bank peaked at 6.5 percent of GDP in 1969 and in Gaza it peaked at 10 percent in 1975.[23] In 1987, housing accounted for 78 percent of private-sector investment and 68 percent of total investment. Public-sector investment was very low: in 1987 it equaled only 17 percent of total investment. Between 1987 and 1991, government investment fell by 32 percent.

In Gaza the investment pattern, like much else, was more extreme. Although in 1991 total investment accounted for about 25 percent of GDP, 80 percent of it was in housing. (In comparison, in 1991, during the height of Israel's construction boom that accompanied the huge immigration from the former USSR, housing accounted for 57 percent of total investment.) The very large share of housing in total investment in Gaza was a permanent feature of the economy after 1967. By 1991, housing accounted for 66 percent of total investment in the West Bank. Furthermore, the share of the public sector in total investment fell from 16 percent in 1987 to 16 percent in 1987. The combined effect of a weak private sector, political and economic uncertainty, and little government initiative meant that overall

[23] Calculated from Arnon, Spivak, and Weinblatt. 24, 122, 125.

investment levels were low. This meant that infrastructure development was limited and that economic growth was severely restricted.

The Oslo Agreement

In 1992 and 1993, Israeli and Palestinian negotiators held secret talks in Norway that led to the Declaration of Principles on Interim Self Government Arrangements (also known as the Oslo Agreement), signed on 13 September 1993 in the White House in Washington, D.C. It included mutual recognition: Israel recognized the Palestine Liberation Organization (PLO) as the legitimate representative of the Palestinian people and the PLO recognized Israel's right to exist. The declaration stated that negotiations would begin to establish a Palestinian Authority that would have limited powers for an interim period of five years. During that period a permanent settlement was planned to be reached. These negotiations were concluded with the Cairo Agreement of 4 May 1994. This defined the West Bank and Gaza as a single territory and began the first phase of Palestinian autonomy in Gaza and Jericho.

The Paris Protocol of 1994

An economic agreement between Israel and the PLO was signed in Paris in April 1994. It was largely determined by the political framework. As no border between Palestine and Israel was defined (an issue that was supposed to be determined later), the economic options were limited. A free-trade agreement (FTA), under which each party maintained its own external tariff, would have required a border between the two parties. This would have been needed to prevent imports into the party with the lower external tariff leaking into the one with the higher external tariff, given that no internal tariffs are possible in an FTA. As no border was fixed in the Oslo Agreement this option was rejected. Another option would have been complete separation (as has largely happened since 2000). This would also have required a border and would also have prevented Palestinians from working in Israel, something that the Palestinian negotiators in Paris were anxious to avoid. As a result, a customs union (in which the countries or parties in the union maintain a common external tariff and remove restrictions on trade between them), or something close to it, was the only option. Under the Paris Protocol, Israel and the Palestinian Authority were to have similar import policies. The Palestinian Authority was allowed to import mutually agreed-upon goods at customs rates differing from those prevailing in Israel and to import goods from Arab countries in agreed-upon limited quantities.

The agreement provided for the free movement of goods manufactured in the autonomous areas into Israel and vice versa. Agricultural produce from the autonomous areas could enter Israel freely for the first time, with limited and temporary exceptions for which there would be quotas. Tourists would be allowed to move freely between Israel and the autonomous areas. The Palestinian Authority was permitted to establish a monetary authority whose main functions would be the regulation and supervision of banks, but there would not be a Palestinian currency. The Palestinian Tax Administration would conduct its own direct tax policies. Israel would transfer to the Palestinian Authority 75 percent of the revenues from income tax collected from Palestinians employed in Israel. Israel would continue to collect import duties on goods destined for the Palestinian Authority but would transfer those funds to the Authority. A value-added tax (VAT) would be operated by the Palestinian Authority with rates up to 3 percent higher or lower than in Israel. Finally, Israel agreed to keep its labor market open for Palestinian workers, while reserving the right to place restrictions on the inflow for security reasons.[24]

Critiques of the Paris Protocol

There have been a range of critiques of the Paris Protocol by Palestinians, Israelis, and others. One Palestinian critique was that the protocols served tactical political interests: They were designed to support the political agreements that gave the Palestinians autonomy in limited areas of the West Bank and Gaza. It was not clear whether peace would bring about improvements in the Palestinian standard of living or vice versa. In the end neither was achieved. The mechanics of the protocol also enabled Israel to avoid transferring funds fairly to the Palestinians and, as a result, the stronger side had the capability to bankrupt the weaker one. Although a full political agreement was not necessarily a precondition for economic success, the economic agreement needed to be fairer and more equal if it was to support political moves toward a final settlement.[25] Another critique was made by two Israelis. They stated that the agreement was drawn up on the basis of

---

[24] Israel, Ministry of Foreign Affairs. http://www.mfa.gov.il.
[25] Kanafani, Nu'man. "Economic Foundations for Peace" in Hakimian, Hassan and Jeffrey B. Nugent (eds.), *Trade Policy and Economic Integration in the Middle East and North Africa*. London: Routledge Curzon, 2004. 271–89.

political (and economic) inequality between the parties and in effect froze them in that inequality. The economic agreement did not take into account Palestinian political aspirations. It set custom duties at rates that suited Israel rather than Palestine (or at rates weighted by their relative needs). It enabled Israel to close its labor market to Palestinians when security concerns prevailed, leaving the Palestinians without control over either their trade or employment. It was what has been called an "incomplete contract," because it failed to specify what was to happen in all contingencies. This was not because the political agreements were transitory and designed to be followed by negotiations on final status agreements, but because they did not specify what was to happen in all eventualities. As a result, the Paris Protocol was doomed. Although a full political agreement did not have to precede economic agreements, the latter required major political changes for it to succeed.[26]

Between 1967 and 1994, the trading pattern between Israel and the West Bank and Gaza partly resembled that between the Arab states in the Mediterranean with European Union (EU) partnership agreements and the EU. The main Arab–Palestinian export (agricultural products) was restricted, or even banned, while the main EU–Israeli export (industrial goods) was permitted. In the case of the EU, this was implemented immediately; in the case of Israel it was implemented from 1967. Palestinian industry was fully exposed to Israeli competition while its agricultural production was barred from Israeli markets until 1994. Although the Paris Protocol opened Israeli markets to Palestinian produce, the extremely weak state of Palestinian industry meant that it had little to export. Furthermore, in the early 1990s, Israel liberalized its foreign trade, which meant that Chinese and other cheap sources entered its markets, making it harder for the Palestinians to compete.

The Palestinian Authority

The Palestinian National Authority, usually known as the Palestinian Authority (PA) was established in May 1994 following the Declaration of Principles signed by Israel and the Palestinian Liberation Organization in September 1993. It took control of Gaza and Jericho in May 1994 and of other West Bank towns in December 1995. The way in which it has functioned since then has added another set of obstacles to economic development, the first of which was the increase in public-sector employment.

[26] Arnon, A. and J. Weinblatt. "Sovereignty and Economic Development: The Case of Palestine." *Economic Journal* Vol 111, number 472 (June 2001). F291–F308.

In 1993, the last full year of Israeli direct rule in the West Bank and Gaza, the civil administration had 22,000 employees, 95 percent of whom were Palestinian.[27] By 1999, this had increased to 104,000 in central government alone, of whom 49,300 were employed in the security forces. Between 1995 and 1999, the number of civil servants doubled, and by the end of June 2003 had risen by a further 13 percent, despite the *intifada*. The rise was partly because of the very limited provision of public services by Israel, but was also due to the expansion of the public sector in transparent and nontransparent ways by the PA. By the second quarter of 2006, there were more than 142,000 government employees, of whom 81,000 were civilian and 61,000 were security.[28] In addition, the United Nations Relief and Works Agency (UNRWA) had 14,000 employees who provided health and education services to the 42 percent of the population that was officially classified as refugees. UNRWA's employees were nearly all Palestinian.[29]

The PA's economic policies were notable in two other respects. According to the IMF, from the outset of the Oslo peace process and the creation of the PA, significant volumes of revenue did not go through the PA's budget: petroleum tax revenues were transferred to an account in an Israeli bank under the joint control of Arafat and his financial advisor Mohammad Rachid. Tobacco and alcohol excises collected by the PA, as well as revenues from PA monopolies and other commercial activities, were also channeled to accounts outside the Palestinian ministry of finance. This lasted from 1995 until 2000 and the total volume of revenues diverted equaled $591 million.[30] The diverted revenues were largely invested in commercial activities owned by the PA. These generated profits that were also diverted away from the budget. In the period 1995–2000, excise revenues and profits from commercial organizations that were diverted away from the budget were estimated by the IMF at $898 million.[31] In addition, the various security forces were told to raise part of their funding by charging for border crossings into Israel, something that added to transport costs and created a bandit-like atmosphere.

The second feature of the Palestinian economy in the 1990s was the emergence of PA-sponsored private monopolies. The monopoly in the supply of cement had its origins in that held by the Israeli company Nesher during

[27] World Bank. *Developing the Occupied Territories: An Investment in Peace.* 1. VIII.
[28] IMF: *West Bank and Gaza, Recent Fiscal and Financial Developments, October 2006.* 10.
[29] IMF. *West Bank and Gaza, Economic Performance and Reform under Conflict Conditions,* 2003. 91, 92.
[30] Ibid. 88.
[31] Ibid. 91.

Israeli rule. (Nesher also had a monopoly of the Israeli cement market.) Nesher's monopoly was transferred to the PA, with the ostensible aim of providing it with quasi-fiscal revenues.

The Palestinian Commercial Services Company (PCSC) was a government-owned, private-sector holding firm that owned the cement and other monopolies. Its chairman was Yasser Arafat, chairman of the PA. The PCSC was the organizational predecessor of the Palestine Investment Fund. PCSC's investment portfolio included interests in a wide range of economic sectors, including hospitality/tourism, insurance, construction, real estate, power utilities, telecommunications, consumer products, aviation, and aviation-facilities management. Its holdings and investment-management activities were designed to lay the groundwork for the creation of profitable economic partnership between the Palestinian public and private sectors and the international investment community. In 2000, and more significantly in 2002, the PA enacted reforms in the budget process and in the way in which monopolies were controlled.

In 1996, the petroleum monopoly was transferred from the Israeli company DOR to the Palestinian Petroleum Commission. Although the Petroleum Commission was meant to act as a regulatory agency, it sold products in the West Bank and Gaza with an exclusive contract with DOR. Petroleum prices were similar to those in Israel, while there were reports of fraud, extortion, and smuggling at much lower prices.[32] In 2005, petrol prices were subsidized by $98 million, the cost being born by the PA.[33]

In the early years of the PA, the economy performed badly. In 1994–6, gross national income per capita fell by an annual average of 7.8 percent. This was because of the fall in earnings of Palestinian workers as a result of security-led closures of the labor market in Israel. An increase in foreign aid and higher spending by the PA partly mitigated the effects of the fall in earnings. In 1997–9 there was a recovery and income per capita rose by an annual average rate of 4.9 percent.[34]

The Budget

After 1967, the Israeli authorities took over responsibility for economic management in the West Bank and Gaza. As has been said, public-sector

---

[32] Ibid. 103–4.
[33] World Bank. *West Bank and Gaza Public Expenditure Review*, Report No. 38207-WBG. 2007. 11.
[34] Arnon, and Weinblatt. F291–F308.

investment was very limited, but between 1968 and 1994 public-sector consumption declined. As a result, in the West Bank public investment and consumption fell from a peak of 24.5 percent of GDP in 1969 to 10.6 percent in 1994. In Gaza, where investment levels were higher, it fell from a peak of 30.3 percent in 1969 to a low of 14.2 percent in 1992. The limited nature of public-sector activity meant that the infrastructure was grossly neglected and the private sector was not encouraged either through demand for its services or by specific incentives, such as prevailed in Israel. In a broader sense, budgetary policies as well as monetary and trade policies were not designed with development in mind. They were designed to maintain basic services and prevent competition with Israel.[35]

From 1994, the revenues of the PA came from several sources. First, it collected taxes within the territories under its authority. Second, it received what were called clearance revenues that Israel collected on its behalf under the Paris Protocol. These were customs duties on foreign goods entering Palestinian Territories via its airports and ports and value-added tax on Israeli goods sold in the PA. These revenues were transferred on a monthly basis to the PA and formed a large share of total revenues. The outbreak of the Second *Intifada* in the autumn of 2000 had dramatic effects on the PA's revenues. Between July and December 1999, PA revenues fell by 50 percent as a result of the fall in the movement of goods in and out of the West Bank and Gaza. In December 2000, Israel suspended the transfer-of-clearance payments until late in 2002. (These payments were suspended again in 2006 following the installation of the Hamas-led government.) In 2003, there was an economic recovery and by December of that year, monthly revenues had reached their pre-*intifada* level for the first time. Israel then deducted funds owed by Palestinian local authorities for electricity, water, and sewage from the clearance payments. The $5 billion of assistance that the Palestinians received in 1994–9, $300 per capita annually, was the highest granted anywhere since World War II.

In 1999, domestic revenues accounted for only 38 percent of total revenues. This was because the PA imported most of its needs via Israel and the latter collected taxes for it. It also reflected the importance of employment in Israel as a source of income that was taxed there. Since then, total revenues have fallen even with the restoration of tax payments by Israel on goods imported via Israel to the PA. The share of wages in spending increased and this helped to push up total spending as did pensions and subsidies (nonwage expenditures). Under the PA, there has been virtually

[35] Arnon, Spivak, and Weinblatt. 122, 125, 136.

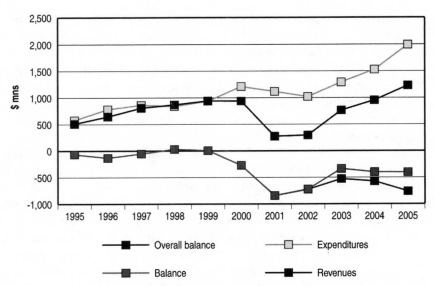

Figure 9.1. Palestine: Palestinian Authority Budget, 1995–2005. *Source:* World Bank, West Bank and Gaza Public Expenditure Review Volume 2, Report No. 38207-WBG, 2007.

no investment. Foreign aid has played a major role but has not prevented economic collapse. By 2003 the public sector accounted for 26 percent of all employment and 34 percent of wages paid. The share of the public wage bill in GDP was 15.2 percent and in the budget 49 percent, by far the highest shares in the Middle East.[36]

The fiscal position became untenable as a result of increasing government spending that outpaced the rise in revenues (see Figure 9.1). Spending on wages, pensions, and utility bills to Israeli providers (mainly electricity) and to Palestinian local authorities has risen sharply. In 2005, the budget deficit, after allowing for foreign aid, came to $406 million, about 11 percent of GDP. In 2006, revenues collected by the PA fell sharply and banks reduced their credit lines to the PA. The decline in revenues was partly offset by an increase in foreign aid. Most of this came from Arab donors and additional amounts were given by other countries. The total volume of foreign aid received in 2006 was reported at $1.2 billion, compared with $1 billion in 2005, despite the international embargo of the Hamas government. Some $740 million was in direct budgetary support, more than double the amounts received in 2004 and 2005. In addition, funds – estimated at more than

[36] World Bank. *West Bank and Gaza Public Expenditure Review.* Report No. 38207-WBG. 2007. 2.

$100 million – have been received in cash from Arab countries and Iran, including cash smuggled in by Hamas officials.[37]

Effects of the Second *Intifada*

At the end of September 2000, armed conflict between the Palestinians in the West Bank and Gaza and Israel broke out. Since then, thousands of Palestinians and Israelis have been killed and wounded and there has been extensive damage to the Palestinian infrastructure. According to the World Bank, between 2000 and 2004, Palestinian society lost its economic dynamism and experienced a recession of historical proportions. As a result, the strong social cohesion cracked, and the PA lost credibility and control in several parts of Gaza and the West Bank.[38]

As well as the loss of nongovernment employment, incomes have fallen and there has been widespread physical destruction. These effects are summarized in Figure 9.1. It shows that the large fall in income in 2001–02 was followed by an improvement in 2003–05. GDP in 2005 was estimated to be 13 percent lower than in 1999 and GDP per capita, 35 percent lower. In the first three quarters of 2006, there was a further fall in GDP estimated at 5–6 percent on an annual basis[39] (see Figure 9.2). The reasons for the fall in GDP were the collapse in government revenues following the installation of the Hamas government and the fall in labor incomes earned in the West Bank, Gaza, and in Israel because of Israeli restrictions on movement within the West Bank and between Israel, the West Bank, and Gaza.

The Hamas Government, 2006

Following its victory in the January 2006 general elections, the Islamic Fundamentalist Hamas party formed a government. The new government refused to accept the Oslo Agreement or recognize Israel. This led to a boycott by the international community and the withholding of aid to the Palestinian government. Also, Israel withheld the refund of taxes collected on behalf of the PA. These measures led to a drastic fall in revenues, partly ameliorated by the transfer of funds to organizations not controlled by Hamas, such as the Temporary International Mechanism and the office of President Mahmud Abbas. Following the withdrawal of all Israeli

[37] *New York Times*. 21 March 2007.
[38] World Bank. *27 Months: Intifada, Closure, and Palestinian Economic Crisis: An Assessment.* 2002. 16, Table 31. http://www.worldbank.org.
[39] World Bank. *West Bank and Gaza Public Expenditure Review*. 2.

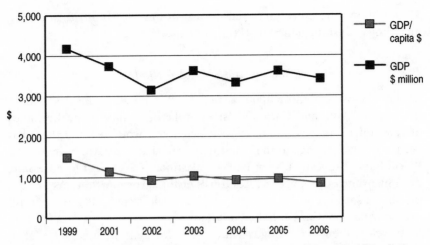

Figure 9.2. Palestine: GDP and GDP per Capita, 1999–2006. *Source:* World Bank: Four Years-*Intifada,* Closures and Palestinian Economic Crisis, October 2004 and World Bank, The Palestinian Economy and Prospects for Its Recovery, Economic Monitoring Report to the Ad Hoc Liaison Committee, Number 1, December 2005; IMF: Macroeconomic Developments and Outlook in the West Bank and Gaza, 2005; United Nations Economic and Social Commission for West Asia, Estimates for GDP Growth in the ESCWA Region Document No. E/ESCWA/EAD/2007/Technical Material. 2007. 1.

settlements from the Gaza Strip in the summer of 2005, the Israeli army left and the area reverted to Palestinian control. Palestinian rocket attacks on Israel and on border crossing points (including those designed as joint Israeli–Palestinian industrial zones) led Israel to close the border with Gaza, thereby preventing the movement of people and limiting trade. This had severe effects on the economy in Gaza. The situation in the West Bank was less severe. At the beginning of 2006, the Palestinian Authority, which was the largest employer in the territories, faced a fiscal crisis that resulted in it being unable to pay the salaries of its officials and security staff. Failure to make the salary payment in full and on time affected hundreds of thousands of people and it swelled the number of unemployed.

International aid has increasingly been used to support Palestinians, including the payment of wages to thousands of PA employees. Very little has been spent on development and there are increasing anxieties that a culture of dependence has been created. Given that by 2007, almost 50 percent of Gaza's population was unable to feed itself without aid, this was a very real danger.[40]

---

[40] *New York Times,* 21 March 2007.

Conclusions

There is widespread, if not universal, agreement on the need to create a Palestinian state in the West Bank and Gaza. This will require maximal territorial continuity: Complete contiguity will not be possible because the West Bank and Gaza are separated by Israeli territory. Given the geographic division between Gaza and the West Bank, contiguity within the latter is even more important. Israeli settlements in the West Bank and the roads leading to them threaten this.

The Palestinian economy needs to grow to survive for several reasons. First is the rapid growth of the population: Palestine will have to provide for natural population growth and also for immigration. The population is growing by more than 3 percent a year. Assuming that the "right of return" will be activated within a future Palestinian state, those most likely to take it up are the more than 300,000 refugees in Lebanon whose status is inferior to that of Palestinian refugees in any other Arab country. This return will pose major challenges in terms of providing basic services and employment. The United Nations, in its 2004 population forecast, predicted that the Palestinian population in the West Bank and Gaza will increase by 17 percent to 4.33 million by 2010 with major immigration.

The second challenge is unemployment. The *intifada* has wreaked havoc on the labor market. Employment in Israel has dried up and the economy in the West Bank, and even more so in Gaza, has been damaged to such an extent that thousands of jobs have been lost. Unemployment averaged 40 percent in 2006. Furthermore, the growth of the population adds thousands of young people to the labor force every year. Unemployment among the young is even higher, as in the rest of the Arab world, with severe social and political consequences. Between 1999 and 2003, the labor force grew by about 4.5 percent a year, or 30,000. That is the number of jobs that have to be created to prevent unemployment rising, assuming that the participation rate does not change. In 2004, 48 percent of the population lived in poverty, defined as not having enough income for the basics of survival. This equaled more than 1.7 million people. The third reason why growth is an imperative is that the new state will operate in a competitive environment.

In 2003, gross national income per capita in the West Bank and Gaza was 44 percent lower than in Jordan and 15 percent lower than in Egypt.[41] This suggests that wages were lower than in the neighboring Arab states, giving the Palestinians a competitive advantage. This cost advantage has

[41] World Bank. *World Development Indicators.* http://devdata.worldbank.org/data-query.

been outweighed by the damage to Palestinian infrastructure. A future Palestinian state also faces competition from cheap sources of supply in South, East, and Southeast Asia. In December 2004, Egypt, Israel, and the United States signed an agreement on the creation of eight Qualified Industrial Zones (QIZs) in Egypt. The agreement permits goods made in Egypt, with a specified minimum Israeli content, to enter the United States without import duties. At present, in the absence of a free-trade agreement between Egypt and the United States, Egyptian exports to the United States are subject to duties and other restrictions. The QIZ agreement has made possible the creation of thousands of jobs in Egypt and has expanded industrial exports, two vital needs of the Egyptian economy. It follows the creation of similar QIZs in Jordan that have greatly benefited the Jordanian economy. Israel and Jordan both have free-trade agreements (FTAs) with the United States. Jordan's FTA, which came into effect in December 2001, together with the operation of QIZs, has led to a dramatic increase in Jordanian exports to the United States.[42]

Economic viability means growth in real income and growth at a rate that will reduce unemployment. This will not be easy to achieve. Another condition for long-term viability is economic independence: Palestine will need to avoid reliance on both the export of labor and on imports of capital, with the exception of foreign investment. A precondition is the improvement in governance. Closely related to this is the question of centralization. As far as is possible, the private sector should be encouraged to develop without the kinds of links to government that existed in the past and that had such disastrous effects in, for example, South Korea: what has become known as crony capitalism. The government will have to be involved in economic development because the challenges facing the economy are so great. Furthermore, the infrastructure is weak as a result of years of neglect and war damage.

Palestine will have to become an exporter of goods and services. This will take time and until it happens there will be a severe shortage of employment and income. It is unlikely that Israel will allow substantial numbers of Palestinians to work in its economy. The easy option of exporting labor to Israel was a function of the occupation: Israel did not permit industrialization out of fear that Palestinian goods, with free access to Israeli markets, would undercut Israeli ones. Only after the signing of the Oslo Accords did the Israeli authorities issue licenses for some factories to be set up.

---

[42] Rivlin, Paul. "The Economics and Politics of the Egypt–Israel Trade Agreement." December 2004. *Tel Aviv Note.* No. 119. http://www.dayan.org.

In exchange for continued free access to Israeli markets for labor and goods, the Palestinians signed a customs union agreement in Paris in 1995. This meant that all goods imported into Palestine were charged the same rate of customs duties as Israel charged. As Palestinian labor no longer has access to the Israeli labor market this quid pro quo no longer holds. If Palestine wishes to open its borders to imports from countries other than Israel, and not charge Israeli rates of customs duties, then an economic border will have to be set up between Israel and Palestine. This could be one that involves Palestinian goods having duty-free access to Israel and vice versa.

Palestine has lost much, if not all, of its middle class. In order to develop it will need to attract it back. The most powerful incentive is the economic one: the opportunities that development offers. This will require very careful implementation of government policies: incentives without domination, another challenge facing the future state. The option exists because the human capital and entrepreneurial skills exist, although at present much is abroad. Whether there is the will to provide economic space and freedom remains to be seen.

TEN

Saudi Arabia

Oil Wealth and Unemployment

Saudi Arabia's economic development is perhaps the most dramatic in the Middle East. Since the early 1970s, it has been transformed from a backward and isolated desert kingdom to the largest economy in the region with massive oil income, investment projects, and financial reserves. Between 1970 and 2005 the national income increased nearly eightfold, while the population grew more than fourfold, from nearly six million to over 25 million (see Table 10.1).

Rapid economic growth has had mixed results in terms of development and one of the consequences is that Saudi Arabia now suffers from a high rate of unemployment. In the 1970s and early 1980s, oil income was used to develop the social and economic infrastructure and create a huge bureaucracy. Saudis were encouraged to have large families because it was believed that the country's large geographical area and oil resources could not be defended with such a small population. Population growth was accompanied by urbanization, especially in the largest cities. In 1960, 30 percent of the population was urbanized; by 2000, the share was 86 percent.[1] Improved health services had dramatic, beneficial effects on longevity and infant mortality and thus on the size of the population. In the 1970s and 1980s, increased oil wealth was channeled in ways that maintained loyalty to the regime. This loyalty depended on a continuous flow of funds, and the role of key families was crucial. They were rewarded with business contracts so the oil wealth did not undermine the social structure. Social and educational services were provided free to the population and many well-paid jobs became available in the public sector.

In the early stages of this development the population and the economy remained small; tribal leaders played a key role in distributing largesse

---

[1] UN. *World Population Prospects: The 2004 Revision.* http://www.un.org.

Table 10.1. *Saudi Arabia: Population and dependency ratios, 1950–2005*

	Population (millions)	Working-age population	Dependent population	Dependency ratio*
1950	3.20	1.75	1.45	83
1960	4.08	2.17	1.91	87
1970	5.75	3.01	2.74	91
1980	9.60	5.08	4.52	89
1990	16.38	9.07	7.31	79
1995	18.25	10.24	8.01	78
2000	21.45	12.34	9.11	69
2005	24.57	14.80	9.77	60

* The total dependency ratio is the ratio of the sum of the population aged 0–14 and that aged 65+ to the population aged 15–64. This is expressed as number of dependents per 100 persons of working age (15–64).

Source: Population Division of the Department of Economic and Social Affairs of the United Nations Secretariat. *World Population Prospects: The 2004 Revision* and *World Urbanization Prospects: The 2003 Revision.* http://esa.un.org/unpp.

and maintaining political stability. The government was able to allocate resources using traditional means, reinforcing traditional patterns of control in society. Over time, however, the population and the economy became too big for traditional systems and the bureaucracy played an increasing role in allocating resources.[2] Power also moved from the western Hijaz region of the two holy cities of Mecca and Medina to the central Najd region that included the capital, Riyadh.[3] There were two threats to economic, social, and political stability: sharp fluctuations in oil revenues and growing unemployment, especially among young people. These are the main themes of this chapter.

Demographic Developments

Between 1950–5 and 1980–5, annual population growth accelerated from 2.31 percent to 5.87 percent. This was the result of improvements in health, the development of the economy, and then, in the 1970s and 1980s, of pro-natal policies adopted by the government. The extent of change was manifest in the urbanization of the population. In 1950, 82.5 percent of the population was rural; in 2005 only 11.5 percent. Life expectancy for both

[2] Aziz Chadhry, Karen. *The Price of Wealth.* Ithaca and London: Cornell University Press, 1997. 140.

[3] Champion, Daryl. *The Paradoxical Kingdom.* London: C. Hurst, 2003. 91–2.

Table 10.2. *Saudi Arabia: Demographic trends, 1980–2005*

	1980–5	1985–90	1990–5	1995–2000	2000–05
Population change per year (thousands)	655	700	461	560	618
Population growth rate % p.a.	5.87	4.81	2.63	2.80	2.69
Crude birthrate per 1,000 of population	41.0	38.2	34.6	31.2	28.5
Crude death rate per 1,000 of population	7.6	5.7	4.6	4.1	3.9
Total fertility rate (children per woman)	7.05	6.26	5.65	4.86	4.09

Source: Population Division of the Department of Economic and Social Affairs of the United Nations Secretariat. *World Population Prospects: The 2004 Revision* and *World Urbanization Prospects: The 2003 Revision.* http://esa.un.org/unpp.

sexes rose from 39.9 years in 1950 to 70.5 years in 1995–2000. The total fertility rate (number of births per woman) rose from a very high 7.18 in 1950–5 to a peak of 7.30 in 1970–5 and fell to 4.09 by 2000–05. The size of the total population was also a function of immigration: large numbers of foreign workers were imported to fill vacancies in the economy first from the Arab world and then from East and Southeast Asia. (It should be noted that UN and official Saudi population estimates vary; this is reflected in the difference of nearly 900,000 in the figures for 2000 shown in Tables 10.1 and 10.2.)

The population is now growing at about 2.7 percent a year, one of the fastest rates in the world. Another important consequence of demographic growth is the large share of young people in the population. In 2005, about 40 percent of the population was 14 years old or younger; almost 56 percent was 24 years old or younger.[4] Demographic transition is, however, taking place: between 1995 and 2005, the total population increased by 34.6 percent, the working-age population by 44.5 percent, and the dependent population by almost 22 percent (see Table 10.1).

Immigration

The import of workers has been a major characteristic of the Saudi economy since the oil boom of the 1970s. There were several sources of labor. First, skilled workers came from developed countries and were involved in large development projects, such as the construction of airports, hospitals, and housing. They worked on turnkey projects that foreign companies carried out for the Saudi government. Some left when the projects were completed

[4] UN. *World Population Prospects: The 2004 Revision.*

Table 10.3. *The Saudi population by origin,*
1974–2005 (millions)

	Total	Saudi citizens	Foreigners
1974	7.01	6.22	0.79
1995	18.23	13.25	4.98
2000	20.57	14.98	5.59
2001	21.08	15.35	5.73
2002	21.60	15.74	5.86
2003	22.13	16.13	6.00
2004	22.67	16.53	6.14
2005*	23.23	16.94	6.29

* Estimate.

Source: SAMBA.org and National Commercial Bank, *Market Review and Outlook.* 26 April 2005.

while others stayed to run them. Another group was those who were needed for their Arabic language skills, such as teachers. In addition, huge numbers of unskilled workers were imported, initially from Arab countries. As a result of political tensions between Arab countries following the Iraqi invasion of Kuwait, Saudi Arabia increased imports of workers from outside the region at the expense of Arab workers in 1990. In 1990–1, hundreds of thousands of Yemeni workers were expelled from Saudi Arabia as a result of Yemen's support of Saddam Hussein following the Iraqi invasion of Kuwait. Migrants from South and Southeast Asia now form the bulk of the immigrant workforce and together with their families, form the majority of foreign residents.

The Labor Market

Table 10.3 shows that in 2005, foreigners accounted for an estimated 27 percent of the population; 74 percent of foreigners or 4.55 million were of working age (aged 15–64), while only 51 percent or 8.44 million were Saudis. The total labor force of 12.99 million consisted of 65 percent foreigners and only 35 percent Saudis. When a calculation of actual employment is made, the Saudi share shrinks even further. There were 6.1 million in employment in 2005, of whom 1.3 million were Saudis (21 percent) and 4.8 million were foreigners (79 percent).

Table 10.4 shows how the employment of Saudis has concentrated in the service and government sectors and foreigners are concentrated in the

Table 10.4. *Saudi Arabia: Employment, 2004–2005*

	2004	%	2005	%	2004–05 change %
Public sector	763,265	100	783,276	100	2.6
Saudis	694,494	91	712,835	91	2.6
Non-Saudis	68,771	9	70,441	9	2.4
Private sector	4,648,530	100	5,362,288	100	1.4
Saudis	485,726	10.4	623,465	11.6	28.4
Non-Saudis	4,162,804	89.6	4,738,823	88.4	13.4
Total	5,411,795	100	6,145,564	100	13.6
Saudis	1,180,220	21.8	1,336,300	21.7	13.2
Non-Saudis	4,231,575	78.2	4,809,264	78.3	13.7

Source: Economist Intelligence Unit, Country Profile, Saudi Arabia, February 2007. 26.

production sector. The government has been the major source of employment for Saudi citizens. In 1970, it employed 97,000 Saudis and 20,000 non-Saudis. By 1980, the number had risen by nearly 90 percent to 183,500 Saudis and 69,000 non-Saudis. In the 1980s, the growth rate was even faster: the employment of Saudis rose by 148 percent. In the 1990s, as recession hit the economy, the growth rate slowed and public-sector employment rose by 59 percent. A further deceleration occurred in the beginning of the current century. By 2004 there were more than 760,000 employed in the public sector, 91 percent of whom were Saudi citizens (see Table 10.4). This occurred in a country that did not adopt socialism as an economic policy, but in which the state played a key role. The growth of the civil service represented a form of welfare system for Saudis and a basis for maintaining loyalty to the regime.

Saudi employment figures should be treated with caution, but Table 10.4 shows that foreigners dominated employment, especially in the largest sector: the private sector. The one optimistic figure in Table 10.4 is the rapid growth of Saudis employed in the private sector (again we should be cautious because these figures only compare two years). The employment of non-Saudis grew at a much lower, but still considerable rate.

Table 10.5 provides a breakdown of private-sector employment. It shows that the two sectors – agriculture and manufacturing – that have been the main sources of economic development in most of the world provided only 16 percent of total employment. Saudis accounted for more than 8 percent of the employment in these two sectors.

During the period 1994–2004, the service sector dominated employment, while industry and agriculture accounted for about 16 percent. Outside oil,

Table 10.5. *Saudi Arabia: Private-sector employment, 2005*

	Saudis	Non-Saudis
Agriculture, forestry, fishing	8,261	371,839
Mining, oil, natural gas, and quarrying	53,558	26,212
Manufacturing	72,889	539,677
Electricity, gas, water	13,631	16,308
Construction	170,386	1,773,084
Wholesale and retail trade	158,268	1,257,084
Transport and communications	19,533	105,418
Financial services, insurance, real estate	28,457	65,483
Social services	91,782	533,789
Other	6,710	52,839
Total	623,465	4,738,823

Source: *Middle East Economic Digest*, 20–26 April 2007.

refining, and petrochemicals, the development of industry was limited. Agriculture was also limited by harsh natural conditions. As a result, consumption was largely met by imports. This is one of the reasons why the service sector was so large. In 1994, foreigners accounted for more than 60 percent of civilian employment. In 1999, their share was 56 percent and by 2004 it had fallen to almost 47 percent. The Seventh Development Plan, for the period 2000–05, envisaged the creation of 328,600 new jobs and the replacement of about 490,000 non-Saudis by Saudis in the labor market.[5]

The labor-force participation rate among Saudi citizens is one of the lowest in the Arab world. In 1999, the overall rate was officially estimated at 19 percent, compared with a Middle East average of 33 percent. Among men it was 32 percent, compared with a Middle East average of 49 percent and among women, only 6 percent compared with a Middle East average of 17 percent. These very low rates were made possible by the presence of millions of foreign workers who had very high participation rates. Imported skilled labor was required to construct large infrastructure projects and then to run them. Unskilled labor was required to do the many jobs that Saudis did not want or could not do.

In 1999, unemployment among Saudi citizens was officially estimated at 8.1 percent (or about 225,000); in 2002 it was 9.66 percent.[6] A credible, unofficial estimate for 2002 was that unemployment among men was

---

[5] Ministry of Planning. *Saudi Human Development Report 2003.* 84–5. http://www.planning.gov.sa.

[6] Saudi Arabian Monetary Agency. *Annual Report 2005.* http://www.sama.sa.

11.9 percent. During the period 2000–02, 175,000 new jobs were created while 340,000 males entered the job market. Male unemployment therefore rose by 165,000 or by 55,000 a year and reached 450,000 in 2002. The number of jobs created is likely to have increased as a result of the boom in the economy of recent years and so the annual increase in unemployment is likely to have decelerated, but the gap has not been eliminated. This assumes that the female participation rate did not rise significantly.[7] In 2004, unemployment among Saudi citizens was officially estimated at 6.9 percent and in 2006 at 9.6 percent.[8]

Why is unemployment so high? The first reason is the low demand for labor in an economy that relies so much on oil. The oil industry has very limited employment capacity as do the large refining and petrochemical sectors. The growth of manufacturing, which is more employment-intensive, has been limited by, among other things, Dutch Disease effects. This refers to the situation in which the strong balance of payments that has resulted from oil wealth has resulted in a relatively strong exchange rate. This has been one of the factors encouraging imports and discouraging non-oil exports. One key result is that manufacturing has been discouraged, limiting employment growth.

On the supply side there are a number of factors. First, many Saudis have inappropriate or inadequate skills. This is highlighted in the subjects chosen by university students: in 2004, only 9 percent of Saudi graduates qualified in science or technology. Of these, 1 percent qualified in engineering and related subjects. These were the lowest figures for science and technology graduates in the Arab world and compared with 19 percent in Bahrain, 29 percent in Iraq, 25 percent in Jordan, 22 percent in Lebanon, and 19 percent in Morocco. In absolute terms, the number of Saudi graduates in 2004 was 81,868 and the number in engineering was only 817.[9] Two-thirds of Saudi students graduate with degrees in the humanities for which there is an oversupply in the labor market.[10] Second, Saudi citizens preferred to work in the public sector where salaries, benefits, and social status are all higher than in manufacturing or other private-sector employment. As a result, manufacturing and many other parts of the private sector employ mainly foreigners.

---

[7] Ibid.

[8] Saudi American Bank. *Saudi Arabia's Employment Profile* (8 October 2002). http://www.samba.com.

[9] Saudi Arabian Monetary Agency. *Annual Report 2005*. http://www.sama.sa; *Saudi Gazette*. 30 July 2006.

[10] UNESCO. *Global Education Digest 2006*. 138–9. http://www.uis.unesco.org.

Table 10.6. *Saudi Arabia: The structure of GDP, 1984–2005 (% of GDP)*

	1984	1994	1999	2005*
Oil	38.2	32.7	31.1	32.9
Non-oil	81.8	67.3	68.9	67.1
Of which				
-Private	37.4	49.0	50.6	44.1
-Government	24.4	17.8	17.8	22.9
Agriculture	3.3	8.9	7.3	3.3
Industry	7.9	9.6	9.5	9.6
Of which				
-Oil refining	4.0	3.2	3.6	3.4
Other manufacturing	3.9	6.4	5.0	6.2
Electricity, gas, and water	2.4	1.3	1.4	0.9
Construction	9.2	7.2	6.6	4.8
Services	39.0	40.3	44.1	48.5

Items do not add to total in source.

* preliminary estimate.

Source: *Ministry of Planning and SAMA Annual Report 1988* (1989) and *2005* (2005).

The figures for scientific and technological education confirm the view of a former senior finance ministry official that decisions made in the early 1970s have had lasting and negative effects. The increase in oil wealth of 1973–4 was not expected by the finance ministry and in response it put forward two sets of proposals to the king and the government. The first placed emphasis on the development of human capital and the second on physical capital. The choice was not one or the other. It was possible to invest in both, but the choice made was that of physical capital.[11] Much was done in education but only within tight ideological constraints and these severely limited the development of science and technology.

Structural Change in the Economy

Table 10.6 shows that in the period 1984–2005, the share of oil in the economy fell by 5.3 percent. The share of government declined by 1.5 percent and as a result the joint government-oil sector fell from 62.6 percent of gross domestic product (GDP) in 1984 to 55.8 percent in 2004. The two sectors should be considered together because the government owns the oil sector. This change reflected fluctuations in the price and quantity of oil,

[11] In conversation with the author, 1995.

attempts to reduce the role of the government in recent years, and increases in production outside the oil sector.

The share of other manufacturing (excluding oil refining and petro-chemicals) was very small. Despite gradual growth, it accounted for only an estimated 6.2 percent of GDP in 2005. The share of agriculture rose between 1984 and 1994 as a result of the government's wheat production program, but it declined thereafter when subsidies were cut (see Table 10.6). The two productive sectors, which in many economies supply most employ-ment, thus accounted for less than 10 percent of GDP. The difference between total private-sector output and that of industry and agriculture was accounted for by construction and services.

The influence of oil goes beyond its direct share in national income. Oil and oil refining accounted for more than 36 percent of GDP in 2005. If petrochemicals are added then the share was about 40 percent. Oil-export revenues have a dominant role in the state budget and that enables the government to play a major role in the economy, including the private sector. The availability of cheap natural gas and feedstock to the private sector influences the choice of investment in favor of capital-intensive plants that inevitably provide limited increases in employment. The huge rise in oil revenues has been used to improve the government's finances and increase investment. This is being done with private-sector involvement on a larger scale than in the past. The non-oil private sector grew by an annual average growth rate of 3.9 percent between 1999 and 2003 and by an estimated 6.4 percent between 2004 and 2007. The non-oil private sector includes oil-related activities and these are very capital-intensive. The employment gains from this growth have therefore been limited. The private sector was estimated to have grown by about 7 percent in 2007 despite the collapse of the equity market in 2006.[12]

Agriculture

Despite its large area, Saudi Arabia has very little arable land and as most of it is desert, it has few water resources. About 2 percent of the land area is irrigated, where there is rainfall, in oases, and in limited irrigated areas.[13]

Although, since the 1980s, it was a favored sector and benefited from large-scale government assistance, agriculture accounted for less than

[12] Saudi American Bank. *The Saudi Economy 2006 Performance; 2007 Forecast.* (2007). 9. http://www.samba.com.
[13] Economist Intelligence Unit. *Country Profile Saudi Arabia 2005.* London: EIU, 2005. 43.

10 percent of national income. The main policy changes were designed to encourage wheat production and reduce the country's dependence on imports. This followed Saudi Arabia's brief oil boycott of the United States in 1973 and was partly driven by fears of retaliation. In 1980, wheat production in Saudi Arabia amounted to about 266,000 tonnes; by 1985, it reached more than two million tonnes, more than domestic demand. Wheat production peaked in 1991 at 4.035 million tonnes and the area under cultivation peaked at 973,880 hectares. In 1991, Saudi Arabia was the world's sixth largest wheat exporter with sales abroad of two million tonnes, worth $275 million, as output has exceeded both domestic demand and even storage capacity.[14] Following the Gulf War of 1991, the government changed its policies to reduce subsidies and cut water consumption.[15] The wheat production program, like others designed to develop food production, was enormously expensive. Wheat was grown in the Ha'il and Qasim areas northwest of Riyadh, using water from underground aquifers. Farmers received subsidized loans, subsidized inputs, free land, and benefited from a protected market. They were paid relatively high prices for their products compared to those prevailing on world markets. In 1991, the government paid $2.2 billion to farmers for wheat and procurement prices were about four times the international level. This meant that instead of importing wheat at a price of $100 to $125 per tonne, the government paid local farmers between $400 and $533 a tonne.[16] The costs of this and other agricultural support programs became a growing burden on the state budget at a time when oil revenues were weak. The wheat production program also resulted in the depletion of water resources. In 1987, agriculture accounted for 10 percent of Saudi Arabian water consumption. Wheat accounted for 5.3 billion cubic meters (bcm), and total agricultural use came to 14 bcm. With very little rainfall and little desalination for agriculture, water was drawn from underground aquifers and these may be exhausted in twenty to thirty years if they continue to be used at current rates.[17] Wheat was the main cereal crop and in 2001–03 the annual average volume of cereal imports was 5.678 million tonnes, twice that of domestic production.[18] By 2005, wheat production had

---

[14] United Nations Committee on Trade and Development (UNCTAD). *Commodity Yearbook.* New York: UN, 1993. 125.

[15] Food and Agriculture Organization (FAO). *The State of Food and Agriculture 1997.* 3. Calculations from FAOSTAT database. http://.faostat.fao.org.

[16] Food and Agriculture Organization. *Statistical Yearbook 2005–2006.* http://www.fao.org/statistics/yearbook/vol_1_1/pdf/b01.pdf.

[17] FAO. *The State of Food and Agriculture 1992.* 100.

[18] FAO. *The State of Food and Agriculture 1992.* 99.

Table 10.7. *Saudi Arabia: Agricultural and food production indices, 1990–2004*
(1999–2001 = 100)

	Agricultural production	Agricultural production/capita	Food production	Food production/capita
1990	103.8	139.1	104.1	139.5
1995	87.0	101.8	87.0	101.8
2000	92.8	93.0	92.7	92.9
2001	115.4	112.2	115.5	112.3
2002	112.9	106.5	113.0	106.6
2003	116.4	106.7	116.5	106.8
2004	118.5	105.5	118.6	105.6

Source: www.fao.org.

fallen to 2.648 million tonnes and the area under cultivation was 490,070 hectares[19] (see Table 10.7).

The Oil Industry and Saudi Arabia's International Role

Saudi Arabia has such an important role in the international oil market that it is necessary to examine it in a broad context. It is the world's largest producer and exporter of oil and also has about 25 percent the world's largest oil reserves. It also has the fourth largest gas reserves. In 2006, Saudi oil production was estimated at 10.7 million barrels a day (mb/d) of which about 7 mb/d was exported, earning some $162 billion. Saudi exports to the United States were 1.4 mb/d, about 14 percent of U.S. imports and it was its third largest supplier.[20] The increase in oil revenues of recent years in Saudi Arabia and other states in the Gulf Cooperation Council resulted in a large accumulation of financial reserves and as a result the region has become a much more important player on international capital markets.

Oil Revenues

Oil is the dominant sector in the Saudi economy. In 2005, it directly accounted for 32.9 percent of GDP (excluding import duties). Its indirect effects were also large: It supplied most government revenues and enabled the government to play a dominant role in the economy. Figure 10.1 shows

---

[19] Food and Agriculture Organization. FAOSTAT database. http://.faostat.fao.org.
[20] Energy Information Agency. Country Analysis Brief. Saudi Arabia, January 2007; OPEC Revenues Fact Sheet. January 2006. http://www.eia.doe.gov.

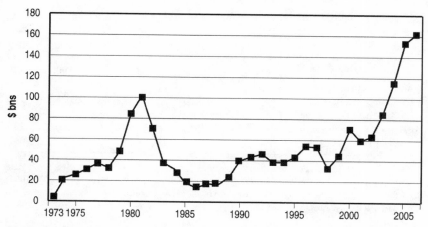

Figure 10.1. Saudi Oil Revenues, 1973–2005. *Source:* 1973–2002: SAMA, Annual Reports 1998, 2003. www.sama.gov.sa. 2003–06, EIA, OPEC Revenues Fact Sheet, January 2006.

the huge growth of oil revenues in 1974–7 and in 1979–80, in current prices. It also shows how they fell in the early and mid-1980s (the 1986 level was only 13.3 percent of the 1981 peak) and then how they have risen since 1998, almost fivefold in nominal terms.

The oil sector drew Saudi Arabia into the world economy in a very selective way. It provided access to modern technology and skilled workers from abroad and it generated ever-increasing revenues. The employment effects were not great: even with the reduction in the number of U.S. citizens and the increase in the number of Saudi citizens employed by Aramco and then by Saudi Aramco, the total number was small and often physically isolated from the main centers of population.

As a result of the rise in oil revenues, Saudi Arabia's balance of payments on current account has moved into strong surplus. Its foreign-exchange reserves have risen sharply as shown in Table 10.8. The assets held by Saudis abroad, as measured by deposits in banks in the Bank for International Settlements region (most of the industrialized economies and many international banking centers) also rose. Saudi imports increased as economic growth accelerated but the country's role in the international economy was much smaller than it had been in the 1970s and 1980s during the oil price booms.

The recent oil price boom has been marked by much more caution. The government, mindful of the legacy of the 1980s, has been reluctant to overcommit itself. Government spending has risen faster than revenues

Table 10.8. *Saudi Arabia: The external sector, 1995–2006*

	1995–9	2000–02	2003	2004	2005	2006
Current account ($bn), annual average	−2.9	11.5	28.1	51.9	90.7	95.5
Current account balance as % GDP, annual average	−2.7	6.3	13.1	20.6	28.3	27.5
Foreign exchange reserves ($bn)	14.0	46.2	59.8	86.8	150	270
Assets in BIS banks ($bn)*			56	82	83	106

* Excluding deposits in U.S. banks.
Source: World Bank. *Middle East and North Africa: Economic Developments and Prospects*, 2006, 106;7; Bank for International Settlements. Provisional Locational and Consolidated Banking Statistics at end. March 2007. www.bis.org.

and surpluses have been recorded in the state budget; these have been used to reduce domestic debt. Following September 11, 2001, Saudis have deposited less in U.S. banks, and repatriated funds from there. The Institute for International Finance reported that at the end of 2006, Saudi Arabia had total foreign assets worth $450 billion (see Table 10.8). This was equal to 29 percent of the total foreign assets of Gulf Cooperation Council member states.[21]

Fiscal Crises

The oil boom of the 1970s and early 1980s transformed the Saudi economy. Huge investment projects were carried out in industry and in the infrastructure. Imports increased sharply as the country could supply neither the investment goods needed for development nor the demand for consumer goods that higher incomes made possible.

Following the fall in oil prices in the early 1980s, a financial crisis developed. In 1988, Saudi Arabia had a budget deficit of 50.2 billion riyals (about $13.7 billion) (see Figure 10.2). This was before the Gulf crisis and war that resulted in a huge increase in spending and oil revenues. The budget deficit was not new; it had been part of the economic scene since 1982–3. The cause of the budget deficits were not just a shortage of revenues, but also the inability of the authorities to control spending that included subsidies, huge defense imports, and other undisclosed items. The fact that the king was

[21] Organisation for Economic Cooperation and Development (OECD). *Middle East Oil and Gas.* Paris: OECD, 1995. 84. Calculated from Figure 80.

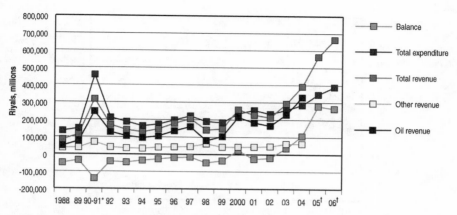

Figure 10.2. Saudi Arabia: The Budget 1988–2006. *Sources:* Annual Report Saudi Arabia Monetary Agency. www. sama.gov.sa; www.samba.com. Saudi Arabia's 2005 Budget, 2004 Performance; The Saudi Economy: 2006 Performance, 2007 Forecast.
*Two financial years amalgamated because of the war.
†Forecast.
These figures are budget proposals and not actual outcomes.

head of the government made it harder to take unpopular austerity measures because he would have been too closely related with them. As members of the royal family were major beneficiaries of public spending programs, there were strong incentives not to make cuts. One of the major ways in which they benefited was from the subsidization of wheat production.

Figure 10.2 shows the major role that oil plays in total government revenues and the correlation between changes in the former and those in the latter. Oil revenues have fluctuated sharply in nominal and real terms, resulting in periods of budget deficits and in surpluses. The deficits have, in turn, been financed by government borrowing (see Figures 10.2 and 10.3).

The deficit was not the product of the Gulf War: It developed as a result of forces that had been at work for many years. In 1988, for example, the budget deficit was equal to more than 18 percent of GDP and this was only reduced in 1989 because oil revenues rose. The level of expenditure in a particular year was related to the higher levels of oil revenue received in previous years and for the reasons given earlier it proved hard to make cuts. The government has argued that the cost of the Gulf War (more than $55 billion) was the main cause of the crisis since 1990. During the period 1990–4, oil income amounted to more than $205 billion, about $95 billion higher than in the period 1985–9. These extra revenues exceeded the total

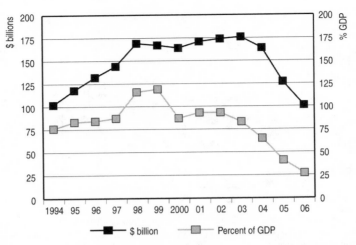

Figure 10.3. Saudi Government Debt, 1994–2006. *Source:* Arab Oil and Gas Directory 1999 Arab Petroleum Research Center, Paris 1999, and Economist Intelligence Unit Country Profile Syria, 1996–6, 1996–7, IMF: Syrian Arab Republic: Statistical Appendix, IMF Country Report No. 05/355, 2005; IMF: Syrian Arab Republic, Staff Report No. 05/356, 2005.

costs of the war and the Gulf crisis that preceded it. Through its control of oil revenues, the government was able to fund a welfare state that had become very costly. Spending on social services and the subsidies on many goods and services that increased after the oil boom of the mid-1980s gave rise to new claims on the budget. An additional problem, which affected all oil-rich states, was the instability of oil revenues. Market forces and autonomous computerized, internationalized trading markets increasingly determined the price of oil and the quantity. As a result, it was hard to forecast the size of large sectors of the national income, export revenues, and budget revenues.

Because the government monopolized natural resources, the demarcation between public goods and services on the one hand, and private markets and initiatives on the other, was determined exclusively by the state. In the West, the burden of taxes is measured against the benefits generated by public services. In Saudi Arabia, where the welfare state has been financed by oil income rather than by taxation, citizens have not felt the costs and therefore the pressure to reduce government spending is limited. Thus, the distinction between the individual and the state, as well as the role of public budgets, has become blurred.

Between 1988 and 2004, oil income accounted for an average of 74 percent of total state revenues. The government did not try to develop other sources of domestic revenues to compensate for the instability of these revenues. In the period 1986–9, non-oil revenues decreased from an annual average of 38 billion riyals ($10.8 billion, or 37 percent of total revenues), to 36.5 billion riyals ($9.75 billion, or 24 percent of total revenues) a year on average in 1990–4. In 1995–2002, they averaged 46 billion riyals ($12.5 billion, or 24 percent of total revenues). Although capital expenditures fluctuated widely, current spending increased at a high rate. A large portion of the rise in current expenditure was accounted for by public services, provided free of charge or at subsidized prices. The growth of the budget deficit also derives from capital expenditure, which can be controlled more easily than other spending. Saudi Arabia has attained standards of basic infrastructure and public services applicable to high-income societies in the West, and correspondingly high-investment commitments are required to maintain them. Unless the private sector takes up at least part of these investments, the replacement investment costs will continue to fall on the overburdened public sector.

Between 1973 and 1982, the accumulated budget surplus came to about 316 billion riyals ($90 billion). In the period 1983–93, there was a deficit of 517 billion riyals ($148 billion) and between 1994 and 2002 the deficit came to 207 billion riyals ($59 billion). Between 1973 and 2002, these deficits came to 408 billion riyals, or $117 billion, and were financed by government borrowing. This formed the national debt, the domestic part of which has become a serious problem. Until 1988, Saudi budget deficits were financed by drawdowns of government deposits with the Saudi Arabian Monetary Agency (SAMA). As a result, there was no significant accumulation of domestic debt. Despite the decline in SAMA's reserves, government spending continued to exceed revenues, resulting in large deficits. In 1988, domestic debt was $11.2 billion, equal to 15 percent of GDP. By the end of 1994, the government and public-sector agencies and companies had a total domestic debt of more than $86 billion, equal to 71 percent of GDP (see Figure 10.3).

Until 1995, the government was unwilling to impose new taxes or reduce subsidy levels that formed part of the extensive welfare system. Despite cuts in spending during the period 1992–4, the budget deficit did not decline and averaged about $11 billion a year. In 1993 and 1994, the budget deficit was higher than officially stated. This is because the official figures exclude the accumulated arrears of payments owed to domestic suppliers and contractors. Consequently, the accumulated domestic debt is also higher than the official figure.

In the early 1980s, the government's domestic borrowing has increased at a pace that has even alarmed the International Monetary Fund (IMF) and the domestic banks. Furthermore, the accumulation of debt arrears to domestic contractors and suppliers has aggravated existing pressures on the banking system and has had a negative effect on the suppliers and contractors involved. In 1983, the budget deficit equaled about 7 percent of GDP. By 1987, it had reached 25 percent. It fell to 12 percent in 1989 as a result of higher oil prices. In 1991, it peaked at about 23 percent before falling to 7 percent in 1992.[22] The improvement in 1992 suggested that steps were taken to bring the deficit under control, but the reduction was due to other factors.

The deficit was mainly financed by sales of government bonds, much of which were sold to government institutions such as pension funds. At the end of 1989, there were 71 billion Saudi riyals (SR; $19 billion) of bonds outstanding, two-thirds of which had been sold to government institutions. By the end of 1992, the volume of outstanding bonds had increased to SR 178.6 billion ($47.6 billion).[23] The increase in the debt resulted in larger volumes of debt repayments and thus further pressure on the budget. By 1995, the government was having difficulty paying the private sector for goods and services that it had ordered. This was despite the fact that the budget had been cut. The Grain Silos and Flour Mills Organization (GSFMO) owed SR 9.7 billion to 23,000 farmers. Some banks were willing to buy these promissory notes, at a small discount, which meant that they, rather than the government, made cash payments to farmers.[24] The government delayed payments to domestic suppliers for two to three years since 1986 when international oil prices fell. In early 1996, these debts accumulated and total domestic debt was reported at SR 375 billion (about $100 billion), equal to 76 percent of GDP. Most of the debt consisted of borrowing from the state pension fund and Social Security systems. The total included funds owed by public-sector companies to each other and more than SR 75 billion held by the private sector and commercial banks and owed by the government and public sector.[25]

Measures to deal with Saudi Arabia's financial problems were slow and partial. In 1988, plans to introduce an income tax for foreigners were announced in the budget. Following an outcry from employers, these proposals were withdrawn within days. In 1992, some of the subsidy cuts previously announced were abandoned following complaints about the amount being paid to the United States in connection with the Gulf War.[26] Although

---

[22] *NCB Economist.* Vol. 3, No. 1 (January 1993). 5.
[23] *Financial Times.* 4 April 1996.
[24] *Financial Times.* 4 April 1996.
[25] Field, Michael. *Inside the Arab World.* Cambridge, Mass.: Harvard University Press, 1995. 330.
[26] *Financial Times.* 4 April 1996.

the king is also prime minister and announced changes himself, economic policy has been very reactive. This is largely due to the fact that the monarchy has no mandate to make conditions harsher for the population as a whole or for members of the royal family in particular. Members of the ruling family owned several of Saudi Arabia's largest wheat-producing companies that benefited from water subsidies and high procurement prices paid by the government. Subsidies for wheat production fell from more than $1.7 billion in 1993 to $850 million in 1994.[27]

In 1993, oil prices and investment income declined and the budget deficit increased. The IMF issued a report that expressed anxiety over the state of the economy and this was followed by the announcement of a 19-percent cut in spending in the 1994 budget. This resulted in a reduction in subsidies for wheat production and for water, defense, and new projects, but only part of the reduction was achieved and as a result another attempt was made in 1995. The prices of many services provided by the public sector were raised so as to reduce the dependence of the budget on oil revenues.[28]

Developments since 2000

The state budget has been transformed since 2003. Since then, surpluses have increased sharply from the equivalent of 4.5 percent of GDP to an estimated 20.3 percent in 2007 (see Figure 10.2). This was because of the massive rise in oil revenues accompanied by a significant but smaller increase in public spending. Despite this, between 2000 and 2006, government spending in current prices almost tripled. As a result of the turnaround on the budget, the government's domestic debt fell from $176 billion in 2003, equal to 83 percent of GDP, to $98 billion in 2006, equal to 28 percent of GDP.

Although its revenues have risen faster than spending, the government has taken steps to increase the role of the private sector. In July 2002, the Supreme Economic Council passed a resolution setting that would permit private-sector involvement in developing large-scale water and power projects. The aim was to attract private-sector investment for up to 60 percent of the equity in these projects, with the remainder split between two public-sector organizations: the Public Investment Fund and the Saudi Electricity Company (SEC). In March 2004, plans were announced to launch ten projects by 2016, at a total cost of $16 billion. By early 2006, the SEC had approved four projects, worth more than $8 billion. The combined capacity

[27] Economist Intelligence Unit. *Country Profile, Saudi Arabia.* London: EIU, 1997. 15.
[28] EIA. Country Analysis Brief, Saudi Arabia. February 2007.

of the four projects will produce more than 7,000 megawatts of power and 600 million gallons of water daily, boosting the total desalination capacity of the kingdom by 80 percent when they come online between 2008 and 2010.[29] The Eighth Development Plan for 2005–09 places emphasis on the non-oil sector and includes measures to encourage increased private-sector involvement. An estimated $80 billion worth of projects were reported to be under way in April 2007 with another $190 billion being planned. They include the construction of four new cities. A total of 107 oil and gas projects and 404 non-oil projects were at different stages in April 2007. Only thirty-nine projects were in the manufacturing sector, accounting for about 5 percent of total investment.[30]

In October 2007, a groundbreaking ceremony of the King Abdullah University of Science and Technology, fifty miles from Jeddah, was held. The project that will cost some $12 billion (much of which will come from the king's private funds) is of great potential significance because it is designed to address the weakness of Arab technological capacity. Breaking a taboo, the king acknowledged that the Arabs have fallen "critically behind much of the modern world in intellectual achievement and that his country depends too much on oil and not enough on creating wealth through innovation."[31] The new university will be groundbreaking in allowing men and women to work together, the religious police will not operate in the campus, and the university will be built by Saudi Aramco rather than by the Ministry of Education. The project is an acknowledgment of the problems facing Saudi Arabia and the Arab world more generally and the constraints under which it operates. The king has the wealth to create a new university but the fact that he had to circumvent the Ministry of Education is an indication of the power of conservatism and ultimately the threat it poses to the country's future. The huge oil resources now available give Saudi Arabia a second opportunity to build a more balanced economy, but whether the new university has a dynamic effect or remains, like other institutions, an isolated island, remains to be seen.

The System of Government

Saudi Arabia is ruled by a royal family of more than 5,000 princes. It is one of the most conservative regimes in the world, both in terms of the

---

[29]   The Institute for International Finance. *Regional Briefing Gulf Cooperation Council.* 21 May 2007. 3. www.iif.com.
[30]   National Bank of Kuwait. *Saudi Arabia Economic and Financial Review.* April 2007. 16.
[31]   *New York Times.* 28 October 2007.

policies that it follows and in terms of the centralization of power. These factors have given rise to tensions as many Saudis realize that they live in one of the most restrictive societies in the world and have a government that is virtually unanswerable to the public. There are, however, others in the country who feel that the regime has abandoned the country's sacred role as the guardian of Islam and there are also religious fundamentalists who are waging a terrorist war against the regime. Given its extremely unrepresentative nature, the regime finds it hard to make or justify changes. As has been shown, although economic changes are needed, the incentives have been muted, at least temporarily, by floods of oil revenues such that have been experienced in recent years.

The entry of members of the Saudi royal family into the business world occurred during the reign of King Faysal, who ruled from 1964 until his death in 1975.[32] This reduced the need for the state to support the royal family directly, or at least reduced the level of direct support required. Faysal also decreed that the royal family's take from oil revenues would not exceed 18 percent.[33] In the period 1973–2005, 18 percent of Saudi Arabia's oil revenues came to $287 billion.

The founder of modern Saudi Arabia, Abd al Aziz ibn Abd ar Rahman Al Saud, had forty-one male children.[34] Initially, members of the royal family were involved in setting up manufacturing industries, which was considered a patriotic duty, during the relatively early stages of economic development in the late 1960s and early 1970s. Others then became involved in international contract negotiations and attracted international attention and criticism for the mediation fees that they charged. This was made possible by the greater tolerance of the regime toward the activities of the princes since the death of the relatively austere King Faysal in March 1975. The entry of the princes into business has also enabled the royal family to maintain direct control over the economy, both through ownership and control. The royal family, through its control of oil resources, the public sector, and its integration into the business elite, can block any attempt by commoners, or any other identifiable group, to dominate any sector of the economy and thus gain excessive economic or political influence.

Another important feature of the monarchic economy is the way in which the ruling family disposes of land, credits, government contracts, subsidies, and licenses. These are allocated in accordance with royal wishes within a

[32] Field, Michael. *The Merchants*. London: John Murray, 1984. 112.
[33] *The Economist*. "A Survey of Saudi Arabia," 7 January 2006. 5.
[34] Hudson, Michael. *Arab Politics: The Search for Legitimacy*. New Haven and London: Yale University Press, 1977. 165–6.

closed system, with no accountability to parliament or the public. The way in which land is allocated is, in some respects, the most interesting because of the perpetual nature of landownership. Business contracts are often one-off and not repeated, financial assets can collapse in value but ownership of land often yields permanent economic benefits in terms of rents and capital gains. In Saudi Arabia, Public Land Development Ordinance carries out the granting of land, previously done by the king himself. Between 1964 and 1991, 509 beneficiaries received 29,736 dunams of land.[35] Between 1970–1 and 1974–5, a total of 2,146,000 hectares (100 hectares = 1 square kilometer) of public land was distributed in 10-hectare plots.[36] Although land is not in short supply in the Gulf, the price in urban areas is relatively high. A gift from the state of land near a city on which development will take place can lead to large capital gains and future streams of rent.

Conclusions

As a result of oil, the Saudi economy has been transformed. It is now able to offer much if not all of its citizenry comprehensive social services and a modern economic infrastructure. In 1993–8, oil revenues came to $505 billion. In 2000–06, they were an estimated $710 billion. The extra $280 billion earned was equal to more than $23,000 per Saudi citizen. In contrast to the 1970s and 1980s, government spending has been kept under control and large reserves have accumulated. The incentives for reform have declined, but overspending has been avoided and attempts have been made to increase the role of the private sector, especially in sectors such as water desalination and electricity generation. Despite huge oil wealth and the move toward more cautionary economic policies, Saudi Arabia suffers from a major unemployment problem. This is because it failed to use its oil revenues to create employment-intensive sectors that would attract Saudi citizens. It also failed to provide sufficient education in areas that would yield well-paid private-sector employment. Employment in the private sector went to foreigners, while better paid but less productive jobs in the public sector were reserved for Saudi citizens.

Saudi Arabia is the most important example of a rentier state in the world because it receives a larger income from oil than any other country. In absolute, if not in relative, terms, the king and government receive more

---

[35] Hajrah, Hassan Hamza. *Public Land Distribution in Saudi Arabia*. London: Longman, 1992. 79.
[36] Hajrah. 113.

income as a result of the high rents that oil earns (defined as the difference between the price of oil on world markets and the cost of pumping it out of the ground) than anywhere else. Little of this income is the result of work or production in the economy and as a result the regime is not answerable to a tax-paying population. It has huge resources at its disposal and as a result major resources are allocated without the use of the market mechanism. The government has done a great deal to develop the economy but the fact that it distributes oil wealth means that the allocation of resources is politicized and bureaucratized.

ELEVEN

Syria

Lost Potential

Syria's population is growing by nearly 2.5 percent a year and the labor force by 4 percent, which is among the fastest rates of growth in the region. Economic growth has been sustained by high oil revenues, but oil production has fallen and is expected to continue. The economy suffers from massive government intervention despite elements of reform over the past twenty years. Economic growth has decelerated since the late 1990s and has barely matched that of the population.[1] Syria's involvement in Lebanon remains extensive but the economic implications, while significant, are difficult to quantify. It is one of a number of political and military factors that have to be considered to understand the country's serious plight.

Population Growth

The rapid growth of population has been the most serious problem facing Syria. In 1960, Syria had a population of just 4.6 million, in 1970, 6.4 million, in 1990, 12.8 million, and in 2000, 16.8 million. The population growth rate declined over the last quarter of a century from an annual average 3.76 percent in 1980–5 to 2.49 percent in 2000–05 (see Table 11.1). The rate remains fast and poses formidable problems in terms of providing basic services and employment. Between 1995 and 2005, the total population increased by 29 percent, the working-age population by 48 percent, and the dependent population by only 7.5 percent.

Table 11.1 also shows how the dependency ratio fell by nearly 40 percent. This reflected the change in the age structure of the population with the

---

[1] United Nations Development Program (UNDP). *Macroeconomic Policies for Poverty Reduction: The Case of Syria, 2006.* 13. http://www.undp.org/poverty/docs/sppr/Syria%20Macro%20Report.pdf.

Table 11.1. *Syria: Population and dependency ratios, 1980–2005*

	Population (millions)	Working-age population	Dependent population	Dependency ratio
1980	8.98	4.33	4.65	107
1985	10.84	5.21	5.62	108
1990	12.84	6.25	6.50	104
1995	14.75	7.77	6.99	92
2000	16.81	9.61	7.20	77
2005	19.04	11.53	7.51	66

Source: Population Division of the Department of Economic and Social Affairs of the United Nations Secretariat. *World Population Prospects: The 2004 Revision* and *World Urbanization Prospects: The 2003 Revision.* http://esa.un.org/unpp.

working-age group (aged 15–64) growing much faster than the dependent groups (aged 0–14 and aged 65 and older). This occurred in a country with one of the fastest growing populations, which meant that between 1980 and 2005, the dependent population rose from 4.64 million to 7.50 million, a rise of 62 percent.

Table 11.2 shows that although the rate of population growth has decelerated, the absolute annual increase rose by almost 20 percent between 1980–5 and 2000–05. According to the United Nation's medium variant forecast, this will only begin to change in the period 2010–15 and then only very gradually. The birthrate fell from 46.2 per 1,000 to 28.7 per 1,000 – a fall of 38 percent. This reflected the decline in the total fertility rate (the number of children born per woman) of more than 50 percent. The effect of lower birthrates was, however, outweighed by the fact that the number of women

Table 11.2. *Syria: Demographic trends, 1980–2005*

	Population change/year (thousands)	Population growth rate (%)	Crude birthrate/1,000	Crude death rate/1,000	Total fertility rate
1980–5	372	3.76	46.2	7.2	7.25
1985–90	401	3.40	40.4	5.7	6.15
1990–5	382	2.78	32.7	4.6	4.61
1995–2000	412	2.61	30.3	3.9	3.95
2000–05	446	2.49	28.7	3.5	3.47

Source: Population Division of the Department of Economic and Social Affairs of the United Nations Secretariat. *World Population Prospects: The 2004 Revision* and *World Urbanization Prospects: The 2003 Revision.* http://esa.un.org/unpp.

aged 15–49 increased sharply, from 1.9 million in 1980 to 2.8 million in 1990 and to 5.1 million in 2005.[2] The fall in the death rate also added to demographic growth.

In the 1970s, fertility did not decline with increased education because economic growth was not accompanied by increased employment opportunities for women. Rising real wages for men limited the need for women to work outside the home. The decline in Syrian fertility rates came in the early 1980s, when there was an increased need for women to work outside the home. Education per se did not, therefore, reduce fertility. Furthermore, high fertility levels among the highly educated meant that there was little chance of the less educated being influenced to have fewer children by more successful sections of society.[3]

Syria was one of the last countries in the Arab world to experience an end to the demographic explosion.[4] Population growth rates in most of the Arab states of North Africa, including Egypt, stabilized and began to decline in the period 1985–90. The slowing down of the rate of population growth was because of lower birthrates. Demographic growth was also the main factor behind pressure on food and water supplies as well as on government spending. It has and will result in a large increase in the labor force for many years to come with serious consequences for employment and for socioeconomic stability.

The Labor Market

The increase in the number of people entering the labor market was a function of the growth of population and the rate of participation in the labor force. There has been an increased recognition of the dangers of fast labor-force growth in recent years: evidence of this was a report in the Syrian press at the beginning of 1997 that the labor force would rise from 4.225 million in 1994 to 7.29 million in the year 2011. This was based on a forecast total population of 21 million in 2011 and an increase in the share of women in the workforce from 16 percent in 1995 to 25 percent in

---

[2] UN. *World Population Prospects: The 2004 Revision* and *World Urbanization Prospects: The 2003 Revision.*

[3] For evidence of higher fertility among better educated women in Egypt, see Chapter 5. Courbage, Youssef. *New Demographic Scenarios in the Mediterranean Region, National Institute of Demographic Studies.* Paris: INED (undated). http://www.ined.fr. Chapter 2, Section III. 5.

[4] Fargues, Philippe. "Demographic Explosion or Social Upheaval" in Ghassan Salame (ed.), *Democracy without Democrats: The Renewal of Politics in the Muslim World.* London: I. B. Tauris, 1994. 156–7.

Table 11.3. *Syria: Labor market trends, 1999–2003 (thousands)*

	1999	2000	2001	2002	2003
Working-age population	8,893	9,702	9,958	10,398	10,861
Labor force	4,967	5,164	5,275	5,459	5,083
Employment	4,559	4,468	4,844	4,822	4,469
Employers	369	418	394	403	358
Self-employed	1,103	1,250	1,228	1,333	1,147
Wage earners	2,398	2,250	2,329	2,300	2,449
Of which public sector	1,185	1,205	1,259	1,169	1,217
Of which civil servants	804	834	867	873	987
Other (mainly unpaid family members)	688	550	893	786	514
Unemployment	408	696	431	637	614
Labor-force participation rate (%)*	55.8	53.2	53.0	52.5	46.8
Employment rate (%)*	51.3	46.2	48.6	46.4	41.1
Unemployment rate (%)[†]	8.2	13.5	8.2	11.7	12.1

* Percent of working-age population.
† Percent of labor force.
Source: IMF. *Syrian Arab Republic: Statistical Appendix, 2005.* 13, Table 11.

2011.[5] According to a Syrian source, the cost of providing employment for an additional three million people by the year 2011 would be $60 billion.[6] Most recent UN forecasts suggest that these population growth figures were underestimates.

In 2001, the government set up the Agency for Combating Unemployment with the aim of mobilizing $1 billion from local and foreign sources to create 440,000 jobs in 2003–07. The government provided 20 percent of the funds. In 2002, 30,000 jobs were reported to have been created, less than half the annual number needed to fulfill the five-year target.[7]

Population growth is the first factor determining how fast the labor force grows. The potential number of those seeking first-time employment equals the annual increase in the number of workers aged 18–23 (the age of entry into the job market increases as educational opportunities expand). In 2003, an estimated 380,000 entered the labor market. This large number was despite a fall in labor-force participation rates that has been apparent in recent years (see Table 11.3). The number of new jobs that have to be created annually equals the number of entrants minus the number retiring. An estimate of the latter is 60,000 and so the net addition for which employment

---

[5] *Ha'aretz.* 28 February 1997.
[6] *Ha'aretz.* 28 February 1997.
[7] Economist Intelligence Unit (EIU). *Country Profile, Syria, 2005.* London: EIU, 2005. 34–35.

has to be found – if increased unemployment is to be avoided – is about 320,000.[8] In 1980 there were 996,000 in the 18–23 age-group; in 1990 1,474,000 and in 2005, 2,619,000.[9] If a wider definition is given, allowing for the fact that those younger than age 18 and older than 23 may be first-time labor-market entrants, then the number is larger.

In 2003, some 600,000 Syrians were employed on a seasonal basis, mainly in agriculture. Another 600,000 were intermittently employed. The official definition of unemployment excluded those who had done more than one hour's work a week. In a survey carried out in March 2003, a busy month in agriculture, there were 581,000 unemployed, equal to 11.6 percent of the labor force. A less restrictive definition would have been up to two days of work a week and this would have yielded 812,000 unemployed or 16.2 percent. Combining these figures gives a total of almost 68 percent of the labor force either underemployed or unemployed.

Table 11.3 shows that between 1999 and 2003 unemployment increased and employment declined by almost 2 percent. The public sector was the only one that experienced growth as a result of increased recruitment into the civil service where employment rose by 183,000 or 23 percent. Between 1999 and 2003, private-sector employment fell from 3.37 million to 3.25 million, a decline of 3.6 percent. As a result of these very weak employment trends, labor-force participation rates have fallen. Although they were much lower for women than for men, both female and male participation rates fell in the period 2001–03.

Poverty

In 2003–04, some 2 million people (11.4 percent of the population) had an income of up to $1/day and thus could not meet their basic needs. If the limit of $2/day is used then 10.4 percent of the population is defined as poor. These measures, which are often used for making international comparisons, do not allow for regional differences in consumption patterns and prices and for the different needs of household members. Using different methodology that allows for these differences, we get a figure of 5.3 million who were defined as poor (30.1 percent of the population).[10]

[8] Courbage. 13.
[9] UNDP. 57–65.
[10] Ibid. 119.

The poor were mainly rural and poverty was concentrated in the northeast of the country. The poor tended to be poorly educated and employed in marginal and unskilled work. Poverty was not deep: most of the poor had incomes just below the line used to define poverty. Although poverty decreased between 1996–7 and 2003–04, economic growth between those years tended to benefit those who were not poor, increasing inequality in the distribution of income.

Economic Growth in the 1990s

Many of the problems that affected the economy in the 1970s and 1980s continued in the 1990s and the early 2000s. Apart from rapid population growth, they included reliance on rental incomes such as workers' remittances and foreign aid; a very small manufacturing sector; formidable bureaucracy and politicization of the public sector; high defense spending and a large military establishment; economic isolation; water and electricity shortages as well as environmental degradation.

The early 1990s were years of fast economic growth, with the gross domestic product (GDP) increasing by an annual average of 7.5 percent in 1990–04. In the period 1995–6, the average rate was 6.5 percent but in the period 1999–2003, the average rate was estimated at only 1.25 percent.[11] The deceleration was due to a number of factors. The manufacturing sector suffered from increased competition from imports that resulted from the liberalization of foreign trade. The adoption of more stringent financial policies by the government squeezed demand and thus helped to slow the rate of growth. Crude oil production and refining output declined since 1996. A liquidity crisis in 1994, which developed when a number of pyramid financial schemes in the informal capital market collapsed, caused financial losses and reduced confidence in the economy.[12] These trends were reinforced by a drought that had severe effects on agricultural production in the late 1990s.[13] Underlying all this was the slowdown of the economic reform program that discouraged the private sector and reduced investments by Syrians living abroad.

---

[11] IMF. *Syrian Arab Republic Staff Report for the 2005 Article IV Consultation.* 5.
[12] Embassy of the United States of America. *Doing Business in the Syrian Arab Republic: A Country Commercial Guide for US Companies.* 1996. http://damascus.usembassy.gov/uploads/images/xbWE230070xAoKXPyztogQ/ccg-syria-2007.pdf.
[13] EIU. *Country Report, Syria, 3rd Quarter 1999.* 21–3.

Syria has traditionally depended on a number of external sources of income. These included aid from Arab states (in the form of loans and grants) and remittances from workers abroad. Changes in aid and remittance flows as well as oil revenues had significant effects on the economy, but their levels were largely outside the control of the government. (Between the 2002 peak and 2004, oil-export revenues declined nearly 30 percent.) There has also been an inflow of capital from Syrian residents abroad who have been investing in new projects under the Investment Promotion Law No. 10 of 1991, averaging about $180 million a year between 1999 and 2004 through registered channels. Resources available to the economy from abroad have been used to increase investment. In 1990, investment equaled 13 percent of GDP; in 1995 it was 16 percent and in 2003 an estimated 23 percent.[14]

Although economic reforms have not been comprehensive, there have been some changes in recent years. These have had ideological significance in that the regime wants the private sector to play a major role, especially in investment. Private capital has been invested in sectors of the economy that were previously closed to it. In 1994, private investment was permitted in heavy industry, cranes, turbines, generators, iron and steel, cement, and also in flour milling. In the same year, subsidies on electricity and fuel oil were reduced and the government announced that public-sector firms should begin to operate on a commercial basis with much less interference from the state. In 1996, a private concern was permitted to build an electricity-generating plant and a sugar refinery. Interest was also expressed by the private sector in investing in a petroleum refinery.

The efficiency of investment may have improved as market forces and the private sector played a greater role in the economy and investment decisions were made more on an economic rather than on a politico-bureaucratic basis. There are, however, no accurate measures of the efficiency of investment. Large investments were made in the transport sector, with a huge increase in the number of minibuses imported. This was a response to shortages that had been experienced and led to economic improvements, but investment needed to be concentrated in industrial productive capacity to have a sustained effect on the economy. The failure to invest more in sectors where the payoff was in the medium or long term reflected the private sector's lack of willingness to take risks.

In the period 1986–9, there was a nearly 40-percent decline in the volume of investment. In 1990, a recovery began, but by 1995 the level of investment

---

[14] IMF. *Syrian Arab Republic: Statistical Appendix, 2005.* 7, 50.

was still 2 percent lower than in 1985.[15] Since 1990, investment (mainly in the private sector) has increased but domestic savings have not. In 1990, savings and investment were in balance: domestic savings equaled 16.9 percent of GDP, while investment came to 16.5 percent. By 1994, savings were 16.2 percent of GDP, while investments equaled 30.3 percent and were increasingly funded out of the external deficit. The gap between domestic savings and investment rose from 0.4 percent of GDP in 1990 to 14.2 percent in 1994, which meant that the economy had become reliant on foreign funding to maintain its rate of growth. Both the public and private sectors imported capital to fund investment projects. One of the objectives of economic policy was to encourage the repatriation of Syrian funds and this occurred after the introduction of the Investment Promotion Law No. 10 in 1991. The open question was whether the sources of funds would be available in the future. The weakness of the economy was the low level of domestic private savings, which was related to the lack of development of the banking sector and the low level of average incomes. The share of investment in GDP fell from 29.3 percent in 1995 to 18.3 percent in 2001.[16]

Structural change takes time and it is therefore necessary to measure development over a period of five to ten years. United Nations' figures for the period 1990–2001 show little structural change with the exception of a rise in the share of mining and quarrying. This was because of the rise in oil prices, the effect of which exceeded that of falling quantities of oil production. The share of manufacturing was low in 1990 and remained so throughout the period (see Table 11.4).

Economic Developments since 2000

In 1999–2003, economic growth averaged only 1.25 percent, one of the slowest growth rates in the region. The slow rate of growth was the result of the virtual ending of the economic reform program and an adverse external environment. This occurred despite the rise in oil revenues that resulted in, among other things, a large increase in government spending.[17] In 1999–2003, crude oil and petroleum accounted for an average of 72 percent of total merchandise exports and an average of 48 percent of government revenues. In 1999, oil exports accounted for 13 percent of GDP; in 2003

---

[15] Calculated from the Syrian Arab Republic. *Statistical Abstract 1994*. 514–15 and *Statistical Abstract 1995*. 526.

[16] IMF. *International Financial Statistics*. November 1997; UN, *National Accounts Statistics: Main Aggregates and Detailed Statistics, 2001 Part 1*. New York: UN, 2003. 708–09.

[17] IMF. *Syrian Arab Republic, Article IV Consultation Staff Report*, 2005. Report No. 05/356. 5.

Table 11.4. *Syria: GDP: Value added by sector 1990–2001 (%, current prices)*

	1990	1995	2000	2001
Agriculture, hunting, forestry, and fishing	28.3	28.2	24.7	25.9
Mining and quarrying	15.0	6.7	27.5	20.3
Manufacturing	5.5	6.2	1.5	5.6
Electricity, gas, and water	–	0.9	1.1	0.9
Construction	3.8	4.3	3.2	3.2
Services	47.4	53.7	42.0	44.1
Of which government	9.7	9.3	8.5	10.0
GDP	100.0	100.0	100.0	100.0

Source: UN. *National Accounts Statistics: Main Aggregates and Detailed Statistics, 2001.*
Part 1. UN: New York, 2003; UN. *National Accounts Statistics: Main Aggregates and Detailed Tables, 1994.* Part II. UN: New York, 1997.

they were estimated at 18 percent.[18] Given the fall in oil production and exports recorded in 2004 (following the decline in 2003), the International Monetary Fund (IMF) estimated that the economy grew by 3.1 percent and 2.9 percent in 2006. The forecast for 2006 was 3.2 percent.[19] These figures, based on official statistics, should be treated with caution given the fall in the volume of oil production and exports. At the same time, Syria absorbed several hundred thousand refugees from Iraq, which later resulted in a large increase in domestic demand that was covered without a significant acceleration of inflation. The economy benefited from the reforms of recent years: the exchange rate has been effectively unified and most restrictions on access to foreign exchange for import financing have been removed. Most sectors of the economy have been opened to private enterprise and, according to official sources, this boosted the contribution of the private sector to non-oil GDP to more than 80 percent. A more dynamic private banking sector is now leading financial-sector growth. The complex and opaque tax system has been partly replaced by more efficient and equitable taxes and its administration has been modernized. Investment Promotion Law No. 51 of October 2006 unified tax incentives for investment. Local industry has been exposed to greater international competition through tariff cuts – which brought the average tariff rate to 14.5 percent compared to almost 20 percent in 2003. The maximum tariff rate fell from 225 percent

[18] IMF. *Syrian Arab Republic: Statistical Appendix, 2005.* Country Report No. 05/355. 26, 53.
[19] IMF. *Syrian Arab Republic: 2006 Article IV Consultation-Staff Report,* August 2006. Country Report No. 06/294. 22.

to 60 percent; there was a reduction in the number of prohibited imports and a relaxation of import licensing procedures, and customs procedures were simplified. Attempts to implement fiscal discipline have been attempted against the background of a large fall in oil revenues.[20]

The Public Sector

The public sector continues to play a dominant role in the economy. The public sector employs about 18 percent of the labor force, including the majority of those who have higher education. Almost 66 percent of public-sector workers were university educated, compared with 28 percent in the private sector and 6 percent in the unorganized private sector. The concentration of graduates in the public sector meant that a vested interest in maintaining the status quo and avoiding reforms such as privatization was present.[21] In 2002, it accounted for 40 percent of GDP mainly because of its ownership of the oil sector. It directly accounted for 23 percent of non-oil GDP. Public ownership of the oil sector meant that the public sector accounted for 79 percent of exports. However, it only took 23 percent of imports.

In 1985, the private sector accounted for 34 percent of total gross fixed investment and the public sector accounted for 66 percent. By 2000, the private sector accounted for 40 percent of investment but by 2003 it had fallen to an estimated 34 percent. Between 1999 and 2003, total gross fixed capital formation rose by 40 percent in real terms. Investment by the private sector rose by 18 percent while that by the public sector rose by 55 percent. In 2002, the public sector carried out 66 percent of gross investment and nearly 19 percent of consumption. The public sector accounted for 30 percent of domestic spending. If allowance is made for public-sector exports and imports, then, in 2002, its share of GDP came to almost 53 percent, a figure boosted by the peak in oil exports recorded that year.[22]

The Fiscal Balance

In other ways the government's influence was even greater than these figures show. The government provided subsidies to public-sector firms, thus

---

[20] Syrian Arab Republic. *Article IV Consultation, Mission Preliminary Conclusions.* 16 May 2007. 1.

[21] UNDP. 148.

[22] IMF. *Syrian Arab Republic: Statistical Appendix.* 6, 8, 15, and 57.

Table 11.5. *Syria: Fiscal operations, 2000–2006 (% of GDP)*

	2000	2001	2002	2003	2004	2005*	2006[†]
Revenues	27.2	30.1	26.2	28.5	27.4	26.5	27.5
-Oil related	12.3	17.9	12.5	14.6	11.2	8.8	10.4
-Non-oil tax revenue	9.8	9.0	10.3	10.4	11.6	10.4	10.4
-Income and profits	4.9	3.4	3.7	3.4	4.7	3.6	3.7
Expenditures	28.7	27.8	28.4	31.1	31.6	30.7	30.7
-Defense	5.5	4.7	4.2	5.2	5.9	4.8	4.2
-Subsidies	4.1	3.4	2.9	2.6	2.4	2.5	2.5
Balance	−1.4	2.3	−2.0	−2.6	−4.2	−4.2	−3.2
Non-oil balance	−13.8	−15.6	−14.5	−17.2	−15.4	−13.0	−13.1

* Estimate.
[†] Projected.
Source: IMF. *Staff Report, Syria 2005.* 32; IMF; Syrian Arab Republic: 2006. Article IV. Consultation-Staff Report, August 2006. Country Report No. 06/294.

covering much of their investment without receiving an economic return with the exception of the oil sector. It also subsidized consumers in different ways. Explicit subsidies are those given by the government to lower prices for consumers. In 2004, these were estimated at about $1 billion, or 3.8 percent of GDP. The most important explicit subsidy was for wheat. Implicit subsidies (differences between prices charged in Syria and international prices equaled 10.8 percent of GDP in 2004. Nearly half of this was because of the low domestic price of petroleum products. These implicit subsidies encouraged domestic consumption and thus reduced the volume available for export.

Despite these expenditures, Syria's state budget has, in recent years, been broadly in balance. This was possible because of the large volume of oil revenues that accrued. In 2003, oil revenues (in the form of taxation, royalties, surcharges, and profits from the Syrian Petroleum Company) equaled half of total budget revenues. The non-oil budget deficit would have come to 17.9 percent of GDP instead of an actual deficit of 2.7 percent. (This includes an allowance for oil subsidies.) The non-oil balance is an important guide to the extent of adjustment that will have to be made as oil production falls.[23]

Table 11.5 gives details of the state budget in the period 2000–06. It shows that oil accounted for 45 to 57 percent of revenues. The budget deficit rose between 2002 and 2006 because spending increased faster than revenues

[23] IMF. *Syrian Arab Republic: 2005 Article IV Consultation-Staff Report* No. 05/356. 31.

and was financed largely from domestic borrowing. The non-oil deficit was large throughout the period although it fell after 2003.

The Defense Burden

During the last decade the spending on the military, as measured by the defense budget, has failed to increase in line with inflation. As a result, the real volume of defense spending has fallen as has its share in GDP. The share of defense in GDP fell from 11.2 percent in 1986 to 7.0 percent in 1994 and 5.3 percent in 2003. The fall was because of the failure to increase the budget in line with inflation and because of the depreciation of the exchange rate. Defense spending accounted for 16 percent of budget expenditure in 2004, 32 percent in 1990, 39 percent in 1994, and 28 percent in 1994. Arms imports were not included in the defense budget and were funded with foreign aid. In the 2006 budget, national security accounted for 14.5 percent of total spending.[24]

The burden of defense was larger than budgetary figures suggest, not only because arms imports are excluded. Syria conscripts men and women for the armed forces and has large paramilitary and state-security forces. It also has about 35,000 troops in Lebanon. Although military personnel is cheap, in that conscripts earn minimal amounts, the military complex has spread into other sectors of the economy, especially construction and trading. This military industrial complex has to be supplied and appeased when policy is made and this has economic as well as political costs.

Banking

The banking system is dominated by the state in terms of ownership, control, direction of credit, application of technology, and services available to depositors. It shows more than any other sector how backward and isolated Syria's economy is. The number of branches is small and the number of bank accounts per 100 of the population is low. Until recently monetary policy has been largely passive with very little response of interest rates to economic and financial developments.[25] As a result, Lebanon has provided Syrians with many banking facilities, not only those who worked there, but others working in Syria.

---

[24] IMF. *Staff Report: Syria*, 2005. 32.
[25] UNDP. 17.

Since nationalization in 1963, the banking system has been organized by sector. The Commercial Bank, with three quarters of bank deposits and half of the credit extended, finances internal and external trade. Most of its lending is to the public sector. The Agricultural Cooperative Bank is largely financed by the Central Bank and lends farmers working capital to buy inputs in accordance with government plans. There are four other state banks, each of which concentrates on a particular sector.

Changes in the structure of the economy and the liberalization of the financial sector resulted in the growth of credit to the private sector. At the end of 2001, the private sector accounted for almost 25 percent of the credits made available by local banks. By September 2006, this had risen to almost 50 percent. As a result of opening up of the banking system to the private sector, in 2001–02 six private banks started operating and by 2006 they had a total of forty-three branches. As a result, the total number of branches in Syria's very small banking network rose by about 20 percent.[26]

The Manufacturing Sector

One of the most remarkable features of the Syrian economy was the very small size of the manufacturing sector. In 1992, manufacturing accounted for less than 6 percent of GDP, a very low share even by Middle East standards. In Turkey its share was 23 percent, in Jordan 15 percent, in Egypt 12 percent, in Morocco 19 percent, and in Tunisia 17 percent. In 2002, it was 3.7 percent.[27] Another was that output in manufacturing fluctuated sharply. In the 1980s, and especially between 1986 and 1989, the economy as a whole was subject to severe fluctuations but changes in manufacturing output were even more severe. During the period 1970–80, value added in manufacturing rose by an annual average of 5.9 percent. In the 1980s, it rose by only 0.7 percent and in the period 1990–3 by 6.7 percent, but that was not enough to increase its share of the total. No figures on value added in manufacturing in constant prices are available for the period since 1993. It is not, therefore, possible to calculate growth rates. Between 1999 and 2003 (preliminary estimate), manufacturing output measured in constant prices rose by less than 0.5 percent annually. Output fluctuated sharply in 2000 and 2001 and was estimated to have been 28 percent lower in 2003 than in 2002. The IMF noted that these estimates should be treated with caution given methodological problems, but the trend is clear: the manufacturing sector

[26] Central Bank of Syria (Damascus). *Quarterly Bulletin* 44, No. 3 (2006). 20, 27.
[27] IMF. *Syrian Arab Republic: Statistical Appendix.* 15.

stagnated over a period of four years. The third feature was the low ratio of value added to gross output. Value added is a measure of the relationship between output and inputs. It measures the original contribution of the sector in question, net of the value of inputs. In 1991, value added equaled 17.8 percent of gross output in manufacturing; by 2001 it had fallen to 15.8 percent. The low level of value added reflected the state of development in Syria. In South Korea, by way of contrast, there was an increase in the share of value added in gross manufacturing output from 26 percent in 1991 to 27 percent in 2001.[28] Even more than in the rest of the Arab world, the manufacturing sector in Syria has failed to act as a motor for economic growth, employment, and exports. As a result, unemployment has risen, many are underemployed in other sectors, and economic growth has suffered.

Manufacturing was dominated by chemicals, food, beverages, tobacco, textiles, clothing, and leather. They accounted for 78 percent of manufacturing output in 2002 and almost 83 percent in 1991. The decline in their joint share suggests that a modest diversification of output occurred but high technology is nonexistent and even middle-level technology is very limited.[29]

Oil

If manufacturing is the weakest sector, then oil is in some respects the strongest. It has been the leading sector in the Syrian economy in the last ten years in terms of generating economic growth. In 1992, the level of oil production was more than three times its 1982 level. In 1986, oil revenues were $336 million; in 1995 they rose to $2.4 billion (see Figure 11.1). In 1995, oil accounted for about 20 percent of GDP and 60 percent of exports. As is shown in the section on fiscal issues later in the chapter, it also accounts for a substantial part of government revenues. Oil, more than any other factor, permitted the economy to grow and gave the government unprecedented room for maneuver. In 2004, oil accounted for about 60 percent of exports, compared with 69 percent in the peak year of 2002.[30] Since its peak in 1995, oil production has slumped and by 2006 it was an estimated 35 percent.

---

[28] UN. *National Accounts, 1992,* New York: UN, 1992. 1140–1; *National Accounts, 1993,* New York: UN, 1294; *National Accounts,* 2001, New York: UN, 2001. 713.

[29] UNDP. 85 and Appendix. IV, T.5.A.7.

[30] IMF. *Syrian Arab Republic: 2005 Article IV Consultation-Staff Report* No. 05/356. 35.

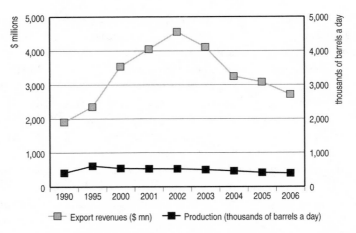

Figure 11.1. Syria: Oil Production and Revenues, 1990–2006. *Source:* Arab Oil and Gas Directory 1999 Arab Petroleum Research Center, Paris 1999, and Economist Intelligence Unit Country Profile Syria, 1996–96, 1996–99, IMF: Syrian Arab Republic: Statistical Appendix, IMF Country Report No. 05/355, 2005; IMF: Syrian Arab Republic, Staff Report No. 05/356, 2005.

More than a dozen foreign oil companies have explored for oil in Syria since the late 1980s. They were encouraged by Shell's discovery in the Furat (Euphrates) area in Dayr al-Zur in eastern Syria. The other companies failed to discover oil outside Dayr al-Zur and their exploration contracts expired. In some cases, other companies took over the areas being explored. Between 1991 and 2003, remittances of profits by foreign oil companies from Syria averaged $1 billion a year.[31]

At the end of 2006, Syria had estimated proven oil reserves of three billion barrels, which at the rate at which it was used in that year, would last for 19.7 years.[32] The future volume of exports will depend on domestic consumption levels. A growing economy will consume more oil, assuming no change in the relative price of oil inside Syria. A stagnant economy would result in little growth or a decline in consumption. Under the first scenario, oil-export revenues would fall because of both falling production and increasing domestic demand; under the second, they would decline because of falling production.

When allowance is made for the repatriation of profits by foreign oil companies, then the net contribution of the oil sector is much smaller than its export revenues. In 2002, for example, repatriated profits accounted for

[31] IMF. *Balance of Payments Yearbook,* various issues. Washington, D.C.: IMF.
[32] British Petroleum. *BP Statistical Review of World Energy, 2007.* http://www.bp.com.

25 percent of oil export revenues. That was the peak year for oil revenues; since then they have fallen but the repatriation of profits has not.[33] The other limitation was that oil did not generate significant amounts of employment. The fact that foreign oil companies did much of the development work meant that they brought their own personnel from abroad, thus limiting the benefits to the Syrian economy.

Gas

Proven reserves in 2004 were estimated at 370 billion cubic meters (bcm).[34] At the current rate of use, these reserves will last for about seventy years. Syria's gas reserves are, by Middle East standards, relatively small and this means that its export potential is very limited. Given plans to increase domestic use of gas in generating electricity, there is unlikely to be a surplus for export. The government wants to use gas in power stations and in industrial plants to increase the availability of oil for export, but the process of conversion has been slow. In 2004, gas production was 5.2 bcm, up from 1.5 bcm in 1994. All of domestic output was domestically consumed.[35] The government sells gas to final users and power plants at cost and so earns no revenues from it. Infrastructure to export gas to Lebanon has been constructed.[36]

Agriculture

Syria has one of the strongest agricultural sectors in the Arab world and it accounts for a larger share of employment in Syria than any other Arab country. In 1992 the food gap or difference between food imports and exports was $187.6 million or $14 per capita.[37] This compares favorably with a food gap in the United Nations' Economic and Social Commission for West Asia (ESCWA) area as a whole (Lebanon, Syria, Yemen, Bahrain, Kuwait, Oman, Qatar, South Arabia, Egypt, Jordan, UAE, and Iraq) of $10.6 billion or $82 per capita. According to ESCWA, Syrian agriculture

---

[33] Calculated from IMF. *Balance of Payments Statistics 2006.* Washington, D.C.: IMF, 2006.
[34] British Petroleum. *BP Statistical Review of World Energy.*
[35] British Petroleum. 2005. http://www.bp.com and Energy Information Agency. *Country Analysis Brief Eastern Mediterranean.* 2008. http://www.eia.doe.gov/emeu/cabs/East_Med/NaturalGas.html.
[36] IMF. *Syrian Arab Republic: 2005 Article IV Consultation-Staff Report* 2005. 40.
[37] United Nations Economic and Social Commission for West Asia (ESCWA). *Agriculture and Development in West Asia.* 1994. 18.

Table 11.6. *Syria: Agricultural and food production, 1990–2004 (1999–2001 = 100)*

	Agricultural production	Agricultural production/capita	Food production	Food production/capita
1990	68.1	89.4	71.3	92.9
1995	85.8	97.4	88.6	100.6
2000	103.0	103.1	77.8	78.2
2001	107.0	104.5	151.8	149.1
2002	118.3	112.9	134.6	129.1
2003	115.2	107.2	141.2	132.2
2004	118.8	108.1	121.3	110.9

Source: Food and Agriculture Organization. FAOSTATS. http://www.fao.org.

progressed because of increased investment, reforms of agricultural pricing, and other policies.[38]

Syria has a cultivated area of 5.7 million hectares, mainly rain-fed. Agriculture accounted for 30 percent of employment and a similar share of national income.[39] Industries closely related to agriculture – textiles, leather, tobacco, and food processing – accounted for 25 percent of output in the economy and about 50 percent of manufacturing employment. Agricultural production rose by 51 percent in the decade to 2000; on a per capita basis, it rose by 15 percent. In 2000–04, output rose by 15 percent and output per head by 4.8 percent (see Table 11.6).

A major emphasis was placed on the production of cereals for domestic use and this resulted in a 40 percent increase in the area planted with cereals between 1979–81 and 1995; a 26-percent rise in yields and a 90-percent jump in production. Production of cotton lint rose by 55 percent over the same period.[40] In 1992 Syria achieved self-sufficiency in wheat with a harvest of 3 million tons; in 1996, wheat production reached 4.2 million tons. Wheat is grown in the private sector but the state-run General Establishment for Cereal Processing and Trade is responsible for marketing. About 60 percent of wheat produced is durum (which is better suited to the manufacture of pasta than bread) and this together with the lack of milling capacity means that wheat imports are necessary. The large increase in wheat production has not been accompanied by an expansion of storage facilities. The country suffers a chronic shortage of storage silos; much grain is stored in the open

---

[38] ESCWA. *Survey of Economic and Social Developments in the ESCWA Region.* 1994. 86–7.

[39] Ibid. 100; Economist Intelligence Unit (EIU). *Country Profile: Syria 2005.* 35.

[40] Food and Agriculture Organization (FAO). *Quarterly Bulletin of Statistics* 8, No. 3/4 (1995). 110.

with large consequent losses. Large investments are being made in both milling and storage.

The total cropped area equals 4.8 million hectares and this has changed little in the last decade.[41] Less than 20 percent of the cultivated area is irrigated, the rest being rain-fed. Efforts to increase irrigation depend on the volume of water in the Euphrates but this has been affected by Turkey's use of its water and poor canal structures for distributing water in Syria. Between 70 percent and 75 percent of the cropped area is taken up with wheat, the main staple crop, and barley, the main feed grain. Cotton was the main export crop and in 2003 accounted for 18 percent of agricultural exports.

Government policy was aimed at reducing reliance on imports and increasing exports. It did this through trade, production, and pricing policies. It set procurement prices for major crops and controls interest rates, agricultural input prices, and energy and transport prices. The government also favored one crop over another by changing input and the procurement of state purchasing agencies. Bread, rice, sugar, and tea prices were controlled by the government; fruit and vegetable production and prices are market determined. Agricultural exporters are now allowed to retain all of their earnings.[42] Increased production of cereals has not been accompanied by a sufficiently rapid expansion of storage facilities. Given the limited quantities exported, this has resulted in excess wheat, barley, and lentils being stored out of doors in jute bags with large losses because of bad weather and infestation. Investments in silos have increased, but not at fast enough rates to store the amounts produced.[43]

Large investments have been made in irrigation. In 1983, 580,000 hectares were irrigated; in 1993, an estimated 906,000 hectares.[44] It has accounted for up to 75 percent of the state budget for agriculture. The objective was much higher production: the 15 percent of cultivated land that was irrigated produced 50 percent of total agricultural output. The other incentive was that production on rain-fed land (85 percent of the total) fluctuated greatly each year. A total of 1.25 million hectares could potentially be irrigated from surface water. In 1992, the total area irrigated with surface and groundwater was 900,000 hectares. In 1991, farmers also irrigated 451,000 hectares from wells. Cotton, sugar beet, tobacco, and sesame crops were produced only

[41] Food and Agriculture Organization (FAO), *The State of Food and Agriculture*, 1993. 189.
[42] Ibid. 163.
[43] EIU. *Syria Country Profile*, 3rd Quarter 1997. 20.
[44] FAO. *Yearbook 'Production'* 48 (1994). 15.

on irrigated land. More fruit and vegetable production was on irrigated land. Exports of fruit and vegetables rose from $165 million in 1990 to $236 million in 1994. In 2000, they were $243 million, having averaged $366 a year in 1997–9.[45]

Landownership in Syria is dominantly private and this has been a major strength. When combined with government purchases of major products at prices above those prevailing on international markets, production has increased. Despite this, serious problems remain in that sector. The pressure of population has, along with other factors, resulted in the use of land, water, and forests beyond their natural limit and the result has been environmental degradation. This has meant deforestation, desertification, overcultivation, soil damage and erosion, overpumping of groundwater, and pollution. All these factors threaten the long-term sustainability of the agricultural effort. The trade-off has been between higher current output and threats to future output.[46]

Water

In 1993, agriculture accounted for 85 percent of water use in Syria. The industrial demand for water rose by almost 900 percent in the 1980s and the rapid growth of population was also a competing source of demand.[47] Syria's water supply is derived from rainfall, from rivers crossing its borders, and from groundwater that is pumped to the ground and is mainly used to irrigate crops. It should be noted that figures for Syrian water resources are poor and there are large differences between those used by, for example, the World Bank and the UN's Food and Agriculture Organization (FAO).

According to the World Bank, renewable water resources per capita fell from 1,196 cubic meters per capita in 1960 to 439 in 1990 and will fall to 161 in the year 2025.[48] Public irrigation projects have been large in scale; the main example is the Euphrates River project. This river is the main source of Syria's irrigation water, and development plans aim to add 650,000 hectares of irrigated land. Salinity, water logging, and reduced river flows have hampered this. Salinity and water logging date back to the 1960s.

[45] FAO. Yearbook 'Trade' Vol. 48 (1994). 331; *UN International Trade Statistics Yearbook, 2000.* New York: UN, 2001.

[46] UN, ESCWA, and FAO. Resource Conservation, 1996.

[47] FAO. *The State of Food and Agriculture,* 1993. 174.

[48] Berkoff, Jeremy. *A Strategy for Managing Water in the Middle East and North Africa.* Washington, D.C.: World Bank, 1944. Table A-4.

Private projects operate on a very small scale. Individual farmers have been encouraged to drill wells. They have received subsidized credits to buy subsidized fuel to operate imported pumps bought with an overvalued currency. With urban demand for fruit and vegetables increasing, the incentives to drill have been strong. This has helped to increase the irrigated area and expand agricultural production, but at a cost. Overpumping of aquifers for irrigation has caused saltwater to be absorbed in the coastal plains. The irrigation system itself is inefficient: 40 percent of water is lost.[49] Syria faces acute shortages of water for domestic use in its large cities.[50]

The flow of water into Syrian territory from the Euphrates River at the Turkish border was estimated at 26.3 billion cubic meters (bcm) in 1997. Turkey has agreed to supply 15.75 bcm to Syria; the rest was kept by Turkey using the dams constructed under its South East Anatolian Development Project, known by its Turkish acronym, GAP.[51] Syria has agreed to share the water of the Euphrates crossing its border with Iraq on a 58 percent (Iraq), 42 percent (Syria) basis. As a result, it supplies Iraq with 9 bcm annually.

The internally derived surface flow added 0.5 bcm and 12 bcm was lost in outflow to other countries and the sea. As a result, 5.5 bcm of surface water was available for use in Syria. A total of 1.5 bcm of groundwater was drilled, giving a total supply of 7.0 bcm. Rainfall equaled 7.0 bcm, of which 6.0 bcm was available for agriculture. Syria is a country with a significant water deficit and limited ability to mobilize investment to improve the water-management system. In the future it will have to generate foreign exchange in nonagricultural sectors to pay for food imports and thus reduce pressure on water resources.[52]

The Balance of Payments and Foreign Debt

Figure 11.2 shows that Syria's balance of payments has experienced many changes over the last quarter century. Despite this, there was a current account surplus during most of the period from 1989 to 2004. This was

---

[49] Sadik, Abdul-Karim and Shawki Barghouti. "The Water Problems of the Arab World: Management of Scarce Resources" in Rogers, Peter and Peter Lydon (eds.), *Water in the Arab World: Perspectives and Prognosis.* Cambridge, Mass.: Division of Applied Science, Harvard University, 1994. 20.

[50] Bakour, Yahia and John Kolars. "The Arab Mashrek: Hydrologic History, Problems and Perspectives" in Rogers and Lydon, *Water in the Arab World.* 1994. 133.

[51] Allan, J. A. "Overall Perspectives on Countries and Regions" in Rogers and Lydon, *Water in the Arab World: Perspectives and Prognosis.* 1994. 72.

[52] Allan, J. A. "Economic and Political Adjustments to Scarce Water" in Isaac, Jed and Hillel Shuval (eds.), *Water and Peace.* Amsterdam: Elsevier, 1994. 376–80.

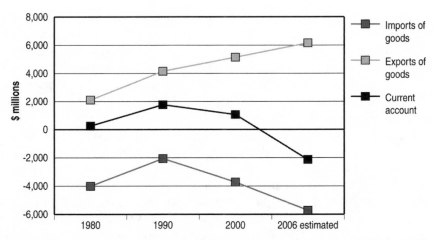

Figure 11.2. Syria: Balance of Payments, 1980–2006. *Source:* IMF, International Financial Statistics Yearbook, 1999; IMF, Syrian Arab Republic: 2005 Article IV Consultation-Staff Report no. 05/356; IMF, Syrian Arab Republic: 2006 Article IV Consultation-Staff Report, August 2006, Country Report No. 06/294, IMF, Syrian Arab Republic: 2007 Article IV Consultation – Staff Report; and Public Information Notice on the Executive Board Discussion, Country Report No. 07/288.

the result of squeezes on imports that restricted the growth of the whole economy and increased oil revenues. Once the restrictions on imports were lifted as a result of increased oil revenues, they rose sharply. The current account had a deficit of $800 million in 2004 but this increased sharply to $2.1 billion in 2005. The balance of non-oil goods and services was in continuous deficit ($2.1 billion in 2000 and an estimated $3.1 billion in 2005). The oil balance (oil exports minus imports) fell from a peak of $3.6 billion in 2002 to an estimated $2.2 billion in 2004 and an estimated $243 million in 2006.

Syria's foreign debt rose sharply in the 1980s (see Table 11.7). This was a period in which oil revenues and aid from abroad declined. The government replaced it with foreign borrowing for as long as it could. This included aid from the Soviet Union. In the 1990s, Western sources were unwilling to lend funds to Syria, partly because of its dispute with the World Bank on outstanding debt and the dissolution of the Soviet Union meant an end to Soviet aid. In 2005, Russia wrote off Syria's debt to it and this resulted in the massive fall in total debt recorded in Table 11.7.

One of Syria's main debtors was the World Bank and in July 1997, Syria agreed to repay $526.4 million that it owed the World Bank. A total of $256.9 million was to be paid in August 1997 and $1.6 million was to be paid each

Table 11.7. *Syria: Foreign debt, 1980–2005 ($ millions)*

	Total	Long term	Short term	Total debt servicing/exports (%)
1980	3,548	2,917	631	11.4
1990	17,259	15,108	2,151	21.8
2000	21,657	15,930	5,727	4.8
2005	6,508	5,640	868	1.9

Source: World Bank. *Global Finance Development, 2006.* Vol. 2. 2007. Washington, D.C.: World Bank, 2006, 2007.

month over a five-year period. This was considered to be a milestone in improving Syria's international creditworthiness.[53]

In 1996, Syria and France agreed on a deal under which France would write off 30 percent of the $370 million owed to it with the balance to be repaid after a five- to seven-year grace period. Negotiations with Germany have been stalled because of Syria's refusal to accept German demands that it repay debt owed to the former German Democratic Republic. In 2005, Syria and Russia reached an agreement on Syria's debt to the former Soviet Union. Of the total outstanding debt of $13.4 billion, $9.8 billion was cancelled, $1.5 billion was to be repaid over ten years, and the balance of $2.1 billion was to be converted into Syrian pounds, deposited in a Russian bank in Syria, and used to finance Russian imports of Syrian goods and Russian investment in Syria.[54]

Syria in Lebanon

Syria benefits in different ways from its domination of Lebanon. Beirut is a liberal financial center that provides Syrians with banking services lacking at home. Lebanon provided a source of employment for hundreds of thousands of surplus Syrian workers. This reduces pressures on the labor market at home and provides foreign currency. There are no official figures on the number of Syrians working in Lebanon, but unofficial estimates are up to one million. In 2005, earnings of $7–$12/day for unskilled work and $25/day for skilled work were reported.[55] If we assume – for the purpose of illustration – that 750,000 Syrians worked in Lebanon 200 days a year,

[53] *Middle East Economic Digest* (MEED). 29 August 1997.
[54] IMF. *Syrian Arab Republic: Statistical Appendix*, 2005. 52.
[55] *Middle East Report.* Washington, D.C.: Middle East Research and Information Project, No. 236 (Fall 2005). 28–33.

earning an average of $9.5/day, then their annual earnings came to $1.43 billion. If we assume that they remitted two-thirds of this home, then the capital going to Syria equaled almost $1 billion. This is considerably more than the amount recorded in balance-of-payments data. The IMF projection for 2005 was $679 million and that included funds from countries other than Lebanon, where Syrians work. It is, of course, likely that much is remitted outside the banking system. The Syrian military and intelligence forces benefit from legal, illegal, and illicit trade between the two countries as well as from exports of drugs from Lebanon's Bekaa Valley.

What Might Have Been

In 1960, Syria and Tunisia had populations of similar size, 4.6 million and 4.1 million, respectively. By 2005, Syria's population had increased nearly fourfold to 19 million, while Tunisia, which has gone further than any other country in the Arab world in terms of population transition, experienced a 2.46-fold increase to 10.1 million. Between 1960 and 2004, Syria's GDP rose from about $1 billion to $23 billion, while Tunisia's GDP increased from $800 million to $28 billion. In 1960, GDP per capita in Syria was $217 and in Tunisia, $195. In 2004, GDP per capita in Syria was $1,190 and in Tunisia $2,790. If Syria's population had increased at the same rate as Tunisia's, its 2004 GDP would have been divided between 10.1 million people, giving a GDP per capita of $2,772. If Syria's economy had grown at the Tunisian rate, its actual 2004 population would have had income per head of $1,897, 57 percent higher than actual GDP per capita.[56]

These are obviously simplistic calculations, but they illustrate the differences between the two countries as well as the costs of the policies that Syria has followed. Tunisia's demographic and economic achievements have been the most impressive in the Arab world, but they too are modest compared with the accomplishments of many countries in East and Southeast Asia.

Conclusions

In April 1997, the United Nations Industrial Development Organization (UNIDO) published a report on the prospects for Syrian industry. It stated that the development of private-sector investment banks, the creation of a

---

[56] Calculated from IMF. *International Financial Statistics Year Book,* various editions; World Bank. *World Development Indicators.* Various editions. http://www.worldbank.org.

stock exchange, and other financial measures would enable Syria to generate the employment needed to cope with the increase in the labor force in the coming years. It would also attract billions of dollars in investment, strengthening the balance of payments as well as bringing foreign technology and expertise to the country.[57] This advice, like much else, has not been taken, or at least has not been acted on to generate a critical mass of reforms.

The pace of economic reforms has largely been influenced by changes in the volume of rental incomes. The combination of a decline in foreign aid, falling remittances from Syrians in the Gulf, and bad harvests led to a serious economic crisis in the early 1980s. In 1985, the government's initial reaction to the crisis was to take steps to reduce imports; the exchange rate was reduced and private-sector firms were encouraged to finance imports with funds held abroad. Since then reforms have been introduced, but never at a pace or on a scale that would create confidence among private investors, as has taken place in Egypt in recent years.[58]

In the late 1990s, economic reform virtually came to a halt, partly because the balance of payments was healthy and did not exert pressure for change. Since the introduction of the 1991 Investment Law No. 10, there has been limited progress toward a more liberal economic system. There have been calls for a loosening of restrictions on foreign-exchange transactions, but as of the time of this writing, these have not been agreed to. As well as a large public sector, transfers to the public and private sectors, a lack of bank lending, and no capital market, the budget has run a sizeable budget deficit that has been financed in part by printing money. This has been inflationary and as economic growth rates have declined, the country is now suffering from inflation of about 20 percent a year and rising unemployment.

These measures helped to boost the economic growth rate but the real source of growth was oil, which took the place of capital imports. The foreign currency earned from oil exports was invested in the infrastructure and in public-sector industry. Agriculture was liberalized and farmers were offered prices that provided greater incentives to produce. As in China, these reforms were introduced within the tight constraints of the existing political and

---

[57] *Middle East Economic Digest.* 29 August 1997. 18.

[58] Rivlin. Paul. "Structural Adjustment in Egypt, Morocco, and Tunisia, 1980–96" in Bruce Maddy Weitzman (ed.), *Middle East Contemporary Survey, 1996,* Vol. XX Boulder, Colo.: Westview Press, 1998. 169–96.

economic infrastructure, but unlike China, Syria has not reduced the ruling party's involvement in the economy and it has not established significant contacts with international firms and multilateral organizations.[59]

Syria faces two looming economic problems. The first is that oil revenues are declining and there is no other source of foreign exchange that could replace it on a stable and sustainable basis. The second, even more serious problem is that of rapid population and labor-force growth that forces the economy to run in order to stand still. Without *increasing* oil revenues, the economy is likely to cease growing and as a result per capita incomes will fall. This leaves the government with only one option: economic reform.

The problems faced by Syria's economy are in large part those of management. If it moved toward a more market-oriented system then the gains in terms of productivity would be considerable. Reforms in agriculture have resulted in an export surplus of fruit and vegetables and this would apply to other sectors if the right steps were taken. The government is not short of ideas on how to reform the economy; the question is whether it actually wants reforms that would strengthen the private sector at the expense of the state and the party. The answer, at the time of writing is no. Reforms took place when rental incomes were low; when rental incomes rose, the government avoided making changes that would unsettle key groups that support it. These include the Alawite minority, the peasantry, the Ba'ath party, government bureaucracies, and the army and security forces. Syria has yet to experience a combination of reforms and high rental income. The irony is that reforms designed, inter alia, to make the economy more self-sufficient would attract both Syrian and foreign capital, which would bring vitally needed technology and know-how.

Syria has a number of economic advantages. It has oil that is expected to yield significant export revenues for at least the next sixteen years, at current rates of extraction, and sizeable gas reserves.[60] It also possesses one of the strongest agricultural sectors in the Arab world. The potential exists to obtain economic rents in exchange for political changes; some of the benefits of a peace treaty with Israel would be aid and investment from the West. Tourism has a large potential, given the wealth of Syria's archaeological sites. Even more significant would be the gains from domestic reforms.

[59] Perthes, Volker. "Syria: Difficult Inheritance" in Perthes, Volker (ed.), *Arab Elites Negotiating the Politics of Change.* Boulder, Colo.: Lynne Rienner Publishers, 2004. 87–114.

[60] British Petroleum. *Statistical Review of World Energy 2005.* http://www.bp.org.

Syria has maintained macroeconomic stability, achieved without the intervention or instructions of the IMF. It has achieved major improvements in socioeconomic indicators such as longevity, literacy, and disease control. The provision of subsidized basic services and a powerful social network have helped the poorest and ameliorated the effects of worsening labor market conditions.[61]

[61] UNDP. 142–3.

TWELVE

Tunisia

Unhappy Economic Leader

In comparison with most Arab states, Tunisia is a small country both geographically and demographically. Its population is relatively homogenous, both ethnically and linguistically, and the distribution of income is one of the most equal in the region.[1] Tunisia has the highest level of income per capita among the non-oil states. In 2005 it was $2,890, 29 percent higher than the Middle East and North Africa average, including the oil states of the region.[2] The number of people living in poverty (defined as living below a minimum consumption expenditure level) fell from 800,000 (8 percent) in 1995 to 400,000 (4 percent) in 2000. The economically vulnerable (defined using a more generous definition) fell from 17 percent of the population to 10 percent.[3]

Tunisia has suffered little political instability in recent years, partly the result of vigorous and successful attempts by the government to root out opposition. The government has followed a liberal economic policy that has reduced budget deficits, cut inflation, and opened the economy to foreign trade. Tunisia also has very close links with the European Union (EU), which dominates its exports and imports. It has a relatively large industrial sector and has very limited oil and gas resources. Perhaps because of that it has had to invest in other, more labor-intensive activities with the result that living standards are relatively high. For many years, the Tunisian model was one that other Arab states could follow to advantage, but today problems are apparent.

---

[1] Morrisson, Christian and Bechir Talbi. *Long-Term Growth in Tunisia*. Paris: OECD Development Centre, 1996. 136.

[2] World Bank. *Tunisia at a Glance*. 5 March 2007. http://devdata.worldbank.org.

[3] Anos-Casero, Paloma and Aristomene Varoudakis. *Growth, Private Investment, and the Cost of Doing Business in Tunisia: A Comparative Perspective*. Washington, D.C.: World Bank, 2004. www-wds.worldbank.org. 4.

Table 12.1. *Tunisia: Population and dependency ratios, 1950–2005*

	Population (millions)	Working-age population	Dependent population	Dependency ratio*
1950	3.53	1.96	1.57	80
1960	4.22	2.22	2.00	91
1970	5.13	2.56	2.57	100
1980	6.46	3.50	2.96	84
1985	7.33	4.09	3.24	79
1990	8.22	4.71	3.51	74
1995	8.98	5.38	3.60	67
2000	9.56	6.10	3.46	57
2005	10.11	6.84	3.27	48

* The total dependency ratio is the ratio of the sum of the population aged 0–14 and that aged 65+ to the population aged 15–64. This is expressed as number of dependents per 100 persons of working age (15–64).

Source: Population Division of the Department of Economic and Social Affairs of the United Nations Secretariat. *World Population Prospects: The 2004 Revision* and *World Urbanization Prospects: The 2003 Revision.* http://esa.un.org/unpp.

Demographic Developments

Demographic trends are outlined in Tables 12.1 and 12.2. Table 12.1 shows that between 1995 and 2005, the total population increased by 12.6 percent and the working-age population by 27 percent, while the dependent population declined by 9.2 percent. Tunisia was the only Arab country to

Table 12.2. *Tunisia: Demographic trends, 1980–2005*

	1980–5	1985–90	1990–5	1995–2000	2000–05
Population change per year (thousands)	176	177	151	117	108
Births per year (thousands)	233	236	207	172	165
Deaths per year (thousands)	55	54	52	51	53
Population growth rate (%)	2.55	2.28	1.76	1.27	1.10
Crude birthrate (per 1,000 population)	33.8	30.3	24.1	18.6	16.8
Crude death rate (per 1,000 population)	8.0	6.9	6.0	5.5	5.4
Total fertility rate (children per woman)	4.92	4.14	3.13	2.32	2.00
Infant mortality rate (per 1,000 births)	64.1	48.9	34.2	26.6	22.2
Life expectancy at birth (years)	64.1	66.9	70.0	71.9	73.1

Source: Population Division of the Department of Economic and Social Affairs of the United Nations Secretariat. *World Population Prospects: The 2004 Revision* and *World Urbanization Prospects: The 2003 Revision,* medium variant, http://esa.un.org/unpp.

experience such a decline. The deceleration is forecast to continue: according to the United Nations' medium-variant forecast, between 2005 and 2015, the population will increase by 10.9 percent.

Table 12.2 provides the background to these trends. It shows the sharp decline in the birthrate since 1980–5. Combined with the much more modest fall of the death rate, the population growth rate fell rapidly. As a result, the absolute increase in the population declined from 176,000 a year in 1980–5 to 108,000 in 2000–05. The indicators of health – infant mortality and life expectancy – showed improvements throughout the 1980s and 1990s, and are expected to go on improving. The key to demographic change was the decline in the number of births per woman. This fell sharply, from an average of 4.92 in 1980–5 to 2.00 in 2000–05.

The Tunisian population is very young, a characteristic shared with all Arab countries, including those with much faster demographic growth rates. In 2000, more than 51 percent of the population was aged 0 to 24, down from 63 percent in 1980. This was due to the fall in the birthrate that led to a sharp fall in the percentage of the population under age 4. The high proportion of young people (up to age 24) in the population means that there is a large, young labor force. It also means that the ratio of dependents to workers or potential workers is relatively low; Tunisia is benefiting from the demographic gift referred to in Chapter 2.

Economic Development and Structural Change

Following its independence in 1956, Tunisia established a public sector, a planning framework, and government investment programs. The state took control over wages, prices, trade credit, and foreign exchange; emphasis was placed on investment in education, health, and social security. In the late 1960s, import substitution policies were implemented. Between 1962 and 1971, despite the many controls that it was subject to, the private sector accounted for 22 percent of fixed investment. This was stimulated by the overvaluation of the exchange rate that made imports of capital equipment cheaper than they would otherwise have been and by low tariffs on intermediate goods and capital equipment. These factors, together with a well-developed banking system, encouraged economic growth.[4]

As a modest oil producer, the rise in oil prices during the early 1970s increased government revenues and permitted an increase in public-sector wages. The 1970s were years of fast and broadly based economic growth, averaging 7.4 percent a year; real value added in the manufacturing sector

---

[4] UN. *World Economic and Social Survey 1996*. New York: UN, 1996. 160.

increased by 11 percent annually. Investment rose from 20 percent of gross domestic product (GDP) in 1970 to 29 percent in 1980 and savings rose from about 17 percent of GDP to nearly 25 percent. The budget deficit was low, averaging 2 percent of GDP in the 1970s and the balance-of-payments current account deficit was manageable at about 6 percent of GDP. This was made possible by successful demand management policies and by a real depreciation the exchange rate of the Tunisian dinar. Aid from abroad was largely concessional and so the burden of debt servicing rose only modestly between 1970 and 1980.

In 1981, the international oil price fell and there was a decline in the estimate of Tunisia's oil reserves. Furthermore, Tunisia's phosphate production and manufacturing output declined and exports fell. Agricultural output fell because of bad weather and agro-industries suffered as a result. The fall in petroleum and phosphate prices worsened the terms of trade. The official response to the deterioration in economic conditions was to tighten price controls and restrict imports. This added to the rigidity of the economy and increased distortions but fiscal and monetary policies remained expansive. Between 1981 and 1984, domestic demand rose faster than GDP, resulting in pressure on the balance of payments. Tourism revenues and remittances declined and interest payments on foreign debt rose. The foreign exchange reserves declined. Problems experienced in the budget because of the fall in oil prices reduced government revenues: In 1982, the petroleum sector contributed 20 percent of government revenues and in 1986, 12.0 percent.[5] In addition, aid from official Arab sources declined as a share of GNP from 1.9 percent in 1977 to 0.2 percent in 1983.[6] The private sector and the balance of payments were also affected by a fall in remittances from 4.6 percent of GNP in 1982 to 3.2 percent in 1985.[7] In 1985, the budget deficit was cut, domestic price controls were liberalized as were imports and investment, but the terms of trade continued to deteriorate as did agricultural production and tourism revenues. The government was left with no alternative but to change course.

The 1986 Reforms

In August 1986, the government announced a new economic strategy. This was designed to improve the efficiency of the economy and improve financial

[5] Nsouli, Saleh et al. *The Path to Convertibility and Growth: The Tunisian Experience.* IMF Occasional Paper, No. 109. Washington, D.C.: International Monetary Fund, 1993. 2.

[6] Ibid. 6, Table 1.

[7] van den Boogaerde, Pierre. *Financial Assistance from Arab Countries and Arab Regional Institutions.* Occasional Paper, No. 87. Washington, D.C.: IMF, 1991. 41, 89.

stability by ending controls on prices, trade, investment, foreign exchange, and by adjusting the exchange rate to a more realistic level by devaluation. More resources would be made available for the private sector by reducing government spending and by improving monetary management. A stand-by loan arrangement was negotiated with the International Monetary Fund (IMF) and this was followed by a four-year extended arrangement. A loan was also negotiated with the World Bank for the agricultural sector. In 1987, an industrial and trade-policy adjustment loan was made available, and structural adjustment and other loans followed in 1988, 1989, and 1991. Tunisia did not seek debt rescheduling and serviced its debt on schedule.[8] The reforms in economic policy covered fiscal policy, monetary policy, and the banking system; changes in the management of the public sector; reforms of the investment code designed to encourage the private sector; reforms and rationalization of the foreign trade regime; and the foreign currency systems.

Fiscal policy reforms included the introduction of a value-added tax, a single personal income tax system, and a simplified corporate tax. These changes were designed to improve efficiency, equity, and the elasticity of the system. Tax incentives to the private sector were improved and numerous distortions removed. Measures were introduced to slow the growth of public-sector wages. Steps were also taken to gradually reduce subsidies.

The budgetary system was reformed with all public spending and revenues coming under the budget. During the period 1982–6, only 76 percent of public revenues and 37 percent of total government expenditures had been recorded in the budget.[9] The net effect of these measures was a reduction in the ratio of total government spending and lending to GDP from 40.7 percent in 1982–6 to 33.4 percent in 1987–91. The budget deficit, including grants from abroad, fell from an annual average of 5.4 percent of GDP in 1982–6 to 4.1 percent in 1987–91.[10] These reductions were much less dramatic than those experienced in Morocco in 1983 or in Egypt in 1991 because the fiscal imbalance prior to the reforms was less severe. Public-sector investment was reduced with the expectation that private-sector investment would take its place. Efforts were made to increase the efficiency of investment by eliminating potentially unsuccessful projects and concentrating public resources on infrastructure, education, and health.

[8] Ibid. 84.
[9] Nsouli et al. 5.
[10] Ibid. 6, Table 1.

Monetary policy was designed to reduce the growth of domestic credit and the money supply and to move financial resources from the public sector toward the private sector. In 1987, interest rates were increased to encourage the holding of interest-bearing local currency deposits and to discourage that of cash and foreign currency. Measures were also taken to strengthen the banking system and increase the role of market forces by reducing administrative controls. New financial instruments, including treasury bills, were introduced to deepen the capital market by providing an instrument for medium-term financial investments.

Structural reforms were designed to liberalize the economy by ending, or reducing government controls, and to open the economy toward exports. The measures included decontrolling prices at the production and distribution stage and reducing subsidies. In 1990, the share of agricultural and manufactured goods subject to price controls was 30 percent; in 1994, it was 13 percent.[11] Public-sector enterprises were transferred to nongovernment shareholders either through privatization or by liquidating nonviable firms. By early 1993, forty public enterprises had been privatized. Controls in private-sector investments were eased and the investment code was unified with the effect from 1994.

Foreign trade was liberalized through the lifting of restrictions on imports of raw materials, some finished products, spare parts, and capital goods. From 1985, imports of consumer goods were also liberalized. The tariffs on imports were lowered and their range was reduced in 1987–8. In 1990, 74 percent of the economy was protected by quantitative restrictions on imports; in 1995 this had fallen to only 8 percent. The average tariff rate was reduced from 40 percent in 1986 to 33 percent in 1994.[12] Finally measures were taken to make the dinar convertible. This involved increasing the allowances for invisible transactions carried out and by the banks. In January 1993 it was announced that the dinar would be convertible for current account transactions. The only restriction remaining was on transferring capital abroad.

Tunisia's reform program consisted more of structural adjustment than stabilization. This was because the deficits in the budget and the balance of payments were less serious than in Egypt and Morocco. There was, therefore, less need to stabilize the economy by reducing demand, especially in the public sector. The structural adjustment program was implemented in 1986 with the assistance of loans from the World Bank for different sectors and

[11] World Bank. *Trends in Developing Countries* 1996. 506.
[12] World Bank. *Trends in Developing Countries* 1996.

with support from the IMF. Although the financial pressures were less intense than elsewhere, Tunisia went further than any other Arab country in liberalizing its economy, both in terms of domestic policies and opening it to international trade. Despite this, problems remained.

Between 1976 and 1985, the economy grew by 11 percent a year; between 1986 and 1996, growth averaged 4.3 percent a year.[13] The slowdown was due to a number of factors. In 1990–1 the Gulf crisis affected the level of economic activity throughout the Middle East; in 1992–3 there was a recession in Western Europe, Tunisia's largest market, and, as a result of drought, there were three bad harvests in the years 1993–5.

Investment as a share of GDP was lower after 1986 than before. In 1988 it fell to its lowest level, as a share of GDP, since 1960.[14] This was because of the reduction of public investment and the inability of the private sector to fully compensate. From 1988 to 1993 there was an increase in investment from 22 percent of GDP to 31 percent. Although these were higher levels than in many Arab states, they were lower than those experienced in the 1960s and 1970s. There may, however, have been an increase in the efficiency of investment, with the ratio of capital to output falling by 40 percent between 1987 and 1992.[15] In 1988–9 drought resulted in slow growth of GDP of 1.8 percent and relatively fast inflation: 7.5 percent. During the 1994–5 drought the economy grew at 3.5 percent and inflation peaked at 5.5 percent. In 1996 the economy benefited from good rainfall and an upturn in the European economy and growth was estimated at 7.1 percent and in 1997, 5.4 percent.[16]

Positive achievements of the stabilization program included a reduction in inflationary pressures and an improvement in the balance of payments. The volume and burden of external debt also declined. Despite this, Tunisia's economic reform program was slow and as a result it is falling behind competitors such as China and Turkey. Between 1990 and 1994, Tunisian exports per head increased by an annual average of 2.5 percent in real terms, compared to a 5-percent average in the developing world. GDP per capita rose by an average of only 2 percent a year, also less than the average for developing countries. The World Bank urged the government to accelerate the liberalization of foreign trade, continue privatization, and increase the flexibility of the labor market.[17]

---

[13] IMF. *International Financial Statistics Yearbook 1997* and *International Financial Statistics, August 1998*.
[14] UN. *World Economic and Social Survey 1996*. 163.
[15] Ibid.
[16] IMF. *International Financial Statistics, August 1998*.
[17] Economist Intelligence Unit. *Country Profile Tunisia*, No. 4 (1996), 15.

In 1996, the World Bank agreed to provide $250 million of loans to help Tunisia implement its Association Agreement with the EU. These loans were designed to help fund employment services and retraining. They were also to be used to help private entrepreneurs improve the quality of their products and to help the government cope with the loss of revenue from import duties because of the agreement with the EU. In addition the World Bank agreed to provide $250 million in return for a government promise that 122 companies would be privatized.

Tunisia's reform program has been praised as one of the most successful in the Arab world. It has succeeded because the government has lived up to its commitments. It has worked closely with the IMF and the World Bank in implementing very orthodox proposals. The president, Zine al-Abidine Ben Ali, backed decisions taken by Western-trained and oriented technocrats who were given the authority to develop reforms.[18] The significance of presidential support for the reforms was considerable and contrasted with the weaker economic policy-making system in Egypt.[19]

After three disappointing years, 1993–5 in which GDP rose by an annual average of only 2.6 percent, 1996 and 1997 saw a recovery with an average annual rate of 6.3 percent. This took place against a background of low inflation, averaging less than 4 percent a year, despite rises in administered prices. The balance of payments remained manageable with imports rising as a result of higher investment, which accounted for 26.1 percent of GDP. Gross savings also rose to 22.7 percent of GDP in 1997, one of the highest rates in the Arab world.[20] Between 1997 and 2005, the economy grew by an annual average of 5 percent (see Figure 12.1).

Economic development means that the share of output coming from different sectors changes. Ideally this should be because growth accelerates in more modern sectors rather than just because traditional sectors decline. The latter should be relative rather than absolute. The structure of the Tunisian economy has changed over the last twenty years. The share of the primary sector fell sharply in the decade from 1985 and this was mirrored by an increase in the share of the nonprimary sector. The decline in the primary sector was because of the slower growth of agricultural production than that of industry and the decline in oil production. In many respects,

---

[18] Richards, Alan and John Waterbury. *A Political Economy of the Middle East.* Boulder, Colo.: Westview Press, 1996. 233.

[19] Rivlin, Paul. "Soft and Hard States" in Yafeh, Yishay, Ehud Harari, and Eyal Ben-Ari (eds.), *Lessons from East Asia.* Jerusalem: The Harry S. Truman Research Institute for the Advancement of Peace, 1998. 130–40.

[20] IMF. Press Notice, June 1998.

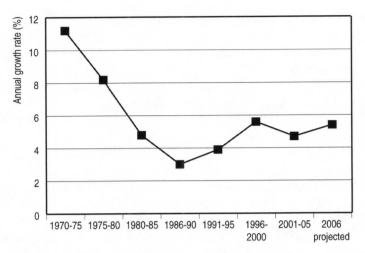

Figure 12.1. Tunisia: GDP Growth Rate, 1970–2006. *Source:* 1981–2004: Calculated from International Monetary Fund, International Financial Statistics Yearbook 1999, Yearbook 2002, IMF, Tunisia Article IV Consultation Staff Report Country Report No. 04/359, and Central Bank of Tunisia 46th Annual Report for 2004. 2005: Preliminary Estimate IMF, Tunisia 2005 Article IV Consultation 20 June 2006, Country Report 06/207.

the modernizing sector is manufacturing. The share of manufacturing in GDP, after increasing from 14.2 percent in 1983 to 17.1 percent in 1993, and to 18.6 percent in 2002, fell to 17.7 percent in 2004.[21] The growth of manufacturing output decelerated from an annual average of 11.8 percent in the 1970s to 6.8 percent in the 1980s. It then declined to 6.4 percent in 1990–5 and to only 4.3 percent in 2000–04.[22] Within manufacturing, the mechanical engineering and electronics sector did well. Between 1990 and 2003, its output increased by 107 percent, compared with 90 percent for manufacturing as a whole. Output in the other leading export sectors (textiles, clothing, and leather) increased by 134 percent, but they accounted for only 20 percent of manufactured output in 2003.[23]

---

[21] Central Bank of Tunisia. *47th Annual Report for 2005.* Tunisia: Tunis, 2005. www.bct.gov.tn. 56.

[22] Amsden, Alice H. *The Rise of the Rest: Challenges to the West from Late-Industrializing Economies.* New York: Oxford University Press, 2001. 293; Central Bank of Tunisia, *46th Annual Report for 2004.* 62.

[23] Republique Tunisienne, Ministere du Developpement et de al Cooperation International, Institut National de la Statistique. *Annuaire de la Tunisie, 2001,* no. 44 (2001), 129–30; *Central Bank of Tunisia, 46th Annual Report for 2004.* 56.

Table 12.3. *Tunisia: Agricultural and food production indices, 1990–2004*
(1999–2001 = 100)

	Agricultural production	Agricultural production/capita	Food production	Food production/capita
1990	81.9	94.9	81.2	94.0
1995	68.7	73.0	68.3	72.5
2000	97.9	97.8	97.8	97.7
2001	87.4	86.3	87.2	86.1
2002	83.6	81.7	83.4	81.5
2003	123.5	119.4	123.9	119.8
2004	101.5	97.1	101.6	97.2

Source: Food and Agriculture Organization FAPSTATS. www.fao.org.

The Tunisian economy faces four structural problems. The first is its reliance on agriculture that in turn is dependent on fluctuating levels of rainfall. The second is the weakness of the private sector, and the third is the unfavorable international economic environment. Finally, and as a result of the first three, it suffers from chronic high levels of unemployment, especially among the young. These are examined next.

Agriculture

The importance of agriculture remained despite the fact that its share in GDP declined from 19 percent in 1965–73 to 14 percent in 1997–9 (see Table 12.3). In 2001, it accounted for 22 percent of employment (see Table 12.4). The share of arable land that is irrigated remains low: in 2002 it was 13.7 percent, up from 10 percent in 1990.[24] As a result, fluctuations in rainfall affect the level of agricultural production and thus the rate of growth of national income.[25] The level of agricultural and food production has fluctuated sharply; six out of the last eight contractions in the level of business occurred in periods of agricultural contraction. In 1988, when there was a severe drought, agricultural output fell by 30 percent and, as a result, GDP growth was zero. In 1990, when there were good rains, agricultural output rose by 32.2 percent and GDP by 7.3 percent.[26] In 2000–02, as a result

---

[24] FAOSTAT. www. fao.org.
[25] Kouame, Auguste T. *Achieving Faster Economic Growth in Tunisia.* Washington, D.C.: World Bank, 1996. 46.
[26] World Bank. *Tunisia's Global Integration and Sustainable Development.* Vol. 4, No. 1 (2003).

Table 12.4. *Tunisia: Labor market trends, 1997–2001*

	1997	2001	1997–2001 growth rate %
Labor force	2,978,334	3,292,736	11
Male	2,255,734	2,468,386	9
Female	722,600	824,350	14
Urban	1,912,800	2,156,459	13
Rural	1,065,534	1,136,277	7
Employment	2,503,572	2,788,780	11
Male	1,906,400	2,095,431	10
Female	597,172	693,349	16
Agriculture	546,166	609,793	12
Manufacturing, excluding textiles	247,289	281,759	18
Textiles, clothing, and leather	259,233	276,909	7
Unemployment	474,762	503,956	6
Male	349,334	372,955	7
Female	125,428	131,001	4
Less than primary education	57,620	57,283	−1
Primary education	253,693	234,603	−8
Secondary education	146,327	180,150	23
Postsecondary education	17,122	31,920	86
Unemployment rate	15.9	15.3	

Source: World Bank. *Republic of Tunisia Employment Strategy*, Vol. 1 (2004), 24.

of drought, average agricultural production per head was 18 percent lower than in 1989–91.[27]

The effect of a change in agricultural output was stronger when agricultural production contracted than when it expanded. Hence a 1 percent fall in agricultural production caused a 0.25 percent fall in GDP; a much larger fall than its share in GDP. A 1-percent rise in agricultural output caused GDP to rise by only 0.17 percent. The difference was because as drought was anticipated, activity in agriculture-related industries and services slowed down, with consequent effects on GDP. When good rains were forecast, it was hard to calculate how far they would increase agricultural production. Caution was thus built into the upswing and investments did not increase commensurately. As a result, the effect of change in agricultural production on the economy was asymmetric. This was also true on the demand side: Declining agricultural incomes affected households' consumption more than increasing incomes did.[28]

---

[27] FAO. Bulletin Working Paper Series No. 20 (December 2000), 2–5.
[28] Kouame. 4.

Table 12.5. *Tunisia: Employment growth, 1989–2001*

	Employment growth (% annual average)	Nonagricultural employment growth (% annual average)
1989–1994	3.2	4.4
1994–1997	2.6	2.5
1997–2001	2.7	2.6

Source: World Bank. *Republic of Tunisia Employment Strategy,* Vol. 1 (2004), 3.

Between 1994 and 2004, food production increased by 45.2 percent (see Table 12.5). This reflected the fact that 1994 was a base with low output. Compared with the average for 1999–2001, output increased by only 1.6 percent, not enough to keep up with the rate of growth of the population.

The Weakness of the Private Sector

Although Tunisia has gone further in terms of economic reforms than most Arab countries, it has not been able to break through a glass ceiling and achieve the higher growth rates and lower unemployment rates prevailing in fast-developing countries outside the Middle East. According to the IMF, Tunisia's economy needs more reforms, including a more flexible labor market.[29] There is, however, another problem that prevents growth and this is the weakness of the private sector. If this thesis is true for Tunisia then it is even more so in other, less developed Arab countries, with the obvious exception of Lebanon.

To understand this weakness, it is worth looking at the way in which the private industrial sector developed in Tunisia. During the modern colonial period from 1881, the French bought agricultural products from Tunisia and sold industrial products there. Virtually no French investment was made in Tunisian industry. In 1904, this pattern was formalized with the creation of a customs union between France and Tunisia that ensured free access for French industrial products in Tunisian markets. The situation changed in the late 1930s and during World War II, when the absence of French goods encouraged industrial production in Tunisia. France started to promote industrial development in 1942 to maintain the economy, but French personnel dominated the industries set up, thus preventing the

[29] IMF. *Article IV Consultation and Staff Report Tunisia, 2006.* 18.

creation of a locally based private sector. This continued until independence in 1956.

Tunisia's independence was followed by a debate on how the economy should be run. There were two main schools of thought: one favored the private sector and the other favored the public sector. In the early years, the private sector was encouraged with loans, tax, and other benefits. However, its response was weak and in 1962, in an attempt to encourage economic growth, a state-led policy was implemented. Although the state invested in public-sector industries, it never wholly discredited the private sector as happened in other Arab countries during their socialist phase. The aim of the policy was to concentrate economic decision making in the government rather than implement socialism. During the period 1962–71, the public accounted for 72 percent of gross fixed investment.[30] All this took place within the context of import substitution: tariffs and other restrictions on imports meant that local markets were reserved for domestic production, something that was to continue until the 1980s.

Failures in agricultural production and a fiscal crisis resulted in a change of direction in the early 1970s. Emphasis was placed on the private sector; extensive help and encouragement were provided. In the words of the minister of national economy, the state would create a generation of private-sector industrialists who would take over economic leadership in the future.[31] The results were dramatic: in the 1970s, industrial growth grew rapidly.

These patterns of development show that the private industrial sector was neither parasitic nor dominant. The early 1980s brought economic crisis when oil revenues fell as a result of lower Tunisian production and lower world prices. Agricultural production fell as a result of drought and as a result of the combination of these factors, both the state budget and the balance of payments deteriorated. In 1986, the government announced comprehensive reforms designed to stabilize and restructure the economy. These were based on agreements with the IMF and the World Bank and included a liberalization of foreign trade. This reduced the extent of import substitution, gradually exposing parts of industry to foreign competition. With the signing of an Association Agreement with the EU in 1995, Tunisia committed itself to much more extensive reductions on taxes on imports from its major market.

---

[30] Bellin, Eva. "Tunisian Industrialists and the State" in Zartman, I. William (ed.), *Tunisia: The Political Economy of Reform.* Boulder, Colo. and London: Lynne Rienner, 1991. 49.
[31] Ibid. 50.

Compared to other high-growth developing economies, Tunisia suffers from a lack of private investment. Despite satisfactory macroeconomic conditions and structural reforms, growth has relied more on public investment, and private investment remains limited, at around 14 percent of GDP in the early 2000s. This was even a lower rate than in the 1980s and early 1990s. One reason for the low private-investment ratio is the limited openness of services markets and network industries, particularly in information technology and transport. This kept the cost of key services high, hindered competitiveness, and deprived Tunisia from significant opportunities for private investment. Another reason was the uncertainty of the business environment, reflecting the risks in Tunisia's international economic environment. However, these factors only partly explain the large private-investment gap in Tunisia. The World Bank provides a further explanation. Interference by the government was often arbitrary, limited competition, and favored those who had personal connections to officials. The regulatory framework lacked transparency and predictability as did that for government contracts. All this limited competition, efficiency, investment, and production.[32]

The weakness of the private sector notwithstanding, the fact that it is more developed than in many other Arab countries has meant that total investment, as a share of GDP, was lower after the economic reforms of 1986 than before. In 1988, it fell to its lowest level as a share of GDP since 1960.[33] From 1988 until 1993, there was an increase in investment from 22 percent of GDP to 31 percent. Although these were higher levels than in many Arab states, they were lower than those experienced in Tunisia in the 1960s and 1970s. The share of private-sector investment in GDP rose in the 1970s from 11–12 percent to 15–16 percent. In the 1990s it fell, reaching 12–13 percent in 1995–9.[34]

The private sector faces government-imposed limitations. First, privatization of the telecommunications, transport, and other sectors has been limited. In other developing countries, including Arab ones, these sectors have attracted substantial private capital and foreign investment. Partly because these sectors remain publicly owned or dominated, competition is limited and so costs and prices are high. This is closely related to weaknesses in the regulatory environment. Government officials retain a high degree

[32] World Bank. *Country Assistance Strategy for the Republic of Tunisia, 2004*. 7–8.
[33] UN. *World Economic and Social Survey 1996*. 163.
[34] Anos-Casero, Paloma and Aristomene Varoudakis. *Growth, Private Investment, and the Cost of Doing Business in Tunis: A Comparative Perspective*. Washington, D.C.: World Bank, January 2004. 19.

of discretion in regulating economic activity. The arbitrary powers used by government officials reflected the state of play in government–private sector relations. Although the government has long recognized its limitations as an entrepreneur and financier, it has not been willing to share power with the private sector. One of the ways in which it maintains its control is to act arbitrarily, and avoid excessive transparency and clarity.[35]

Tunisia's rulers have maintained a large bureaucracy and public sector so that they can dispense patronage and retain control. As the domestic market is small, economies of scale in production are limited and so the development of manufacturing industry for the local market is limited. Tariffs on imports offer opportunities for rents, but they are threatened by international trade agreements. As a result of its relatively high living standards, Tunisia does not receive much foreign aid, so the government has encouraged the development of an export manufacturing sector.

Tunisia has failed to integrate the export sector into the oligarchy close to the ruling elite. As the regime lacks legitimacy, it has hesitated to open the doors to either full economic or political competition. The regime favors trusted, individual capitalists, rather than the capitalist class as a whole.[36] The uneven resuscitation of capitalism has been too incomplete and discontinuous to create a new class of independent capitalists and so the accumulation of capital has not translated into political power.[37] The new capitalist class is reliant on the state for licenses and even access to capital.

During the period of economic liberalization, since 1986, Tunisia's ruling party has abandoned its traditional attempt to represent a broad segment of society and has become a vehicle representing the interests of the rural bourgeoisie and urban manufacturers, many of whom were previously rural notables. As a result, the regime now represents the rural bourgeoisie and the urban bourgeoisie is merely an offshoot. At the same time, an increasingly globalized economy and stagnant state-led growth strategies within Tunisia led to constraints on state autonomy, as international forces pressed for increased market reforms. Currently the Islamist movement serves as the strongest organized resistance to the ruling party. The party's increasing link with the rural bourgeoisie and its urban offshoot, as well as its ties to transnational capital, has brought to an end the era in which the

[35] Henry, Clement M. and Robert Springborg. *Globalization and the Politics of Development in the Middle East*. Cambridge: Cambridge University Press, 2001. 136.

[36] Ibid. 156.

[37] King, Stephen J. "Economic Reform and Tunisia's Hegemonic Party: The End of the Administrative Elite – Beyond Colonialism and Nationalism in North Africa." *Arab Studies Quarterly* Vol. 20, no. 2 (Spring 1998). 1.

administrative elite in Tunisia was willing and able to challenge the interests of the most powerful social forces within and outside of the country.[38]

Social conflict has been depoliticized or privatized and this has disciplined and divided the business community and the trade unions. The business community is split between the state orientated, anti-liberalization group and the market-orientated, pro-liberalization group. The latter is a tiny minority of private entrepreneurs, although it does control the Tunisian Union of Industrialists, Merchants, and Artisans (UTICA) and export industries.[39]

The International Environment

The implementation of the Association Agreement with the European Union (AAEU) by 2008 and the phasing out of the Multi-Fibre Arrangement (MFA) at the end of 2004, which consisted of bilateral agreements establishing quotas to protect domestic textile industries, pose competitive challenges for Tunisia. More than 40 percent of Tunisia's exports have been concentrated in clothing, and 75 percent of exports go the EU countries. Between 1991 and 1995, the manufacturing export growth rate averaged 12.9 percent per annum but between 1996 and 2002, export performance worsened and the growth rate of manufactured exports decreased to 3.7 percent.[40]

Tunisia suffers from a chronic trade deficit, which averaged $2.2 billion a year between 1993 and 2003. In 2004–06 it averaged an estimated $2.3 billion. The trade deficit was partly financed by tourism revenues and by the remittances of Tunisian workers abroad. There was also a deficit on the service account, and the volume of transfers did not cover the deficit. As a result, the current account of the balance of payments was in deficit throughout the period, but could be financed by inflows of funds including foreign investment. Since 1993, food imports have accounted for a decreasing share of total imports: In 1993, they took 14 percent, and in 2003, they accounted for only 6.7 percent.[41] In 2005, Tunisia's foreign debt came to

---

[38] Erdle, Steffen. "Tunisia: Economic Transformation and Political Restoration" in Perthes, Volker (ed.), *Arab Elites Negotiating the Politics of Change*. Boulder, Colo.: Lynne Rienner, 2004. 227–8.

[39] World Bank. *Press Release* No. 2004/465/MNA. "World Bank Approves US$36 Million to Boost Tunisia's Exports." 2004.

[40] World Bank. *Country Assistance Strategy for the Republic of Tunisia, 2004.* 78.

[41] European Union. *EU Trade Issues.* www.europa.eu.int; IMF: *Tunisia: 2007 Article IV Consultation – Staff Report; Public Information Notice on the Executive Board Discussion;* and

$17.8 billion, equal to 66 percent of gross national income (GNI). This was double the share of foreign debt in Morocco and much more than in Egypt. Servicing it accounted for 13 percent of exports, double the Egyptian level and much higher than in Morocco. The high and burdensome level of debt persisted despite the stabilization of the economy years ago.[42]

In 2003, the EU accounted for 79 percent of Tunisian exports and 74 percent of its imports. Its exports have been heavily concentrated: clothing and textiles accounted for 48 percent of exports. A total of 82 percent of Tunisia's tourism revenues came from the EU.[43] Its share of European markets for manufactured goods has failed to grow at anything like the rate of its South Asian and East Asian competitors in that market. Furthermore, its position in the EU market for textiles and clothing has deteriorated, as the Multi-Fibre Arrangement (MFA), which gave it privileged access, was phased out. The effects of increased competition on international textile and clothing markets were felt in 2003 and 2004. Added value in the textile, clothing, leather, and footwear industries fell in 2003 by 3.7 percent and in 2004 by 0.4 percent. As a result, their share in GDP declined from 6 percent to 5.6 percent. Textile and clothing as a share of total exports fell from 41.1 percent in 2003 to 37.2 percent in 2004.[44]

The agreements that have been signed with the EU mean that Tunisia will reduce its taxes on imports. This will expose the economy to increased competition from EU goods and, at the same time, government revenues will decline. Like other Arab states, Tunisia is under great pressure to make its economy more efficient. If they cannot cope with the competition, then firms will close and jobs will be lost. This could prove disastrous, given current high levels of unemployment.

There has been a lack of integration of the offshore export sector that produced clothing and textiles for the EU and those sections of the economy supplying the domestic sector. Companies producing for export benefit from duty-free imports of inputs. The domestic economy continues to operate on an import substitution basis: despite reductions in import

Statement by the Executive Director for Tunisia, Report No. 07/302. 20; IMF: Tunisia: *2006 Article IV Consultation – Staff Report; Staff Statement; Public Information Notice on the Executive Board Discussion*; and *Statement by the Executive Director for Tunisia*, Report No. 06/207. 23.

[42] IMF. *Global Development Finance 2007*. Washington, D.C.: IMF, 2007. 396–7.

[43] Central Bank of Tunisia. *46th Annual Report for 2004*. 67.

[44] Page, John. *Structural Reforms in the Middle East in The Arab World Competitiveness Report 2002–3*, New York: Oxford University Press for the World Economic Forum, 2003. 69.

duties, they remain high by international standards.[45] European companies invested in Tunisian plants that produced textiles and clothing for the European market. These plants did not have free access to the domestic market, which remains protected. In 2003, Tunisia had an unweighted average import tariff of 30 percent, double that for lower middle-income countries worldwide.[46] As a result, a dual system has developed: one for export and another for the domestic market. Because of the protection offered to producers for the domestic market and restriction on entry into the domestic market placed on exporters, their technologies, cost, and efficiency levels vary. Although manufacturing has been fairly dynamic, the sector remains small compared to those in other developing countries that have achieved fast income growth. Textiles and mechanical/electrical equipment have performed well as export sectors but have only made a modest contribution to GDP. This is explained by the fact that both these groups of industries rely on imports and add little value to inputs before they are exported.

The Labor Market

Insofar as Tunisia is the most industrialized and best performing non-oil Arab state, it is worthwhile examining developments in the labor market in some detail. Employment growth accelerated slightly from 2.6 percent a year in 1994–7 to 2.7 percent a year in 1997–2001, but this was less than the 3.2 percent recorded in 1989–94. In 1997–2001 this meant that 71,000 jobs were created a year while 79,000 were needed to prevent unemployment increasing. There were two reasons why employment did not grow fast enough to prevent unemployment rising: first, the economy did not grow fast enough and second, there was a fall in the employment intensity of growth in all sectors except agriculture. Significantly, manufacturing experienced a decline in employment intensity.[47] Although the population is growing at only 1.2 percent a year, the labor force is increasing by 2.5 percent a year. Despite its relatively good growth record, unemployment in Tunisia is very high. The economy has not grown fast enough or in the right way to reduce this rate.

---

[45] World Bank. *Trade, Investment, and Development in the Middle East and North Africa.* http://www.worldbank.org. 2003. 136.

[46] IMF. *Tunisia: 2004 Article IV Consultation-Staff Report.* 2004. 6.

[47] World Bank. *Republic of Tunisia, Employment Strategy, Volume 1.* 2004. 3–4, 24.

As in other Arab countries, unemployment is a major problem. In 2001 it was 15.3 percent, down from 16.2 percent in 1999. In 2005 it was estimated at about 14.5 percent.[48] In 2004, the labor force was 3.3 million and so an unemployment rate of 13.9 percent meant that 458,700 were unemployed. In 2004, job creation outside agriculture was 74,000 and between 2000 and 2003 it averaged 66,200. In 2001, 82 percent of the unemployed had completed primary education or had completed primary and secondary education. The unemployment rate among those who had completed secondary education was 17 percent; among those who had no education or an incomplete primary education it was 9.6 percent. More than half of the unemployed were aged 20–29. The unemployment rate fell from 34 percent among those aged 15–29 to 5.8 percent among those aged 50 and older.[49]

In 2004, the labor force increased by about 82,500 and unemployment rose by some 8,500. This was in a year in which industrial output growth accelerated and in which the economy grew by 6 percent.[50] The pattern of employment generation was also problematic. The generation of employment in the manufacturing sector has slowed down in recent years, and the government has been responsible for most job creation.[51] The labor force has become more educated and the number of women looking for employment outside the home has increased because of successful programs to improve and expand women's education. However, the demand for highly skilled workers has declined and this seems to be resulting in a rise in unemployment among the better educated. This phenomenon, which has been detected in other Arab countries, is very worrying because it puts a question mark over one of the most important tools that has been used to bring about economic development. Another reason why unemployment is high among the better educated is that they are educated in the wrong skills.

In the 1990s, employment growth was concentrated in the public sector and in other low-productivity sectors. Job creation for the skilled population declined leading to higher rates of unemployment among those with more education. To meet the employment challenges of the current Tenth Development Plan (2002–06), 80,000 jobs will need to be created annually

[48] IMF. *Tunisia: 2007 Article IV Consultation Mission, Preliminary Conclusion,* 2007. http://www.imf.org.

[49] Central Bank of Tunisia, *46th Annual Report for 2005.* www.bct.gov.tn/english/publication/index.html. Chapter 5.

[50] www-wds.worldbank.org/servlet/WDSContentServer/WDSP/IB/2004/07/28/000012009_20040728105627/Rendered/PDF/25456110v.pdf.

[51] Central Bank of Tunisia, *Annual Report 2004.* http://www.cbt.gov.tu.

to absorb the rise in the labor force. This will require nonagricultural output to grow by 10 percent a year, compared with 5.7 percent experienced in the 1990s or 6.2 percent projected in the Plan. If unemployment is to be reduced, growth will have to be even faster.

Job creation in private services and manufacturing declined from 50,000 a year in 1989–94 to 37,000 a year in 1994–7 and to 34,000 a year in 1997–2001. In manufacturing, the number of jobs created fell from 20,600 in 2000–01 to 18,500 in 2003–04. Within the manufacturing sector, job creation in electromechanics rose from 1,000 a year in 1989–94 to 4,000 a year in 1994–7 and 1997–2001 while that in textiles fell from 10,000 to 6,000 and then to 4,000.[52] This suggests that there was a process of structural change within manufacturing but that it was not strong enough to increase job creation. One of the factors behind the deceleration of employment growth in manufacturing was an acceleration of productivity growth. This reflected the modernization of manufacturing within and between its subsectors.

According to the IMF, unemployment fell from 15.3 percent in 2001 to an estimated rate of 14.3 percent in 2005 and to a projected rate of 13.9 percent in 2006.[53]

Conclusions

Tunisia is in many respects a model for other Arab countries to follow. It has a stable economy with growth, good human development indices, a relatively large manufacturing sector plus exports, but it also has high unemployment. As the Tunisian economy has become more sophisticated it has become harder to control. The costs of overcontrol have grown and resulted in distortions and economic losses. Tunisia's economic future is constrained by government control. It has taken many of the steps advocated by the IMF and the World Bank to stabilize its economy and also introduced structural adjustment measures. It now needs to extend these reforms but hesitates because it fears that economic reform, privatization, and greater liberalization will lead to political change. How far Tunisia has to go on the political front is revealed in data from the Arab Human Development Report. The UN's human development index (HDI) combines information on life expectancy, adult literacy, school enrollment, and GDP per

---

[52] IMF. *Executive Board Concludes 2006 Article IV Consultation with Tunisia.* Public Information Notice. No. 06/62. 8 June 8 2006.

[53] Murphy, Emma C. "The Tunisian *Mise à Niveau* Programme and the Political Economy of Reform." *The New Political Economy*, Vol. 11, No. 4 (December 2006). 519–40.

capita. Tunisia's 2002 HDI was 0.745, placing it as the 92nd country in the world. In Tunisia illiteracy was relatively low: 37 percent among women and 17 percent among men.[54] The Alternative Human Development Index added data on lifelong knowledge acquisition, availability of information technology, women's access to societal power, and measures of human freedom. When these additional criteria were included, in 2002, Tunisia's ranking was ninety-three, behind Jordan (sixty-seven), Lebanon (seventy-three), Morocco (seventy-nine), and Egypt (ninety-two). The highest was Sweden and the United States came in at number eleven. Tunisia's political freedom score was very low at 0.18. (Sweden's was 1.00 and the lowest in the world was Congo with 0.03.[55]) This reflects the fact that in the 1990s and the early 2000s, Tunisia became a much more repressive society. According to the World Bank, the UN Development Fund, and others, Tunisia's lack of democracy is, or will be, a factor that retards its economy over time.

The state in Tunisia has, like that in other Arab countries, developed with considerable autonomy from society. It has used selective coalitions to achieve reforms but the patrimonial, personalized, and authoritarian tendencies of the president have undermined this. This includes the use of the police and security forces. The system has become one of rent-seeking, by the state and the private sector with the resultant blurring of the border between them. As elsewhere in the region, it has become an obstacle to reform. The size of the state has shrunk because of the economic reforms, but its power remains dominant through its network of connections in the public–private sector. As Tunisia experiences the loss of its textile markets in Europe as the result of Chinese competition following the end of the MFA, it will need to find new sources of economic growth and that will require political change.[56]

---

[54] IMF. *Tunisia 2006 Article IV Consultation and Staff Report*. http://www.imf.org. 22.
[55] World Bank. *World Development Indicators 2004*. 85–6.
[56] United Nations Development Program. *Arab Human Development Report 2002*. New York: UN, 2002. 166–7.

THIRTEEN

Conclusions

The Arab Equilibrium

The Arab world is experiencing demographic transition: the population of working age is increasing faster than the dependent population. The growth of the labor force provides the opportunity to increase production and thus income but the condition for this to take place is faster employment growth. The rise in oil income over the last decade, plus the effect of limited economic reforms, has resulted in somewhat faster employment growth in recent years, but it has not been enough to reduce unemployment significantly. The very high levels of youth unemployment pose a serious threat to social and political stability and have persisted for years. Given the severe imbalances that exist in the labor markets of all Arab countries, the central question posed in this book is "Why have reforms been so limited?" This chapter examines the reasons why. The basic concepts outlined in Chapter 3 were chosen because of their relevance in explaining the weak economic development of the Arab world. There are overlaps between the works of those cited as well as contradictions. My interpretation uses these ideas eclectically.

The ideas examined in Chapter 3 suggest a number of conclusions. The first is that what happens today and what people plan for the future (or do not plan) is affected by past events and maybe by those in the distant past. This is largely because institutions, ideas, and knowledge are formed over time. Furthermore, experience, one of the main conduits for the acquisition of knowledge and understanding, takes time to acquire. Generations learn from their predecessors and adapt and change what they receive in the light of their own experiences. These processes are universal, but they work differently over the globe. In certain periods change is rapid; in others it is slow. There is also geographical variation as regions simultaneously develop, but at different speeds.

The second is that geography had initial and indirect effects. Hydraulic despotism was geographically determined and was a means to survive in the river valleys of the Middle East and other parts of the world. To operate it required centralized administration to organize the irrigation system. These geographical factors have remained ever since and all the cultural and other changes that have occurred since then have been added to the legacy influenced by geography.

The third conclusion is that political factors are central. The Arab or Islamic Empire that unified much of the Middle East from the eighth century on had centralized rule, even though there were periods of decentralization. For many people in the region, it was foreign rule. Government was therefore something alienating if not alien. The Arab/Islamic Empire was succeeded by the Ottoman Empire, which was operated on similar lines: periods of decentralization with Mamluks and others ruling for the Ottomans. The Mamluks were chosen for their loyalty to the sultan, not for the closeness to the ruled, and so the tradition of alien rule and alienation continued. The two empires ruled in the Middle East for some eleven hundred years until the First World War and the effects of such a long and recent period of imperial rule were immense. The Arab/Islamic Empire was created by the Prophet and his immediate successors in the name of God. As a result there was an identity between state and religion. The implications of this are examined next.

The collapse of the Ottoman Empire had a dual effect in the region. On the one hand it resulted in the end of foreign rule and this was welcomed as furthering Arab aims.[1] On the other hand, the abolition, in 1924, of the caliphate was condemned as a betrayal of Islam by some, particularly in the region that became Saudi Arabia. The end of Ottoman rule was followed by the period of genuinely foreign rule as Great Britain and France took over parts of the region and maintained indirect control over others.

The experience of Western colonialism in the Middle East differed from that of Latin America in one key respect. With the notable exception of Algeria, Western settlers were insignificant compared with the Spanish and Portuguese settlement in Latin America. The Westerners who settled in Latin America played a dominant role in the political economy of the region. They killed, or caused the death, of most of the native population, imported millions of slaves, and later formed the main group pushing for independence from the Spanish and Portuguese thrones. This was largely true for those

---

[1] Hourani, Albert. *Arabic Thought in the Liberal Age.* London, Oxford, New York: Oxford University Press, 1962. 183–4, 267–8.

parts of North America that became the United States, although there were many differences between the northern and southern states. The Western presence in the Arab world was largely rejected or ejected following Arab independence. This applied to groups such as the Jews, Armenians, and Greeks whose presence preceded the arrival of Napoleon in Egypt. The migration, from the 1880s, of Jews from Europe to Palestine as part of the Zionist enterprise was also rejected, as was the state of Israel. Arab relations with their former rulers in the West have, in many respects, not progressed beyond the hostility stage. This stands in strong contrast to the reaction of East Asian and Southeast Asian states to Japan. The expulsion of foreigners following Arab independence resulted in economic losses as it weakened the middle class and the region's trading links.

One similarity with the colonization of Latin America was that Western countries exploited the Middle East's natural resources. The British controlled much of the Gulf that was rich in oil reserves and, from the 1940s the United States played an increasingly important role there. (This also applied to Iran.) It took the Arab states many years to gain control of their oil and gas resources and so when they did, in the 1970s, the effect was dramatic.[2] The economic and political implications of oil are discussed later, but one point should be made here. The British, in creating the states of the Gulf, handed the oil fields over to the rulers as the private property of the latter. The structure of power and wealth in the Gulf States was therefore partly a legacy of the colonial period.

Between the 1930s and the 1960s, Arab countries gained their independence. The process varied by country with peaceful evolution in parts of the Gulf and major conflict in Algeria. In most of the monarchies the political system survives to this day, the most notable exceptions being Iraq and Libya. In Iraq and Egypt, the period of liberal democracy under a monarch in the mid-twentieth century was brought to an end by the military, the dominant group in the politics of the region since independence. By their very nature they were unrepresentative and ultimately alienating, if not alien. From the 1950s to the 1970s, the economic policies that they adopted were influenced by the Soviet Union. Since then, they have been influenced by the United States and the West. None of them have had successful economies and this has caused alienation, frustration, and dissent. It has also provided the context in which terrorism within and outside the region has become potent.

---

[2] Rivlin, Paul. *World Oil and Energy Trends: Strategic Implications for Israel, Jaffee Center for Strategic Studies*, Memorandum No. 57. Tel Aviv: Jaffee Center for Strategic Studies, 2000. 15–21.

The military and the regimes that they spawned, as well as the monarchies, were all notable for throttling opposition either partly or totally. This meant, among other things, that debate and discussion were restricted. For many, all that was left as a source of comfort, support, or inspiration was Islam.

We, therefore, need to examine the role of Islam in more detail. There has been much debate about the role of religion in the economic development of the region. Islam is no more intrinsically harmful to economic development than Judaism or Christianity, to which it is closely related. A key difference is that Islam created an empire, and Arab states today share that as a source of identity and unity. Although the unity of the Arab states has weakened over time, the shared Islamic past has become a more important symbol for many. The second difference is that Judaism and Christianity, as practiced by most of their adherents, has changed significantly. This was most dramatically manifest in the Protestant Reformation, and later the rise of secularism. Islam was not subject to anything like the Reformation and the process of secularization was much narrower and perhaps shallower. There were changes, but they were not unidirectional. The Golden Age of Islam was followed by restrictions that stifled debate, creativity, science, and technology. In the Christian world, there were attempts to restrict thought with consequences for development, such as the persecution of Galileo, but over time the trend was to an opening of the mind and a reevaluation of the past that permitted the development of science and technology, bringing huge economic benefits. The problem in the Arab world was the use made of Islam and this was essentially a political matter. As rulers had a monopoly (or near monopoly) of power they could use Islam as they wished. It was also possible because it formed the belief system of the vast majority of the population. Acting against the state was an act against Islam when the ruler was the caliph. The battle was therefore over the interpretation of Islam and in this, as in so much else, the state was dominant.

The Arab/Islamic and Ottoman Empires were remarkable for their duration: seven hundred and four hundred years, respectively. This was due to their military success in putting down threats from abroad and at home. The latter reflected the uneven nature of the power structure: there was very little to oppose the state from within. A crucial group that is almost always the source and transmitter of change – the middle class – was marginalized throughout. This had profound implications for economic development.

The balance of political forces that prevails at the beginning of the twenty-first century does not encourage economic development. The forces for economic change are weak, while those favoring the status quo are strong. As a result, recommendations for economic, social, and political reform are largely ignored by Arab governments. The most powerful force acting against change is the fact that the regimes are, in Ayubi's terminology, fierce but weak. They feel that major economic reforms might lead to a change in the balance of political forces that would diminish, or even extinguish, their power. They have formidable resources to maintain themselves in power: modern technology has made armies, police, and secret police forces very effective in dealing with opposition when warnings do not work. The huge scale of Arab armies and paramilitaries testifies to this.

If it retarded growth, why was there no significant exit from Islam until the abolition of the caliphate in 1924?[3] The reason was that Islam was a secular force as well as a religious one; rejecting Islam, reinterpreting it, or limiting its role was a political act that no individual or group could easily contemplate. The state gained its legitimacy from Islam: the state was Islamic. Here we need to look at the role of the state over a long period, from the decline of the Golden Age, through the Ottoman period to the creation of independent states in the Arab world. Islam has not lost its centrality in the Arab world and the state does not need to enforce religion. Rather the opposite: governments in the Arab world have had in recent years to restrain fundamentalism.

Islam affected the belief system or it may have been *the* belief system. This determined people's willingness to accept or reject the decisions of government that were imposed in an undemocratic way. As opposing the state was to oppose Islam – the belief system – it was not only the actions of the state that counted, but also their perception or context among the population. The identity of religion and state in the Arab and Ottoman Empires was of great political and economic significance. It influenced the way in which people thought and reacted and this became part of the culture in much of the Middle East. The fact that Islam came to parts of Southeast Asia so much later may well help to explain the differences in economic performance between the Arab countries and Malaysia and even Indonesia.

Economies exist in competitive systems: the companies or corporations within them compete among themselves and to the extent that there is international trading, they compete with those abroad. The imbalance between companies in the Middle East and those in Europe has been noted. As time passed, European companies and banks grew, specialized, and created trading networks. Those in the Middle East lagged behind because of legal

---

[3] Montgomery, James. "Toward a Joint Theory of Religion and Economic Development Comment on Timur Kuran, Islam and Underdevelopment: An Old Puzzle Revisited." *Journal of Institutional and Theoretical Economics*, 153. (1997). 74.

problems analyzed in Chapter 3. As a result, a gap developed in the level of economic activity that became ever harder to close. This is yet another reason why comparative economic analysis is essential. The unwillingness of many in the region (as well as many who study it) to accept this is in itself the symptom of a malaise, an unwillingness to accept reality. Greif notes that cognitive dissonance has played a major negative role in the Muslim world.[4]

In the last twenty or thirty years, the most important force pushing for economic liberalization has been the international community led by the World Bank and the International Monetary Fund (IMF). Their role in the Arab world increased when economic crises hit parts of the region in the 1970s and 1980s. Their power lay in the fact that they controlled the purse strings and they usually laid down strict conditions in exchange for aid. The U.S. government and, more recently the European Union, have played a similar role on a bilateral basis.

With the exception of foreign donors, no interest group has been able to stop the state from adopting its chosen path. It should be noted that in Egypt strategic rents eased the conditions imposed by the IMF: The United States intervened to soften IMF decisions regarding conditions for aid. In Syria, foreign loans were not taken, and the speed of liberalization has been slow and its direction and content unclear.

Another foreign interest has been the reliance of Western and other countries on Middle Eastern oil. The willingness, in 1991, of the United States to send five hundred thousand troops halfway around the world (albeit with the costs paid by Saudi Arabia and Kuwait) to liberate Kuwait was due to its fears that Iraq would gain control of Saudi, as well as Kuwaiti, oil fields. Alliances between Western powers and Gulf rulers go back to the creation of the Gulf States. Today those regimes, and many others in the region, receive explicit or implicit Western support to help them deal with Islamic fundamentalist forces. Thus, while the West advocates economic and political decentralization, or a weakening of the state vis-à-vis society in Arab states, it reinforces the state by buying oil (the oil sector is government-owned in all Arab states), providing military aid or sales of defense equipment.

The very sources of stability in Arab countries were also those of economic malaise. The first source was the role of rents. During the period 1980–2000, the region earned about $2.5 trillion in rents ($125 billion a year on

---

[4] Greif, Avner. *Institutions and the Path to the Modern Economy: Lessons from Medieval Trade.* Cambridge: Cambridge University Press, 2006. 191–2.

average), 90 percent from oil. In 2001–07, oil revenues in the seven Arab members of OPEC were estimated at $1.77 trillion ($253 billion a year on average).[5] This was possible with very limited economic activity within the region: fewer than one million people were employed in the oil, refining, and petrochemical industries. Oil revenues, along with foreign aid, went to the state or to the ruler. As a result, much of the nation's production was concentrated in the state sector. It was the state that distributed the wealth generated. The oil-rich states were not socialist, nor, with the exception of Iraq, did any of them go through a socialist phase. Yet in some respects they behaved like socialist states.

The volume of oil wealth that has been accumulating since 1999 has led to an increase in Arab funds held abroad. These now yield billions of dollars of income in the form of interest, profits, rents, and dividends. If the estimate of Gulf Cooperation Council (GCC) foreign reserves of $1.55 trillion of overseas assets is accurate (and not an underestimate as the authors of the estimate believe) then a 5-percent return brings in $77.5 billion annually. This can be added to rental incomes from other sources.[6] Total rental incomes from oil and interest may therefore have been as high as $330 billion a year in recent years.

The second source of stability was the political system. Dictatorships of various kinds, varying from the "bunker states" of Algeria, Iraq, Libya, Sudan, and Syria to the "bully praetorian states" of Egypt and Tunisia and the monarchies of Jordan, the GCC states, and Morocco all survive by force, or the threat of force, against their own citizens.[7] Egypt is one of the more open societies in the region, although it seems to be moving backwards toward the bunker states. All major decisions about the allocation of resources are made by the government with only very narrow consultation or democratic decision making. This was the situation under Nasser and it remains true under Mubarak and is the ideal environment for rental agreements to be concluded. The leader's aim is not to produce economic growth but to survive. If growth is the only way for the system to survive then attempts will be made to encourage economic growth, but if those steps threaten the system through a loss of power by the government, they will be avoided.

---

[5] Calculated from Energy Information Agency, Department of Energy. *OPEC Revenues Fact Sheet*. January 2006. http://wwwww.eia.doe.gov.

[6] Institute of International Finance, Gulf Cooperation Council Regional Briefing, 2007. http://www.iif.com.

[7] The terminology is from Henry, Clement M. and Robert Springborg. *Globalization and the Politics of Development in the Middle East.* Cambridge: Cambridge University Press, 2001.

This is how economic policy has muddled through in Egypt and elsewhere in the Arab world.

Third, the political system operates without checks or balances. One reason for this is the lack of a strong middle class, the weakness of civil society, and the ability of the state to penetrate nonstate activities. Ayubi called the Arab state fierce rather than strong: it is stronger than other groups in society but its attempts to mobilize the society around development objectives have been weak. Because of its undemocratic nature, the Arab state has relied on force to obtain resources (nationalization, expropriation) rather than on taxation, which requires a greater degree of representation. The prevalence of rents has helped to sustain the lack of accountability of the state. Forces pushing for reform have been relatively weak and the state, while not short of power, has been unable and unwilling to use it as a galvanizing force in the development process. For Arab leaders the issue is simple: The system works in terms of ensuring political stability defined as regime continuity, so why fix it? The decision not to undertake fundamental economic and political reforms is, from the viewpoint of the regime, quite rational. However, for the economy and the society, it is not true. Given the lack of incentives, or to put it more accurately, the presence of incentives for leaders *not* to make changes, Arab states remain trapped in what economists call a low-level equilibrium. In some respects this has been true for hundreds of years and has survived changes in rule from the Ottomans to the Western powers to independence in the mid-twentieth century.

Little that has happened since the Arab states gained their independence has increased pluralism, decentralization of political power, and the free expression. All governments make mistakes, but in an undemocratic environment, the opportunity to criticize and suggest alternatives is limited. The incentives to make corrections are also lacking. Reform in Islamic countries has high costs because of the legacy of Islam and the availability of cheap default options for the regimes. Reforms mean embracing more explicitly the ideology of the West (at least its economic part) and this is unacceptable to many who feel that they have been defeated, abused, or betrayed by the West. In the face of this kind of ideological opposition, which has a religious aspect, governments in the region are cautious.[8]

The default options have, ironically, been partly made available by the West. The most important is the sale of oil that, until recently, went mainly to Western countries or those closely linked to the West. Another was military

---

[8] Platteau, Jean-Philippe. "Religion, Politics, and Development: Lessons from the Lands of Islam." 60; http://www.fundp.ac.be/pdf/publications/61703.pdf.

and economic aid. This was extended to countries that decoupled from or opposed the Soviet Union and later it went to those that favored an accommodation with Israel and to those threatened by Islamic fundamentalism or by Iran. (These groups overlap.) Within the region there were aid flows and large movements of emigrants' remittances, largely made possible by oil.

A useful concept for understanding the political economy of Arab states is one favored by many economists: "equilibrium." The word *equilibrium* is frequently used in economics in a very restricted form to describe a situation in which there are no incentives or opportunities to change. This exists in conditions of perfect competition in the neoclassical model. In such a state, consumers lack incentives to change spending because their maximum utility has been achieved. As producers maximize their profits in such a situation, they lack incentives to change.[9] Following Hahn, we can use the term *equilibrium* in a broader sense to describe a situation in which self-seeking agents learn nothing new and so their behavior becomes routinized. The economy generates messages that do not cause agents to change the theories that they hold or the policies that they follow.[10] Equilibrium implies continuity and this is precisely the point to be made about the Arab economies. Despite changes in policy, ownership, and control, ideology and even political rule, there have been strong elements of continuity in their performance.

How might this equilibrium change? Positive reasons would be when powerful enough groups or coalitions decide that it is in their interest to change the status quo. They could do this as a result of domestic pressures arising from high levels of unemployment, especially among the young. Another causal factor might be a large, prolonged, or even permanent fall in income from hydrocarbons such as happened in the mid-1980s.

---

[9] Leftwich, Richard H. *The Price System and Resource Allocation*. London: Holt, Rinehart & Winston, 1970. 358.
[10] Hahn, Frank. *On the Notion of Equilibrium in Economics*. Cambridge: Cambridge University Press, 1973. 25.

References

Abed, George T., and Hamid R. Davoodi. 2003. *Challenges of Growth and Globalization in the Middle East and North Africa.* Washington, D.C.: IMF. http://www.imf.org/external/pubs/ft/med/2003/eng.abed.htm.

Abdel Jaber, Tayseer. 1995. *Key Long-Term Development Issues in Jordan.* Working Paper 199522, Cairo: Economic Research Forum.

Acemoglu, Daron, Simon Johnson, and James A. Robinson. 2001. The Colonial Origins of Comparative Development. *American Economic Review* 91, No. 5: 1369–1401.

Al Ahram Weekly online. 11–17 July 2002. http://www.weekly.ahram.org.eg.

Al Chaleck, Al Fadel. April 2004. "Challenges to the Economy and State in the Middle East." In *Looking Ahead Challenges for Middle East Politics and Research,* Perthes, Volker (coordinator), EuroMeSco Paper No. 29. http://www.euromesco.net.

Allan, J. A. 1994. "Overall Perspectives on Countries and Regions." In *Water in the Arab World: Perspectives and Prognosis,* eds. Peter Rogers and Peter Lydon, Cambridge, Mass: Harvard University, 65–100.

Allan, J. A. 1994. "Economic and Political Adjustments to Scarce Water in the Middle East." In *Water and Peace,* eds. Jed Isaac and Hillel Shuval, Special edition of *Studies in Environmental Sciences* m58, 375–387. Amsterdam: Elsevier.

Alnasrawi, A. 1994. *The Economy of Iraq: Oil, Wars, Destruction of Development, and Prospects, 1950–2000.* Westport, Conn. and London: Greenwood Press.

Alnasrawi, Abbas. 2002. *Iraq's Burdens: Oil, Sanctions, and Underdevelopment.* Westport, Conn.: Greenwood Press.

Amsden, Alice H. 1989. *Asia's Next Giant: South Korea and Late Industrialization.* New York: Oxford University Press.

Amsden, Alice H. 1994. Why Isn't the Whole World Experimenting with the East Asian Model to Development?: Review of *The East Asian Miracle. World Development* 22, No. 4: 627–633.

Amsden, Alice H. 2001. *The Rise of the Rest: Challenges to the West from Late-Industrializing Economies.* New York: Oxford University Press.

Amsden, Alice H., and Ajit Singh. 1994. The Optimal Degree of Competition and Dynamic Efficiency in Japan and Korea. *European Economic Review* No. 38: 941–951.

Anderson, Perry. 1974. *Lineages of the Absolutist State.* London: New Left Books.

Anos-Casero, Paloma, and Aristomene Varoudakis. 2004. *Growth, Private Investment, and the Cost of Doing Business in Tunisia: A Comparative Perspective.* Washington, D.C.: World Bank.

Arnon, Arie, Israel Luski, Avia Spivak, and Jimmy Weinblatt. 1997. *The Palestinian Economy.* Leiden: Brill.

Arnon, A., and J. Weinblatt. June 2001. Sovereignty and Economic Development: The Case of Palestine. *Economic Journal* No. 111: F291–308.

Ashtor, Eliyahu. 1976. *A Social and Economic History of the Near East in the Middle Ages.* London: Collins.

Assaad, Ragui. August 2000. *The Transformation of the Egyptian Labor Market, 1988–1998.* Cairo: Economic Research Forum for the Arab Countries, Iran, and Turkey.

Ayad, Mohamed, and Farzaneh Roudi. *Fertility Decline and Reproductive Health in Morocco: New DHS Figures.* 10.5.2006–10 MAY 2006?. http://www.prb.org./Articles/2006/Fertility Decline and Reproductive Health in Morocco New DHS Figures.aspx.

Ayubi, Nazih N. 1995. *Overstating the Arab State: Politics and Society in the Middle East.* London and New York: I. B. Tauris.

Aziz Chadhry, Karen. 1997. *The Price of Wealth.* Ithaca, N.Y. and London: Cornell University Press.

Bakour, Yahia, and John Kolars. 1994. "The Arab Mashrek: Hydrologic History, Problems and Perspectives" in Rogers, Peter and Peter Lydon, *Water in the Arab World.* Cambridge: Harvard University Press. 121–146.

Bank, Andre, and Oliver Schlumberger. 2004. "Jordan: Between Regime Survival and Economic Reform." *In Arab Elites Negotiating the Politics of Change,* ed. Volker Perthes, 35–60. Boulder, Colo.: Lynne Rienner.

Bellin, Eva. 1991. "Tunisian Industrialists and the State." In *Tunisia: The Political Economy of Reform,* ed. I. William Zartman, 45–66. Boulder and London: Lynne Rienner.

Berkoff, Jeremy. 1994. *A Strategy for Managing Water in the Middle East and North Africa.* Washington, D.C.: World Bank.

Bloom, David E., and Jeffrey G. Williamson. 1998. Demographic Transitions and Economic Miracles in Emerging Asia. *World Bank Economic Review* 12, No. 3: 419–455.

Blue Carroll, Katherine. 2003. *Business as Usual? Economic Reforms in Jordan.* Lanham, Md.: Lexington Books.

Boogaerde, Pierre van den. *Financial Assistance from Arab Countries and Arab Regional Institutions.* Occasional Paper No. 87 (Washington, D.C.: International Monetary Fund, 1991).

British Petroleum. *Statistical Review of World Energy, 2003.* http://www.bp.com.

British Petroleum. *Statistical Review of World Energy, 2005.* http://www.bp.com.

British Petroleum. *Statistical Review of World Energy, 2007.* http://www.bp.com.

Bulmer-Thomas, Victor. 1994. *The Economic History of Latin America since Independence.* Cambridge: Cambridge University Press.

Cassing, James H., Samih Fawzy, Denis Gallagher, and Hanaa Kheir-El-Din. 2000. "Enhancing Egypt's Exports." In *Catching up with the Competition: Trade Policy Challenges and Options for the Middle East and North Africa,* eds. Bernard M. Hoekman and Jamal Zarrouk, 207–226. Ann Arbor: University of Michigan Press.

Central Bank of Syria. 2006. *Quarterly Bulletin* 44, No. 3. Damascus: Central Bank of Syria.

Central Bank of Tunisia. *46th Annual Report for 2004.* http://www.cbt.gov.tu.

Central Bank of Tunisia. *47th Annual Report for 2005*. http://www.bct.gov.tn.

Central Intelligence Agency. August 2008. World Factbook. https://www.cia.gov/library/publications/the-world-factbook/geos/tw.html#Econ.

Champion, Daryl. 2003. *The Paradoxical Kingdom*. London: C. Hurst.

Choucair, Julia. "Illusive Reform: Jordan's Stubborn Stability" Carnegie Paper No. 76. Washington, D.C.: Carnegie Endowment, December 2006. http://www.carnegieendowment.org/files/cp76_choucair_final.pdf.

Cippola, Carlo M. 1993. *Before the Industrial Revolution*. London: Routledge.

Cochrane, Susan H., and Ernest E. Massiah. "Egypt: Recent Changes in Population Growth, Their Causes, and Consequences" Human Resources Development and Operations Policy Working Paper 49. Washington, D.C.: World Bank Working Paper, 1995.

Council for Foreign Relations and James Baker III Institute, Rice University. 2003. Guiding Principles for US Post Conflict Policy in Iraq. http://www.cfr.org/content/publications/attachments/Post-War_Iraq.pdf.

Courbage, Youssef. 1999. Economic and Political Issues in the Fertility Transition in the Arab World – Answers and Open Questions. *Population and Environment: A Journal of Interdisciplinary Studies* 20, No. 4: 353–380.

Courbage, Youssef. 1999. *New Demographic Scenarios in the Mediterranean Region, National Institute of Demographic Studies*. Paris: INED. http://www.ined.fr.

Crone, Patricia, and Michael Cook. 1977. *Hagarism: The Making of the Islamic World*. Cambridge: Cambridge University Press.

Dhonte, Pierre, Rina Bhattacharya, and Tarik Yousef. "Demographic Transition in the Middle East: Implications for Growth, Employment and Housing" Working Paper WP/00/41. Washington, D.C.: IMF, 2000.

Dillman, Bradford. Spring 2001. "Facing the Market." *Middle East Journal* 55, No. 2: 198–215.

Easterly, William. 2001. *The Elusive Quest for Growth*. Cambridge, Mass.: MIT Press.

Easterly, William. 2001. The Middle Class Consensus and Economic Development. *Journal of Economic Growth* 6, No. 4: 317–336.

The Economic Research Forum for the Arab Countries, Iran, and Turkey. 2002. *Economic Trends in the MENA Region, 2002*. Cairo: The American University in Cairo Press.

The Economic Research Forum for the Arab Countries, Iran, and Turkey. 2004. *Egypt Country Profile*. Cairo: Economic Research Forum for the Arab Countries, Iran, and Turkey. www.erf.org.eg.

The Economist. "Leaving the Door Ajar: Oil in Venezuela." 8 April 2006. London.

The Economist. "A Survey of Saudi Arabia." 7 January 2006.

The Economist. "Up from the Bottom of the Pile: Latin America's Economies." 18 August 2007. London.

Economist Intelligence Unit. 1996. *Country Profile Tunisia*. London: Economist Intelligence Unit.

Economist Intelligence Unit. 1997. *Country Profile Saudi Arabia*. London: Economist Intelligence Unit.

Economist Intelligence Unit. 1997. *Syria Country Report*, 3rd Quarter 1997. London: EIU.

Economist Intelligence Unit. 1999. *Country Report, Syria*, 3rd Quarter 1999. London: EIU.

Economist Intelligence Unit. 2003. *Country Report: Egypt, February 2003.* London: EIU.
Economist Intelligence Unit. 2005. *Country Profile Jordan.* London: Economist Intelligence Unit.
Economist Intelligence Unit. 2005. *Country Profile Saudi Arabia 2005.* London: EIU.
Economist Intelligence Unit. 2005. *Country Profile, Syria, 2005.* London: EIU.
Elbadawi, Ibrahim A. 2005 (2006). Reviving Growth in the Arab World. *Economic Development and Cultural Change* 53 No. 54: 293–326.
Embassy of the United States of America. 1996. *Doing Business in the Syrian Arab Republic: A Country Commercial Guide for US Companies.* http://damascus.usembassy.gov/uploads/images/xbWE230070xAoKXPyztogQ/ccg-syria-2007.pdf.
Emerging Textiles.Com. 21 November 2006. Egypt's QIZs attract Apparel Investment from Turkey Country Report. http://www.emergingtextiles.com/?q=art&s=061121Egypt&r=free&n.
Energy Information Agency. January 2006. OPEC Revenues Fact Sheet. http://www.eia.doe.gov.
Energy Information Agency. 2007. *Country Analysis Brief, Saudi Arabia.* http://www.eia.doe.gov.
Energy Information Agency. 2008. *Country Analysis Brief Eastern Mediterranean.* http://www.eia.doe.gov/emeu/cabs/East_Med/NaturalGas.html.
Engerman, Stanley L., and Kenneth L. Sokoloff. "Factor Endowments, Inequality, and the Paths of Development among New World Economies" Working Paper no. 9259 (National Bureau of Economic Research, 2002). http://www.nber.org/papers/w9259.
Erdle, Steffen. 2004. "Tunisia: Economic Transformation and Political Restoration." In *Arab Elites Negotiating the Politics of Change,* ed. Volker Perthes, 207–236. Boulder, Colo.: Lynne Rienner.
European Union. EU Trade Issues: Tunisia, http://ec.europa.eu/trade/issues/bilateral/countries/tunisia/index_en.htm.
Evans, Peter. 1992. "The State as Problem and Solution: Predation Embedded Autonomy, and Structural Change." In *The Politics of Economy Adjustment,* eds. Stephen Haggard and Robert Kaufman, 139–181. Princeton, N.J.: Princeton University Press.
Fargues, Philippe. 1994. "Demographic Explosion or Social Upheaval." In *Democracy without Democrats: The Renewal of Politics in the Muslim World,* ed. Ghassan Salame, 156–182. London: I. B. Tauris.
Fargues, Philippe. 1997. State Policies and the Birth Rate in Egypt: from Socialism to Liberalism. *Population and Development* 23, No. 1: 115–138.
Fargues, Philippe. 2000. Protracted National Conflict and Fertility Change: Palestinians and Israelis in the Twentieth Century. *Population and Development Review* 26, No. 3: 441–481.
Fargues, Philippe. 2006. *International Migration in the Arab Region: Trends and Policies.* Beirut: UN Secretariat, Department of Economic and Social Affairs, Population Division.
Fergany, Nader. 1995. *Egypt 2012 Education and Employment.* Economic Research Forum for the Arab Countries, Iran, and Turkey. 2. http://www.erg.org.eg.
Field, Michael. 1984. *The Merchants.* London: John Murray.
Field, Michael. 1995. *Inside the Arab World.* Cambridge, Mass.: Harvard University Press.
Financial Times. "Oil Set for Big Boost in Next Ten Years." 4 April 1996.
Financial Times. "London. Iraqi Oil Demand Can Help Meet Rise in Demand." 15 April 2005.

Food and Agriculture Organization. FAOSTAT. *Food and Agriculture Indicators.* http://www. fao.org.

Food and Agriculture Organization. *The State of Food and Agriculture, 1992.* http://www. fao.org.

Food and Agriculture Organization. *The State of Food and Agriculture, 1993.* http://www. fao.org.

Food and Agriculture Organization. 1994. *Yearbook 'Production'* 48. Rome: FAO.

Food and Agriculture Organization. 1994. *Yearbook 'Trade'* Vol. 48. Rome: FAO.

Food and Agriculture Organization. 1995. *Quarterly Bulletin of Statistics 8,* no. 3/4: 110.

Food and Agriculture Organization. *The State of Food and Agriculture, 1997.* http://www. fao.org.

Food and Agriculture Organization. "Bulletin" Working Paper series no. 20 (Rome: FAO, December 2000).

Food and Agriculture Organization. 2003. *Bulletin of Statistics 4,* No. 1.

Food and Agriculture Organization. 23 September 2003. *Special Report: FAO/WFP Crop, Food Supply, and Nutrition Assessment Mission to Iraq.* http://www.fao.org.

Food and Agriculture Organization. *The State of Food and Agriculture, 2004.* http://www. fao.org.

Food and Agriculture Organization. *The State of Food and Agriculture, 2005.* http://www. fao.org.

Food and Agriculture Organization. *Statistical Yearbook 2005–2006.* http://www.fao. org/statistics/yearbook/vol_1_1/pdf/b01.pdf.

Foreign Affairs. September/October 1996. Industrialization. Sponsored section by Republic of China Government.

Forum Euro-Méditerranéen des Instituts Economiques (Femise). *Jordan Country Profile, The Road Ahead from Jordan.* http://www.femise.org/PDF/cp/cp-jordan-0508. pdf.

Furtado, Celso. 1970. *Economic Development of Latin America.* Cambridge: Cambridge University Press.

Galal, Ahmed. 2002. *The Paradox of Education and Unemployment in Egypt.* Cairo: The Egyptian Center for Economic Studies.

General Agreement on Tariffs and Trade. *International Trade 1994.* Geneva: GATT.

El-Ghonemy, M. Riad. 1998. *Affluence and Poverty in the Middle East.* London: Routledge.

El-Ghonemy, M. Riad. 2003. *Egypt in the Twenty-First Century.* London and New York: Routledge Curzon.

Gilbar, Gad. 1997. *Population Dilemmas in the Middle East.* London: Frank Cass.

Gill, Indermit, and Homi Kharas. 2007. *An East Asian Renaissance.* Washington, D.C.: The World Bank.

Greif, Avner. 1994. Cultural Beliefs and the Organization of Society: A Historical and Theoretical Reflection on Collectivist and Individualist Society. *The Journal of Political Economy* 102, No. 5: 912–950.

Greif, Avner. 2006. *Institutions and the Path to the Modern Economy.* Cambridge: Cambridge University Press.

Ha'aretz. "Syria Needs $60 Billion to Generate Jobs." (Hebrew). 28 February 1997. Tel Aviv.

Ha'aretz. "Without Investments There Will Be No Security; Without Security There Will Be No Jobs." by Zvi Barel (Hebrew). 30 July 2003. Tel Aviv.

Hajrah, Hassan Hamza. 1992. *Public Land Distribution in Saudi Arabia*. London: Longman.

Hakura, Dalia S. "Growth in the Middle East and North Africa" Working Paper No. 04/54, 2004.19 (Washington, D.C.: IMF, 2004). http://www.imf.org.

Hammond, Andrew. 15 May 2001. Reuters. http://archives.his.com/populations-new/msg02003.html.

Handoussa, Heba. 2002. "A Balance Sheet of Reform in Two Decades." In *Institutional Reform and Economic Development in Egypt*, eds. Noha el-Mikawy and Heba Handoussa, 89–104. Cairo: American University Press.

Hansen, Bent. 1991. *Egypt and Turkey: The Political Economy of Poverty, Equity, and Growth*. Oxford: Oxford University Press.

Henry, Clement M. 1997. *The Mediterranean Debt Crescent*. Cairo: The American University in Cairo Press.

Henry, Clement M., and Robert Springborg. 2001. *Globalization and the Politics of Development in the Middle East*. Cambridge: Cambridge University Press.

Herrara, Marianna. 2005. *Land Tenure Development and Policy Making in Latin America*. Organization of American States. 2. http://www.oas.org/dsd/Documents/LTDpolicysummary_LATIN%20AMERICA.pdf.

Hourani, Albert. 1962. *Arab Thought in the Liberal Age 1789–1939*. London: Oxford University Press.

Hudson, Michael. 1977. *Arab Politics: The Search for Legitimacy*. New Haven, Conn. and London: Yale University Press.

Ikram, Khalid. 2006. *The Egyptian Economy, 1952–2000, Performance, Policies, and Issues*. London and New York: Routledge.

The Institute for International Finance. 21 May 2007. *Regional Briefing Gulf Cooperation Council*. www.iif.com.

International Bank for Reconstruction and Development and International Finance Corporation. 2005. *Country Assistance Strategy for the Arab Republic of Egypt for the period FY06–FY08*. Report No. 32190-EG. http://www-wds.worldbank.org/external/default/WDSContentServer/IW3P/IB/2005/06/24/000012009_20050624102618/Rendered/PDF/321900rev3.pdf.

International Herald Tribune. "Trade Minister Fears Economic Backlash: Iraqi Urges Caution on Free Markets." By Thomas Crampton. 13 October 2003. Paris.

International Labour Office. *Global Employment Trends 2004*. http://www.ilo.org/public/english/employment/strat/global04.htm.

International Labour Office. *World Employment Report 2004–5*. http://www.ilo.org/public/english/employment/strat/wer2004.htm.

International Labour Office. June 2005. *Global Employment Trends Brief*. www.ilo.org.

International Labour Office. *Global Employment Trends Brief. February 2005*. http://www.ilo.org/public/english/employment/strat/download/get05en.pdf.

International Monetary Fund. *Balance of Payments Yearbook*, various issues. Washington, D.C.: IMF.

International Monetary Fund. November 1997. *International Financial Statistics*. Washington, D.C.: IMF.

International Monetary Fund. 1998. *Directions of Trade Statistics Yearbook, 1998*. Washington, D.C.: IMF.

International Monetary Fund. April 1998. *Morocco Statistical Appendix*. Report No. 98/02. http://www.imf.org/external/pubs/ft/scr/1998/cr9842.pdf.

International Monetary Fund. August 1998. *International Financial Statistics.* Washington, D.C.: IMF.

International Monetary Fund. 2002. *International Financial Statistics. 2002 Yearbook.* Washington, D.C.: IMF.

International Monetary Fund. 2003. *West Bank and Gaza, Economic Performance and Reform under Conflict Conditions.* http://www.imf.org/external/pubs/ft/med/2003/eng/wbg/wbg.pdf.

International Monetary Fund. 2004. *Jordan: Fifth Post-Program Monitoring Discussions-Staff Report; and Press Release on the Executive Board Consideration,* Country Report no. 07/284. 17. http://www.imf.org/external/pubs/ft/scr/2007/cr07284.pdf IMF. *Jordan Selected Issues and Statistical Appendix,* 2004. http://www.imf.org.

International Monetary Fund. May 2004. *International Financial Statistics.* Washington, D.C.: IMF.

International Monetary Fund. May 2004. *Jordan. Selected Issues and Statistical Appendix.* Country Report no. 04/121. http://www.imf.org/external/pubs/ft/scr/2004/cr04121.pdf.

International Monetary Fund. June 2004. *Morocco Statistical Appendix.* Report No. 04/163. http://www.imf.org/external/pubs/ft/scr/2004/cr04163.pdf (http://www.imf.org).

International Monetary Fund. (September) 2004. *(Country Report), Iraq Use of Fund Resources-Request for Emergency Post-Conflict Assistance,* 04/325 http://www.imf.org/external/pubs/ft/scr/2004/cr04325.pdf.

International Monetary Fund. November 2004. *Tunisia: 2004 Article IV Consultation Staff Report.* Report No. 04/359. http://www.imf.org/external/pubs/ft/scr/2004/cr04359.pdf (http://www.imf.org).

International Monetary Fund. 2005. *Arab Republic of Egypt: Selected Issues,* Country Report No. 05/179. http://imf.org/external/pubs/ft/scr/2005/cr05179.pdf.

International Monetary Fund. 2005. *Directions of Trade Statistics Yearbook, 2005.* Washington, D.C.: IMF.

International Monetary Fund. 2005. *Jordan Post-Program Monitoring Discussions-Staff Report No. 05/100.* http://www.imf.org/external/pubs/ft/scr/2005/cr05100.pdf.

International Monetary Fund. June 2005. *Arab Republic of Egypt, 2005 Article IV Consultation-Staff Report,* Country Report No. 05/177. http://www.imf.org/external/pubs/ft/scr/2005/cr05177.pdf.

International Monetary Fund. October 2005. *Syrian Arab Republic, Article IV Consultation Staff Report.* Report No. 05/356. http://www.imf.org/external/pubs/ft/scr/2005/cr05356.pdf.

International Monetary Fund. October 2005. *Syrian Arab Republic: Statistical Appendix,* Country Report no. 05/355. http://www.imf.org/external/pubs/ft/scr/2005/cr05355.pdf.

International Monetary Fund. November 2005. *Morocco: 2005 Article IV Consultation – Staff Report; Public Information Notice on the Executive Board Discussion; and Statement by the Executive Director for Morocco.* Report No. 05/418 http://www.imf.org/external/pubs/ft/scr/2005/cr05418.pdf (http://www.imf.org).

International Monetary Fund 2006. *Arab Republic of Egypt: 2006 Article IV Consultation-Staff Report.* Country Report No. 06/153. http://www.imf.org/external/pubs/ft/scr/2006/cr06253.pdf.

International Monetary Fund. 2006. *Balance of Payments Statistics 2006*. Washington, D.C.: IMF.

International Monetary Fund. 2006. *Tunisia: 2006 Article IV Consultation – Staff Report; Staff Statement; Public Information Notice on the Executive Board Discussion; and Statement by the Executive Director for Tunisia*. Report No. 06/207.

International Monetary Fund. June 2006. *Article IV Consultation and Staff Report Tunisia*, Report No. 06/207. http://www.imf.org/external/pubs/ft/scr/2006/cr06207.pdf.

International Monetary Fund. August 2006. *Syrian Arab Republic: 2006 Article IV Consultation Staff Report*, Country Report no. 06/294. http://www.imf.org/external/pubs/ft/scr/2006/cr06294.pdf.

International Monetary Fund. October 2006. *West Bank and Gaza: Recent Fiscal and Financial Developments*. http://www.imf.org/external/np/wbg/2006/eng/rr/pdf/fis_1006.pdf.

International Monetary Fund. (March) 2007. Iraq: Third and Fourth Reviews Under the Stand-By Arrangement, Financing Assurances Review, and Requests for Extension of the Arrangement and for Waiver of Nonobservance of a Performance Criterion – Staff Report; Staff Supplement; Press Release on the Executive Board Discussion; and Statement by the Executive Director for Iraq (*Country Report, Iraq*) Report No. 07/115. http://www.imf.org/external/pubs/ft/scr/2007/cr07115.pdf.

International Monetary Fund. 2007. *Iraq: Third and Fourth Reviews under the Stand-By Arrangement, Financing Assurances Review, and Requests for Extension of the Arrangements and for Waiver of Nonobservance of a Performance Criterion-Staff Report, 2007*. Country Report No. 01/115.

International Monetary Fund. 2007. *Arab Republic of Egypt: Selected Issues*, Report no. 07/381. http://www.imf.org/external/pubs/ft/scr/2007/cr07381.pdf.

International Monetary Fund. 2007. *Global Development Finance 2007*. Washington, D.C.: IMF.

International Monetary Fund. May 2007. *Syrian Arab Republic. 2007 Article IV Consultation, Mission Preliminary Conclusions*. http://www.imf.org/external/np/ms/2007/051607.htm.

International Monetary Fund. 2007. *Tunisia: 2007 Article IV Consultation Mission, Preliminary Conclusion*. http://www.imf.org/external/np/ms/2007/062907.htm (http://www.imf.org).

Iqbal, Farrukh. 2006. *Sustaining Gains in Poverty Reduction and Human Development in the Middle East and North Africa*. Washington, D.C.: The World Bank.

Israel Radio. 16 December 2005. News report on Israeli-Egypt trade relations.

Israel, Ministry of Foreign Affairs. The Gaza-Jericho Agreement Annex IV Protocol on Economic Relations. http://www.mfa.gov.il/MFA/Peace+Process/Guide+to+the+Peace+Process/Gaza-Jericho+Agreement+Annex+IV+-+Economic+Protoco.htm.

Israel, Central Bureau of Statistics. July 1996. *Demographic Characteristics of the Arab Population in Judea, Samaria and the Gaza Area, 1968–1993*, Publication No. 1025.

Israel, Central Bureau of Statistics. 1994. *Demographic Characteristics of the Arab Population in Judea & Samaria and the Gaza Area, 1968–1993*. Jerusalem: Central Bureau of Statistics Special Series no. 1025.

Issawi, Charles. 1982. *An Economic History of the Middle East and North Africa.* London: Methuen.

Issawi, Charles. 1995. "Iraq: A Study in Aborted Development." In *The Middle East Economy: Decline and Recovery,* ed. Charles Issawi, 143–163. Princeton, N.J.: Markus Wiener Publishers.

Issawi, Charles. 1995. "The Adaptation of Islam to Contemporary Economic Realities." In *The Middle East Economy: Decline and Recovery,* ed. Charles Issawi, 185–206. Princeton: Markus Wiener Publishers.

Issawi, Charles. 1995. "The Japanese Model and the Middle East." In *The Middle East Economy: Decline and Recovery,* ed. Charles Issawi, 165–184. Princeton: Markus Wiener Publishers.

Issawi, Charles. 1983. "Why Japan." In *Arab Resources: The Transformation of a Society,* ed. I. Ibrahim, 283–300. Washington, D.C.: Centre for Contemporary Arab Studies.

Issawi, Charles. 1989. "The Middle East in the World Context: A Historical View." In *The Middle East Economy: Decline and Recovery,* ed. Charles Issawi, 1–30. Princeton: Markus Wiener Publishers.

Jones, Eric L. 1987. *The European Miracle: Environments, Economies, and the Geopolitics in the History of Europe and Asia.* Cambridge: Cambridge University Press.

Jordan, Ministry of Finance. 21 December 2005. Budget Speech 2006, Amman. http://eng.mof.gov.jo/english/inside1.asp.

Jordan, Prime Minister's Office. 2005. *National Agenda 2006–2015,* Amman: Prime Minister's.

Jordanian Embassy in Washington, D.C. 19 October 2007. U.S. *Assistance to Jordan.* http://www.jordanembassyus.org/new/aboutjordan/uj1.shtml.

The late Abdul Moneim Kaissouni interviewed by the author, 1980.

Kanaan, Taher H., and Marwan A. Kardooh. 2002. *Employment and the Labour Market in Jordan.* http. www worldbank.org.

Kamil, A. (ed.). 2002. *Iraq's Economic Predicament.* Reading: Ithaca.

Kanafani, Nu'man. 2004. "Economic Foundations for Peace." In *Trade Policy and Economic Integration in the Middle East and North Africa,* eds. Hassan Hakimian and Jeffrey B. Nugent, 271–290. London: Routledge Curzon.

Kardoosh, Marwan A., and Riad al Khouri. 2004. *Qualifying Industrial Zones and Sustainable Development in Jordan.* http://www.erf.org.eg.

Kindleberger, Charles P. 1996. *World Economic Primacy: 1500 to 1900.* New York and Oxford: Oxford University Press.

King, Stephen J. Spring 1998. Economic Reform and Tunisia's Hegemonic Party: The End of the Administrative Elite – Beyond Colonialism and Nationalism in North Africa. *Arab Studies Quarterly* 1: 59–86.

El-Kogali, Safaa E., and El Daw A. Sulim. "*Poverty, Human Capital, and Gender: A Comparative Study of Yemen and Egypt*" Working Paper 0123 (Cairo: Economic Research Forum, 2003).

Kouame, Auguste T. 1996. *Achieving Faster Economic Growth in Tunisia.* Washington, D.C.: World Bank.

Krugman, Paul. 1994. The Myth of Asia's Miracle. *Foreign Affairs* 73, No. 6: 62–73.

Kuran, Timur. Forthcoming. Explaining the Economic Trajectories of Civilizations: Musings on the Systemic Approach. *Journal of Economic Behavior and Organization.*

Kuran, Timur. 1997. Islam and Underdevelopment: An Old Puzzle Revisited. *Journal of Institutional and Theoretical Economics* 153: 41–71.

Kuran, Timur. 2003. The Islamic Commercial Crisis: Institutional Roots of Economic Underdevelopment in the Middle East. *Journal of Economic History* 63, 2: 414–446.

Kuran, Timur. 2005. *The Absence of the Corporation in Islamic Law: Origins and Perspectives.* CLEO Research Paper Series C04–16 Law.

Kuwait, Ministry of Planning, *Annual Statistical Abstract,* 1988.

Lal, Deepak. *The Hindu Equilibrium: Cultural Stability and Economic Stagnation, India c1500–AD 1980.* Oxford: Clarendon Press, 1988.

Landes, David. *The Wealth and Poverty of Nations.* New York: W.W. Norton, 1999.

Landes, David. 2000. Culture Makes Almost All the Difference. In *Culture Matters,* eds. Lawrence E. Harrison, and Samuel P. Huntington, 1–13. New York: Basic Books.

Leahy, Elizabeth, with Robert Engelman, Carolyn Vogel Gibb, Sarah Haddock, and Tod Preston. 2007. *The Shape of Things to Come: Why Age Structure Matters to a Safer, More Equitable World.* Population Action International. http://www.populationaction.org.

Lewis, Bernard. 1950. *The Arabs in History.* London and New York: Hutchinson's University Library.

Lewis, Bernard. 1993. *Islam in History.* Chicago and La Salle, Ill.: Open Court.

Lewis, Bernard. 1996. *The Middle East.* London: Phoenix.

Looney, Robert. 2003. Bean Counting in Baghdad: Debt, Reparations, Reconstruction, and Resources. *Middle East Review of International Affairs Journal* 7, 3: 60–72.

Lydon, Ghislaine. A 'Paper Economy of Faith' without Faith in Paper: A Contribution to Understanding the Roots of Islamic Institutional Stagnation. *Journal of Economic Behavior and Organization* 68. 329–351.

Mabro, Robert, and Samir Radwan. 1976. *The Industrialization of Egypt.* Oxford: Oxford University Press.

Mahdi, Kamil A. 2002. "Iraq's Agrarian System: Issues of Policy and Performance." In *Iraq's Economic Predicament,* ed. Kamil A. Mahdi, 321–342. Reading: Ithaca.

Mattione, Richard. 1985. *OPEC's Investments and the International Financial System.* Washington, D.C.: Brookings Institute.

McNeill, W. H. 1963. *The Rise of the West.* Chicago: Chicago University Press.

Middle East Economic Digest. 29 August 1997. London: EMAP.

Middle East Economic Survey. 16 January 2006. Nicosia: Middle East Petroleum and Economic Publications, XLIX, 3: 21.

Middle East Report. Fall 2005. Washington, D.C.: Middle East Research and Information Project. No. 236.

Migdal, Joel S. 1988. *Strong Societies and Weak States.* Princeton: Princeton University Press.

el-Mikawy, Noha. 2002. "State/Society and Executive/Legislative Relations." In *Institutional Reform and Economic Development in Egypt,* eds. Noha el-Mikawy and Heba Handoussa, 21–36. Cairo: American University Press.

Mokyr, Joel. 2002. *The Gifts of Athena.* Princeton and Oxford: Princeton University Press.

Moore, Pete W. 2004. *Doing Business in the Middle East: Politics and Economic Crises in Jordan and Kuwait.* Cambridge and New York: Cambridge University Press.

Morocco. Premier Ministre. 2002. *Annuaire Statistique du Maroc,* Departement de la Prevision Economique et du Plan, Direction de la Statistique.

Morrisson, Christian, and Bechir Talbi. 5 March 2007. *Long-Term Growth in Tunisia.* OECD Development Centre, 1996. World Bank. *Tunisia at a Glance.* http://devdata. worldbank.org.

Murphy, Emma C. December 2006. The Tunisian Mise à Niveau Programme and the Political Economy of Reform. *The New Political Economy* Vol. 11, No. 4: 519–540.

Mustafa Naquib, Fadle. 2004. Economic and Social Commission for West Asia (ESCWA). *Linking Aid to Development in the Current Palestinian Situation.* Beirut: ESCWA.

Myrdal, Gunnar. 1968. *Asian Drama: An Inquiry into the Poverty of Nations,"* vol. II. New York: Pantheon, Random House.

Nabli, Mustapha, Jennifer Keller, Claudia Nassif, and Carlos Silva-Jauregui. 2005. *"The Political Economy of Industrial Policy in the Middle East and North Africa."* ECES Conference paper, Cairo. http://www.worldbank.org.

National Bank of Kuwait. April 2007. *Saudi Arabia Economic and Financial Review.*

Nelson, Richard R. 2005. *Technology, Institutions, and Economic Growth.* Cambridge: Cambridge University Press.

New York Times. "An Ugly Side of Free Trade: Sweatshops in Jordan." By Steven Greenhouse and Michael Barbaro. 3 May 2006. New York.

New York Times. "Aid to Palestinians Rose Despite an Embargo." By Steven Erlanger. 21 March 2007. New York.

New York Times. "New York. Saudi King Tries to Grow Modern Ideas in Desert. By Thanassis Cambanis. 28 October 2007. New York.

Noland, Marcus, and Howard Pack. 2007. *The Arab Economies in a Changing World.* Washington, D.C.: The Peterson Institute.

North, Douglass. 1990. *Institutions, Institutional Change, and Economic Performance.* Cambridge: Cambridge University Press.

Nsouli, Saleh et al. *"The Path to Convertibility and Growth: The Tunisian Experience"* IMF Occasional Paper No. 109. Washington, D.C.: International Monetary Fund, 1993.

National Commercial Bank. January 1993. *NCB Economist* 3, 1: 1–7.

Nybery Sorensen, Ninna. "Migrant Remittances as a Development Tool: The Case of Morocco" Working Papers Series, no. 2. Geneva: International Organization for Migration [IOM], June 2004). http://www.iom.org.

Organisation for Economic Cooperation and Development (OECD). 1995. *Middle East Oil and Gas.* Paris: OECD.

Owen, Roger. 2001. *The Uses and Abuses of Comparison.* Al-Ahram Weekly Online, 27 Dec. 2001–2 Jan. 2002, Issue No. 566.

Harvard Owen, Roger, and Sevket Pamuk. 1998. *A History of the Middle East Economies in the Twentieth Century.* London: I. B. Tauris.

Page, John. 2003. *Structural Reforms in the Middle East in the Arab World Competitiveness Report 2002–3.* New York: Oxford University Press for the World Economic Forum.

Palestine National Information Center. *Population in Palestine.* http://www.pnic.gov.ps.

Park C. H. 1962/1989. *Our Nation's Path: Ideology for Social Reconstruction.* Seoul: Dong- A. 1962, quoted by Amsden, Alice. *Asia's Next Giant: South Korea and Late Industrialization.* New York: Oxford University Press.

Pedersen, Jon, Sara Randall, and Marwan Khawaja. (eds.). 2001. *Growing Fast: The Palestinian Population in the West Bank and the Gaza Strip.* Oslo: FAFO Institute for Applied Social Science.

Perkins, Dwight H. 1994. There Are at Least Three Models of East Asian Development. *World Development* 22, 4: 655–661.

Perthes, Volker. 2004. "Syria: Difficult Inheritance." In *Arab Elites Negotiating the Politics of Change*, ed. Volker Perthes, 87–116. Boulder, Colo.: Lynne Rienner Publishers.

Platteau, Jean-Philippe. Forthcoming. Religion, Politics, and Development: Lessons from the Lands of Islam, *Journal of Economic Behavior and Organization.*

Radwan, Samir. 1997. *Towards Full Employment: Egypt into the 21st Century.* Cairo: The Egyptian Center for Economic Studies.

Radwan, Samir. "Employment and Unemployment Rates in Egypt: Conventional Problems, Unconventional Remedies" Working Paper No. 70. Cairo: The Egyptian Center for Economic Studies, 2002. 3.

Ragui, Assaad. 2004. *The Transformation of the Egyptian Labor Market, 1988–1998.* Cairo: Economic Research Forum for the Arab Countries, Iran, and Turkey.

Republique Tunisienne, Ministere du Developpement et de al Cooperation International, Institut National dela Statistique. 2004. *Annuaire de la Tunisie, 2001*, no. 44. 129–130 and Central Bank of Tunisia, *46th Annual Report for 2004.*

Richards, Alan. 1995. "Economic Pressures for Accountable Governance in the Middle East and North Africa." In *Civil Society in the Middle East*, ed. Augustus Richard Norton, 21. Leiden, New York, Koln: E. J. Brill.

Richards, Alan. 2004. "Economic Reform in the Middle East: The Challenge to Governance." In *The Future Security Environment in the Middle East*, eds. Nora Bensahel and Daniel L Byman, 57–128. Santa Monica: Rand.

Richards, Alan, and John Waterbury. 1990. *A Political Economy of the Middle East.* Boulder, Colo.: Westview.

Richards, Alan, and John Waterbury. 1996. *A Political Economy of the Middle East.* 2nd ed. Boulder, Colo.: Westview Press.

Rivlin, Paul. 1985. *The Dynamics of Economic Policy Making in Egypt.* New York: Praeger.

Rivlin, Paul. 1998. "Soft and Hard States." In *Lessons from East Asia*, eds. Yishay Ehud Harari Yafeh and Eyal Ben-Ari, 130–138. Jerusalem: The Harry S. Truman Research Institute for the Advancement of Peace.

Rivlin. Paul. 1998. "Structural Adjustment in Egypt, Morocco, and Tunisia, 1980–96." In *Middle East Contemporary Survey 1996*, Vol. XX, ed. Bruce Maddy Weitzman, 159–185. Boulder, Colo.: Westview Press.

Rivlin, Paul. 2001. *Economic Policy and Performance in the Arab World.* Boulder, Colo.: Lynne Rienner.

Rivlin, Paul. 2003. Egypt's Demographic Challenge and Economic Responses. *Middle East Review of International Affairs* 7, No. 4.http://meria.idc.ac.il/journal/2003/issue4/rivlin.pdf.

Rivlin, Paul. February 2003. Iraq's Economy: What's Left? *Tel Aviv Notes* no. 65: 2.

Rivlin, Paul. 2004. "Arab Economies and Political Stability." In *Political Stability in Arab States: Economic Causes and Consequences*, eds. Paul Rivlin and Shmuel Even, 9–26. Tel Aviv: The Jaffee Center for Strategic Studies. http://www.inss.org.il.

Rivlin, Paul. December 2004. "The Economics and Politics of the Egypt–Israel Trade Agreement." *Tel Aviv Note* no. 119. http://www.dayan.org.

Rivlin, Paul. September 2004. The Reconstruction of the Iraqi Economy and the Weight of Economic History. *Orient* 45.

Rodinson, Maxime. 1974. *Islam and Capitalism*. London: Allen Lane.

Rodriguez, Francisco. (undated). *The Political Economy of Latin American Growth*. www.gdnet.org/pdf/322_F.Rodriguez.PDF.

Rodrik, Dani. "*King Kong Meets Godzilla*" *Discussion Paper 944*. London: Centre for Economic Policy Research, 1994.

Rodrik, Dani. 1995. Getting Interventions Right: How South Korea and Taiwan Grew Rich. *Economic Policy* 20.

Rostow, W. W. 1960. *The Stages of Economic Growth*. Cambridge: Cambridge University Press.

Ruppert, Elizabeth. 1999. The Algerian Retrenchment: A Financial and Economic Evaluation. *World Bank Review* 13, No. 1: 155–183.

Ruppert, Elizabeth. *Algeria: Statistical Appendix*. Report no. 01/163 (Washington, D.C.: IMF, 2001).

Sachs, Jeffrey. 2001. Long Term Perspectives in the Economic Development of the Middle East. *The Economic Quarterly* 48, No. 3: 417–440. Tel Aviv: Am Oved. Hebrew.

Sadik, Abdul-Karim, and Shawki Barghouti. 1994. "The Water Problems of the Arab World: Management of Scarce Resources." In *Water in the Arab World: Perspectives and Prognosis*, eds. Peter Rogers and Peter Lydon, 20. Cambridge, Mass.: Division of Applied Science, Harvard University.

Sadowski, Yahya M. 1991. *Political Vegetables*. Washington, D.C.: Brookings Institution.

Safir, Nadji. 1999. "Emigration Dynamics in the Maghreb." In *Emigration Dynamics in Developing Countries IV, The Arab Region*, ed. Reginald Appleyard, 89–127. Aldershot: Ashgate Publishing Ltd, for the UN Population Fund and the International Organization for Migration.

Saudi Arabia. 2003. Ministry of Planning. *Saudi Human Development Report*. http://www.planning.gov.sa.

Saudi American Bank. 8 October 2002. *Saudi Arabia's Employment Profile*. http://www.samba.com.

Saudi American Bank. 2007. The Saudi Economy 2006 Performance; 2007 Forecast http://www.samba.com.

Saudi Arabian Monetary Agency. 2001. *Annual Report*. No. 37. Riyadh: Saudi Arabian Monetary Agency.

Saudi Arabian Monetary Agency. *Annual Report 2005*. http://www sama.sa.

Singh, A. "*How Did East Asia Grow so Fast: Slow Progress Towards an Analytical Consensus*" Discussion Paper No. 97 (Geneva: UNCTAD, 1995).

Singh, A. "*How Did East Asia Grow so Fast: Slow Progress Towards an Analytical Consensus*" Discussion Paper No. 97 (Geneva: UNCTAD, 1998).

Springborg, Robert. 1986. Infitah, Agrarian Transformation and Elite Consolidation in Contemporary Iraq. *Middle East Journal* 40, No. 1: 33–53.

Springborg, Robert. 1993. The Arab Bourgeoisie: A Revisionist Interpretation. *Arab Studies Quarterly* 15, No. 1: 13–39.

Stauber, Zvi, and Yiftah Shapir. (eds.). 2005. *Middle East Military Balance 2004– 2005*. Brighton, Portland: Sussex Academic Press for The Jaffee Center for Strategic Studies.

Stiglitz, Joseph E. 1992. Some Lessons from the East Asian Miracle. *The World Bank Research Observer* 11, No. 2: 151–177.

Stockholm International Peace Research Institute. 2006. *SIPRI Yearbook 2006.* Oxford: Oxford University Press.

Syrian Arab Republic. 1994. *Statistical Abstract 1994.* Damascus: Prime Minister's Office.

Syrian Arab Republic. 1995. *Statistical Abstract 1995.* Damascus: Prime Minister's Office.

Temin, Peter. 1997. Is Culture Kosher? *Journal of Economic History* 57, No. 2: 267–287.

Tignor, Robert L. 1984. *State, Private Enterprise, and Economic Change in Egypt, 1918–1952.* Princeton, N.J.: Princeton University Press.

United Nations. 1992. *National Accounts, 1992.* New York: UN.

United Nations. 1993. *National Accounts, 1993.* New York: UN.

United Nations. 1996. *World Economic and Social Survey 1996.* New York: UN.

United Nations. 2000. *International Trade Statistics Yearbook, 1999.* Vol. 1. New York: UN.

United Nations. 2001. *Egypt Human Development Report, 2000–2001.* 97. http://undp.org/en/reports/nationalreports/arabstates/egypt/Egypt_2001_en.pdf.

United Nations. 2001. *International Trade Statistics Yearbook 2000.* New York: UN.

United Nations. 2001. *National Accounts, 2001.* New York: UN.

United Nations. 2004. *International Trade Statistics Yearbook 2002.* Vol. 1. New York: UN.

United Nations. 2004. *World Population Prospects: The 2004 Revision and World Urbanization Prospects: The 2003 Revision.* New York, UN.

United Nations. *National Accounts Statistics: Main Aggregates and Detailed Statistics,* 2001 Part 1. UN: New York, 2003. *ESCWA Region 2006–2007,* document no. E/ESCWA/EAD/2007/TechnicalMaterial.1, 4 January 2007.

United Nations Committee on Trade and Development (UNCTAD). 1993. *Commodity Yearbook.* New York: UN.

United Nations Development Program. 2002. *Arab Human Development Report, 2002.* New York: United Nations.

United Nations Development Program. 2002. Regional Bureau for Arab States. *Arab Human Development Report, 2002.* New York: UN.

United Nations Development Program. 2005. *Human Development Report 2005.* http://hdr.undp.org/reports/global/2005.

UNDP. 2005. *Macroeconomic Policies for Poverty Reduction: The Case of Syria.* http://www.undp.org/poverty/docs/prm/syriamay22.pdf.

United Nations Development Program (UNDP). 2006. *Macroeconomic Policies for Poverty Reduction: The Case of Syria.* http://www.undp.org/poverty/docs/sppr/Syria%20Macro%20Report.pdf.

United Nations Economic and Social Commission for West Asia. 1994. *Agriculture and Development in West Asia.* Amman: UN, 1994.

United Nations Economic and Social Commission for West Asia (ESCWA). 1994. *Survey of Economic and Social Developments in the ESCWA Region.* Amman: UN, 1994.

United Nations Economic and Social Commission for West Asia. *Estimates and Forecasts for GDP Growth in the ESCWA Region 2006–2007,* document no. E/ESCWA/EAD/2007/TechnicalMaterial.1, 4 January 2007. http://www.escwa.un.org/information/publications/edit/upload/ead-07-tm2-e.pdf.

UNESCWA and FAO. 1997. Resource Conservation Policies and Strategies for Agriculture: The Case of the Syrian Arab Republic. New York: UN, 1996. Report number E/ESCWA/AGR/1995/12/REV.1

United Nations Educational, Scientific, and Cultural Organization. 2006 *Global Education Digest 2006*. http://www.uis.unesco.org.

United Nations Industrial Development Organization. 2005. *Industrial Development Report 2005*. http://www.unido.org.

United Nations Population Division of the Department of Economic and Social Affairs of the United Nations Secretariat. *World Population Prospects: The 2004 Revision and World Urbanization Prospects: The 2003 Revision*. http://www.esa.un.org/unpp.

United Nations Population Fund. 2003. "The Arab Population." In Schwab, Klaus and Peter Cornelius eds. *The Arab World Competitiveness Report 2002–2003*. New York: Oxford University Press. 34–61.

United Nations Relief and Works Agency (UNRWA). *Medium Term Plan 2005–2008*. un.org/unrwa/news/mtp.pdf.

UN/World Bank. October 2003. Joint Iraq Needs Assessment "Livelihoods, Employment, and Re-integration" Working Paper 31543. UN/World Bank, 2003. http://www-wds.worldbank.org/external/default/WDSContentServer/WDSP/IB/2005/05/06/000160016_20050506114042/Rendered/PDF/315430IQ0LIVELIHOODS01public1.pdf.

UN/World Bank. October 2003. Joint Iraq Needs Assessment. http://www-wds.worldbank.org/external/default/WDSContentServer/WDSP/IB/2007/12/26/000020953_20071226134206/Rendered/PDF/419690ENGLISH011Assessment01PUBLIC1.pdf.

United States Agency for International Development (USAID). *Budget Jordan*. http://www.usaid.gov/policy/budget/cbj2006/ane/jo.html.

U.S. Census Bureau. *Foreign Trade Statistics*. http://www.census.gov/foreign-trade/statistics/country/sreport/country.txt.

U.S. Embassy, Amman, Jordan. 13 March 2008. Press Release: "QIZs Provide an Engine for Export-Led Growth in Jordan." http://amman.usembassy.gov/user/NewsDetail.aspx?NewsId=1379.

Wade, Robert. 1990. *Governing the Market: Economic Theory and the Role of Government in East Asian Industrialization*. Princeton: Princeton University Press.

Waterbury, John. 1983. *The Egypt of Nasser and Sadat*. Princeton: Princeton University Press.

Waterbury, John. 1999. "The State and Transition in the Middle East and North Africa." In *Prospects for the Middle East and North Africa: From Boom to Bust and Back*, ed. Nemat, Shafar, 159–177. London: Macmillan.

Watson, Andrew M. 1974. "The Arab Agricultural Revolution and Its Diffusion, 700–1100." *Journal of Economic History XXXIV*: 8–36.

Weiss, Dieter, and Ulrich Wurzel. 1998. *The Economics and Politics of Transition to an Open Market Economy in Egypt*. Paris: OECD.

White, Gregory W. 1996. "The Mexico of Europe." In *North Africa: Development and Reform in a Changing Global Economy*, ed. Dirk Vandewalle, 111–128. Basingstoke: Macmillan.

Williamson, Jeffrey G., and Tarik M. Youssef. 2002. "Demographic Transitions and Economic Performance in the Middle East and North Africa." In *Human Capital: Population Economic in the Middle East*, ed. Ismail Sirageldin, 16–36. London and New York: I. B. Tauris.

Wittfogel, Karl. 1957. *Oriental Despotism: A Comparative Study of Total Power*. New Haven and London: Yale University Press.

World Bank. n.d. *Republic of Korea Data Profile.* http://devdata.worldbank.org/external/CPProfile.asp?CCODE=KOR&PTYPE=CP.

World Bank. *World Development Indicators.* http://devdata.worldbank.org/data-query.

World Bank. *World Development Indicators.* Various editions. http://www.worldbank.org.

World Bank. *World Development Indicators.* http://devdata.worldbank.org/data-query.

World Bank. 1978. *World Development Report 1978.* New York: Oxford University Press.

World Bank. 1979. *World Development Report 1979.* New York: Oxford University Press.

World Bank. 1981. *World Development Report 1981–82.* Washington, D.C.: World Bank.

World Bank 1993. *East Asian Miracle.* New York and Oxford: Oxford University Press.

World Bank. 1993. *Developing the Occupied Territories,* Vols. 1, 4, 6. Washington, D.C.: World Bank.

World Bank. 1993. *World Development Report 1993.* New York: Oxford University Press.

World Bank. 1994. *Peace and the Jordanian Economy.* Washington, D.C.: World Bank.

World Bank. 1994. Memorandum of the President of the International Bank for Reconstruction and Development and the International Finance Corporation to the Executive Directors of the World Bank Group for the Kingdom of Morocco.

World Bank. 1995. *The Evolving Role of the World Bank.* Washington, D.C.: World Bank.

World Bank. 1996. *Trends in Developing Countries 1996.* Washington, D.C.: World Bank.

World Bank. 1996. *Trends in Developing Countries 1996.*

World Bank. 2001. *Global Development Finance 2001.* Washington, D.C.: World Bank.

World Bank. 2001. Kingdom of Morocco Poverty Update. 1.

World Bank. 2002. *World Development Report 2002.* New York: Oxford University Press.

World Bank. 2002. *Long-Term Policy Options for the Palestinian Economy.* Washington, D.C.: World Bank.

World Bank. 2002. *27 Months: Intifada, Closure and Palestinian Economic Crisis, An Assessment.* http://www.worldbank.org.

World Bank. 2003. *Inequality in Latin America and the Caribbean: Breaking with History.* http://www.worldbank.org.

World Bank. 2003. *World Development Indicators 2003.* Washington, D.C.: World Bank. 39, 43.

World Bank. 2003. *Trade, Investment, and Development in the Middle East and North Africa.* Washington, D.C.: The World Bank. 3, 136.

World Bank. 2003. *Trade, Investment and Development in the Middle East and North Africa.* http://www.worldbank.org.

World Bank. 2003. *Tunisia's Global Integration and Sustainable Development,* Vol. 4 No. 1.

World Bank. 2004. *Doing Business in Tunisia: A Comparative Perspective.* Washington, D.C.: World Bank. www-wds.worldbank.org.

World Bank. 14 January 2004. *Interim Strategy Note of the World Bank Group for Iraq,* Report No. 27602. http://www.worldbank.org. 11.

World Bank. 14 January 2004. *Interim Strategy Note of the World Bank Group for Iraq.* 11. http:// www.worldbank.org.

World Bank. 2004. *Unlocking the Employment Potential in the Middle East and North Africa.* Washington, D.C.: World Bank.

World Bank. 2004. Press Release No. 2004/465/MNA. "World Bank Approves US$36 Million to Boost Tunisia's Exports."

World Bank. 2004. Memorandum of the President of the International Bank for Reconstruction and Development to the Executive Directors on the *Country Assistance Strategy for the Republic of Tunisia*, 2004. Report no. 28791-tun http://www-wds.worldbank.org/external/default/WDSContentServer/WDSP/IB/2004/07/13/000012009_20040713125947/Rendered/PDF/287910rev.pdf (IMF: Tunisia: 2007 Article IV Consultation – Staff Report; Public Information Notice on the Executive Board Discussion; and Statement by the Executive Director for Tunisia, report no. 07/302).

World Bank. 2004. World Development Indicators *2004*. http://web.worldbank.org/WBSITE/EXTERNAL/DATASTATISTICS/0,,contentMDK:20420198~hlPK:1365919~menuPK:64133159~pagePK:64133150~piPK:64133175~theSitePK:239419,00.html.

World Bank. 2004. *Republic of Tunisia, Employment Strategy, Volume 1*. www.wds.worldbank.org/servlet/WDSContentServer/WDSP/IB/2004/07/28/000012009_20040728105627/Rendered/PDF/25456110v.pdf.

World Bank. June 2004. *Country Assistance Strategy for the Republic of Tunisia*. report No. 28791-TUN http://www-wds.worldbank.org/external/default/WDSContentServer/WDSP/IB/2004/07/13/000012009_20040713125947/Rendered/PDF/287910rev.pdf.

World Bank 2005. *Middle East and North Africa Region, Economic Development and Prospects* 2005. http://siteresources.worldbank.org/INTMENA/Publications/20451730/MENA%20Economic%20Developments%20and%20Prospects%202005.pdf.

World Bank. 2005. *World Development Indicators 2005*. Washington, D.C.: World Bank.

World Bank. 2005. *Jordan Quarterly Update, First Quarter 2005*.

World Bank. 2005. *World Development Indicators 2005*. http://www.worldbank.org.

World Bank. December 2005. *The Palestinian Economy and Prospects for its Recovery, Economic Monitoring Report to the Ad Hoc Liaison Committee, Number 1*. http://domino.un.org/pdfs/PalEcoWB_AHLCrep.pdf.

World Bank. 2006. *Economic Developments and Prospects 2006*. http://www.worldbank.org.

World Bank. 2006. *Rebuilding Iraq: Economic Reform and Transition*. Report No. 35141-IQ. 31. http://www.worldbank.org.

World Bank. 2006. *Jordan Quarterly 2006*. Washington, D.C.: World Bank.

World Bank. 2006. Kingdom of Morocco, Country Economic Memorandum.

World Bank. 2006. Kingdom of Morocco, Country Economic Memorandum, I, II. Report No. 32948-MOR. 12. Washington, D.C.: The World Bank.

World Bank. 2006. Kingdom of Morocco Country Economic Memorandum.

World Bank. 2006. *Global Development Finance 2006*. Vol. II. Washington, D.C.: World Bank.

World Bank. 2006. West Bank and Gaza Country Economic Memorandum. 1. Report no. 36320 WBG. Washington, D.C.: World Bank.

World Bank. 2006. West Bank and Gaza Country Economic Memorandum.

World Bank. 2007. *Economic Developments and Prospects, Middle East and North Africa Region*. http://siteresources.worldbank.org/INTMENA/Resources/EDP_2007_REPORT_Aug7.pdf.

World Bank. 2007. *Middle East and North Africa Region, Economic Prospects and Developments.* http://siteresources.worldbank.org/INTMENA/Resources/EDP_2007_ REPORT_Aug7.pdf.

World Bank. 2007. *World Development Indicators 2007.* http://www.worldbank.org.

World Bank. 2007. *West Bank and Gaza Public Expenditure Review 2.* Report No. 38207-WBG. 2.

World Bank. 2007. *West Bank and Gaza Public Expenditure Review.* http://domino.un. org/pdfs/38207WBGVol.1.pdf.

World Bank. Egypt Data at a Glance. http://devdata.worldbank.org/AAG/egy_aag.pdf. accessed 17 January 2008.

World Trade Organization. 2006. *International Trade Statistics 2006.* Geneva: WTO. 38. http://www.wto.org/english/res_e/statis_e/its2006_e/its06_byregion_e.pdf.

Yadav, Vikash. March 2007. The Political Economy of the Egyptian–Israeli QIZ Trade Agreement. *Middle East Review of International Affairs* Vol. 11, No. 1: 1. http://meria.idc.ac.il.

Young, A. 1994. Lessons from the East Asian: A Contrarian View. *European Economic Review* 38, No. 3/4: 964–973.

Yousef, Tarik M. 2002. *Macroeconomic Aspects of the New Demography in the Middle East and North Africa.* http:/www.worldbank.org.

Yusuf, Shahid. 2001. "The East Asian Miracle at the Millenium." In *Rethinking the East Asian Miracle,* eds. Joseph E. Stiglitz and Shahid Yusuf, 1–54. New York: Oxford University Press and the World Bank.

Zerhouni, Saloua. 2004. "Morocco: Reconciling Continuity and Change." In *Arab Elites, Negotiating the Politics of Change,* ed. Volker Perthes, 61–86. Boulder, Colo.: Lynne Rienner.

Index